CW00701807

Evenings in the Duffrey

EVENINGS

IN

THE DUFFREY.

BY PATRICK KENNEDY,

Author of "Legendary Fictions of the Irish Celts", "The Banks of the Boro",
" Fictions of our Forefathers", etc.

DUBLIN:
M'GLASHAN AND GILL, SACKVILLE STREET.
PATRICK KENNEDY, ANGLESEA STREET.

LONDON: BURNS, OATES, AND CO.,
PORTMAN STREET, PORTMAN SQUARE.
1869.

J. F. FOWLER, PRINTER,
3 CROW STREET, DAME STREET,
DUBLIN.

To the Revered Memory

OF THE

RIGHT HONOURABLE THE LATE LORD CAREW

THESE RECOLLECTIONS OF A HAPPY PERIOD OF LIFE

SPENT ON THE CASTLEBORO ESTATES,

ARE DEDICATED BY THE WRITER THROUGH A

DEEP FEELING OF RESPECT FOR HIS LORDSHIP'S

INDULGENT AND JUDICIOUS TREATMENT OF HIS TENANTRY,

AS WELL AS A DEEP FEELING OF GRATITUDE

FOR MANY KINDNESSES RECEIVED,

BOTH AS PUPIL AND TEACHER,

IN TWO OF THE EXCELLENT SCHOOLS ESTABLISHED BY

HIS LORDSHIP.

PREFACE.

THOSE who favoured the *Banks of the Boro* with a perusal, and were at all interested in the fortunes of a certain character in that rambling story, could not remain satisfied with the condition in which he was left at its close. They will find as much done for him in the present narrative as I ever intended; however, it was not my chief object to excite interest in the career of Edward O'Brien. It was rather to present a truthful picture of one or two phases of the domestic life and condition of the farming class in that portion of my native county which lies in the shadow of Mount Leinster. The preservation of some fireside conferences at which I assisted, the traditionary and legendary lore, and the rural minstrelsy, chiefly entered into my design. Any story connected with such a plan could only be slight, and not at all interesting to the patrons and patronesses of exciting fictions.

The present is in all probability my last collection of country reminiscences. I am not gifted with ability, nor indeed well inclined, to compose mere fictions, and have in the two works now abroad, embodied everything which seemed to me interesting in the fireside literature of my native district.

A word in the ear of sensitive folk of either sex, and of every age. If they or any of them think well of questioning me on the relative proportion of fact and fancy in the fortunes of my candidates for marriage, I hereby solemnly announce my fixed resolve not to satisfy their indiscreet curiosity. On all other points they may be assured that there is not a fictitious character nor incident in the mere narrative, nor legend nor tradition related, nor ballad sung, which was not current in the country half a century since. The fireside discussions were really held, and the extraordinary fishing and hunting adventures detailed, as here set down.

I have embodied in the present work a few local sketches in my first literary venture, the *Legends of Mount Leinster*, and retained the initials (H. W.) of the assumed author of that collection.

For the many hearty and encouraging notices of the *Banks of the Boro* I take this opportunity of expressing my most grateful acknowledgments to the different writers.

Patrick Kennedy

CONTENTS.

EVENINGS IN THE DUFFREY.

CHAPTER I.

A DAY AT PADDY DONOVAN'S.

Two years have passed since the dance was held in O'Brien's barn, and Pat Neil chaunted his nuptial song. Mr. Maher has left our seminary at Cloughbawn to prosecute his clerical studies, and our Latin and Greek classes have separated like ropes of sand, and H. W.'s classic exercises are at an end, and he does not know how to dispose of the large stock of vacant time on hands. Kind Father James of Davidstown has proposed to ordain him monarch of the Courtnacuddy gymnasium; but his acceptance would smack of ingratitude towards his literary chief, Mr. O'Neil, and the offer is thankfully declined.

So on a day in the spring of 1820, when I was at the funeral of our late bishop, Dr. Ryan, in Enniscorthy, I met Edward, who had come from Tombrick to witness the ceremony. After the solemnities we set out in company for the Iron Forge, and were little troubled with hiatuses in our conversation.

He had become more steady and reserved since his heart-disappointment; and he now dwelt with great satisfaction on the good nature of the people among whom his life was passing. He had given up his little tenement, for its loneliness was intolerable, especially when he called to mind the associations formerly connected with it; and had taken up his residence at my godmother's, Mrs. K. of Coolgarrow, or at the Donovans' or Lucas's, or Kennedys' of Tombrick. A school house was now about being

2

built, and a piece of ground set apart for him by Lord
Carew ; and he was to be sent up to the training school
in Dublin.   So he proposed to me to fill his place during
his three months' absence, and thus try my 'prentice hand
in the occupation which seemed allotted to me by circumstances.   I embraced the proposal very willingly ; and it
was settled that we should meet again next Saturday at
Paddy Donovan's of Tombrick, if my people approved of
the step.

I enjoyed a fine, dry, windy spring morning on the
appointed day, as I measured the road through Scobie,
the Iron Forge, and along the hill side of Ballyorril
towards Scarawalsh.   From Scarawalsh bridge I took the
fine level road upwards, the river flowing at my right
hand, about the breadth of a meadow away, admired the
old manor house of Munfin with its grey front, the little
lawn between itself and the road, and its shaded avenue
leading down to the Slaney at its back ; wished for an
hour or two to explore the little wood on my left ; pushed
on between the large trees on either hand of the road, so
nicely furnished with green banks on each side; and was
prepared to do my duty on the good dinner to which I
sat down on my arrival at Mr. Donovan's about half past
twelve o'clock.

The farm house of the Donovan family was pleasantly
situated in the shelter of a gently inclined hill, at a field's
breadth from the road.   The interior resembled the old
familiar residence of the Roche's, and being on a slope,
its good clay floor was always dry.   The barn and stable
ran at right angles from its upper or parlour end, and in
the corner was a style over which we scrambled into the
haggard.   The cow house and piggery was on the south
side of the yard opposite the dwelling house ; beyond
them lay the orchard ; and at the eastern or lower side of
the bawn reposed the heap of manure.   A sewer in the
fence conveyed the superabundant moisture down to the
neighbouring field, which was truly thankful for what
might otherwise send a fever into the family some fine
summer's day or other.

Mrs. Donovan was of the best blood of the farmocracy on either bank of the Slaney, and had been a very handsome young woman, I am sure. At my first introduction, I could have fancied her a lady by birth and education, whom fate or fancy had sent to preside at a farmer's table. Her gentle manners were inherited by her eldest and youngest sons and daughters. The master of the house, with three of the sons, were of brusquer manners.

Edward met me on the road near Munfin and introduced me to the family, and we sat at dinner at a table necessarily large, for it had to accommodate twelve individuals. The heads of the house and the eldest daughter used a smaller one near the fire. One distinguishing feature of the meal-hour was, that the conversation never ceased. A subject was started probably at the upper table; it travelled to the lower one, and passed from tongue to tongue, every one adjusting it after his or her peculiar taste; and finally it was rounded off, or got the finishing touch, from one of the labourers, or Owen Jourdan, the hereditary faggot cutter of the Duffrey.

Being asked if I had met many going to Enniscorthy, and answering that I had seen several; "Ah then", said Pat, "you must have met Murtagh Horan". "Perhaps I did, but I knew no one". "You must recollect him, he was in full dress". "I do not recollect any one particularly well dressed". "But this is a remarkable case; he had a pin in his collar". "I suppose he is gone a courting", said Martin. "I wish him better success, than when he was sitting one side of the fire at Jemmy Lucas's, and Margaret Lucas sitting at the other, and when he found that he could not invent a single thing to talk about. At last a lucky thought came into his head. He took a coal in the tongs, popped it at her, and asked in his most captivating manner, 'Will I burn you, Maggy?' 'Yes', said Mosey, 'and when she screeched and jumped away, he cried out, 'Musha, but you are as wild as a puckawn, and so you are, aroon'. "Ah it is himself that 's the spirited young courtier", said Pat. "Last fair day of Scarawalsh, he was treating

a few of the neighbours' daughters to some beer and peas
in a tent, and when the drink was running short, and
the peas were demolished, and Murtagh was at a loss for
talk to entertain the girls, he struck the table, and cried
out so courageously : ' Hang the expense ! while we 're
in it, let us be in it : send us another ha'porth o' pays'' ''.

Now the reader must know that Murtagh was an
estimable young fellow enough, but certainly not particular about his dress. He denied to his dying day the
imputation of the peas. Pat's assertion was a mere piece
of waggery of some one's invention, so was the anecdote
of the courting tongs.

Mary now secured the ball (we are going down the
succession according to age). A more guileless, less selfish,
or better conditioned little girl never came under my
notice, than Mary. It was easy to embarrass her in her
narratives by a roguish or ill-natured gesture ; and then
the succession of incidents was disturbed. She essayed
to describe how Murtagh and his sister were employed a
day or two before, repairing a fence in one of the fields,
and how they set Betty the young servant girl to prevent
the sheep and goats from trespassing on the wheat in
the next field, as the gap of the knoc where they were,
was in a very shaky condition. Cunning Pat grinned at
the story teller at this point and disturbed her not a
little. However, she managed to let us understand that
the day was cold, and that Bet, after doing duty for a
while, ran to shelter, and her roguish charge taking a
mean advantage of her neglect, cleared the gap, and
devoured various shoots, and trampled on many more,
before poor Bet could induce them by the persuasion
of a few two-year old stones, to re-enter their proper
domain.

The little historian was pretty consistent so far, but
now getting another encouraging grimace from Pat, and
finding the general silence oppressive, she got embarrassed,
and soon made it a doubtful point, whether the next foray
on the wheat field was owing to Bet getting tired for want
of company, or the goats getting away, and the sheep

pursuing them for want of company; or the sheep striving to quit company with the goats, or both combining to rid themselves of their negligent guardian. But as the silence was now succeeded by general tittering and a few little explosions, she brought the master and mistress to the chastisement of the imprudent herd, and her own relief, winding up the tangled skein in these words, " Bet run away from Mary, and Mary run after her, to beat Bet".

Now came the turn of dear little black-eyed, small-fingered, impulsive, beautiful, good-natured little Catherine. " Yes indeed, and so she did run away, and shewed me the mark of a clod on her fat shoulder; and I saw Murtagh myself to-day going to the market with the corker pin in his shirt; and there was a great big car coming after him, and such a load of men and women as were on it, ay up to the sky. I'm sure there was twelve any way, and a fiddler and a piper; and the women with big bow-ribbons in their bonnets, and the fiddler was playing, and the piper squeezing his bellows, and the music squeeling and buzzing, and the men smoking, and the women laughing and waving their hats, the men I mean; and one woman giving a screech that was near the piper, yes indeed the piper, a piper, a piper, indeed and so he was a piper !"

Poor Catherine's story was nipped in the bud by Pat's waggery, even as Mary's was. Thomas, the youngest child, seemed the most seriously disposed personage in company. He might smile at some conceit or practical jest, but seldom laughed; and when he was obliged to speak, did it with the composure of a young judge. Dear little Thomas! I feel proud of my young pupil, when I reflect on all the good you have been permitted to do, since your call to the priesthood; on the many sinful and erring creatures you have reconciled to their Father; and on the aids you have unceasingly given to the unsteady but sincere steps of your flock towards their final home.

After dinner, the elder boys went to their spring labours; the womenkind were at no loss for domestic occupation; and Edward, and the younger children, and I were indulged with a walk by the Slaney; and the children chased each other along its velvety banks, and Edward and I thought with some sadness on the Banks of the Boro, and the happy careless season of boyhood for ever gone by. This was but a fleeting shade, however: both were too much interested in looking forward to spare much sentiment to the past.

Night came, and labour was suspended, and the master and mistress were seated in the cozy recess at the fire-place farthest from the door, her hands employed knitting, and his employed doing nothing whatever.

Owen Jourdan rested in a state of sublime repose on the griddle which covered the ash-pit on the other side of the fire-place; and others of us were on stools and bosses in front of the fire, and the rest on the turned up settle-bed lying by the side wall.

Thomas inquires how long will it be till the apples come again on the trees; Catherine is curious to know if she will be soon let to sampler work; and Mary requests information about the rings of deep green in so many places in the inches by the Slaney. Owen, wrapped in his long grey coat, and with his thin bronzed face shining in the blaze, tells her that they are caused by the dancing of the "*Good People*" at the dead of the night; and that if she wishes to see them at their sport, she has only to make a ring out of a thraneen, and look at them through it, and she will see them in all their bravery with their fox-glove caps and green jerkins, capering to the sound of a bag-pipe, with a lurikeen playing it, and he sitting on a fairy mushroom; but she will never see a *stim* with that eye again.

Mosey was reminded by this explanation, that he dreamed one night that he was standing in one of these rings, and that he was frightened by a great she-fox swimming from Mr. Derinzy's side of the river, straight across to him, with a weed in her mouth; and that he woke in a fright, and that it turned out a very unlucky dream for him. For the next day he was in the knoc as you go up the lane to the wood, and he almost fell across a fine partridge sprawling on the sod, with every wing and leg she had broken. He stooped down to pick her up, but she fluttered just out of his grasp, and kept on, struggling, till she got him a couple of perches away; and then she sprung up into the sky, and flew off as if there wasn't a ha'porth amiss with her.

Mosey's fox reminded Alice of the loss it was to the neighbourhood for Captain Carey to keep a fox-cover so near his place; such numbers of ducks, and geese, and hens as were lost by the farmers every season; and H. W. began to praise the fine appearance of the old manor house, and the shady avenue, and the lawn, and the fine road with the green banks and the large trees on either side.

"Myself often wonders", said Owen, "when I'm all by myself in the knoc or the ditch, with my back aching, and my arms tired, and no one in the world to care about me, what I done before I was born to be tied down to poverty and labour; or what Captain Carey done, that he should have full and plenty about him, and fine furniture, and *sofias*, and carpets, and dogs and horses for hunting, and wine, and whiskey-punch, and might sleep till twelve o'clock every day if he liked; and if he was too lazy to chew his meat, he might have people to do it for him".

"Perhaps, Owen", answered Mrs. Donovan, "if you could be transformed into Captain Carey for a week, you would not find the change so very pleasant after all. But suppose he was to live a happy life for a hundred years, and you a life of labour and want; at the last moment your past hardship and his past happiness would not be of the value of a withered faggot. You both would have an endless eternity before you, and the only thing to be thought of would be, did you do your duty to God and your neighbour, or did you not? The longest life does not seem the length of a minute when it is past; and we may rest assured that every one who does his best to please God, will meet with that state of life best suited for his happiness here and hereafter".

" Still and all ma'am, I would n't be a bit sorry to find
a crock of gold or even silver some day in the dyke of an
old ditch when I 'd be cutting furze. Be me word I
would n't be frightened the way poor Thummaus the tailor
was, when he came on one in the rath. But yez all heard
about that, I suppose".

" May be not", said Edward, " especially as it happened
on the borders of Bantry, and the Duffrey. Even if they
did, the second telling by you is worth the first telling of
any other genius. So fire away, Owen".

" Thank you, master! Ah, if I knew grammar and
rethoric and elocution like you it would be worth listening
to some things I know. Well I 'm too old to go to school
now, so I must only do the best I can. Here goes".

THE CROCK FOUND IN KNOCMORE.

" I dont go very often out of the Duffrey here to follow
my business, but one time that I was so far as the near
part of Bantry, I cut a good deal of faggots for a very
rich family in the rank of gentlemen-farmers. When I
came home, a very knowledgeable woman that lived in
Cromogue there beyond, told me of the queer way the
father and mother of the people that I was working for,
got their first rise.

" Once when he was only a little sculloge of a farmer,
a poor sprishan of a tailor was making clothes for the
family. The mistress of the house often took notice of
him while he was sitting cross-legged on the kitchen table,
stopping the needle or the goose, and putting his hand under his chin, and pausing ever so long. ' What's the matter
with you, Thummaus?' says she at last, 'are you sick, or
is there any thing troubling you?' ' You may say trouble,
ma'am', says he, 'and be this an' be that, I 'll not let it
trouble me any longer till I make a cat or a dog of it.
Last night was the third time that I dreamed there was
a crock of gold and silver in the Rath of Knocmore, and
I 'd know the place between a stone overgrown with moss
and an old *skeoch* tree. Begonies, I 'll take a spade and

shovel with your leave, ma'am, and see what luck God sends'. She laughed at the notion, but he persevered, and off he set a little after dinner-time towards the rath.

"Three hours after, the mistress saw him come into the bawn as pale as ashes, and his limbs hardly able to carry him. When he got inside the door, he says, 'ma'am dear, will you let me go to bed? My inside is all *threenacheala*, and I think I'll faint'. She gave leave with a good heart, and soon after brought him a bowl of whey with a glass of wine in it, and bedad he found himself much better after it, and fell asleep. Next morning he was up at the flight of night, and away somewhere, but at breakfast time he was back crying and shouting to the mistress to give him his crock of money. He did not stop even for the servants and labourers being gathered round the table. 'What crock of money are you talking of?' says she. 'Ah, you know well enough: the crock I told you about', says he, 'and that I dug up yesterday afternoon. Did n't I tell you of my dream before I left the house? and sure enough, I found the stone and the skeoch just as I dreamed of them. Ah, ma'am honey, give me my crock, and I'll make you a handsome present'. 'Oh, the poor man is mad', says she, 'to say such things'. 'Not a bit mad except with grief. Sure when the spade struck the *led* of the crock, I felt like as if fire was darting through my veins, and when I dug round it, and got it lifted up on the sod, I felt a turn in my inside, and a weakness all over me, and a kind of fright. I fell in a stugue on the grass, and when I came to myself, I could not touch the crock if I was to get a hundred pounds for it. I crawled home, and got to bed, where I won't deny that you gave me a good drink that put me to sleep. O my treasure! my treasure! what's become of you! When I went there this morning, there was the hole, and the spade and shovel, but not the smallest sign of crock nor money. I'll lose my senses if you have n't the heart nor the goodness to let me have my money that I dhramed about and dug up with hard labour'. She and her husband stoutly denied that they had any thing to do about it; but he

held abusing them, and asking for his crock, and bawling
and roaring till he had all the neighbours gathered about
the door.   Bedad they had at last to get the constable to
relieve themselves from him ; but as soon as ever he got
his liberty, he came to torment them again.   He was now
completely out of his senses, and staid that way till the
day of his death.   The family were good enough about
giving him his meals, and cast-off clothes, *and that*.   The
neighbours suspected that the woman and her husband
got the money.   That same evening none of their family
nor near neighbours saw them about the place for an hour
and a half after the tailor fell asleep.   They seemed to
thrive by degrees.   They took a large farm some time
after, and their children were the richest gentlemen
farmers in that part of the country, and are so at the
present day.   If the money came ill, it did not go ill.
There are not more religious or better conducted men and
women in the barony of Bantry than they are, nor more
charitable to the poor".

As a horse with winkers on each side of his head, sees
his way straight before him well enough, but feels no
interest in its connection with the prospect on either hand,
so Owen could see a part of a subject sufficiently clear ;
but his mental powers were too limited to take in its
relations with other things.   So as in the case of the
horse, his hearers were occasionally obliged to turn his
head suddenly to one side, or remove his winkers, to make
him aware of the dangers besetting his theories.   He
resumed :—
    " I often felt something like them thoughts you were
speaking of while ago, ma'am, when I would be sitting on
the edge of the river of a Sunday, resting my bones, and
watching the straws, and bits of stick, and weeds, all
floating on the top, and running away with the current,
just as the days and nights runs away with ourselves,
Howandever we are better off than the straws, for we
have a kind of guidance over ourselves, and they are at

the pleasure of the water. The Slaney is the finest river
I ever *see*. I often wonder where such a heap of water
comes from, and why it does not all run away to the *say*
sometime or other. Ah, if the bottom was dry, would n't
we have the sport, *ketching* the trouts, and eels, and
salmons?"

"And wouldn't there be a fine pullaluing in a week or
so among the people", said Martin, "when the meadows
would be as dry as the road, and the cattle dying for want
of water? You remind me, Owen, of the wise man that
set fire to the thatch of his cabin to give him light at his
supper".

"Yes", said Pat, "or the other wise man of Gotham
that was going into town on horseback one day to sell a
cheese. His cheese dropped; and his sword was so
short, that he could not stick the point deep enough into
it to raise it up. Owen, I suppose, would alight and
seize it bodily, but that wise man was above acting like
any common person. He rode into town and bought a
sword six inches longer in the blade, and by the time he
got back he had no use for it".

"Well, well", answered Owen, "the heap of fish hid
the calves and the kids. Ach! it would be a queer
world if it was left to the likes of us to get sunshine, and
rain, and frost by only wishing for them. But about the
Slaney—what 's the meaning of the word? May be somebody knows: we say '*Slaintha*' for health, when the
Irish gets uppermost".

None of the family appearing to be aware of the reason,
Edward said he would endeavour to account for it from a
bit of legendary history in Keating, and a tradition which
he had heard from his mother. All were silent in a
moment, and he commenced his tradition.

CHAPTER II.

THE MILK BATH OF THE WHITE COWS.

" Long ago a chief or little king named Crovan, lived
in a strong fort or rath with two deep trenches round
it; and this fort occupied the highest part of Enniscorthy
on our side of the Slaney. He was rather surprised one
afternoon when the sentinel who was posted on the
highest point of the fortress, sent him word that ever so
many *corrachs* (skin-covered boats) were making their
way up the river, and that fighting men were landing
from them as fast as fast could be.

" Crovan did not wait to be attacked in his stronghold.
War horns were blown, all the fighting men seized their
arms, the gates were opened, and the trenches crossed,
and down rushed the Wexford men on the invaders.
These were called the *Wood People*. They came from
Wales, and had done mischief at Wexford town (Wexford
Bay was then called Loch Carmain) before they sailed up
the river.

" The two forces fought with swords, spears, bows
and arrows, and the women and the children on the ramparts thought the ringing blows of the swords on the
helmets a terrible kind of music you may be sure. They
did not give up fighting till the sun was over Cooliah, and
the Irish would not have stopped then only they saw that
every man that had got the slightest wound, found himself getting sick immediately, and his flesh becoming
quite purple, and all his strength gone. Scores on scores
were lying on the ground dying or dead, though most of
the wounds were only slight gashes or arrow pricks.

" Crovan gave orders to retire and carry into the fort
every man that still had any remains of life. So, strong
unwounded men made a wall of defence with their shields,
and others carried their dying comrades over the moats.

" In that battle were killed the king's three sons-in-law,
Breas, Buas, and Buaine. Buas died just as they were

carrying him in, and his young wife stooped over him crying piteously, and strove to draw the head of an arrow from his breast. In doing so she wounded her own wrist with the barb, and it was not long till she fell down in a faint sickness, and a purple colour began to creep up her arm. This added to the general grief, and nothing was heard but the cries of women and children, the men leaning on their spears, and looking on with anger and sorrow in their hearts.

"There was a bustle at the entrance, and two old men and one young man entered the big wooden hall. The young man dropped on his knee beside the dying princess, and putting her wrist to his mouth, he began to suck it and spit out. One of the old men spoke in a voice of authority to the people around, and ordered them to milk all the white cows they owned, and fill baths with it and Slaney water mingled, and be quick. A large vessel was soon ready, and the wounded lady put into it, and as many more were got ready as could be. She soon began to recover, and so did all that had any life left, and every one set to work with such good will that not a wounded man was left uncared for.

"Well, all this was great relief, and now every one began to find their appetite, and a dinner or supper, whichever you like, was got ready, and the strangers and some followers who had come in later, conducting the daughter of one of the old men, were treated with Irish welcome, the three men and the young lady being set next Crovan and his queen.

"The meal was roast and boiled beef and venison, with flat cakes, water cress, and a kind of sour preparation of milk. The drink was wine, which in those times came from France and Spain, and they had spirits, and mead, and something resembling beer. When the meal was over, one of the old men who was a druid told where they came from and all about them. 'Our ancestors', said he, 'were driven some hundred years ago from the north of this country, and sailed to Greece, from which their own fathers had come. There our people have since lived, but

latterly they have been badly treated, and the young prince
of the country attempted to carry away this lady, sister to
our young chief Cathluan. Her brother returning from
an expedition on which he had been sent by the same
young libertine, met the party, and his sister shrieked to
him for aid. He gave it so well that the prince lost his
life in the struggle. When they reached home the whole
tribe held counsel, and judging that the king would seek
revenge, they seized as many ships as they needed, and
set sail. It was revealed to me by our gods that the
chief's daughter would be healed of a lingering illness by
drinking the waters of that river of Erin which flows into
Loch Carmain, and that we should be the means of saving
the lives of many warriors of a Scottish tribe, whose fortress lay on its banks. We sailed westwards through
the great central sea, and out into the still greater one
that bounds the world on the west. We landed at a
little harbour on your eastern coast yesterday in the
afternoon, and it is a pleasure to us to have done you
some service. Our followers have settled themselves
beyond the river for this night, but their hands will be of
use to-morrow'.

"Watches were kept up on the mounds, and as many
as could, snatched some hours of sleep. Before day pits
were hollowed in the ground outside the fort, lined with
tough clay tempered, and filled with Slaney water and the
milk of white cows. The new comers were sent for by
their chief, and they crossed the river in corrachs, and
joining the native Scots, as the Irish were then called,
they raised three shouts that might be heard miles off,
and rushed down on the woodmen who were lying around
where you may still see the ruins of the old abbey. They
received them with a shower of poisoned darts, but wherever these pierced the mail coats, the wounded men
hastened to the pits, and came out as fresh as ever. The
arrows were collected and sent back with sure aim, and
the woodmen fell like stalks of corn. The parties soon
closed and a terrible fight was waged, for the woodmen
were fierce and strong. They wondered much why the

poison was not doing its work, but still fought like men in despair. The day went against them. Scarcely a man escaped, and their remains were not treated like those of honourable foes. They were burned on the bank of the river, and the ashes and fragments of bones flung into it to be carried out to the sea.

"The druid Trosdane had a vision some months afterwards, in which his gods revealed to him that the appointed resting place of his people was a land to the north and east of the great Causeway of the Giants. So the strangers made their way to the west of Scotland, then called Alba, Cathluan persuading the lady whose life he had saved to accompany him as his wife, and as many of his warriors as had pleased the eyes of the young women of the tribes imitating his example. They swore to Crovan that the sons born of the Scottish women should have precedence of those of any others. Old historians say that the Picts were the descendants of the people of this colony, and that their country took the name CALEDONIA from the young chief Cathluan".

When the story was over, and the story teller thanked, all sorts of criticisms were made, and the children, to whom belongs the inconvenient privilege of finding their appetite for the marvellous increase in proportion to the quantity consumed, petitioned for another legend: but it being Saturday night, the womankind preferring our room to our company, opposed the prayer, and no other story was told. However, Catherine being disappointed of a story, should have a song, and to gratify her, Edward sung the *Indifferent Damsel*, which it is to be hoped the reader recollects as warbled by the susceptible maiden at Mr. Dick Greene's Harvest Home. If not, he 'll find it in the " Banks of the Boro", p. 120. As Edward's version is fuller than that one, we quote it except the last two verses, which are identical with those of the Bantry Girl's.

> " It was on a fine summer's morning in June,
>   Abroad as I did walk,
> I laid my back close to a garden wall
>   For to hear two lovers talk;—

To hear two lovers talk, my dear,
    And to mark what they would say,
That I might know a little more of their minds
    Before I would go away.

" ' Come sit you down, my darling', said he,
    ' Upon this meadow so green,
For 't is full three quarters of a year and more
    Since together you and I have been'.
' I 'll not sit down by you', my dear,
    ' Now nor at any other time,
For I 'm told you 're engaged to another fair maid,
    And your heart is no longer mine.

" 'For when your heart it was mine, my dear,
    And your head laid on my breast,
You made me believe what a false lover said,
    When the sun shone over the east'. "

" Well", said John, "that was never composed by an
Irishman. It 's a pity there 's not better sense in it, the
air is so sweet". " It is one of those songs", said Edward,
" that have come to us from over the water, and to say
truth they have a charm for me for which I can't account.
No one seems to know how old they are. I have a claim
now for another song, and I 'm sure, Mosey will gratify
me". Mosey grinned, but did not require much pressing,
and out came the egregious lay of—

" THE STAR OF SLANE.

" You brilliant muses, who ne'er refuses,
    But still infuses in the poet's mind,
Your kind sweet favours to his poor endeavours,
    If his ardent labours but appear sublime.
Preserve my study from getting muddy,   .
    My ideas ready to inspire my brain,
My quill refine whilst I write those lines,
    On a nymph divine, called the Star of Slane.

" In beauteous spring, when the warblers sing,
    And their music rings thro' each silent grove,
Bright Sol did shine, which did me incline,
    By the river Boyne for to go to rove.

I was contemplating and meditating,
  And ruminating as I paced the plain,
When a charming fair one beyond compare,
  Did my heart ensnare near the town of Slane.

"Had Paris seen this young maid serene,
  The Grecian Queen he would soon disdain,
And straight embrace this virgin chaste,
  And peace would grace the Trojan plain.
If great Julius Cæsar would on her gaze, sir,
  He'd stand amazed for to view the dame.
Sweet Cleopather he would freely part her,
  And his crown he'd barter for the Star of Slane.

"To praise her beauty, it is my duty,
  But alas, I'm footy in this noble part,
And to my sorrow, sly Cupid's arrow
  Full deep did burrow in my tender heart.
In pain and trouble, I still will struggle,
  Tho' sadly hobbled by my stupid brain,
Yet backed by nature, I will tell the features
  Of this lovely creature, called the Star of Slane.

"Her eyes, 't is true, are an azure blue,
  And her cheeks the hue of the crimson rose;
Her hair behold, does shine like gold,
  In fine flowing rolls it so nicely grows.
Her skin as white, as the snow by night,
  Straight and upright is her portly frame,
The chaste Diana, or fair Susanna,
  Are eclipsed in grandeur by the Star of Slane.

"Her name to mention, might cause contention,
  And its my intention for to breed no strife,
But for to woo her, as I'm but pooer,
  Really I'm sure she wont be my wife;
In silent anguish I here must languish,
  'Till time does banish my love-sick pain,
And my humble station I must bear with patience,
  Since great exaltation suits the Star of Slane".

There was some suppressed laughter during the performance, which the singer did not accept as complimen-
ary, and he took occasion to state at the conclusion that
he bought the ballad in Bunclody, and hadn't made the
slightest mistake in singing it.

It was a feature in Mr. Donovan's household, that we

used to sit up too long on occasions; and sometimes the small men and women were overtaken by sleep in manner as they sat or lay on settle bed or form; and at the hour of final retirement, the grown children charged them on their shoulders; carried them to bed; and consigned them to the care of their ever-waking guardian spirits.

How pleasing soever the recollections of my abode with that estimable family, I will say that the conduct of John the senior in regard to family prayer was not entirely judicious.   Not calculating the power of attention in his hearers, he commenced with the Rosary, continued with the Litanies, went on with other prayers, and did not stop when he came to an end.   All this would be a very desirable thing among devout adults if commenced at a reasonably early hour.   But the poor little men and women of twelve years and under, after an evening spent in listening to songs, and traditions, and country topics, were not able to go through the exercise in a befitting spirit.   So heads in some instances drooped, and eyes closed, without sin on their parts—as we trust—poor weary little souls!   If two afterwards devoted their lives to the services of God in religious houses, and one became an exemplary clergyman, we are not to thank John's long exercises for the family blessing.   He and the seniors were supported by a strong devout feeling, and as we hope, are now enjoying the reward which awaits God's faithful on earth.

CHAPTER III.

A VISIT TO MY BIRTH PLACE.

Next morning after breakfast, the family set out for Castle-Dockrell to attend Mass.   In due time and place the impatient reader shall be conducted to that unpicturesque locality, but on this particular occasion he or she will please to accompany Edward and myself to the cross of

Kilmeashil. I was anxious to visit my earliest playmate, and to look again on the localities of my childhood. Having abundance of time before us, we took the Bunclody road, admired the great meadow by the Slaney, where all the Tombrick farmers were privileged to send their cows in autumn, and noticed the openings on either hand of the road for the extraction of pebble limestones. On passing the Glasha at the Mill of Moyeady, we had a shake-hands with the gigantic miller and his handsome wife, who was as good natured as she was good looking, and had a heart that matched her well-developed person. I was introduced then and there to my future little favourites, John, Mary, Catherine, and Honora. I also was introduced to that fast friend of country teachers, Paddy Lennon, the weaver, now unable from blindness to follow his business, but still keeping a good trade alive by employing skilful hands. We shall shortly renew our intercourse with him.

We continue our journey near the Slaney banks till we meet the great road, which traversing the Duffrey in a north-east direction, comes here down hill from the old church yard of Kilmeashil, and crossing the river at Cloghamon, keeps on towards the sea. We get glimpses of the wooded hills that encircle Bunclody through the tall trees by the road side, turn up the hill to the old church yard, and I am greatly mortified at its bare appearance, for I had been there at a *Patron* when about four years old, and had brought away an imposing picture of trees or posts, with big curtains hanging between, and an old sacred well, and gigantic tomb-stones, and tents, and gingerbread stalls and beer barrels. A quarter of a mile farther on we enter the *Crosses*, the village where the chapel stands, and from which a bridle road leads over a small eminence towards Bunclody. I had heard my first mass in this chapel, when the walls were rough, and the altar nothing but a frame, held up by stakes driven into the wall. I told Edward how on that occasion, I got under the temporary altar, and with my face to the congregation read the prayers with much care,

looking up occasionally to see how the priest was occupied.   Father Stafford used afterwards to mention the
ludicrous effect my small inquisitive face had on him, as
I peeped up from under the altar.   After mass we found
out my earliest companion, Terence O'Brien, and went
home with him to dinner.

We passed the little cabin where I received my first
lessons; and I attempted to give my companion a notion
of the strange impression made on me by the first sight
I had of the LORD's PRAYER in print.   I had known it
previously by sound, and now I was introduced to it by
sight, and the relation between the two modes of percep-
tion was most bewildering.

It seemed as if many scores of years had intervened
since my eyes last met the objects now before me, so far
had entire absence from the place thrown back my former
existence. There was the ruined farm house, on the edge
of the bog below the road; there were its neglected garden and little grove, where I had often strayed about; and
I had so often dreamed about them, that it was not now
in my power to distinguish between the images remaining from the dreams, and those produced by the realities.
We passed the narrow stony lane that led to the top of
the little ridge, and I called to mind my early explora-
tion of that unknown and awful pass.   I approached the
highest point with something like the awe that must have
enveloped Balboa as he neared the summit of the last
eminence at Panama, with the expectation of beholding
in a few moments the wide expanse of the western ocean
spread before him.   Not small was my own delight and
surprise, when beyond the down sloping fields before me,
I had a clear prospect of the high ridge running west
from Bunclody to join the broad imposing mass of the
eastern face of Mount Leinster with all the grey, reddish
purple, and green tints of the picture, harmoniously combining in the light of the clear summer morning.   It was
my earliest impression of the sublime.

My dear old playmate and his mother gave us a cordial welcome, and we spent three hours as if they were

but three minutes, talking over early recollection,—how we made moss-houses in the garden in the full belief that the birds would shelter in them during the night; and how the mistress shewed us an improvement on these dwellings, by sticking some twigs in a circle, tying their tops, and filling the interstices with moss. Also how we used to fasten the cavalry sword to one of our buttons by the ring of its metal sheath, and so trail it along the ground; and how the gander once beset me in the evening going home, bit my legs, slapped me with his wings, and nearly frightened the life out of me.

If I had thought on the present scene early that morning, my mind would have been filled with images of long reaches of lane or road, of gigantic trees, high houses, high fences, and immense fields. Now every object seemed dwarfed and insignificant in comparison, but still very interesting; the green above the farm house, the wide yard, the grove, kitchen garden, and bee hives opposite the dwelling, the haggard at the rere, where we had often played *hide and seek* among the ricks, and the stony lane connecting the lower side of the bawn to the bog of Cashel.

After dinner we strolled up the crooked lane that served for communication with the high road before mentioned. Some perches to the west of the junction on the left, lies the extensive rath of Cromoge, with Kennystown bog approaching it on the south. Some of the legends and traditions that follow are connected with this old fort. The village of Kennystown and Tobinstown, watch each other's movements across the bog. Going eastwards, along a very stony lane, we pass the avenue gate of the fine old manor house of Ashgrove, the once rich and hospitable residence of the Fitzhenrys. Leaving its fine garden and lawn, and the tall slate-roofed building itself down below us on the right, we follow the same lane until we get into the lonely village of Lower Gurteen, which seems to have retired into that out-of-the-world locality from some very urgent motive. The remains of strong walls and massive gate-posts imply that it must have boasted of some importance in

times past. We are now only a short distance southwards from where we dined. We see beyond the Glasha
the hill of Coolgarrow; and looking up a ravine through
which a little rivulet tumbles and foams, we get a sight
of the comfortable farm-house of my Godmother. We
are not now going to pay her a visit, we mean to do so
anon. We cross the lower part of the bog of Cashel, and
get over the Glasha stream. We are now in Upper
Tombrick, and moving up the hill-side through a defile,
and below our scarped path lies a sheltered farm-house.
The position is most snug and picturesque, but when the
farmer yokes his horse I will not undertake to explain
how he and his load get up the steep lane to meet the
main road from my Godmother's village down to the
road by the Slaney.

At this part of our narrative we beg our readers to
indulge in a retrospect of the longest remembered portions of their lives, especially if raths, or rushing waters,
or meadows with thorn fences, or mountains, made up the
landscape. Let them indulgently consider this piece of
map-work while under the pleasant influence of childish
recollections.

As we proceeded leisurely up the hill-side, our discourse turned to Bantry, and I began to sound my companion on the state of his heart. I learned that for a
long time after the disappointment already chronicled, his
mind was much disturbed and his spirits depressed; but
that by dint of prayer and close application to his business, the fascinating image so long present to his thoughts
had at last become faint, unless when an unwelcome
dream brought it back in all its former freshness, and
then for a couple of days he felt the wretched longing
left by disappointed affection.

From the spot which we had now reached, we had a
fine prospect over the wood of Tombrick, the clear, winding Slaney, and its green inches, the house and wood of
Munfin, Clobemon, the seat of the Derinzy's beyond the
river, the fine country in its rear overlooked by Slieve-
bui, the hills on the near border of Wicklow, the old

castle of Ferns, the rugged Carrick-ruadh, and far to
the south, the cone of Vinegar Hill over Enniscorthy.
"There", said Edward, pointing out a farm-house lower
down, "is Mr. Lucas's, one of my chief patrons. I do
not think I have ever seen a more industrious family
than he has, from the eldest daughter Margaret to the
youngest, nice little Sarah, whom you will be delighted
to have for a pupil.

"Mr. Lucas himself is a very intelligent and shrewd
man, though not overburthened with literary information.
His powers of observation and memory are very great.
The sons, Peter and Bernard, are cheerful, humorous
young fellows, and I have passed some very pleasant
evenings in the family. Margaret's school days were
over before my arrival".

"Edward, take care of her beauty getting entangled
with you, as Sleeveen said". "Oh, bother yourself and
Sleeveen! A word or look of love has not passed between
me and any woman, old or young, these two years; and
I think I will have the same story to tell seven years
hence. I will not deny that Margaret Lucas is very
modest, unaffected, and gentle in manner, and sweet-
featured into the bargain. Indeed, it will be a pity if
she is thrown away on that ass of a Murtagh Horan:
though he is a good plodding man of business, and
knows well enough how to manage his farm".

Some among the readers of this narrative are probably
not aware that Tombrick wood covers the south slope of
the eastern portion of Coolgarrow hill, which gradually
sinks from its western summit above my Godmother's
house till it loses itself in the upper part of our townland. As we went down the northern verge of this wood,
we heard voices inside, and were immediately joined by
Mr. Lucas, his eldest and youngest daughters, one of his
sons, and Murtagh. There was much cordiality in their
reception of Edward, not excepting the long wooer himself, who, if mortified by a suspicion of a preference shown
to the stranger, was still sensible of his good qualities.
I had some opportunity here to gather information; and

could not help judging from the animation of the young
lady's countenance, and my friend's demeanour towards
her, that their mutual feelings were of a livelier character
than they themselves suspected.

Margaret Lucas's dress, though neatly made, and serving well enough to follow the outline of her graceful
figure, was of uncostly materials; little silk and less
jewellery being visible. The upper part of her profile
presented a beautifully flowing curve, as in Hogarth's
country beauties. The full face was a charming oval,
the mouth was small, but the lips the reverse of pinched,
and a very sweet expression was the result of the whole.
How she might have looked if offended I do not know,
never having seen her except in a pleasant or serious
mood, and on one or two occasions, under the sway
of sadness. Mr. Lucas had more of the manner of a
citizen, than that of a country farmer, and little Sarah
was one of the prettiest children I ever laid eyes on.

While a mingled conversation was going on, Edward
was taken to task by Margaret, for his absence from
Castle Dockrell; he threw the blame on my eagerness
to revisit my birthplace, and my earliest friends; and
then her brother put in his oar. "Are you quite sure
that there was no sweetheart in question? It is unnatural for a good-looking fellow like the master here,
to be more than two years in the parish, and never found
out sighing for some young girl, or making a song in
her praise. Maybe there is some little goddess about
Kilmeashil or Cromogue?" Here I thought that I perceived on Margaret's face a considerable degree of attention to the expected answer.

"Make your mind easy, Bernard", said Edward. "I
look on courting, when there is no immediate prospect
of marriage, as a very undesirable operation; and I am
very much in awe of handsome heiresses, for my own
fortune is yet to be made".

Here H. W. took the liberty of whispering to the
modest speaker. "Ah! if Graigue, Cooliagh, and
Scollagh were present, and could impart their knowledge

in plain English, I think your face would not have that righteous expression on it". H. W. got a look which extinguished him for a distance of several perches.

"Do n't be too hard on Mr. O'Brien", said Margaret. "Sure he has set all our minds at ease now at any rate. But I remember well about a quarter of a year after he came to this neighbourhood, how he once accidentally dropped a nice little ornamented china box; and when I picked it up, and did my best to keep it, he caught my hand, and squeezed my fingers hard enough, and forced it from me; not, however, until I contrived to open it, and I think I saw a nice twisted lock of brown hair inside. Maybe he will explain, and apologise for hurting my fingers".

Poor Edward was not a little embarrassed; he felt his cheeks burning, and wished himself snugly sitting on Mr. Donovan's griddle beside Owen Jourdan. However, Mr. Lucas came to his relief. "Master, if ever you happen to be alone with a woman, young or old, and find that you cannot make her pay much attention to your discourse, tell her a little bit of scandal about some neighbour, with a spice of love or matrimony in it, and never fear she 'll soon be attentive enough. But where are yourself and countryman—'boy', I should say. bound for?" "To Mr. Donovan's". "Well, Paddy Donovan must do without you for one evening. The old woman has a hot cake on the griddle, and if she finds we let you off, we 'll hear it on both sides of our head". After some thrusting and parrying, Edward obtained a victory, very much against his own wishes, as I could guess; but made a promise to spend next evening with them. We separated, and in due time reached our destination, and spent our evening at Mr. Donovan's; the ordinary fireside gossip being varied with some edifying reading.

CHAPTER IV.

THE BATTLE OF LIFE COMMENCED.

NEXT morning after breakfast, Edward and I set out for school, accompanied by Pat, Mosey, Mary, and Catherine: and our up-hill way was very pleasant through the furzy fields and paths by sheltery hedges, being frequently enlivened by the frolics of the children as they coursed each other round the bushes. Many of these small clumps of furze are clipped by the goats into the semblance of a helmet, with a waving plume. Mary added to our entertainment, blushing, and laughing, and striving to put some story right, after hopelessly embroiling it, her persecution being renewed as we traversed the knoc, where " Bet run away from Mary, and Mary run after her to beat Bet". Dear, innocent little Mary, your blunders were more delightful than the wisest sayings of other children. We got a salute as we passed Lucas's bawn-gate, but Margaret was not visible; and I detected Edward's eyes sounding the depths of shade through doors and windows for a glimpse of her stuff gown, or the tuft of brown hair gathered at the back of her graceful head.

We entered our temporary school room, first getting a jovial salutation from Mrs. Murphy, one of whose out-houses had served for the seminary for three years past. We found about a dozen pupils assembled, and fell to the business of the day with more earnestness than is sometimes found in fashionable academies. During this cold season we had a fire, and we did all the business we could in its neighbourhood. Being very desirous in this my first campaign, to establish a good reputation, I entered on my apprenticeship with the greatest avidity.

I have never since felt anything like the zeal which then upheld me in my arduous duties. My patrons were at best but country farmers, but they and their families were my arbiters, my audience, my world, and I can boast that all turned out real well-wishers and friends. Being of an active and mercurial turn, and nineteen years of age, I exerted myself to give them pleasure, and was rewarded by kindness and confidence. At this distance, I look back with pleasure on that useful span of my life, and think with gratitude, of the affection shown me by the Doyles, the Whittys, the Hogans, the Kehoes, the Kennedys, the Longs, the Murphys, and the Henricks. May some of my surviving pupils, read these lines with something like the pleasurable emotion with which they are written: and the dear little girls and boys—now, alas! careworn women and men—may they forget all instances of discipline in school, and remember only our chatty pleasant walks homewards, when the evening closed our labours. Dear little Mary and Catherine Doyle, Anne and Catherine Whitty, Mary and Catherine Hogan, my Godmother's Mary and Catherine, and the rest, I wish I was possessed of Aladdin's lamp for your sakes. At that time, it seemed no trifling thing to be summoned out of the school-room to enjoy the honour of taking breakfast with Father Cullen, after the station held at Mr. Lucas's house. The priest's notice, the flavour of the tea, the buttered home-made bread, and the agreeable cordiality shown by Margaret, are as fresh in my mind at this moment, as when they occurred.

Our academy was unlike fashionable schools in more than one respect, for our throngest time was the middle of summer; and in the month of August, when city teachers are announcing the re-opening of their academies, our little men and women were helping at harvest work. When this was concluded we had a bustle again for a while, but the cold weather of December and January shut up our bee-hive altogether.

The consciousness of giving satisfaction to our scattered country patrons, was sufficient to make the longest summer day seem too short, and yet the labour was not at all trifling. The hearing of the spelling or grammar-tasks committed to memory at home, interfered terribly

with the ordinary school business, and was very annoying
in other respects, as pandies for mistakes or forgetfulness were in full vogue. By the time that the whole
reading and spelling force could get through three individual lessons, dinner hour had come, and we were
obliged to dismiss our pupils with an uneasy impression
that we had not gone through as much business as could
be wished.

There was quiet in the school for about an hour ; those
who returned first from dinner having the privilege of
playing till all would be assembled, and the proper time
for renewing lessons arrived.

Our favourite play ground was the paddock that lay
between the rere of Mrs. Murphy's house and Mr.
Lucas's bawn ; and under the shelter of the ash trees
when the days were fine, the game of *Prison Bars*
(Prisoners' Base) was delightful. There were two sta-
tions, and a party of five or six at each ; and while boy
or girl touched the stone representing the fortress, and
held one of his party by the hand, and that one held
another, and so on, the person of each was inviolable.
and not to be carried off into bondage. Facing each
other in two parallel lines, the leading principle of the
game was that any one leaving his own station later than
an opponent had quitted his, had the privilege of chasing
him ; and if he laid hand on him before he could touch
any of his own party who were still stationary at their
terminus, he carried him off to prison. Of course these
prisoners were sought in their desolation by their allies ;
and when a captive could touch the hand of a free comrade, before this last was intercepted by a privileged
opponent, he was enfranchised at once, and joined his
friends.

The parties consisting indifferently of boys and girls,
it added interest to the mimic war, when a little girl in
prison was released by a swift and active boy of her own
faction.

After play hour we endeavoured to get through two
lessons with each individual, and what was called the

Class, concluded the secular business. That exercise has been described in the *Banks of the Boro*, page 262.

Now and then through the day, a laugh would arise from such mistakes as one boy asking the king of the class to spell and tell the meaning of LACTATLON, having mistaken the I in the word for an L, or Michael Foley turning "ah me!" into the feeling expression "ah, my eye!" or Neal Kirwan announcing *Gulliver* as the discoverer of America, or Theresa Duffy asserting *chronology* to be the established religion of Denmark. The closing hour being at hand, a portion of Devereux's Catechism was taught, a few common prayers were recited, and all separated for their several homes. I have seldom since experienced the same hearty, satisfactory feelings that these evenings were sure to bring; feelings that arose from the conscientious discharge of a truly sacred duty. But if I had given way to anger in the course of the day, I was pretty well punished by unpleasant sensations during our homeward walk.

CHAPTER V.

AN EVENING AT MR. LUCAS'S.—A TARTAR CAUGHT AGAINST THE WILL OF HIS CAPTOR.—AN UNPLEASANT SPECIMEN OF A GO-BETWEEN.

SCHOOL is at last dismissed; and after giving a hand to Mr. Lucas and his sons at the evening occupation, we are all assembled at the kitchen fire, where the hot cake is in progress of being well baked, and the tea-pot by its presence, diffuses an agreeable anticipation of delicacies by-and-by; and the tea tray is furnished, and carried into the parlour above the kitchen where we will not be uncomfortable, as a fire has been lighted on the hearth, and our happiness is enhanced by the dropping in of Mrs. Murphy. Mrs. Murphy is a widow, provided with a son and two daughters; of moderate means, but furnished with a heart to the full as large as that of our old acquaintance Mrs. Roche.

Dear old friend! my memory will be weak when I forget your general goodness, or your particular kindness to myself. A more unselfish or better-natured heart never dwelt in that home of love and goodness, the breast of a true woman; but still, my estimable lady, you were not faultless. Your temper was short, and when in a passion, your tones were not of a dulcet character. While the preparations were making she entertained us with the woful disappointment that befel her son, on Edward's first coming to the country.

"We all heard Father Cullen after Mass, recommending the master here, and exhorting the parishioners to be diligent in sending their children to school, and seeing them provided with books and catechisms. Garrett took a peep at the new teacher, and seeing such a modest boyish appearance about him, he whispered to Mosey Donovan, 'Oh, won't we have fine sport, if that young fellow is to be over us; we'll do as we like'. My poor Garrett! he had soon to change his tune. I never saw a poor gorsoon so put out of his way as he was, when he found the boy-teacher so resolute in school hours, though he was not afraid to join his scholars at play time. Indeed, master, if you had a little better command of your temper, like myself, *mauryah!* there would not be a better teacher from this to Donaghadee, wherever that place is".

"That's right, ma'am", returned Edward. "Think much of my merits, and little of my defects. I heard Jem Kavanagh the prophecy-man say, that when the Protestants were all dead and gone, at least all the good old stock, the Catholics that did n't care much about them when they were to the fore, would be seen crying at their graves, and even carrying home some of the clay for a memory of them. So, maybe, when I am away in Dublin, and Harry with his rod is extracting tears from the eyes of some of the little urchins, they will devote a few of them to my absence".

" Well, master, whatever your defects may be, you have managed to get the love of most of the youngest of the scholars, though they are pretty much in awe of you. I missed something the other day while you were at dinner, and when I could get no tidings of it, I threatened I'd send the master to gaol if it was not found. Mary Hogan burst out a crying at once, poor innocent little thing! and said, 'Indeed, and if you do, ma'am, I'll go to gaol along with him. I do n't know if the little master will be so successful".

" I assure you, ma'am", said H. W., " I've always been a special favourite with old women, young children, cats, dogs, and simpletons; but no woman between fifteen and thirty-five ever paid the least attention to me".

" Ah, little fear of your having the luck of Murtagh, here", observed Barney Lucas. " You would not believe me if I were to tell you of the number of young girls that paid for a whole winter's night-schooling to Mr. Dan Henrick, to be able to read his love-letters, and answer them".

" Oh, bother your inventions, Barney!" replied Murtagh. " So far is that from the truth, neighbours, that that hanging-bones of a Murtha Cowman (*Comyn*) had the *impedence* to ax me the other day if I had any young woman in my eye, that he might go court for me; and he'd take out the worth of his trouble in meal or malt, money or *marvels* (marbles); any way I'd like".

" I hope, Mr. Horan", said Edward, " you did not give him a good kicking. I do n't think I am unprovided with mere bodily courage, but I assure you, I got no small fright one day by his coming close to me, putting his head on one side in an insinuating style, and making some such proposal. His manner was so fawning, the part about his lips looked so raw and moist, and his beard was so thin and weak, and his face had such a queer appearance as if it belonged neither to a man or woman, that I did not know whether I had better knock him down, or run away".

" Well, boys", said Mr. Lucas, " I entirely approve of

your depending on yourselves when you want to secure a
wife. Indeed your best plan is not to give yourselves too
much uneasiness about it. If you were to work yourselves to oil, or break your necks or hearts, maybe their
choice would settle after all on some gander that did not
care a pinch of snuff about them, nor ever offer them, at
fair or market, a mug of beer nor a pipe of tobacco.
Bother the tobacco! I did not mean it, but it comes in so
naturally with the drink, it slipped from me. I suppose,
let a young woman do all she could to fall in love with a
worthy man that wanted to marry her, she could n't
manage it, if it did not come to her of its own accord.
No one need be frightened, however. Let a pair be only
of good religious dispositions, and their tastes or inclinations not very different, and let each wish to please the
other, and even if that love we read about in story books
is in no hurry to come, a blessing will follow, and good
feelings soon bind them to one another. So let the master
and Murtagh renounce the match-maker and his works,
and when their hour comes, let them not even burthen
themselves with a *Black man*. If I find the hot cake and
tea to my liking, I 'll tell you by-and-by how Mick
Jones went a courting againt his will, and how his black
man did his best for him against *his* will, and how neither
of them got what he was working for. Well, Nanny, is
all ready?"

Here we repaired at our matron's beck to the parlour;
and some people being born under an unlucky planet,
Murtagh got a seat by the vanithee, while Edward had
the happy lot of sitting next Margaret, and helping her
in the pleasant duties of the tea table.

When the statute number of cups were nearly emptied,
Mr. Lucas took up the discourse. " I must say a few
words before I get the story rightly by the horns, for the
information of the little master, as he has been out of the
country since he was a child. You saw several large
holes by the road side, as you went up towards Moyeady
yesterday, and some of them encroaching even on paddocks
and kitchen gardens. The ground near the banks of the

river is full of pebble-limestone, and any one on this part of the estate is privileged to open the land wherever he pleases, and take out these pebbles, provided that he levels the ground when he has done, and replaces the upper soil and the sods.

"Now when the burrower has his limestone ready, the next thing is to get it burned, either on this side the Slaney, or there beyond the river, where you see the kilns with the raw stony-looking banks at each side of them. The nearest colliery is in the Queen's County, and there we must go for culm to burn our lime. Taking a supply of cakes in a bag, we set out; and when we are benighted, and wish for refreshment for ourselves and our cattle, we tnrn into some farmer's bawn on the edge of the road, give hay to the horses, and rest ourselves before the good kitchen fires. We happen to have a good name among the Carlow people, and they never dream of shutting their doors against us.

"Those that are in the habit of going to the colliery, have their horses so well trained that once they clear Bunclody, they throw themselves in the hay in the bottom of the car, and doze or sleep, while the horse, knowing the way by heart, follows his nose.

"And now you won't be at a loss to understand the beginning of my story.

CHAPTER VI.

THE COURTSHIP IN CARLOW.

" WELL, there was a widow woman living there above, between the slate quarries and Rossard, and she had a stout-built *Turk* of a son, that was worth his weight in gold for work, but a special bad hand at the courting; and he would tremble, as if he had the ague, if he was left near a handsome young girl, and thought he was expected to make himself agreeable.

"They had a decent, well-looking servant girl, and she

4

was not long in her new situation when Mick (the family
name was Jones) was suspected by his mamma to be a
trifle more civil and attentive to Bessy Keogh, than young
farmers are obliged to be, to persons in her situation.
So she took counsel with a long-headed neighbour or
two, and started Mick on a courting expedition up into
Carlow, giving him for a *Blackman* a lively fidget of a
neighbouring farmer, Richard O'Connor by name.   Mrs.
Jones was slightly acquainted with the family of the
intended bride; and Mick had stopped a few times there
on his colliery expeditions. Richard had also been on the
spot on a couple of occasions.

"So they mounted their beasts, and set off on a fine
morning in July, and rode up through Bunclody, or, as
your Englified people call it, 'Newtownbarry'. Och! how
I hate to see a title like that, without any meaning, dis-
possessing a fine old name that marked a spot for maybe
more than a thousand years, and had a meaning besides—
Bun Clody, the end of the Clody; for you know it falls
into the Slaney just above the town.   I have heard gentlemen that travelled far and near say, that it is the
finest village (that is what they call it) in all Ireland.
If you stand on the bridge and look up the river, you
have the fine meadow on the right hand, the wood sloping
down to the river on the left, with the nice walk by the
bank; the little waterfall, and the Slaney itself bending
round, with the trees and the hills in the rear.   Then if
you come to the opening into the town, and it be a fine
evening in summer or harvest, how nice the little stream
looks, coming down through the middle of the wide street,
with the mall by the side, and the rows of trees. Maybe
the sun is shining on the white houses on the Slaney side
of the town, while the opposite ones cast a cool shade on
the pavement; and you see out beyond, the hills, and the
woods running down their side to the Ryland road, and
all appearing so cool and purple, when you look at it,
and the bright walls, and sunny side of the street together.
It reminds me of some fine pictures I have seen at
Munfin, Castleboro, and other places.

" I am detaining the travellers too long. They are beyond the bridge over the Clody, and gone up the Ryland road, the hills on their left, and the wooded banks of the Slaney below them; and after passing far beyond Kildavin and Myshall, they are at last on a rising ground, the back of Mount Leinster pretty far to their left, and a farm house half way down the slope of the road before them. They were dressed much alike. Their coats were brown, we are not so partial here to blue as they are in Carlow and Kilkenny. They wore top-boots, cassimere breeches, and good Carolina hats; but their looks and manner were quite different. Richard's face was always ready for a laugh or a smile; and he let nothing nor nobody along the road escape without some observation or joke, while Mick gazed before him with a dogged, disturbed look; and a person that could read faces, would see in his, a kind of weakness, and an inclination to be obstinate when he could.

" ' Musha, Richard', said he looking down towards the house, ' I wish we were safe at home again. Oh, dear! what made me come out at all? and there, as sure as a gun, is the old man watching for us. Could n't my mother find a match for me in my own neighbourhood? and indeed I 'd rather have a quiet wedding with our own servant maid, poor Bessy Keogh, than to have all this bother; clipping my hair, shaving and bleeding myself, and putting on this divel of a cravat that is half choking me, and I 'm afraid, will slice off my ears. And how am I to find talk and compliments for Miss Catherine Murphy that I 'm sent to court, with her cold nose and stand-off airs? And this reminds me that I do n't recollect three out of the thirty nice things that I learned by heart in the *Academy of Compliments* that I paid a tester for last market day in Bunclody. Oh! that 's true! you, being my Blackman, must find talk for me as well as yourself;. but if you leave me a minute alone with the young woman I 'll have your life so I will'.

" ' I pity you much, my poor friend,' says Richard, ' so much that I would have no objection to change places

with you.   It is a great hardship, indeed, to sit down by
a comely young girl, like Miss Murphy, and praise her
beauty, and her fine silken hair, and tell her that you
have seen no one between this and the Duffrey to compare with her, and that she is never out of your thoughts
waking or sleeping, and that——'

"'Oh, talk is cheap', says Mick. "Do you think I'll
be able to please her on so short an acquaintance,
when as you know yourself, not a girl in our own parish
could bear to be joked on about me? Well, well; I
think poor Bessy likes me a little. She cried when I
was coming away, and hid her face when my mother
came in; and, troth, she is good-looking enough, and can
read and write a good hand, and is a good sempstress
and housekeeper, ay, and of a good old respectable family,
though they are reduced now".

"'And can't you take the same method to gain Miss
Murphy's good opinion that you did to make Bessy like
you?'

"'Oh, *sarra* method or plan did I take about it at all;
only when she'd be carrying too heavy a basket, I'd take
one side, or may be I'd hold the skein on my arms when
she'd want to wind it, or drive home the cows for her, or
put in a soft word when her mistress would think of
scolding her, or, may be, buy a bit of a silk 'kerchief or
ribbon for her, of a very odd time; but where is there an
opportunity for any such thing here? And besides,
though Mis Catherine always showed herself civil enough
any time that I stopped at the house going to the colliery, she has some method of freezing a joke or a compliment, before I can open my mouth to make it; and
now, there is the old miser her father, waiting at his gate
for us like a spider. Och, don't I love the sight of his
poverty-bitten face!'

" They now crossed a grass plot that lay between the
bawn-fence and the road, and were welcomed by the old
gentleman. The front of the house looked towards the
pleasant-looking back of Mount Leinster, and the inside
was on the very plan of the house we're in.

"They were soon exchanging compliments with the *Vanithee*, a handsome, contented-looking woman, about forty-five, decked out in her best quilted petticoat and stuff gown; and with the heiress, a serious-looking, well-featured young woman of twenty-four. Poor Mick was sadly flustered, and Richard, for a wonder, felt in want of words, for if he had got time or opportunity, he would prefer to change places with his comrade. Even the lady who shook hands with Mick with very little disturbance, faltered a little when she presented her hand to his Blackman.

"Mr. Murphy had a way of his own of going through this ceremony. He separated his thumb very far from his fingers, the four of which he held out in a most deadly cold manner, and never stirred muscle or joint till you let his paw drop: I 'd as *lieve* handle a frog as touch his excuse for a hand.

"The dinner was now served up, consisting of good floury potatoes, bacon, and cabbage. Our poor Mick, for his sins, was placed beside Miss Murphy; and it would be sorrowful to go over the list of his troubles while he assisted at that awful feast of state, everything being either in his own, or in each other's way: the knife and fork were as often on the ground as in his hands, and if his plate did not go so low, it was owing to good luck.

"Mrs. Murphy, out of pity for him, began to talk to him of different matters, and then expressed her great pleasure at seeing him her guest, and pressed him to eat heartily, and lay shyness aside.

"'Do you think our friend is shy, ma'am?' says Richard. 'Ah, then, if you were at the cross-roads, near Myshal, this day fortnight, his shyness would give you little trouble ever after. We just got there, on our return from the colliery, when we were met by a lazy bodagh of a fellow dozing on the warm hay in his empty car. We were foot-sore, and a little annoyed by the impudent look the bosthoon gave us. So Mick came to the back of his car, and took hold of his hand, and began shaking it as if he 'd pull it off, and asked about his health, and the health of

his family, and how the farm was doing; till at last the
geochach being very uncomfortable, and only half wakened
up, got out of the car, and stood with us till his beast was
a good quarter of a mile ahead. Mick hardly let him get
a word out of his mouth the whole time, but now he
began to return thanks with a very puzzled face, saying,
'Really, I 'm very much obliged to you, but though I 'm
ashamed to own it, you have the advantage of me (*I
have not the pleasure of knowing your name*)'. 'In troth,
says Mick, 'it 's true for you: we are just at home with
our loads while you are only beginning your journey'.
There was no puzzle then in his face, I assure you, for his
look was all for a fight; and he would have gone to search
for the soft part of Mr. Jones's head, only for something
in my friend's eye that did not encourage him, and I think
something also in the appearance of his arms and shoulders, we were in our shirt sleeves at the time. So thinking better of it, and letting a bitter curse at us, he pegged
after his horse and car that were now out of sight.

"Poor Mick's confusion was great at the conclusion of
this small story, and well it might; as it was honest
Richard himself that had disturbed the lazy boy in the
car; and the two women, taking a peep at the troubled
face of the wooer, made a very close guess at the truth.

"The old farmer was a sad miser. Little did he enjoy
the good food before him; and at last, before the natural
conclusion of the meal, and in a fit of spleen and forgetfulness of his company, he began to rub his hands, and
repeat in Irish, 'For what we have received, mumble,
mumble, mumble; *rise* the table'. It was a falling table
they were seated round at the time.

"'Oh, *Mogue* dear', said his wife, 'what are you thinking of? Our Wexford friends ought to be told that since
you had the *sickness* (fever) you sometimes forget all
about you. I suppose you thought just now that we were
done dinner. Mr. O'Connor and Mr. Jones, if you do
not go on, and make a hearty meal, I 'll think you are
offended'. Here she gave her master a quiet but serious
look, which if he readily forgot, I wonder at it, that 's

all, and Mr O'Connor gave her story just the same credit that she had bestowed on his.

"Dinner being over, Mrs. Murphy requested her daughter to shew Mr. Jones the paddocks and near parts of the farm; and then, she and her husband, and Richard, taking seats under the big chimney-piece, arranged the conditions of the marriage portion, it being distinctly understood that no force was to be laid on the inclinations of either of the young people. The old gentleman's purse-strings were rather stiff, but still, after a good deal of talk, they came to terms.

"Meanwhile matters were not as satisfactory abroad as could be desired. The bridegroom, in handing his future bride over a drain, gave her left foot a good wetting, and her wrist was nearly sprained by some manœuvre of his, while helping her across a fence. Catherine remarking the delightful appearance of the mountain side, with the low sun shining so nicely on it, Mick took occasion to express his fears that his workmen would not be sufficiently diligent in the drawing home of the turf in his absence. Catherine's shawl being caught by a briar, he took the opportunity of crying out, 'Ah, that is the way that your beauty is entangled with me'. Seeing how surprised she looked, he cleverly changed the phrase to 'Och, I mean, Miss Murphy, that my beauty is entangled with you'. Finding matters not mended by the alteration, he cried out in despair, 'Oh dear; I 'm sure I do n't know what I mean; but at any rate, it would be a pity to throw you away on the likes of me'. She bade him not to think so meanly of himself, and relieved him by turning the conversation to his friend Richard. This was a theme on which he really could shine, in his listener's opinion at least, for he did not tire of enlarging on his sound judgment, cheerfulness of disposition, real piety, and good conduct. Richard's friendship for himself was the chorus to every verse of his song, and his hearer seemed as if she wished it would never come to an end. They were sitting on a grassy hillock, and as Catherine's ears took in his words, her eyes wandered over a level tract of ripe

corn-fields, potato-stripes of rich dark green, lately mown
meadows of a livelier colour, and the shadows thrown over
these objects by the trees.   When the eye was fatigued by
the glare of the sun, they turned round, and kept them
fixed on the back of the mountain.

"Catherine now took her part in the discourse, and
hinted to her admirer that though she felt as sincere a
friendship for him as their acquaintance warranted, she
did not consider that their union would be particularly
desirable for either; and she expected from his good
nature, that if her parents would press for her consent, he
would give her some help.   Mick was both rejoiced and
embarrassed by this request, and between hypocritical regret for his ill success, and eager offers to give what assistance he could, she readily guessed that a breaking off of
the match would not inflict a heart-break on himself; so
this obstacle being removed, their walk home was much
pleasanter than the outset promised.

"Meanwhile Richard did his friend all the service he
conscientiously could, but certainly felt no particular pain
at Mrs. Murphy's declaration that she and her husband
would leave the choice of marriage or not marriage, freely
to Catherine, after stating their own cordial wishes in
favour of Mr. Jones.

"The wanderers were returned from their walk, the
cows were housed and milked, and the farm servants were
enjoying their rest on benches, stools, and straw bosses
round the fire.   Fresh wheaten loaves were baking in pots
for some time, lighted coals being laid on the lid, as
sometimes with ourselves; and when they were just at the
right point, neither too crusty nor too soft, they were
whipped out, and split open, and I suppose they did not
soon melt the butter that was laid inside.   I won't say
much in praise of the tea.   I have heard that the Royal
Family of China never let the best tea out of the country.
So when the other kings and queens through the world
have picked out the next best quality, and left the Lord
Lieutenant the leavings, you may be sure the gentlemen
and ladies that come after him, take all that's any good

out of what remains in the sack; and Mrs. Murphy and Mrs. Lucas, when they are buying tea, may as well shut their eyes, take what they get, and make no remark. However, neither the Queen nor the Duchess of Leinster had better cream, nor butter, nor wheaten bread that night, nor a better appetite than the Murphys and their visitors.

"Two of the supper party, however, were little benefited by the good fare before them. The master of the house was so annoyed by the extravagance of the feast, that he could scarcely swallow a mouthful; and Mr. Jones was so taken up by joy at his release, anxiety to find compliments, and shyness of the company, that first, the tea-cup scalded his mouth, and then the saucer in its fall, scalded his thighs; then both articles bit the clay floor, and went in smithereens under the table.

"Richard, with the object of doing something for the relief of his friend, asked if the fame of the great Andrew Farrell had come so far north. They said 'No', and he observed that he was quite sure he must be at least seven miles off, for the smell of the present good cheer would have brought him to the spot from any shorter distance. 'The girls of Cashel', he observed, 'when sitting lonesome at their spinning wheels, are in the habit of roasting potatoes in the *greeshach*, but they never venture on the exploit without first getting on the bawn ditch to spy if Andrew be within any unreasonable distance; for no guager in the barony has a sharper nose for a potheen still, than Andrew for a batch of roasted potatoes. Mr. Jones, in a few verses that he made on the subject, sings in this way about it.

> "The girls of Cashel they sit in the ashes,
>   A roasting potatoes their pockets to smoke;
> They must go to brave Andrew to get out a permit,
>   For if they roast private, they'll pay for the joke.

> "Andrew Farrell, he is the head guager:
>   The alphabet's printed upon his shin-bone"—

And no wonder, for as he never does any thing but

watch his neighbours' chimneys at meal-time, and sit by
their fires, all the colours of the rainbow are burnt into
his legs. The only thing besides, that he ever turns his
hand to, is making up matches between the young men
that are too bashful, and the farmers' daughters round
the country. He applied to Mr. Jones here, to allow him
to look out for a good wife for him, but my friend very
properly answered that 'the man was not worthy of a
good wife, who was too lazy or too cowardly to make the
search himself'. So my dirty old boy never forgave him,
but has been ever since pick-thanking, and tattling, and
telling lies of him, to all the girls of Cashel, and Cromogue, and Gurteen, and Tobinstown, and Kennystown:
much we care for him, the contemptible old thief!

"'So, according to your account', said the vanithee,
'Mr. Jones, along with being a wag and a wit, is a poet
too; it is a pity he is so modest'.

"'You may well say that, ma'am', answered the Blackman, 'and although I am putting myself too forward, I
can't help giving you another specimen of his talents in
that way: but mayn't we as well go into the kitchen, and
sit at the fire, and let the people there be amused by my
friend's composition'. While the change was making,
Jones whispered to him, 'Oh, bother your lies, and
praises, and gosther! Won't they find out soon enough,
that I have not a screed of wit, nor waggery, nor poetry
about me?'

"'Be quiet, will you', says the other; 'take every
thing that comes, and don't interfere with what does
not concern you'.

"They took their places at the fire while the farm labourers were finishing their supper of boiled wheat, sea-
soned with butter and salt, and Richard rattled out the
Rogueries of Coley, which, I suppose, you all have by
heart. If the Bantry boys have not heard it, some one
may sing it for them when my story is at an end.

"The company received this simple ballad with great
merriment; Catherine and her mother were obliged to
laugh in spite of themselves, but it is probable that

Richard's comicality and Mick's features had something
to do in it. The poor fellow rubbed his shins, and gave
a stupid laugh now and then; but did not know whether
to keep his eyes on the floor, or the fire, or the ceiling, or
O'Connor's face, or what to do.

" 'Well now, Mr. Jones', says Mrs. Murphy, 'will you
let us hear your voice? Any thing is acceptable, but we
would prefer a song of your own composing, if you
please'.

" 'Oh, Mrs. Murphy! do n't believe Richard. Dickens
a verse of a song could I put together, if you were to
make me heir of Damer's estate; but it would be too bad
to be bad with it, and bad about it, so I 'll strive to give
a few lines made by Tom Blanche, the little tailor: ah!
that 's the boy that has the Dixhenry by heart. Here
goes'; and with a beating at his heart, and a shake in
his voice, he commenced, but, alas! was n't able to
conclude—

The Beauty of Brie.

" Ye sub-celestial deities, ye nymphs of Mount Parnassus,
  With cheerfulness I hope you will attend :
Ye Macedonian muses, ye bards of elocution,
  Conjointly sympathise with a friend :
Your noncupative eloquence incessantly resound
  To praise a blooming *seraphim* whose equals can't be found,
Were I to circumnavigate the earthly globe all round :
  And she dwells in you valley so green".

'O murdher, I 'm so confused that I can't think of the
rest; and troth it 's a pity, for there is a power of beautiful hard words in it: hm—hm—hm.

" It being the limitation of slow approximation,
  And said, ' thou blest charmer divine' "—

'That means, I believe, just as the *courtier* met the lady
he was courting. I can't go on with it, but I 'll give
you some other'; and so he did give them the *Cottage
Maid*, with all the gods and goddesses from east to west
in it.

" As the airs of both songs were good, and the subjects lofty and obscure, there was great attention given; and Mick's praises were sung on all sides, when the performance was at an end.

"The old gentleman in his turn, sung *Peggy Bawn*; and Catherine, *The Banks of Clashavey*, to a mournful air; some punch was drunk, and Mick, gathering courage, made an attempt or two at pleasantry. Your impudent rogue may perhaps act a modest part with success, but the attempts of a bashful man to act the brazen-face are never lucky. This remark I give you from a book which fell into my hands some time or other.

"As the hour was now late, Mrs. Murphy handed a well-used copy of Father Gahan's Piety to Richard, and requested him to recite the Litany. So the faces that were bursting with the laugh a minute or two ago, became serious at once. Some answered devoutly enough; but one or two of the tired or lazy labourers laid their breasts flat on the next stools, and kept looking down through the floor all the time the prayers lasted, giving a spit now and then, by way of variety. If I had my will, I would not grudge to clap a lighted turf to their hind parts, the indevout, lazy thieves!

"After all was over, the servant boys retired to their straw beds in the barn; Richard and Mick to a room below the parlour; Mr. and Mrs. Murphy to one beside it, the separating wall not reaching to the roof; Catherine and her younger sisters to rooms on the other side of the kitchen, and the servant girls to their settle bed that rested by the kitchen wall opposite the door.

"For a while after our two friends lay down, Richard's feelings were far from comfortable. He considered that the intended marriage would scarcely prove a happy one; and, to say truth, a nearer acquaintance with Catherine, had cooled his zeal for his friend, though he determined to play out his part faithfully, whatever it cost him. While he turned over in his mind the amiable qualities of Catherine, and the turn of things that prevented him from endeavouring to obtain a place in her heart, he heard some muttering in the adjoining room, and his hearing being rendered sharp by the discomfort of his feelings, he managed to overhear the following dialogue.

"'*Mauria* dear, I'm afraid I'll be starved before morning, if you can't find something relishing for me to eat'.

"'And *who* have you to blame, Mogue asthore? had n't you full and plenty before you both at dinner and supper?'

"'Ah, you may easy talk; it was a fine piece of expense, the same dinner and supper, and punch. To *Halifax* with it for punch: I have a cutting headache after it, because there was nothing for it to rest on; for I was so *stomached* with the waste going on about me, that I could hardly eat a bit; and now I feel my ribs fallen down on my back bones a'most'.

"'Really, I hardly know what I can get; I gave all that was any good to the poor cottiers to take home to their little families. Well, well, I must only get up and make a cake, and bake it on the hearth-stone under the hot greeshach'.

"'Do so, Molly, and do'nt be long about it. I'm sure I wish it was all over, for a bothering courting and wedding'.

"The unshod feet of the vanithee were soon crossing the parlour into the kitchen; and Richard heard her kneading the cake, and then settling it on the hearth-stone, and piling the red hot sods over it.

"At the moment he felt spent after his singing, and joking, and exerting himself for Mick's honour; and feeling a very strong liking for Catherine, and a wish to make her his wife, he got altogether uncomfortable, just as if the skin of his mind had got a carding. So he got up, quietly slipped on his clothes, and presented himself at the kitchen fire, much to the annoyance of the mistress, though she did not *let on*.

"Taking a seat on the form that ran by the side of the partition wall which separated the fire place from the entrance, and with his back to the spy-hole, the intruder thus commenced his *palinody*:—'Mrs. Murphy, I am afraid I'm troublesome, but if you only knew the dis-

turbed state of my mind at nights, and the trifle of slee
I get, I'm sure you would have some pity for me'.   Here
he took hold of a sharp-pointed stick, and went on. 'You
must know, ma'am, that when my great-grandfather was
dying, he left the three townlands of Bawnard, Rossard,
and Coolycan, to be divided among his five sons. ' The
ill-natured people of our country—for there are ill-natured
people everywhere—call these places the three hells upon
earth, because the women, when they have not much to do
at home, take a stocking under their arm for an excuse,
and go to shanachus in the neighbours' houses; and sitting cozily that way together, and talking about those that
are away, the discourse is not always the most charitable
in the world.   Well, ma'am, these stories are sometimes
repeated, and then they set the women to tear off their
neighbours' caps, and the men to cudgel one another,
when they happen to go look at any one drinking in the
sheebeens.
   " 'But I see I'm straying from my story.   My great-
grandfather, as I said, having left these three townlands
to his four sons'—'You said five just now'.   'Did I,
ma'am ? Well, what a memory I have; and sure enough
there were five: let me see: Pat, and Bill, and Ned, and
Dick, and Jack, and Tim, and Tom; one, two, three,
four, five.—Oh, tare an' ages, that's seven.   Well,
I'm sure there were not seven any how.   Now I recollect, two of them were dead'.   'No matter, Mr. O'Connor, it's all the same'.   'Thank you, ma'am, it is your
goodness to say so.   Well, my five grandfathers—I mean
my grandfather and his four brothers, as soon as the
funeral was over, levelled every *ditch* on the land, just as
I am levelling the greeshach with this kippeen'.   This exploit rubbed the ashes into the soft cake, and disfigured
it mightily; and the poor woman was about springing
over to catch his hand, but she did n't.   'Then, making
a guess, they ran ditches as it might be this way'.   Suit-
ing the action to the word, he made a map on the ashes,
the pointed stick separating the unfortunate cake into as
many pieces as there were fields.

" Mrs. Murphy, whose state of mind was much to be pitied, now addressed her tormentor, representing that it would be a wiser thing to get a sound sleep, and forget these old miseries.

" 'Oh, Mrs. Murphy', says he, ' I did not come to the big misery of all, yet. One of my uncles, that is my grand-uncles, a cantankerous little cur, said that the division was not fair; that his farm was the least, and besides was all rushy and boggy, and too far from the road; and when the rest seemed unwilling to have any more bother, he threatened all sorts of law, and vengeance, and bum-bailiffs, and 'tornies, and tithe-proctors, and hearth-money-men, and process-servers, and latitats, if they did n't make another division. Anything for a quiet life; at it they went again, and re-levelled the fresh-made ditches, so (here the ashes and coals were again rubbed into the wounds of the cake); and then did n't he make them lay out the new bounds quite in a *conthráry* direction, just as if they run here (a new operation with the twig completely destroyed poor Mr. Murphy's last hopes, and not a bit the size of a thimble, was left together); and so with the trouble, and the ill-will, and the destruction of the soil, and the throwing up of the yellow clay, and the ill nature of their different families to one another ever since, you can 't wonder, ma'am, that I 'm not at all comfortable in my mind. However, your agreeable company has been of great service to me to-night: I feel calmer after this pleasant conversation. Good night, ma'am; you know that every careful mistress of a family should be up early to look after her household; and of course, if she does not go early to bed she 'll not get enough of natural rest. Go to sleep, ma'am, I beg; if poor Mr. Murphy is awake, he 'll be feeling lonesome: indeed, may be it 's waking him up out of his sound sleep you 'll be now, and that makes people cross'..

" Mr. Spoil-sport then made his way back to his sleeping apartment, and getting past Mick's bed, which lay next the door, he scrambled into his own pew, and

listened like a fox for the end of his exploit. He was
gratified by hearing an anxious demand for the cake;
and then a whispered conference was held, the tones of
the husband very harsh and cross, those of the wife
apologizing and somewhat resentful. At last a few clear
words rose out of the confused clatter. 'Well, well, let
us have a-noggin of milk any way: may be it will keep
us alive till morning'.

"Mrs. Murphy was in motion once more, but this
time she trod so lightly, though she had on her shoes,
that Richard was hard put to follow her movements;
however, he heard some fumbling among the delf articles
on the kitchen dresser; and then the latch of the outer
door was lifted.

"In about two minutes after Richard heard the latch
raised, he was up again, and was soon within about four
feet of Mrs. Murphy; she at one side of the cow in the
byre, not suspecting any new scheme, and milking
ding-dong, and he squatting down on the other side as if
waiting impatiently for the vessel to be full.

"'Ah, then, Mauria', says he, counterfeiting the old
gentleman's voice and manner, 'arn't you done yet? I
got into such a way that I could n't wait any longer.
Have you a drink ready? hand it over, for goodness sake,
I think I 'll faint'.

"'Here, take it', said she pettishly enough, 'and
much good do you with it. I 'm sure I 'm glad that we
have n't many holidays of this kind in the year'.

"He stretched over his arm under the cow's belly,
seized the noggin, and pretended to take a hearty drink:
for fear of detection, however, he made a hasty retreat
into the kitchen, and putting his vessel into a corner,
stole into his bed once more, without being heard by his
victim, who was enduring his little purgatory in the next
room.

"In a short time he was sensible of a very ungallant
proceeding on the part of the master of the house; for,
instead of welcoming his dutiful partner, he was asking in
a very peevish tone why she did n't bring the refreshment.

"'Did you not drink the whole noggin full, a few minutes ago, there abroad in the cow house?'

"'Me in the cow house! Oh, dear! Oh, dear! What in the world would take me there? I did not stir a foot since you left the bed, woman. It must be some ghost or fairy sent to torment me. Neighbours honey! I'll die dead; the world is come to an end!'

"'Shut your eyes, asthore, and go sleep. After a good breakfast you'll be as fresh as a lark: but Mogue dear, I hope that for the future, you'll never bid the table be lifted again in a hurry; and that when a good meal is laid before you, you'll eat hearty, and be thankful for God's gifts and mercies'.

"'God forgive me! but sure if people do not mind their little substance, it will dwindle away,—bacon and cabbage for a whole week, eat in one day—punch, seven shillings a gallon—I mean whiskey: tay and sugar to no end, and such givings out as there was! Could not mind the workmen, and maybe they did n't idle when they had the opportunity? And how in the world can I spare the fortune? Oh, musha! why do people of sense ever marry and bring such torment on themselves?' Here he fell into a troubled slumber, and had a vision of Andrew Farrell, in a salmon-coloured coat and sky-blue stockings, playing the bag-pipes for a dozen of the Cashel girls: then a puckawn, in a pair of top boots, and with a shepherd's crook in one hand, was looking at himself in a pocket glass, while the dog *Coley*, with turf mould for lather, and an iron hoop for razor, a pipe in his mouth, and a gold-laced, three-cocked hat on his head, was shaving him. Then seeing his white cow sitting on the table, and combing out her tail with one hand, and scratching out his cake from under the embers with the other, he muttered, 'Bother your impudence! do n't rise the table yet a bit'. He spoke some other half words after; but that was all Mrs. Murphy could recollect next morning.

"'O Richard', says Mick, 'I am glad you are quiet at last, I have such news for you. Bad 'cess to the bit of

5

me will Catherine have; aint I ready to jump out of my skin for joy?' Indeed if the same jump was possible, Richard would have been the man for it at that moment. 'But what 'll I do with the old people? Sure I can't inform on her; and with all, it's only right and decent to press for her consent a little, and maybe, then she 'll get their anger by refusing; and maybe, sooner than vex them, she 'll take me after all, and won't we be looking foolish enough at one another then? Oh tundher and turf, Dick, if you do n't lend us a helping hand, we 'll be fairly beat; and sure you ought to do it, if it was only for her civility in asking so much about you, when we were sitting on the hillock in the evening. And it was n't asking like a purse proud damsel about your farm, and cattle, and house, she was; no, but if you were of a sober religious turn, or too fond of wakes or patterns, or looking after the young women. Indeed I think she strove to pick out of me whether you were engaged to any one to be married: but now I think of it; dickens a bit of her asked me a single one of these questions; and I am sure I never thought of giving her any information. Still somehow or other, I know I told her every thing about you. Well, may be it 's best to sleep on it; but how will I go to sleep, for I am as hungry as a hunter? I 'm sure I did n't eat three bits at dinner or supper, with the shyness and the bother I was in, and your confounded gosther and poetry; and now I have a headache, and I 'm famished, and there you lie without a morsel of pity for me'.

"'Well, Mick, you are a bad pattern of a rollicking Wexford bridegroom in a strange county, but it can't be helped now. I saw some of the *gran brie* (boiled wheat) in a pot in the left corner, near the fire; and you 'll find a noggin of fresh milk at the very far end of the lower shelf of the dresser: make no noise going or coming, and do n't waken me when you get back'.

"Mr. Jones got through this manœuvre with tolerable success; he only trod on the cat's tail, and was rewarded by a scratch on the leg. Having partaken of the simple refreshment, he found his feelings relieved, just as if oil and honey were poured on them. At the same time he was sensible of a drowsy confusion creeping over his senses, and his head gave an awful nod or two. Not considering that it would be to the honour and glory of the Duffrey that one of her sons should be found in a strange house next morning, nodding by the cold hearth, half dressed, he made an effort, and got on his legs, but not being strong in plain sailing, or indeed any kind of sailing at all, he turned east instead of west. They say that millions of little threads run from the brain to the muscles and sinews that move the limbs, and bring word back to the head when anything goes wrong in any part of the body. We are not learned enough to know whether this is true or not: we may as well suppose it to be the case. So when Mick knocked his elbow against the partition wall that lay between the door and the fire, the nerve that should convey the tidings to the brain, was too drowsy at the time to deliver the message: so Mick entered and crossed the room above the kitchen, that was opposite to the parlour on the other side; and going into Miss Murphy's room, secured a vacant bed next the door (the young lady being in a curtained one at the far end); and dimly recollecting Richard's caution, quietly undid the few clothes he had on, and getting under the quilt at once, he had hardly time to wink before the sleep that waits on labour and a good conscience descended on him, and he was soon going through all sorts of wild and unconnected adventures by the banks of the clear-flowing Slaney.

"It was some time before Richard could compose himself to rest. The news told him by Mick had sent a feeling of delight through his frame, his hopes were strongly excited, and his fancy at once began to paint a bright picture of future happiness in the society of a dear companion so well fitted to ensure lasting love and esteem. After some time, however, his thoughts began to get mixed; and rousing up once or twice, he tried to settle with himself whether Mick had returned to bed or no. Thinking that he might have done so unperceived, while himself was wrapped in one of his half dreams, and not willing to call out for fear of disturbing the old couple, he gave it up, and resigned himself to sleep.

"Towards morning he was delighted to find himself walking with Catherine on the brown grass that covers the summit of Mount Leinster: their discourse was most interesting and delightful to themselves, but it is very likely that you would find it tiresome enough. After a while they sat by the Cairn, and laid out plans for long years of happiness, but by some sleight for which he could not account, Catherine was presently gone, and himself alone on the near brow of the hill, looking towards his own farm, some miles below him on the Duffrey side.

"A whole herd of bullocks was tearing and trampling a fine field of his wheat, and though he gave a great shout at them, they took no further notice than by a lazy bellow from one or two, and a disdainful shake of their tails. Much annoyed by this mixture of injury and impudence, he spread out his arms, and flew down to take a speedy revenge. He descended delightfully for a while with a triumphant feeling of great power, and saw their eyes upturned in terror, and heard their frightened *lues* (lowings) as they prepared for flight. However, he soon experienced a very unpleasant change; he felt his flying powers gone in a moment, and he was presently tumbling headlong over *Lough-na-Peisthe* (Pool of the worm or serpent). More than twenty serpents of an enormous size, with upturned eyes and fiery tongues, were on the pool, ready to swallow him alive; and their roars were so dreadful that he awoke in a cold perspiration, and with every limb trembling, but after a second or two he felt very glad to find himself safe in bed. Part of Mick's clothes were on the chair beside his bed, but their owner was not to be seen. Richard's ears were, however, still filled with a subdued continuation of the serpents' bellowing, in which his own name was called on for help in Mr. Jones's familiar tones. 'What scrape has this confounded ass got into now?' said he as he huddled on his clothes, and made his way through the parlour and kitchen, to Miss Murphy's bed room, guided by the dismal bawling of his hapless friend. In the far corner was Miss Murphy's curtained bed, with the lady herself inside; near it stood her mother, crying and wringing her hands; in the bed near the door, wriggled and tossed what he supposed to be the body of his friend, wrapped in the quilt, and shrinking, or bouncing. as it was touched by a good hazel kippeen, wielded by the right arm of the enraged master of the house, who was vigorously employed thrashing the poor wooer's corpse. Richard, rushing in on the workman, caught his arms, exhorting him to suspend his labour for a little, and then cried out to the concealed patient, 'What in the world brought you here, you unfortunate disciple?' 'Oh, sure it was hard fortune brought me here at all: but what brings that wicked old man into our bed room, to leather me this way? And why are you letting him beat me, and you having only to jump out of your bed there beyond? Only that he 's old, and that I hear Mrs. Murphy in the room, I 'd be up and give him a good dressing, if he was to be my father-in-law twenty times over'.

" ' Are n't you aware, you omadhawn', said Richard, ' that you are in Miss Murphy's bedroom? You are unlucky at all times; but how in the world did you contrive to fall into this scrape?' 'In Miss Catherine's room! Oh, murdher! what 'll I do now at all! Oh, *Vuya, Vuya!* how will I ever show my face again? I that would n't, for the wealth of Damer, do an ignorant or disrespectful thing to her. Och, I see how it happened. When I was leaving the kitchen, last night, where I happened to have a little business (he omitted the *granbrie*), I felt almost asleep; and so I suppose I took the left hand instead of the right, and thought I was getting into my own bed. I 'm sure, Miss Murphy, you believe what I 'm saying. Och! I wish I 'd never come a coortin', tattheration to it; and that I was a hundred miles under the ground this minute'.

" Richard glanced at Mr. and Mrs. Murphy with a

smile in the corners of his mouth; Mr. Murphy glanced at poor Mick's covering with a puzzled face, and thus spoke. 'How do I know, but that you were afraid Catherine would n't have you, and that you played this shabby trick to prevent any other young farmer from proposing for her?' 'O laws! O laws! She does n't care a ha'porth for me, nor I for her only in the way of friendship. It happened exactly as I tell you; but if Miss Murphy is agreeable, I 'll marry her twenty times, if that will please you'. A voice was at that moment heard from within the curtains. 'Mr. Jones may make his mind easy. I cannot help people's bad construction, but I solemnly declare in the presence of all here, that I will never consent to be his wife, though I am quite sure he has spoken the truth'. 'But do you consider', said her father, 'what people will say, when a lying report goes abroad, and every one sees the match broken off?' 'I 'll bear all with God's help. Yourself, and my mother, and Mr. O'Connor, are sure of my innocence. I will be content with that'.

"Richard interposed at this point. 'Mrs. Murphy, I can now freely say what I would have wished beyond anything to be allowed to say yesterday evening. I feel a most sincere esteem and affection for your daughter, and will think this the happiest journey I ever made, if you receive me into your family with her good will'. There was here a sob or two inside the curtains, and Mrs. Murphy putting in her head made a sign to the men to leave the room.

"They wrapped up Mick and smuggled him into his rightful pew, and a servant girl coming up immediately into the room, found Mrs. Murphy sitting on the edge of the bed, and poor Catherine sobbing on her breast as if her heart would go to pieces. However, as it was not grief entirely, that caused her tears to flow, she recovered from the shock in a reasonable time; and there were smiles on her cheeks again, and a feeling of happiness came all over her; for she felt that the liking she could not help feeling for Richard was returned by him in full measure.

" A word from Mrs Murphy to her husband, made him agreeable to the proposal, which seemed very desirable under the circumstances, especially as he guessed that the new suitor would not look too sharply after the amount of the fortune.

"However agreeably things had turned out, Richard was not indulged the sight of his betrothed till the afternoon; and then he was graciously permitted to take a walk with her, Mick acting the Blackman with much satisfaction to himself, and arranging terms with the elder folk. Catherine, on this occasion, thought the fields were of a finer green, the sky of a more beautiful blue, and the evening altogether the finest she had ever seen. Richard shared her delight, and every object round them looked as if there was a screen of rich-coloured glass between it and their eyes; they spoke of their new-found happiness, and considered that a summer day would not be sufficient for all they had to say about it. Poor Mr. Murphy had like to die of grief on account of the wedding expenses; Mrs. Murphy roasted her son-in-law now and then on the subject of the story he invented when he demolished the cake; and all united in persuading Mrs. Jones to allow her son to please himself in the choice of his wife. Fearing some worse accident might occur from another proof of his cleverness, she yielded at last; and Mick, with his ears almost cut off by his shirt collar, and looking for all the world, according to Owen Jourdan, like a cock rabbit standing on his hind legs, led his bride to the priest's parlour.

" The clergyman, knowing the bridegroom's weak points, took some pains to impress on Mick's mind that he was to repeat the answers after himself. Mick being fully bent on coming off with credit, was in a fever till all was over. However, that did not hinder his head from getting a good thump against the corner of the table in the struggle for the kiss, and an old gray-headed fox that did n't shave for a week, secured the prize".

More than once during the progress of the story, I stole a look at Margaret, and Murtagh, and Edward, mentally identifying them with the personages. The coincidence however was not of design on the part of the story-teller, for, as I afterwards found, it was the wish of Margaret's parents that she should in due time become Mrs. Horan. Murtagh himself was not much at ease during part of the narration; for though self-love and self-esteem were as well developed in him as in others of Adam's sons, there came on his mind at times a glimmering, as it were through a horn-pane, that he was to a certain extent liable to Mick's shortcomings. From some sidelong glances which I caught occasionally on their passage, I judged that self-application was at work with others as well as Murtagh, but in a more agreeable manner.

After the hot cake and tea, Mrs. Lucas brewed a jug of punch, of which every one got as much as was good for him, the young girls merely putting the glass to their mouths, and giving a cough and a laugh at the same time. There was no worshipper of Bacchus among the company; so this part of the evening's entertainment soon ended, and we adjourned to the kitchen, where we found Owen Jourdan entertaining the servant boy and girl with his tough-spoken philosophy. In our ignorance we asked Owen whether he had ever heard about the famous courtship in Carlow, and he answered that he had, and also about the dozen courtships that the great Mr. Rush of the Crooked Bridge had brought to an end (see *Banks of the Boro*, page 158). "But", said he, "the Bantry Puckawn's courtship beat the rest all to sticks. An old shepherd of Ballybawn told it to me. He said he was sittin' on a stone on the side of the White Mountain, and thinkin' o' nothin', when he *hard* a snortin' and prancin'; and there he saw a big Puckawn skelpin' up the stony road that runs from near the Crooked Bridge, through Ballybawn, and across Cooliagh down towards Borris in Carlow. There he was, leapin' and jumpin', and a foot of him hardly touchin' the ground, and I 'm sure if it was night, his horns would be puckin' the stars.

"'Arrah, Puckawn, me boy', says the shepherd, 'what are you about, and where are you goin'?' Puck gave a snort, and a rear, and a dash at the man with his horns, and sputthered out, 'Pruff, pruff, pruff,—goin' to coort, goin' to coort', and away he pegged over the mountain. In about a fortnight after, the shepherd was in the same place one day, and who should he see stalin' back again, dhraggin' one foot after another, and his beard full of the turf *mull*, only my brave goat. 'Ah, then, Puckawn, acushla', says he, ' and where are you goin' now?'

"Poor Puck liftin' his head, and dhrawin' a long sigh, whimpered out, one word afther another; 'Neighbour, I 'm-sthrivin'-to-get-home-as-well-as-I-can'."

O'Brien had heard the "Rogueries of Coley" sung once or twice since he came to the Duffrey, but it was a perfectly new melody to me. So Bernard Lucas, pitying my ignorance, thundered it out in a rollicking style.

The Rogueries of Coley.

" Come, all you good people, I pray you draw nigh;
  The fate of poor Coley will cause you to cry ;
  For feloniously eating a fiddle was tried,
  Condemned by the laws of Court Martial, and died.
                    Down, Down, Coley, lie down.

" You all know John Foley, a sporting young blade,
  Who at dancing and drinking was never dismay'd,
  And pleasing the girls wherever he 'd go,
  Their spirits he 'd cheer with a scratch of his bow.
                    Down, etc.

" But when vagabone Coley his fiddle did eat,
  Says John to his mother, ' My poor heart will break;
  But I 'll have revenge for his sad treachery,
  And like Judas he 'll swing on the old elder tree'.
                    Down, etc.

" He seized on poor Coley, and thus he did say,
  'Make your will and be hanged, for this is your last day';
  But Coley, the traitor, he broke out of jail,
  He hopped thro' the window, and gave him leg bail.
                    Down, etc.

"Poor John in distraction his hair he did pull;
  He stamped and he swore like a roaring mad bull;
  He swore by Moll Allen, Moll Doyle, and Magog,
  That he 'd send for Tim Kerry, and take the black dog.
                    Down, etc.

" Tim Kerry was summoned, and straightway did come,
  And away went young Johnny along with the bum:
  In search of the felon they walked thirteen mile,
  Till they caught him a sleeping at Carrick-na-Phile.
                    Down, etc.

"Says John, ' You vile traitor, I have you again,
  I 'll have you gazetted through France and through Spain;
  I 'll have you transported out of Irish land,
  And I 'll *summons* Tom Neil on your jury to stand !'
                    Down, etc.

"So they tied up the robber, and home they did come,
  Coley, John Foley, and Kerry the bum:
  Tom Neil he was summoned, and straightway he goes,
  With his pipe in his mouth, and his big purple nose.
                    Down, etc.

"So in came Jemmy Ward and his young brother Pat,
  To prosecute Coley for mauling their cat;
  ' The traitor waylaid her on her coming home,
  Her ear he bit off, and he cracked her thigh bone'.
                    Down, etc.

" The next that appeared was the pensioner's wife:
  She swore by Mahomet she would have his life,
  For keeping late hours in her field of peas,
  And plucking the feathers from three of her geese.
                    Down, etc.

" The next that accused him was his master dear,
  That he served true and faithful for many a year;
  ' He first ate his fiddle, and then ate his *mate*,
  He smashed a brown jug and a green-edgèd plate.
                    Down, etc.

" ' And every night, for to please his desire,
  When they'd go to bed, he would scratch out the fire:
  The young hatching goose he attempted to kill,
  And he flittered the gander upon the dunghill'.
                    Down, etc.

" The judge he summed up, and the trial was done,
  And off to the gallows with Coley they run,
  Where Johnny stood sheriff and hangman to be,
  And he tucked up the knave in the old elder tree.
                    Down, etc.

"' As I 'm dying', says Coley, ' without ring of bell,
    To my friend Cæsar Devereux I must bid farewell,
    Tiger Green, Toby Cary, adieu Pincher Clear,
    And poor Cozy Dempsey that loved me so dear'.
                              Down, etc.

"Now Coley is buried, and the crowd gone away,
    He got up from his grave on the very next day;
    For just as old Andrew was opening his door,
    The ghost of poor Coley walked in on the floor.
                              Down, etc.

"' Och Mavrone', says poor Andrew, ' our work is all void;
    By this terrible ghost we 'll be eat and destroyed:
    But I 'll send for Tom Harris, that sportsman so brave,
    And it 's he that will settle this injurious knave'.
                              Down, etc.

"The huntsman soon came, and got him on his back,
    And carried him off to be eat by the pack;
    But Coley turned traitor in the height of the sport,
    He deceived poor Tom Harris, and eat up his shirt.
                              Down, etc.".

Had our present readers, who, perhaps, have not un-
bent a muscle while studying this lay, been present when
Bernard was trolling it off, it would have been a different
matter. We have seldom heard a ballad greeted with
such uncontrolled mirth, the greater part being excited
by the comic power of the singer. After the performance,
he called on Murtagh to indulge the company, and this
he did after some pressing. The lay he selected had not
been very long composed, and was rather popular, owing
to the subject of the poet's praise being in the neighbourhood. There are probably but very few in Tombrick in
whose memories it has continued green.

A New Song in praise of Cloghamon New Mill.

"You lads of brilliant genius, that 's endowed with elocution,
    And by versification have immortalised your name,
To revive my drooping intellects I crave a contribution
    Of assistance for to harmonise with eloquence my theme.
Condemn me not for rashness to attempt impossibilities,
    As I am stimulated by a motive of good will:
Though an inexperienced tyro in the dawn of native literature,
    I intend to state the praises of Cloghamon New Mill.

" This magnific'ent structure of sublime architecture,
     Was founded in Anno Domini eighteen hundred and fifteen,
When by final perseverance it was brought to an accomplishment,
     Its parallel could not be found in Erin the Green.
To give a perfect idea of its spaciousness and symmetry,
     Is far beyond the limits of a feeble poet's skill;
In every direction, 't is a bulwark of perfection;
     Hibernia's boast and glory is Cloghamon New Mill.

" No wonder I should deem it an object of astonishment,
     When men of great discernment arrived from afar,
To view this lofty building, of which it is related
     That it was prognosticated by a great fiery star.
These grand conflagrations—the wonders of creation—
     Were brought to calculation by astron'omic'al skill;
'T was perspicuously expounded, and foretold there would be founded,
     Nigh the town of Newtownbarry, this admirable mill.

" The gentry of the country, for rural recreation,
     The sweet meandering banks of the Slaney do *surnade,*
Where the paintings of nature are arranged in true reality—
     The white trout abounding in each crystal cascade.
When on the noble building they feasted their *curosity,*
     And viewed each grand invention of artifice and skill,
The critical machinery and curious elevation,
     Obtained great approbation for Cloghamon New Mill".

We did not sit up so long as we sometimes did at Donovan's. Edward slept with one of the young men, I myself with the other; and though both, in this instance, found the quarters agreeable, our occasional change of beds or bedfellows was not always attended with pleasant recollections. I remember one night, when a young boy, and a long slim fellow, somewhat short of seven feet, and I, were by the decree of fate to share the same bed. We consulted as to the least unpleasant disposition of our bodies, and at the suggestion of the youngest, this arrangement was made. Nick Thumkin laid himself by the edge, with his back to his fellow-sufferers; his knee, shin bone, and big toe in contact with the foot board; we ensconced ourselves behind him, the soles of our feet resting against or drumming the backs of his legs; and I declare that I have spent more unpleasant nights than the one in question.

CHAPTER VII.

THE FARM HOUSE OF COOLGARROW.

DURING the day the even course of justice was sometimes impeded in our seminary by the presence of our landlady, when chastisement was in question. Indeed when Edward had threatened punishment, and yet was not willing to inflict it, he took good care that the "Intercessor General" should not be left in ignorance of the impending ceremony. His nature was so averse to inflicting pain of any kind, that unless roused to a greater or less degree of anger, he could not use cane or birch; and I consider this as a very serious defect in a teacher. Persons of Edward's diposition are nearly certain, when they set about correction at all, to be more severe than the occasion requires; for they lay on additional stripes out of anger at being made angry.

My Godmother's children—Laurence, Mary, and Catherine—were in school on the next day, and as she naturally wished to see her god-son after thirteen years of absence, she sent a particular charge that I should pay her a visit in the evening, and bring the master with me. So when the scholars were dismissed, we went up by the edge of the wood, along the very back bone of the hill, till we came to Bullaan-a-Rinka, its highest field, with its green fairy rings, its crop of long dry grass, and fence. of loose stones; and if we went on straight, we would be down in the pass of Glanamoin, lying between us and Kilachdiarmuidh hill. We had now a fine view of the face of Mount Leinster. The road on our right a short distance down the hill, goes on its course westwards through sundry villages, along the same side, till it brings its wayfarers to Templeshanbo and Moghurry. Just below us is my Godmother's house, on the edge of this lane, which, dipping just as it passes her bawn, descends to a little stream. This stream dashes down the ravine which Edward and I had noticed on our Sunday walk, and falls into the Glasha opposite the village of Lower Gurtheen.

Descending to the lane, we are before the long, low thatched house, with its many bunches of house leek of the richest red and green hues, and its eaves filled with sparrows' nests.

We enter the bawn by an opening in the wall, unprovided with a gate. In front runs the long, low house; on the right is the barn where the farm servants and benighted travellers enjoy luxuriant sleep on beds in which, if straw is scant, let the blame rest on the laziness or improvidence of the sleepers.

To the left lie the cow-byre, and (truth must be told) the dung-heap; but, as a drain by that end of the house conveys away the superabundant moisture to the kitchen-garden at the rere, and the paddock at the back of it again, we request the delicate-nosed reader to excuse it *for this time only.* A haggart, with hay-ricks and corn-stacks mounted on flag stands, which are again supported by stone posts, lies behind the barn; the surrounding fence is furnished at intervals with fine old ash trees, and a row of well-thatched bee-hives stands on the sunny side of the hedge, and a lovely calf-paddock extends in rear of all.

When one of these stacks is taken down to be thrashed, the labourer hesitates, in order to excite interest among the bye-standers, before he darts his suspended fork into a sheaf; while the cats, and dogs, with burning eyes and cocked ears, are watching the plunge. Down goes the prong; up goes the sheaf; off leap the mice or rats; and helter-skelter after them the cats, dogs, and children. What stag or fox-hunt can equal in interest the chase of the next two minutes, with its accompaniment of barks, shouts, and laughter, and which is to be repeated every five minutes till the bottom layer is removed?

Now, we will just loiter in the paddock, for two minutes, and then go in-doors. From its west and north sides the ground falls in a steep, furze-clad slope to the brook and the Glasha, leaving an uninterrupted view of the imposing mass of the mountain side opposite.

Some opportunity will occur when summer or autumn evenings come round, to sit on the sheltery side of the fence, and look across the hollow of the Duffrey; but this is a harsh spring evening, and the sun has set. We will get out of the exterior cold, and enjoy the comfort of a good turf fire, and a cordial welcome. This we get, and after nightfall we are seated on the huge hearth among a company of fourteen or fifteen individuals of all ages, the turf fire blazing cheerfully under the mighty pot. The children are ensconced in the laps, or between the legs of the seniors, except three, who are performing the ticklish operation of "shaving the White Friar". Having reared a small cone of turf ashes, they stick a straw upright in its summit, and each in turn scrapes away a portion of the side of the heap, repeating at each operation,

> "Shave the White Friar;
> Draw a little nigher;
> If the Friar chance to fall,
> Your back will pay for all".

When the straw falls, which it must do sooner or later, the last operator must suffer in body or goods; a general cuffing being the usual reward of his awkwardness.

You will not mistake my Godmother in that specimen of fat and fair womanhood carding wool: though you might not recognize the master of the house, who sits between her and the end wall, on the farther side of the fireplace. A sturdy, younger looking woman occasionally inspects the progress of the potatoes towards the boiling state, checks any unseemly exhibition among the children, and snubs her husband, a hard-featured, but goodhumoured looking man. This is my Godmother's sister, their husbands are brothers, and the younger folk are the issue of the two marriages.

The two families live in this house, and you may go in and out as often as you please from New Year's Day to next New Year's Eve, without having your ears scorched by an angry or contemptuous word.

Mary, the eldest daughter, is winding a ball of thread

off a spindle; Owen Jourdan is sitting at his ease, making moral observations and smoking; Owen's sister, Hetty, is fumbling among the pots at the bottom of the room, the boundary of which is a partition, about seven feet high, ornamented in front by a dresser, supporting on its shelves no end of dishes, plates, and platters, both wooden and pewter. The lower part protected by a shelf, affords a comfortable asylum to a hatching goose.

The parlour, beyond this partition, is furnished with dark cupboards, dark oak tables, and dark oak chairs. The windows are low and not very large, and with its cool earthen floor, it would be a pleasant place to sit in on a summer morning.

I hope some evening to enjoy a pleasant social evening in the readers' company, with the big fire blazing at the end, and the tea equipage glittering in the light of the candles placed at intervals on the long, dark, polished table.

Leaving the two bed-rooms below the parlour uninspected, we return to the kitchen. The everlasting settle lies along the wall, opposite the door. A strong beam resting in a hole in this wall, its other end supported by the entrance partition wall, bears up the huge structure of the projecting chimney. A post supporting this beam at one third of its length, gets a nick whenever anything unusual takes place, such as Owen passing a day without telling some tremendous lie; or Larry, the eldest son, tying the thongs of his shoes of a morning. Within the shelter of this capacious chimney, all the family may easily sit, without fear of striking their heads when they stand up.

Mr. James K., the younger sister's husband, and a serious wag, amused himself on this evening testing the progress of the children in this wise: "Now, master, is Kitty pretty strong in her spelling?" "Well, she is not to be complained of". "Very well, Kitty; spell me a *red rogue* with three letters?" Kitty is puzzled. "Indeed an' I can't, uncle". "And yet the master praises your spelling! Mary is *coming on* at her grammar?

Mary, why is A put before B in the alphabet?" "I'm sure
I do n't know, uncle. If *you* like you may put B first".
"There's bad attention for you". "Well, uncle, tell us
yourself". "A opens the mouth, you ninnyhammer, and
B shuts it. Kitty, I'll give *you* one more chance to recover your credit. Spell and tell the meaning of *Trans-
magnificandubandandixiality*". "Oh, Lord! uncle, it
would take me the whole night". "I knew I'd find out
weak points in your education. Now, Mary, mind your
figures. A goose before two geese, a goose behind two
geese, and a goose in the middle between two geese, how
many geese is that?" "Nine". "Wrong again. Let's
see are you any better, Larry. A fiddler and his wife,
a piper and his mother, paid each a halfpenny toll over
the bridge of Wexford, and still they were all let across
for three half pence: how did it happen? Ah, master!
You must get up earlier, or make better use of the rod!"
A comment was furnished to Mr. James's text by the
fact of no child in either family ever getting a slap at
home or in school.

I will not waste many words on the kind reception
I met from my godmother, who amused and surprised me
a little by anecdotes of my childhood, which had not
dwelt on my memory. The only personal recollection I
could give in return was, that I went over with her one
Sunday evening to the Rath of Cromogue, beside which
her father's house stood; and I described her beaver bonnet, the silk lining of the hood of her mantle, and the
nice tassel that depended from it. Edward was a welcome guest; good care was taken to prevent him from
feeling himself a stranger, and topics of various sorts
were discussed.

Mr. James went on amusing himself and the company
with the half-puzzled, half-pleased children, till the contents of the pot were approaching the boiling point.

My godmother's sister, who has got her ribbons and
the ears of her cap steamed watching the potatoes, now
gives the signal, Owen and one of the labourers whip off
the enormous weight, and by dint of sleight and strength,

6

toss out the contents into a basket placed over a tub. The basket retains the potatoes; the tub receives the water grateful to the pigs; and now a table frame that has been kept upright along the wall by a hasp at its upper end, and two pivots that fit in grooves at its lower corners, is brought to a horizontal position, and from its front an excuse for feet dangles to the floor, and keeps it up. A cloth is spread on the table, and the overlapping edges are raised up at each side by the youngsters, to prevent the potatoes from falling off when spilled out upon it, after a few seconds' draining.

Noggins of milk that never saw the least drop of the Glasha or Slaney water, are laid at each side; the forms are arranged, the company take their seats, and if any one does not make a hearty supper on the best mealy cups and good milk, I do n't pity him.

Talk and joking go on, such as they are. A standard jest is cracked by Owen, on Bess, sometimes called the bosthoon, because she is so unfortunate as to be fat and good humoured, and not very bright in her intellect. Like Dr. Holloway, or the great Mr. Moses, he began very far from his object.

"Lord be praised!" said the rogue, "what cunnen' crathurs them bees are! I stood watchen their *manuvers* two hours one day, and nothin' could surpass them, barrin' the motions of a poor Christian's limbs. Now if you 'd only watch Bess there for a minute or two, you 'd see that her mouth opens, the minute she bends her elbow".

All eyes being turned for the moment o.. poor Bess, she forgot everything like gentle concord ... ... whose mechanism had been so highly extolled directed a hard hot potato with such skill and force in the direction of Owen's nose, that this unoffending member suffered for the next two hours, for the fault of its wicked neighbour, the tongue.

This may seem an immoral and unedifying incident in our otherwise harmless pastoral; but if we had space we could multiply instances of innocent people suffering chastisement for the faults of their guilty neighbours.

Supper being over, William K., the master of the house, a gentle-mannered and taciturn man, returned thanks, and all crowded round the fire, and conversation went on unflaggingly.

"As I was passing up the Sunday evening before last, to Ballindaggin", said Edward, "I saw from the side of the hill here beyond, a great crowd on Kennystown bog, seeming to be in search of something or other; can any one tell what they were after?"

"Owen will be able to satisfy you", answered Mrs. K., "as I believe that it was some grand discovery of his that put all the country in motion to search for a spawn of the old serpent of Lough-na-Peisthe".

"Be me word, I only repated what I hard from *Matty*, (Mathew) the miller's girl, one evening, when I was sittin' at the fire, afther my day's work".

"Well now, Owen, what did she say in earnest? For once, tell truth, and shame *the old boy*".

"Now did n't yez all hear often and often, of the big eel that used to come out of the Glasha long ago to feed on the *Inch*. Well an' good, Matty's girl, when she was dhrivin' home the cows the other evening, was *freckened* out of her life a'most by some turrible thing that run from the river *thorst* the rabbit burrow, lavin' a wet thrack afther him the whole way. Now, will any of yez tell me what this could be af it was n't the big eel? I axed her if she saw its feet and mane, and she said she thought it had feet and a mane; and that it was about the hoith of Pincher. I thought Pincher was the *big* dog's name and he tould me he is almost the size of a small calf; and when I was repatin' what I hard, next evenin' at Jack Tobin's, I only said that the eel or sarpent, which-ever it was, was not so big as a small heifer. And now what do yez all think, *Shan a Chaiseal* was tellin' the people coming from Mass the Sunday after? Why, that a young spawn of the great ould sarpent had got into Kennystown bog, and that it was as big as an elephant (I never seen an elephant, so I don't know how big he 'is); and that its mane swep' the ground, and that its

eyes were like fiery saucers, and its teeth like twelve-
penny nails. He said likewise, that it was a sign that
the day of judgment, or the French was a comin'; but
first, that the sarpent would begin to eat up people and
cattle, and that Matty's girl saw it risin' out of Lough-
na-Peisthe, and runnin' like wild fire across the counthry,
till it plunged into one of the big bog holes, throwin' up
the wather half a mile in the air. Now how could I
hindher him from adding all that?"

The children had gradually stopped their pastimes,
and when Owen's palaver came to a close, they were
sitting with hands on knees, eyes intent on Owen's face,
and mouths and ears wide open.

Hetty now took the word; she generally gave her
opinions on passing events only once in two or three
days. "And I'll lay my life afther all, that it was only
a rot or an otther that was runnin' aff to the burrow to
lay hands on a sthray rabbit that might be *surnādin'*
about in the cool of the evenin?"

"Rot, indeed!" rejoined Owen. "Do you think any
rot or otther in the Glasha could bring so many sensible
people together, with pitch-forks, and *slanes* (turf-spades),
and salmon-spears, and guns, and bagnets, from the seven
town-lands around, to be lookin' at one another like
fools, if there wasn't some good rason for it?"

"But what about the real old serpent of Lough-na-
Peisthe?" asked Larry. "Does anybody here know the
story of it?"

"I heard it more than once", said his mother, "and it is
not such a story as is easily forgotten. So I'll give it to
you as I received it.

The Serpent of Loch-na-Peisthe.

"Many, many hundred years ago, all the country round
here was laid waste by a huge serpent that made his home
in that pool. If any of you have not seen Loch-na-
Peisthe, you will find it on your right hand as you come
from the bridge of Thuar to where I was born—at the

Rath of Cromogue. He had the power by sucking in his breath to draw man or beast into his mouth, even if they were two miles away. At last the King of Leinster, who lived in the Castle of Ferns, dispatched messengers to the King of Ireland, ever so far away in Munster, begging him to send some great fighting man to kill this devil of a piast or there would n't be left man or woman alive in the three baronies. They went, and gave their message, and bedad, three warriors offered themselves at once,—an O'Brien, an O'Farrell, and an O'Kennedy. One of these was as impatient as the dickens for the day to set out. 'They should n't draw lots at all; he'd fight the baste himself and make mince-mate of him!'

"Ovoch! the very morning they were to set out, my brave boaster was lying sick in his bed. His breast bone was pushed in, or the palate of his mouth was down— some *meea* was on him. Well, all his family were ashamed of their lives: so a brave big bosthoon of a brother of his, that never got any thing better to do at home than thrash or hold the plough, asked the King leave to go in his brother's place for the honour of the family. He got that, and on, on, on the three men and the Leinster messengers travelled till they pitched their tents, there above this house on Bullaan-a-Rinka. They drew lots, and it fell to the big omadhan of a ploughman.

"He and the others then set to work, cut down trees, and made charcoal. He got into a big sack, and they filled all round him with the charcoal, and then tied the mouth leaving him some holes to breathe. They then made the best of their way till they got on the highest point of that arm of Mount Leinster, which you can see from the lane abroad there, and waited for the signal agreed on. They could not have managed all this so snugly only the piast was fast asleep after a great fog meal that came in his way, and they had settled before hand all that was to be done.

"At last the serpent awoke, and began to snuff about. He smelled the men on the mountain, but they were too

far above him, and he began to curse, but as he turned
about in this direction, he felt that there was flesh within
sucking distance, so he lay down on his side and began
to suck like vengeance. Away through the air, like a
bow-arra, came the sack and the man, and struck against
the jaws of the beast with such force that it rolled him
over. That did n't daunt him. He swallowed sack and
man without ever laying a tooth on them. When all was
down he felt rather uncomfortable, and good reason he
had, for the brave boy got out his scian, and cut away
like a man that was in earnest as soon as he felt himself
at rest. The serpent found himself getting worse and
worse every moment, and at last waddled to the rushy
edge of the pool, and tumbled heels over head into it.
However, before he felt the water the boy was out through
his belly, safe and sound, and the first thing he *done* was
to kneel down, and thank God for his deliverance. He
then gathered some withered grass and sticks, and made
a fire, and that was the signal to the men above that he
was safe. They came down, and the good news soon
spread through the country, and there was nothing every
where but rejoicings and bonfires.

"The King of Leinster gave a great many gifts to
the brave Omadhan, but he would keep nothing for himself. He set about building a monastery and a nunnery
near the pool out of gratitude. He had a curious dream
one night, and the next morning he found it verified.
As soon as he came out, he saw a beautiful duck and
drake squatted just at the threshold. They rose in the
air as soon as they saw him, and flew quite leisurely
before him, till they crossed the Glasha at Ballinacoola
ford. Up over the little hill they kept flying, till at last
they lighted at each side of the stream that divides the
grave-yard of Templeshanbo, the duck on the far bank,
the drake on this side. There the two religious houses
were built, and none but women were buried on the west
side, and none but men on the other; and hundreds
of years after Harry the Eighth, or Oliver Cromwell, or
Queen Elizabeth, pulled down the buildings, all the

country kept up the old custom. At last, about fifty
years ago, the *Palentines* of Ballinlugg, not knowing
the custom, buried an old woman on the men's side, and
you know how it fared with her corpse". (*The reader
shall also know it at the proper time*).

Edward, after paying some compliments to the story-
teller, mentioned that he had heard that this thing happened in the reign of Brian Boru, and then an hour was
taken up in inquiries and answers concerning the exploits
of Brian, the details of the battle of Clontarf, the original
use of what are improperly called Danish raths, the
quantity of naked truth contained in the legend, etc.
Then the talk gradually widening in its scope, mention
was made of the early skill of the Irish in agriculture, as
shown by the traces of ridges still extant on hills and
other places uncultivated for centuries; and of the
curious remains of weapons, ornaments, and utensils
found in moats and bogs. Every now and then some
question as to antiquities, or old forms of society, would
arise, that no one could resolve, and then a new game
was started. A general feeling of comfort and coziness
was diffused, from the circumstance of so many people,
all more or less attached to each other, sitting in a narrow compass, within the cheerful influence of the turf-fire
blaze, the limbs reposing from labour, and the mind
pleasantly occupied; every one joining in the conversation as he felt inclined, and no one looking out for set
phrases, in fear of criticism. A timorous proposal being
made of sending the children to bed, it was met by such
vigorous hugging of the knees and necks of the seniors,
and such a preparation of throats for the destined roar,
that no seconder could be found, and the motion was lost
accordingly.

At this point of the evening's occupation, Edward,
who suspected my godmother to have a fine voice of her
own, asked the favour of something in the ballad way

from her.   She, whom some years' experience of married
life had not cured of a leaning to romance, after a faint
denial or or two, gave the fine old country ballad of *Gra
Gal Machree* (Bright love of my heart), and really kept
the company under a spell while she sung, from the combined effects of the genuine feeling of the lay, the fine
air, and her own sweet voice.

Gra Gal Machree.

" I am a young lover that 's sorely oppressed,
  I 'm inthralled by a fair one, I can find no rest;
  Her name I 'll not mention, though wounded I be
  By Cupid's keen arrow, she 's *Gra Gal Machree.*

" I determined to tell that fair innocent dove
  All by a fond letter that she was my love,
  Expecting next morning with pleasure to see
  Some token of love from my *Gra Gal Machree.*

" But that false deceiver, whom I did intrust,
  Above all men breathing he 's surely the worst ;
  He proved a deceiver and traitor to me,
  For he ne'er gave my letter to *Gra Gal Machree.*

" When he got the letter he ran out of hand
  Unto her old father, and told him the plan ;
  When the old man did read it, he swore bitterly
  That he 'd alter the case with his *Gra Gal Machree.*

" He called down his daughter with pride and disdain,
  Saying, ' Here is a letter from your darling swain.
  You cannot deny it, for plain you may see,
  He titles you here his own *Gra Gal Machree'.*

" This tender young maiden fell down on her knees,
  Saying. ' Father, dear father, now do as you please ;
  But if by wild horses I strangled should be,
  I 'll never deny I 'm his *Gra Gal Machree'.*

" A horse was got ready without more delay,
  And to some foreign country she was sent away ;
  And if I do n't find her I 'll mourn constantly,
  And my last dying words shall be *Gra Gal Machree !*"

All kept silence for awhile after the ballad ; for country
folk of that day were not accustomed to stamp feet, or tap

tables by way of applause. The praising was left to
Edward, and myself, and Bess, the fat servant girl, and
this last by way of punishment was called on for another
song. Bess, like some women, and a few men, delighted
in big or strange words, and gave us

The Buncheen of Lucharoe.

" As I roved for recreation down by yon river clear,
  Where pure transparent waters all by the sylvan forest steer,
  The fields being spread with daisies, the fruit spontaneous seemed
    to grow,
  Each bank being decorated with violets and green *lucharoe*.

" I gazed with admiration traversing through the shady grave,
  Felicitating anglers as they the banks did gently rove,
  Till I espied a fair one, more lovely than the falling snow,
  As she was re-arranging her violets and green *lucharoe*.

" As I perambulated, contemplating the works of Jove,
  I thought she was Pandora, Fair Helen, or the Queen of love,
  Her notes when elevated, extirpated my grief and woe,
  As she co-operated her violets and green *lucharoe*.

" The radiance of her beauty so suited her majestic air,
  I thought it too audicious or precarious to approach the fair.
  Her hair hung long and flowing, and did profusely seem to grow,
  And her shape was in proportion to her violets and sweet *lucharoe*".

The songstress or the poet had pitched the key note
too high, he in the poetic, she in the vocal scale; at all
events she got no further. Perhaps a few slight explosions which some of the company were unable to restrain,
contributed to the mischance. " In troth, Bess", said
Mr. James K., " you have shown a right spirit in throwing no more of your fine language on people without taste,
except for common things that the dogs of the town, if
they were sent to school, could understand. I'll engage
they'll relish this ballad that I'm going to sing for them.
It was made by some stupid Englishman that never got
as far as *antherantadrians* or *cozzentiality* in his life".
And to a monotonous air, seconded by a most unmusical
voice, Mr. James sung the following ballad, cheered by

the hilarity of his audience at various passages, as natural
humour supplied vocal deficiencies.

The Boy and the Robber.

"There was a wealthy farmer that lived in Yorkshire land;
And of a fair-morning he called for his boy John.
' There is a fat cow in the byre, go bring her to the fair,
For she is in good order and it 's her that I can spare'.

" John led the fat cow out, and drove her from the bawn,
He drove her to the fair, as you shall understand.
He had not been long there when he met with three men,
And to them he did sell his cow for ten pound ten.

" The men and John along with them went in to take a drink,
And without fail they handed him the purchase in a jink;
Said he to the landlady, ' Advise me, ma'am, I pray,
Where will I put this money to hide it safe away ?'

" ' In the linings of your coat we will stitch it', said she,
' For fraid upon the highway that robbèd you might be'.
But it 's in the room a robber was drinking of his wine,
And he said all to himself, ' Faith that money shall be mine'.

" Now John took his leave, and homewards he did go,
And cunningly the robber did follow him also ;
And soon he overtook him upon the highway ;
' Come and sit behind me, young man !' he did say.

" John jumped behind him, and fast they rode away,
Till they came to a dark lane, when the robber he did say,
' Deliver up your money, and that without strife,
Or this very moment I 'll take away your life!

" So from the lining of his coat the money he tore out,
And in the long grass, faith, he scattered it about.
So the robber he was fain to get down from his horse,
It 's little he did think that he 'd come to such a cross.

For while he was gathering the money was astray,
John shook the bridle rein and quickly rode away ;
The robber followed after him desiring him to stand ;
John took little notice, but gallantly rode on.

Home unto his master he joyfully did bring
Horse, bridle, and saddle, and many a fine thing ;
But when the servant maid saw John a coming home,
It 's to acquaint his master she ran into his room.

"Straightway to the door the master went in haste,
  Saying, 'John, how did my cow turn into a *horse-baste*?'
'Oh, no, my dear master, your cow I have sold,
  And on the road was robbed by a highwayman so bold;

" ' And while he was putting the money in his purse,
  To make you amends, I rode home with his horse'.
The saddle bags were opened, and in them was found
  Three hundred and odd guineas, in silver and bright *gould.*

" ' And three case of pistols are here, I do avow;
  You may see, my dear master, that I well sold your cow !'
The master had a daughter, was beautiful and young,
  The boy he got her for his wife, and so I end my song".

Story and song had excited some of the company to such a pitch that going to bed at all began to assume a problematical air. However, a prosaic member of the party began to tell how he had once sat up a whole night in very agreeable company, and was very cross and unwilling to work the next day. This view of the case seemed to produce an effect; and my godmother making use of the homely expression, " *To bed with the boys, and the goose to the fire*". We were all soon enjoying the sleep of those whose days are spent in useful occupation, and whose consciences are not overburthened.

CHAPTER VIII.

BUSINESS AND PLAY IN ROSE COLOUR:—A KEY-NOTE IN
MORAL EDUCATION.

IT was a lively cold morning as we came down the hill-road next day to school. Before we started, Larry had been out to get a glimpse of the pool, but as he was not successful, he turned and gazed long at the southern spur of the mountain. We stepped out at a lively rate to get into the lower regions where the March wind could not inflict such keen bites on our purple faces. Edward went into Mr. Lucas's as we passed, probably to make the young people aware of the opening of the school; and if he exchanged a few words with Margaret, what more likely than that he was ascertaining whether little Sarah had got her *column* well by heart? Whatever took place, he entered the academy after his visit in a remarkably good humour, and the morning's work was commenced with lively spirits by teacher and pupils.

The writing exercise was executed well or ill, according to limberness of fingers or goodness of pens; and at its termination, Joe Dillon walked in. Joe had been promised something next time he would be late; this was the identical time, and Joe's face was redolent of any thing but mirth. "Joe, what's kept you so late?" "Sir, my *brekest* was n't *bult*". "I have told you frequently that the word is 'boiled', not 'biilt'. Once again, what kept you?" Joe's tongue could not get round "boiled"; and he was afraid to make an attempt for fear "biilt" would drop out. So he ventured on, "Sir, my brekest was n't ready".

"Step out", said Edward to me in a whisper, "and give a hint to Mrs. Murphy, that her presence would be desirable. Joe, I warned you that I would make your fingers smart, if you persisted in coming so late in the morning, and knocking up our business in this way". Joe's looks betrayed a feeling of impending woe. "Hand me the cane, some one. I saw you hiding it just now, Catherine Hogan: do not be playing with edged tools. How far is it from this to your house, Joe?" "About three quarters of a mile, sir". "That is the same as three-fourths, Joe", and then he muttered to himself, "What can be keeping Mrs. Murphy? She would be brisk enough if she was n't wanted. I say, Joe, which would you rather walk three-fourths or three-fifths of a mile?" "I donnow, sir". "Well, which would you rather have— three-fourths or three-fifths of a cake?" "I think I'd rather have it all, sir". "But which?——Ah! (to himself) here she comes. Now, Joe, hold out your hand. Though I am not particularly fond of slapping little boys, you know I promised you a trouncing if you continued to loiter; and I must keep my word". Little Catherine Donovan here approached Edward's ear, and whispered, "But, master, the Catechism says, 'a rash oath is better broken than kept'". "Ah, you little rogue of a casuist: mine was not a rash oath, but a well considered promise; go and rehearse your lesson. Now for it, Joe". Here the cane blew its preparatory whistle, and Mrs. Murphy came to the rescue.

"Ah, master, what is poor Joe going to be slapped for?" "Late attendance on several occasions, ma'am. I promised him this if he did not improve: so I cannot help correcting him". "Joe, you thief", said she, "why do you persist in your laziness, and vex the master in this way, and stop the business of the school?" "Indeed ma'am, I'll ne—ne—never be late again". "Pursuin' to me, but if you do, I'll go all the way to your mother's; and between us, we'll give you such a lambasting as you'll remember. If the master lets you off this time, won't you strive to be early?" "Ye—ye—yes, ma'am, indeed I will". "Well, well, master honey, pass it by this once, if you please. Ah, you lazy sthrōnsuch! catch me going bail for you again. Now, sir, yourself and your new *cōjutor* must take dinner with me to-day. I'll take no refusal; for I want to talk to the little master about his father and mother that I knew before he was born. I'll send in word when it is time to break up. Now, boys and girls, work like little divels in a mud wall. Ach! what would n't I give now, to be attentive when I was a thuckeen; but I was fonder of kicking the *nuckeen* (foot-ball) among the little gorsoons, than study-ing the *Child's new play thing*. I believe I never told you how I asked my grandmother once for a needle to mend a hole in the bladder we were kicking. Ovoch! I think my room here would be better than my company. Be good boys and girls any way, and God will love you"; and many a wistful look is cast after the big, comely, great-hearted woman as she vanishes.

It may be objected that if Edward was uniform in this style of punishment, he would come to be related to King

Log in the fable; but, dear objector, lay aside such apprehension: he was not uniformly too lenient; but, as I hinted before, he was in such a happy frame of mind that morning, that he could not get vexed, nor administer correction at any price.   Apropos to Joe and several of my personages; I am sorry that my space is not sufficient for written likenesses; but as to this particular miching youth, an accurate presentment can be got of him, if the reader only take the trouble of procuring the faces of a yearling fox and a lamb, and skilfully select and combine their features into one portrait, and furnish it with a human expression.

Dinner hour having sounded its warning chime in many a little stomach, and Mrs. Murphy sending word that dinner was ready, the welcome dismissal was given; and for a short distance up and down the road, there was racing, and chasing, and joyous yelling, and banging of schoolbags on each other's shoulders; all the troublesome spirits kept down for four hours, now getting a healthy vent for explosion.

During the dinner at Mrs. Murphy's hospitable board, she burst out into what might be termed a mitigated horse laugh, and when it gave her leave to speak, she cried out, "Oh, Mr. O'Brien! it surely is a great matter to know how to manage children in a wise and sensible manner.   I can never think of what happened in this room the other day without laughing, though the thing was serious enough.   Little Jerr D. and his brother Pat were at the wake at the corner of the Widow Kennedy's long, and the child was greatly taken with the white curtains about the poor corpse, and the ribbons tying them round the bed-posts, and the broken pipe-shanks.   Pat wanted him at last to come home, but he would not budge.   So says the arch young thief, 'Well, Jerr, stay as long as you like. I 'm going home by Mrs. Murphy's, that 's dead; and I 'll go in, and stay there till you overtake me; and I 'm sure she 's laid out much nicer than that corpse'. There was no need of any further coaxing. Jerr came off fast enough, and he felt his legs too short till he got here. I was in that room there when the children came in, and when I opened the door, I was surprised to seee the little boy on his knees in the entry. Poor child! he was saying the Lord's Prayer for my soul. Ochone! my surprise was no more than a fly in Christ Church, compared to his, when he saw me alive and hearty, instead of being stretched on my last bed. He burst out a crying, the disappointment was too great; and I do n't think he 'll look on me with any comfort for a half year to come".

"I wish I was by while the fault was fresh", said Edward. "I 'd surely give Pat a lesson in moral training. It is just a piece of the regular education practised by ignorant, thoughtless servant-maids, and sometimes their mistresses, keeping poor children quiet by threatening them with ghosts and raw-head-and-bloody-bones, and inflicting such injuries on their nerves as are felt through life. Grown up people should set their children an example of truth and sincerity by their own words and actions. Children soon find out, when a lie is said or acted before them". "Well, to do you justice, master, you do all in your power to make your little subjects practise truth-telling by letting them off easy when they acknowledge the fault at once. But, master, you are not a saint: you are too impatient with dull pupils, and your passion is too near you at times. I 'd make you too proud by giving you nothing but praise; but for me to check you for hastiness, is something like Satan correcting sin. God strengthen us both in that respect!"

• ⁣ ⁣ ⁣ ⁣ ⁣ ⁣ the paddock: ⁣ ⁣ ⁣ the hour of study arrived, "Prison Bars" kept every one occupied and happy. The bawn of the Lucas's was divided from this paddock by a low fence studded with the everlasting elder shrubs, and some ash trees. Margaret happened to be near this hedge on one side, Edward, on the other; her mother, or some of her brothers, or grown sisters, were passing backwards and forwards; and her youngest sisters hard engaged in the game. The mingled society of boys and girls in our country schools was productive of good on the whole. The presence of the teacher, both at study and play, was a guaranty for good behaviour; the boys were more gentle in consequence of the arrangement, and the girls less frivolous. They certainly acquired a taste for noisy and active sports; but they were more healthy and robust in consequence. Indeed most of my tomboy little girls were distinguished as they grew up, by sound sense and virtuous conduct.

The conversation of Margaret and Edward was such as could furnish no peg for whispered suspicions among their occasional listeners, large or small; still it was interesting enough to themselves. Margaret's eyes had a habit of laughing at times; and then so engaging and sweet was the expression of her countenance, that poor Edward seemed as if heart, and will, and wish, were fast escaping from his own possession.

CHAPTER IX.

HOW SLENDER STORIES GET BULK AND SHAPE.—A FAMILY CURSE.

MR. DONOVAN's big kitchen fire saw us all assembled again at night-fall round it, or on the settle; and Owen occupied his iron throne over the ashpit. The children were showing off their recollections of what they had lately learned, and succeeded pretty well, only for Holland being occasionally flooded by the Nile, and Germany turning out the most westerly state in Europe. It must be acknowledged that in our seminaries, geography was obliged to make room for arithmetic, grammar, bookkeeping, and geometry. Some topic of history arising, Owen declared that he had not much faith in historians at all; they were so fond of contradicting one another, and moreover they all lived longer or shorter after the things they wrote about. "Besides, if they were on the spot itself, did any of yez ever see five or six people agreeing

about an *accidence* that they were all looking at together?
I 'm sure you did n't. One man will write about it what
pleases himself or his faction; another will do the same;
and such lies as people will tell, even without any bad intention! Father Cullen was talking one Sunday after
Mass, about the 'Prodigal Son', and how he *run* through
all his property, and was obliged to mind pigs, *and that.*
And what did I hear Katty Clarke saying as we were
coming home? 'Oh, dear! who is that unfortunate Prodestin boy, or what did he do, to put Father Cullen in
such a way?' Well, what should another woman that
heard Katty, do, but fix it on poor Jos Maybank, because
she knew no other Prodestin in the parish likely to be a
shuler, and when he is not stuffing his craw at the neighbours' houses, he is making rhymes. The third woman,
not hearing what Jos *done*, and knowing there was no
harm in him but his lampoons, told her gossip that nasty
Jos was after balragging the priest in a ballad he made
about him. So the news flew like the wind; and one day
that Jos was *surnadin* down Neils' street, he was surrounded by all the women and children of the village, and
they 'd have made *gibbets* of him only for Jemmy Whitty
and Long Tom Neil that happened to be near at hand;
and very great trouble they had to clear Jos, and put the
saddle on the right horse".

"Yes, Owen", added Edward, "and you may as well tell,
as your hand is in, how a rat or an otter was changed to
an eel; how the eel grew all at once into a big dog; the
dog became a heifer, and the heifer an elephant, or a big
piast; and how half the barony came to hunt him in
Kennystown bog".

"The cap does n't fit me, master. I only made the one
guess, and that was n't very far from the truth. There
was, I think, some foundation for the story about the
serpent. I once was at a christening up in Cromogue,
and heard Mr. Low, the minister, and Father Stafford,
and Mr. Hackett, that you all know to be so knowledgeable in old histories, talking about this very thing. Mr.
Hackett said that *ramshogues* of stories and fables like

7

this one, have all come down from times before St. Patrick converted the country; and that it was likely there was a temple or grove near the lough, where some old idols or devils were worshipped; and when Christianity came, and the church was built at the *Crosses*, it was dedicated to St. Michael (You sometimes see this great angel in pictures with a spear or sword, trampling on the divel), and was called *Kil-mihäil* in memory of the devil's power being crushed at Lough-na-Peisthe. Neither priest nor minister contradicted him; so if the serpent was not there alive and kicking, I suppose Mr. Hackett was in the right. However that is, the O'Briens, and the O'Farrells, and the O'Kennedys still boast that they are sprung from the three Munster warriors; if it is any comfort to them let them enjoy it".

"It 's not right", said Mrs. Donovan, "to let these old stories be entirely lost, but it 's an uncomfortable thing not to be able to guess what foundation they have. It is easy to see how little we can depend on the report of a thing happening in our own days, and the farther we go back the less dependence there is. I heard when I was young, a story about what happened in a family up among the mountains, that had something very curious about it. It was common enough to hear among their neighbours that every generation of this family wished to make one of the young men a priest, and none of them ever succeeded. It was not a very unnatural thing, because we know the good priest always gets a call in his youth from God Himself. So if people will make one of their sons a clergyman without him having got his vocation, they are rightly served if he turns out bad. The story which went about was always told in whispers.

The Family Curse.

"In the charming little village of * * * * there lived a respectable man named Lowther. He was assistant on a certain year to the high sheriff of the county; and one fine summer morning, when the sun was shining pleasantly on the sides of the hills, he left his house with a big sum in notes and guineas about him.

"His way led by a certain farm-house, whose bawn-gate opened on the highway. The mountain lay at the back, and a bog and some meadows with old thorn fences were on the lower side of the road. As he went by, the farmer and his wife were at the gate. The morning was rather hot, and Mr. Lowther feeling his head uncomfortable, lifted his hat, and began to wipe his forehead with his *Barcelona*. So the conversation ran on the fine weather, and the mistress of the farm-house took the opportunity to ask Mr. Lowther if he was thirsty. He did not deny the fact; so both farmer and wife cordially asked him up to the house, and take his choice between a tumbler of spirits and water and a noggin of mixed milk. He accepted the invitation; the high sheriff did not receive the expected visit of his agent on that day; his wife did not welcome his return on that evening; nor was he ever after seen alive. When enquiry began to be made, one person said he saw him about a quarter of a mile east of the farm-house of * * * *, walking in that direction. A little girl, who had been gathering dry bits of furze bushes in a field below the farm-house, and on the other side of the road, saw a well-dressed man talking to Mr. and Mrs. * * * * at their gate, but no directer evidence could be brought against them.

"Some time after, a lad passing by the neighbouring bog, was horrified by the sight of a human head floating as it seemed on the surface of one of the pools. Running home he gave the alarm, and a crowd soon gathered. The clothes were recognised by Lowther's wife, so of course there could be no mistake about the body, especially as the bog water had done its duty. At that time the custom of caoining was still in force, and the wise women of the neighbourhood gave their services. At a pause, the poor widow took up the lamentation, and as she proceeded, her sorrow and her resentment became deeper and deeper. At last she invoked the curse of heaven on the * * * *'s, and among the maledictions that she uttered, she solemnly prayed that no one of the family to the seventeenth generation should ever receive the gift of the priesthood.

"The present is the fourth generation since the discovery of the body of Lowther, and in every one of these generations an attempt was made to set the prophecy at defiance. The person who told us the history was born within a couple of fields of the farm-house, and has never succeeded in freeing himself from some relics of the awe with which he heard it discussed between his mother and an aged neighbour, who, with their heads close together, and all forgetful of the child's presence, dwelt on the ghastly appearance of the corpse, and the evil fortune that still followed the family. The last student on whom the experiment was tried, was not deficient in talent, nor did his mind dwell on the subject of women or drink. He actually broke the spell, and was ordained. It would have been better if he had never succeeded. After a few years spent in a careful discharge of his duties, he became negligent, and at last, was guilty of irregularities for which he was suspended. He went to America, and after many years returned home to the old place to die, worn out by the effects of a hard life".

The talk that succeeded the recital of this tragedy was grave, and the only melody heard that night was of a tragic character. Connoisseurs in old English ballads may object to the form in which it is here given, but one object of ours in presenting our country pictures to the public, was to preserve the fireside minstrelsy as we *bona fide* heard it, or wrote it down from the mouths of uneducated Leinster people, without endeavouring to account for its migration from its original home, or for the circumstance of its being so long preserved among our people even in a corrupt state.

The Jewess and Harry Hughes.

" It was in May on a fine summer's day,
   As the rain rained down very small,
When little Harry Hughes and all his comrades,
   Went out to play at the ball.

" The very first blow that Harry Hughes gave,
  He drove it against the Jew's wall,
And the very next blow he gave the ball again,
  He broke the Jew's windows all.

" Then the Jew's daughter she came out,
  And she dressed all in green;
' Turn back, turn back, my pretty little boy,
  And play of your ball again'.

" ' I won't turn back, and I can't turn back,
  Without my comrades all,
For if my mother she came out,
  It would be a woeful ball'.

" She took a red apple out of her poke,
  And rolled it along the plain,
The pretty little boy he picked it up,
  And for it he'll suffer the pain.

" She took him by the lily-white hand,
  She led him through room and hall,
Till she brought him into her own close room,
  Where no one could hear him call.

" She laid his head upon her knee,
  She pierced him with a pin,
This pretty little boy began to bleed,
  And he died that room within.

" She wrapped him in a sheet so fine,—
  A sheet with many a fold,
And threw him into yon spring well,
  That was both deep and cold.

" But when the day was sadly spent.
  And when the night came on,
Every mother had her young son,
  But Harry Hughes' mother had none.
*   *   *   *   *   *
" When she came unto the Jew's gate,
  She found they were all asleep,
And then the thought came into her heart
  To search the well so deep.

" ' Are you there, poor little Harry Hughes?
  Oh, God forbid you should be !
Why don't you answer your dear mother,
  That reared you tenderly?'

" ' How can I answer you, dear mother,
   And I so long in pain?
For the Jew's daughter with her pen-knife,
   'T is she that has me slain.

" ' But you will take me up, dear mother,
   And bring me to yon churchyard,
And let my comrades bear my coffin
   Of birch and of oak so hard.

" ' Put my rosary at my head,
   My prayer book at my feet,
My Testament in my right hand,
   That I may soundly sleep' ".

CHAPTER X.

INTRODUCTION OF A BLACK SHEEP INTO OUR STORY. A
DISCOURSE ON THE ROAD FROM CHAPEL, INCLUDING A
HALLOW-EVE TALE.

OUR chapel at Castle-Dockrell in these dark ages, was
of such a bald style of architecture that even Praise-God-
Bare-Bones himself would find a difficulty in detecting an
ornament within or without to hang an objection on. It
was in the form of a T, the altar being attached to the
wall in the middle of the horizontal line, and a window
pierced on each side. Before Mass we arranged the
children for Catechism in one of the transepts; and there
being only one class, and thorough silence reigning, the
instructor's question and the child's answer, were heard
by every one in the half circle.

Both teacher and pupils often felt relieved by the tardy
arrival of Father Cullen's brown surtout—its front still
more embrowned by snuff, his corduroy breeches, and
top-boots. On the Sunday after the last conference,
several of the reader's acquaintance were returning from
Mass, among the others, Jane Lucas, not yet noticed.
She was next in age to Margaret, was of a most industrious turn, and not disposed to look on the life around
her through a medium of romance or poetry. Murtagh

Horan was one of the wayfarers; and when he occasionally strove to secure Margaret's company, and found himself after a few steps deprived of that blessing, I thought I could detect a friendly anxious look, directed by Jane towards his honest face and ungainly figure. Jane's countenance, though not ill-favoured by any means, was destitute of the refinement and sweet expression that prevailed in her sister's. So Murtagh looking on her for a long time in the light of a friendly acquaintance, feeling that they were on a perfect equality as far as intelligence was concerned, and being well disposed, like many others, to secure a partner superior to himself in knowledge and accomplishments, his eyes passed over common place Jane, and rested on her more desirable elder sister. We were on this occasion accompanied by Matt Horan, Murtagh's brother, a worthy, seldom welcome to any of our little evening entertainments. He was selfish, and morose, and disagreeable in manner. He had found some approaches on his part, very badly received by both sisters; his own brother came in for some ill will, on account of his comparative popularity; and judging from incessant attention directed to Margaret, that she felt great esteem, if not affection, for Edward, he distinguished him by much additional dislike. As a boy, he did not care for instruction; and was gifted with an extra quantity of the rudeness and selfishness peculiar to boys. When he grew up, he blamed himself for his past neglect; but he did not the less resent the low estimation in which, on that account, he stood with his neighbours. He would take no pains to render his manners agreeable; and he would meet neglect by rudeness and contempt. He was a hedge carpenter by trade, strongly built, and with a rough and unintellectual cast of features.

A disjointed conversation went on as we proceeded homewards, crossing the little stream at Ath-buidh, and enjoying the fine road through the wood of Tombrick, sheltered by the hill of Coolgarrow, and receiving the full benefit of the sunshine in the lively spring-day.

"Well, girls", said Mrs. Lucas, "how did the little discourse that Father Cullen made, agree with you? You see that you can please God, either as old maids, married women, or nuns".

"Nuns or old maids, indeed!" answered Matt. "I wish I could see a girl refuse an offer from any man that was n't ugly enough to frighten a horse from his oats, if she was sure to better her living, and be mistress of a strong farm by it. They make themselves nuns when they do n't see any chance of a good offer, and they become old maids *belase* they can't help themselves".

"You do n't believe then", said Alice Donovan, "that several girls feel so strong a call to give up their lives entirely to prayer and works of charity, that they have no real comfort or content, till they withdraw into convents?"

"*Baithershin!* How could any one, let her be ever so well inclined, stay on her knees praying for an hour or two, or naturally wish for a life where there is nothing to do but pray, pray? Let me do my best, and I could not stay on my knees *beyant* five minutes, without falling asleep, or letting my mind run on something else. What do you say, Miss Jane?"

"Oh, I'd be sorry that every girl was like me about praying. I'm afraid I could n't stay on my knees long no more than yourself, nor read a pious book long without going to sleep. I am in my element only when I have my hands full, either out in the field, or within the house: but that's no reason that there should n't be girls very devout, and able to pray, and read a long time without being tired".

"Yes, Jane", remarked Edward, "and you will be happier as the wife of a good sensible farmer, when you will have occupation enough for your head and your hands, than if you were obliged to live in a fine grand palace, and spend half the day dressing yourself, and the other half, sitting with your hands before you, or finding polished talk for your grand acquaintance". Jane stole a look at Murtagh at the beginning of this speech, and laughed heartily at the conclusion.

"I think, from what the master says", chimed in Matt, "that if an industrious farmer's daughter, was to marry a man who could not give her such employment as she was used to, she 'd be apt to find the day rather long. What is your opinion, Miss Margaret?"

"Surely there are other occupations, as well as binding sheaves, or carding, or spinning. I think at the very idlest time, she 'd get enough to do, keeping her house neat, preparing the meals for her family, looking after their clothes, and making home comfortable. When all would be in good order, would n't it be pleasant to read an improving book?"

"Ah, ha! and when the husband comes home to dinner, maybe he 'll find his knowledgeable wife crying over an old novel, and a bad fire under the pot. Would *you* like such a wife, Murtagh?"

"Thank you, Matt. If ever I get a wife, 1 hope she 'll have the fear of God in her heart any way, and I 'll engage, she 'll not lose her time over novel or nonsense, when she ought to be at something else".

"Indeed, Murtagh, you are so bad a hand at the *coortin*', that you 'll hardly see yourself married, if you do n't put the *phisharogues* on some girl tired of her service, or some old maid that 's in despair of a husband. May be, if you attended night school for five or six winters, to learn the *Principles of Politeness*, Rhetoric, *Bell's letthers*, Logic, and Navigation, you 'd be able to put the *comhedher* on somebody. Ach! when there 's a well-looking, nice-mannered girl in a townland, she won't give you a civil word, if you do n't dress as neat as hands and pins can make you; and if you are not as genteel in your motions as a dancing master, and speak out of a dictionary. I declare, only for the trouble of learning Latin and Greek, and the fasting, and long praying, and the lonesomeness of it, and the bother of hearing confessions, and getting up out of your warm bed of a cold winter's night to go to anoint sick people, if I was young again, I 'd study for a priest.

"Thank God, it 's too late for you now to set about it",

said his brother. "I am sure that no one would naturally take to these inconveniences you mention, and as we would all be not much better *nor naygurs* or wild beasts, only for our clergy, it stands to reason that God will give a call to as many as will be wanted for priests. I suppose it would be as bad for *them* to stay at farming, or carpenthry, or shoemaking, as it would be for Matt to get himself ordained. It would be a fine feather in the caps of our family, when he 'd be suspended for laziness, or cursing, or thrashing some poor sinners unmercifully; and then be obliged to go live in Back Lane, in Enniscorthy, and turn out a *Father Tackem*, and marry runaway couples for half-a-crown, and have his stockings down about his heels, and a week's beard under his poor moist mouth and purple nose".

"I think, Master Murtagh, if I used an elder brother's rights, and gave you a good kicking, it would *larn* you to give your tongue a holiday, another time".

"Do n't vex yourself, Mr. Horan", said Jemmy Lucas. "Murtagh's remarks, I think, were on the whole right enough, but a little too personal; however he meant it all for the best. And talking of convents, I think I know a neighbour's child or two; and it would be as unwise for them to resist the strong calls they 've got, as it would be for Madge or Jenny, here, to enter one. But, Matt, you 'll make them too proud by putting ' Miss' before their names. I hope you do n't do it by way of disrespect. They are a plain farmer's daughters, and I am sure I would be very foolish if I was to begin to fret about how their future lives are to be spent. God watches over every one; and if he or she does their best in whatever line of life they find themselves, with the the view of pleasing HIM, something will always turn out to guide them into the path of life that 's safest and best for themselves".

"Indeed", said Mrs. Lucas, "Jemmy, you never said a wiser word than that about the folly of being too anxious about things that are to happen. If it was good for us to know them beforehand, God would have laid out some way to reveal them. It's pitiable enough to see the disobedience of young people to their clergy, making tricks on All Hallow Eve to find out who's to be their partners hereafter. I never knew luck or grace to attend such doings, and I'll tell you one that brought ill luck on all that were concerned in it.

Holland-Tide at the Big House.

"There is in our country here, a large old manor house three stories high, with a fine lawn at the back, a large paved bawn before it, and on one side of this bawn a fine kitchen garden. It was the seat of a family of the old English settlers, and the last mistress of it had in her the blood of the O'Byrnes, the O'Tooles, and the O'Kavanaghs. The three 'Torments of the Sassenagh', as they were called. I am sorry to say that the last heir was a person of very loose conduct, and did a good deal of harm in his day. Father Stafford might preach about good conduct and modesty to the girls of the neighbourhood, but there were two or three of the poor things that forgot his sermon when *Master Henry* found an opportunity to put his soft talk on them. Perhaps it's twenty years since there were two servant girls in the house by the names of Oonagh Matthews and Peggy Devereux. Oonah was a smooth-faced, handsome young girl, rather light in the head, and fond of flattery. Peggy was neither so handsome nor so light-headed. Charley Kenny, a tenant's son, who used to do duty work for the house, was as fond as he could be of Winny, who sometimes gave him a fair face, and at other times a cold shoulder, according as she had less or greater hopes of becoming *Master Henry's* wife one day. Peggy felt a great liking for Charley, but he only respected her for her good sense and conduct.

"There was an old *divel* of a woman on the land that had been used more than once by the master for his bad purposes, and she was after laying more than one siege to poor Winny, blowing her brains out with the chance of being the mistress of the *Big House* some day. *All-*

holland Night was coming on, and he and she (that is the old thief of a woman) held two or three *collogues* before it.

" Well, there was a plentiful table spread that evening for the servants and labourers in the big kitchen. There was a fire in the big hearth fit to roast an ox, and the plates and dishes on the big dresser were shining in the blaze that flashed from them. There was but small use for the candles that evening. The mistress of the house and Miss Eliza came and sat at the kitchen fire and talked with the people at the table about their families, and every thing that was happening in the three townlands about them, and every thing was very cheerful.

" Well, when the supper was over, the most of them went out in the yard to commence the ceremonies of the night. They broke up a cake into several parts, and every one took a bit in his hand, and when they were before the door in a line, the first flung his piece against the door and cried out, ' Hunger go away to the Sassenach till this night twelvemonth'; the next person did the same, and so on to the last. They then went in, and sat round the big hearth, and the ladies of the house brought up a bag of apples and another of nuts, and laid them on the table, and bade them enjoy themselves till they were tired.

" ' Glory be to God!' said one of the old women, ' would n't it be an awful thing if the souls of all the people that ever lived in this house were now sitting on the shelves of the dresser and the bars of the bacon-rack, and everywhere they could find a seat, and looking on at what we 're doing. Some people do be saying that that happens on every All Saints' Eve'. Bedad, a good many in the company got rather disturbed, and looked one side and the other, and only every thing was so bright and cheerful, they 'd, I 'm sure, be frightened enough. ' It would be a rather awful thing', said the mistress, ' but you may be certain the departed spirits are very differently employed, some enjoying God's face and the company of angels and saints in heaven, some getting cleansed from the stains they carried on them into the other life, and other unhappy wretches suffering the punishment inflicted on impenitent sinners'.

"This discourse was too serious to last long. The ladies went back to the parlour, and the nuts and apples were shared among the company, and they set up an iron stand in the fire and began to try the fortunes of different couples that were talked of as sweethearts. So with a great deal of laughing, and some wishing, and some hoping, and some faith, and some suspicion, different pairs of nuts were set side by side, one representing a young man and the other his sweetheart. If she burst and flew off, his chance was over; if he burst, it was the same with her. If the both burned side by side they would be married.

"'Be the laws!' said a comical young fellow, a son of Nick Thumkin's, 'here goes to burn *Shebale* (Sybil) with *Shaun-a-chaishal* (John of Cashel). He's a brisk old boy, only going on seventy; he'll live thirty years yet'. 'Ah, then, if you do', said the wicked old creature, 'I'll burn your nose off when I get the opportunity. Take that for earnest!' and only the tongs was caught by the person that sat next her, Thumkin's face would have suffered. 'There's gratitude for you', said he; 'so the dickens a chance I'll give you now. Here goes for Charley Kenny and Peggy Devereux. Poor Peggy blushed, and laughed, and requested him not, but he held on. Ovoch! Charley, like a senseless fellow as he was, bounced away in half a minute. 'Ah, that wasn't a fair offer', said Thumkin, as he saw sadness in poor Peggy's face, 'I did not set them right. She had her head turned away, and he jumped off out of a pet'. Down they went again, and this time they burned down lovingly. 'As sure as a gun I must get the first kiss', said the young wag, 'for that bit of match-making'. Old Shebale was sitting next Winny, and she whispered to her, 'I'm going to put down a pair. You are one, and I need n't say who is the other'; and so she did, but the old knave had a nut ready prepared for Master Henry, with a hole made in it. 'Who's the happy couple?' said Thumkin. 'Divel give you news', said Shebale, and the pair burned delightfully in company.

"'After a wonderful deal of work of this kind, the *grisset* (cresset) was put on, and a good lump of lead inside, and when it was melted, Thumkin took charge of spilling a little into a noggin of water, and putting all sorts of constructions on the shapes that it made. There were spindles, wheels, and other things used by women, when he was trying the men's fortunes; and hammers, sledges, spades, smoothing irons, and every kind of tradesmen's tools fashioned out when he spelled for the girls. Peggy got a plough, and the good-natured young rogue whispered to her, 'There's Charley for you, body and bones'.

"'Give me the grisset, you anointed young *jacknips*', said Shebale at last. 'I want to try my hand for a friend'. 'Oh, musha, and have you a friend at all, at all?' said he. 'D——l thank you whether I have or not!' She tried her luck two or three times before she pleased herself, and then she drew out an article, and hid it in her bosom, to make use of it in her own time'.

"At last all separated for the night, and there was no one left in the kitchen but Winny, Shebale, and a little kitchen helper. Peggy finding that her fellow-servant was about doing a *trick in the devil's name*, would not sleep in the settle bed that night with her, but preferred to go home with her brother, Charley bearing them company.

"When they were alone, 'Now', said Winny, very eagerly, 'show me what the lead *done* for me'. Shebale pulled out the article, but it was n't very easy to know what it was like. 'Ach!' said the old thief, 'would n't any one with *hafe* an eye see that it is a *soord* and belt, the mark of a gentleman! Did n't I tell you? Now do n't open your mouth till the great trick of all is over, or the charm 'll be *bruck*. Be off, yourself and little Cauth, to the meeting of the stream and river there above, where the three townlands meet, and do what I *toult* you'.

"Peggy and her company had a little delay on their going home. When they got to the top of the avenue, instead of turning up the lane to the left, which would have brought them home to their own village, they took the right hand turn to see a young girl, a friend of theirs, safe home at her mother's cabin, for no one, boy or girl, would care to be out by themselves on All Hallow Eve. Well, they were half way back again, when Charley, looking over the *ditch* on the left hand side of the lane, saw a couple of girls, just flitting by inside the field, and bedad, he'd have known the skin of one of them on a bush. 'Do n't mind me', said he to Peggy and her brother. 'I want to look after something here within; I'll tell you about it some other time. Good night, and safe home!' He was over the ditch in a moment. The bushes were very high on it, and they did not see what became of him.

"My brave boy followed the two girls without them seeing him, through another field, and along a path that crossed a knoc, till they came out on a rough bit of ground where the stream fell into the river. He could see all along that they were frightened enough, and now he was not without knowing what they were going to do. Winny took a whitish thing, which he guessed was one of her shifts, and, after looking about in a tremble, drew it three times up the stream, and three times down the stream, and then the two left the bank to go back. Charley kept out of sight behind a big bush, and when they were passing him, he heard their teeth knocking against one another. He was very sorry to see the girl he loved so well do a thing which he knew was a mortal sin. 'Still', said he to himself, 'may be it's out of love to myself she done it. I'll have her opinion, one way or the other, about it to-morrow', said he, 'and give her up *in secula*, if she does not make me a pleasant answer'.

"When the girls came into the kitchen shivering, they found the good fire still kept up, and a small table covered with a clean cloth, and a cake laid out on it. They did not speak a word, but Winny spread out her wet shift

on the back of a chair before the fire, and got into the
settle beside old Shebale.   She covered up her head, and
never stirred till she heard, in about a quarter of an hour,
the latch of the door lifted; and then peeping out, what
did she see but the likeness of the young master in his
bare head, and a whitish loose dress that fell all round
him, walking slow and stately across towards the fire.
After standing quite still, the ghost, or *fetch*, or may be
Master Henry himself, took the shift in his hands, turned
it on the back of the chair, and after another little delay,
sat down at the table.

"He broke a little bit off the cake, and put it in his
mouth, and then got up, turned his face towards Winny,
as she lay almost without drawing her breath, put a
faint smile on his lips, and walked out in the same silent
way as he came.   It might be a ghost for any noise
it made, for there was n't a sound from the feet coming or
going.

"Next day Charley had a few minutes' talk with his
true-love, but she met him with such coldness and dislike
that he never gave her another opportunity of showing
her consequence.

"A twelve month from that day, Poor Winny, instead
of being Master Henry's wife, was nursing an infant in
the cabin of her heart-broken parents.   She got time
enough for repentance, for it 's little of his company
Master Henry ever after troubled her with.   If all our
gentry were like him, may God inspire them to stay
away in London, or Paris, or Moroco, or any place where
they wont bring destruction on our young country girls.

"About the same time Peggy was busy boiling the
stirabout for Charley, her husband, who had sense enough
to make her his wife.   May be young Thumkin did n't
dance and gag to his heart's content at the wedding.
I 'm afraid the abominable old Shebale died without having
time to make her peace with God".

After dinner we took a walk along the sheltery sides

of the farm fences, and the borders of the lower wood; and evening found us assembled round the comfortable fire-place at Mr. Donovan's.

CHAPTER XI.

HOW FERNS CATHEDRAL WAS BUILT. A NOTABLE CON-
TROVERSY.

MARTIN DONOVAN was at Mass on that Sunday at Ferns. He endeavoured in the evening to give us an idea of the amazing strength of the walls of the old castle, and after two or three desultory remarks on the subject, Owen Jourdan took on himself the task of archæologist for the old city and Cathedral.

Saint Mogue and his Brother.

"I believe every one that hears me, knows that it was Saint Mogue built the old cathedral of Ferns. Indeed, I ought to say that he did n't build it, but that was n't his own fault. He was a long time tormented with a wild skithaan of a brother, that nothing could get good of, and at last went away for good. After some time, Saint Mogue got very troubled about him. So he took a short stick in his fist, and *thravelled* the Euro'pean world in search of him, and where did he find him at last but playin' ball again the walls o' Jerusalem! Well, some how he persuaded him to come home, and when they were safe landed, the saint hoped he 'd help him to build the cathedral. But the young fellow was of a conthra'ry disposition, and what did he do but begin to build one for himself *beyant* the Bann in the next parish! Well, to be sure! Saint Mogue was stomached enough at this behaviour, and says he:—' I would n't mind all your former *figaries*, but for this one', says he, ' when the bells of the cathedral I 'm goin' to build will be heard seven miles

8

off, not a *dheeg* o' them will cross the Bann to your parish'.
And I hear people say that it 's so to this day.

"Well, the saint seein' there was no use in expectin'
any help from the brother, set about the work in earnest.
He began in the heel o' the evenin', and about the flight
of night, the walls were up to the eaves, and a white horse
was comin' down Slie Bui with the last load o' stones
that was wanten' to the finish. Just then, as bad luck
would have it, a red-haired woman put her head out
of her bed-room window, and instead of admirin' the
great deal that was done, or sayin', 'God bless the men
and the work!' she bawled out, 'Oh, musha, Saint Mogue
achudh, is that all you done the whole night?' Well,
the saint was so vexed with the *bosthoon*, and the little
value she set on his labour, that he never struck another
stroke on the buildin', and the white horse pitched his
load of stones at the same moment (they say the heap
is the size of three houses), and that 's the reason the
old cathedral of Ferns was never finished. Saint Mogue's
image is lying in a nice alcove inside the church. The
nose of it was broke about eighty years ago, and the
Prodestin' bishop that was then livin', got a man from
Italy, and paid him two hundred pounds for repairin' it".

A discussion followed, in which various shades of
belief in the narrative were expressed, the notion of the
saint being so easily ruffled by what a foolish woman
might think proper to say, being the most unaccountable
incident in the story. Owen himself seldom sought to
separate the probable from the improbable in any of his
legends. He knew most of them from his youth, and by
dint of telling them, all had assumed in his mind the
qualities of true history. Having been struck by the
thickness of one of the ruined walls one day when he
had been so far as the old city, and pondered over it day
after day while at his solitary occupation of tying faggots,
and being gratified on this particular evening by the
general attention paid to his legend, he ventured to air

his notions on ancient buildings, and the life led within them.

"What wonderful strong work they made in them ould ignorant times out of little stones!—work that our most knowledgeable masons can't come within miles of now. They say that they laid the stones little and big in proper order, about four or five feet high, and then poured lime into the work *bilin'* hot: they called it grouting, and you 'd as soon break a stone, as a piece of that same stuff. Well, God is above all: but what hard times some of the old livers had! clearing bits out of the woods and bogs for tilling patches of pyatees and oats, and then looking at an army whipping it all away, or may be jumping over the dikes and fences to kill them selves. And I 'm sure I wonder what did *we* do that God was pleased to send us into the world in peaceable times, when the sight of a red coat going along the road gives no one a fright. And if we have a *chivey* with a Protestant about religion, dickens a worse friends we are after it. I 'm sure you 'd be divarted if you were listening to me and Mrs. Cary, the captain's mother (she is a Mount Loftus herself), arguing Scripture the other day. 'Owen', says she, 'why do n't your priests give you leave to read the Bible?' 'Musha, faith, ma'am', says I, 'if they do n't let me, it 's the first I heard of it. They need n't trouble themselves as far as I am concerned, for I do n't know a B from a bull's foot'. 'Ah', says she, 'it 's the people that can read, I mean'. 'Well, ma'am', says I again, 'it 's odd if they do; for I see Bibles or Testaments wherever the families have any learning or taste for reading: but you know yourself as well as me, that people in country places are not fond of buying books, except "universals", or "Vosters", or "Poor Man's Manuals", or "Keys of Heaven", or almanacks, or books of ballads, *or that*'.

"'But why do you depend so much on every thing the priest says, just as if it was the word of God?' 'Well, ma'am, I know he spent ever so many years studying about religion; and was obliged to lead a regular life, and

show a vocation before he was priested.   And now he
spends a great part of every day reading his office; and
he.'s not bothered with a wife and children.   Then why
should n't he have a great deal more knowledge than me,
and why should n't I be said and led by him?   Besides,
I can see, by what both sides allows, that he has got his
office in regular order, up, up, up, up to the times of the
apostles themselves.   If yourself, ma'am wanted to be
learned to tie a faggot neatly, which would you go to, the
Captain or myself?   Ah, madam! if many Protestants
that have nothing but a hard word for the priests, would
only think what heathens the common people in country
and town would be only for them; what cursing and
swearing there would be; what misconduct among young
people; and what despair and torment poor creatures
would endure when in hunger, and hardship, and sickness, and on the bed of death—if they would only think
on the hell this earth would be, only for them, they
surely would change their way of speaking about them.
But I need n't talk in that way to you, ma'am.   I heard
of a Protestant lady that lives fornent the old *forth* that
bestowed a pair of silver candlesticks to Father Cullen
for the poor little chapel of Castle Dockrell'.

"'Well, well, Owen', says she, 'I'm not the person to
speak ill of your priests, as the few I know of them are
all good men.   We are talking of practices and doc-
trines.   Why are you bound to observe such long fasts?
Most of you Catholics would not touch a bit of meat on a
fast day no more than if it was poison; and you would,
may be, not scruple to get drunk on the same day, or get
your heads broken in a fight.   Now would n't it be better to take such nourishment as God affords us than to do
these things?' ''Deed, ma'am, I think there is neither
better, nor best, nor good about any of them.   But you
may take comfort as to the like of such poor slaves as me
fasting: the priest told myself with his own mouth not
to fast.   But if you, ma'am, or such as you, that have
no trouble or hardship but drinking tay, and making
curtchies, would be obliged to fast and abstain a little, it

s n't to Owen Jourdan you are to come for pity. I heard
a doctor, and he was a Protestant too, say, that a little
voluntary fasting—"voluntary" is the word he used—
" a little voluntary fasting", says he, "is very good for the
health and spirits of lazy people"'. 'Owen', says she
laughing, 'there 's nothing to be got from you but
crooked answers, I see. Your throat I think is dry with
arguing': and the big-hearted gentlewoman gave me a
good jug of beer to drink her health. 'Here 's towards
your good health, ma'am', says myself, 'and a happy death
above all', and that 's the way our controversy ended.

"And like most controversies", said Edward, "it was
only skirmishing. If a person wishes to find out religious truth, or to establish it in the minds of others, let
him confine himself to the subject of *Authority* alone".

"So, Mr. O'Brien", said Mrs. Donovan, "you are to
start for Dublin the day after to-morrow. You will be
sure to spend to-morrow evening with us; and when you
are in the big city, you will write home once a fortnight
at least. We will feel very lonesome till your return".

"Thank you, ma'am, for all your motherly kindness.
I 'm obliged to spend to-morrow evening at Mr. Lucas's,
but I will return here to sleep. I will write regularly to
yourself or my curate here; but we have exceeded our
waking bounds".

" Indeed, master", said little Catherine, "you shan't
go to bed to-night till you sing one of your old English
songs. You have more of them in your place than we
have in the Duffrey, I think".

" Well, if I must I must", said he. " I heard the one
I am going to sing from Father Murphy's niece, who was
a native of the Barony of Bargie. But she had only
scraps of it. The name she gave it was

The Cruel Lady.

. *　　*　　*　　*　　*　　*

" He came unto his lady fair, to kiss her lips so sweet,
　But she had a penknife in her hand, and wounded him full deep.

" ' You 've wounded me, fair Elinor, you 've wounded me full sore,
  Yet not a lord in all Wexford loved a false lady more'.
  She called up her merry maids all, three hours before the day,
  Saying, ' There is a dead knight in my bower, and I wish he was
    away.

" ' Gold will be your hire, my maids, and silver bright your fee;
  And as you are alone, my maids, I 'll bear you company'.
  They booted and they spurred the knight, just ready for the ride,
  With his bugle horn about his neck, and his broad sword by his
    side.

" They brought him through the country round, while all were fast
    asleep,
  They threw him into the Bann Water, was fifteen fathoms deep.

" ' To-night is the birth night of Lord Thomas, to-morrow is his
    day ;
  And I will go to his father's castle, to hear what he will say'.
  ' Did you see your son to-day, or will you see him to-morrow ?
  If I do n't see him before three days my heart will break with
    sorrow'.

" There was a pretty little bird a sitting on the tree,
  And as the lady said her say he sung on merrily.
  ' Go home, go home, false lady', he said, ' and pay your maids
    their fee'.
    *   *   *   *   *   *

" ' Hold your tongue, my pretty bird, and tell no tales of me,
  And your cage shall be of the beaten gold instead of the *sallow*
    tree'
  ' You may keep your cage, false lady', he said, ' and I will keep
    my tree,
  For if you proved false to your wedded lord, you 'd do the same to
    me' ".

CHAPTER XII.

THE MILL OF MOYEADY AND ITS OWNERS. PADDY LENNON'S
REMINISCENCES OF OLD PHILOMATHS.

NEXT day we dined with Mr. and Mrs. Hogan at their
Mill in Moyeady. They were people who seemed to
thrive on the liberality and good treatment they showed
to every one who depended on them. They were never

in a hurry, but never idle; and every thing prospered with them. If Mrs. Hogan wished to direct a labourer's or servant's attention to an animal, it was not, " Now, Jack, take care of the cow", but, " Jack, take care of your cow". How fat, and stout, and well-looking was the good mistress of the family; and what a tall and strong man was the miller! Yet the children, with one exception, had a delicate look. Paddy Lennon, the weaver, who lived on the other side of the road, was invited to meet us, for the characters, abilities, sayings, and doings of schoolmasters, formed the staple of Paddy's thoughts and discourse. He had been blind for some years; but was a hale old man, was in easy circumstances, and was owner of land, and kept a couple of looms at work. He received the new apprentice with much cordiality; but seemed to be in despair of securing any young fellow equal in dignity and self complacency to the old stock.

" I declare, I don't believe there are such sound arithmeticians, or book-keepers, or grammarians made now, as there used to be. A lad laid himself out for one thing, and stuck to it like grim death; and if you had the wit of Solomon, and went to argue with him, he'd sack you.

" Now, there was our last master, a first-rate man at writing, and grammar, and arithmetic, I'm sure, for big sensible boys, though they say he had n't the right method with young children; for he'd merely give them the rule, and not let them into the reason of it; and if they were reading, he would not ask them about the meaning of the words, nor tell them amusing things about the subject.

" I hear that neither of our present masters is much good at writing, so I have brought over Mr. Henrick's advertisement, that I took carefully off the chapel door of Castle Dockrell. My sight was not entirely gone at the time; and I was able to distinguish the fine forms of the letters, and the lively colours, and the flourishes. Look at it as long as you like, but be sure to handle it carefully and not put it in your pocket by mistake".

The following is as near a copy of poor Paddy's trea-sure as can be made with type. The original is in exis-tence and may be seen by the curious at the publisher's. The capitals T. M. are supposed to stand for TEACHER OF MATHEMATICS.

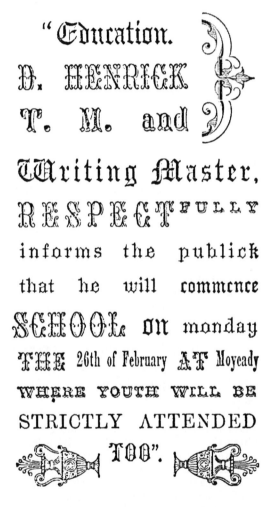

"Education.

D. HENRICK

T. M. and

Writing Master,

RESPECTFULLY

informs the publick

that he will commence

SCHOOL on monday

THE 26th of February AT Moycady

WHERE YOUTH WILL BE

STRICTLY ATTENDED

TOO".

"I can teach MENSURATION and the ELEMENTS of GEOMETRY,
DIALLING, NAVIGATION, and likewise TRIGONOMETRY:
My daily occupation is SURVEYING and ASTRONOMY;
Those branches I perform with the easiest economy".

" But, do you know", continued Paddy, " that I always liked poor Joe Cody's advertisement better. It was simple, and showed so little boast.

> " ' I can teach Voster and old John Gough,
> And for farmers' sons I think that 's enough;
> But if higher pupils come in view,
> I think I could teach book-keeping too'.

" And, indeed, I do n't despise Mr. James MacEnroe's powers either. I 'll repeat as much as I remember of his advertisement, which I saw one Sunday on the chapel wall, written in ornamental hand.

> , " ' School open once more to propagate lore
> At Edward M'Cabe's, where three year old babes
> Instructed shall be in A B C D;
> Pursuing the habit of all the alphabet,
> Until the impression is brought to perfection
> Beyond an objection.
> Of Reynard the Fox, the Frog and the Ox,
> Of profound arithmetic the full of a bed-tick'.

Underneath he wrote, by way of excuse:—

> " ' My pen was not the best,
> My table was my knee,
> I wrote those lines on Friday last
> Upon the lands of Moghurry'.

" But I must n't forget to repeat a few verses of a lampoon that a Mr. Lonergan made on a schoolmaster in Castle Dockrell, who got a few of his scholars from under his fists.

> " ' You celebrated Nine, I pray with me combine,
> And enlighten the weak mind of a feeble Irish bard;
> My talent, wit, and genius, I find are quite unable
> To elucidate this treatise, the task it seems so hard.
> The truth to you to mention, it is my whole intention,
> To give a full description of the base barbarity
> Of a degraded pedant, the dross of human nature;
> He lives in Castle-Dockrell, and basely treated me.

> " ' He did so aggravate me by his false accusations,
> And provoked my indignation by his wicked fraud and guile,

" ' That I 'm forced for to endeavour to search my feeble genius,
      And from its deep recesses these verses to compile.
This despicable upstart is of a mean extraction,
      The marks of which are stamped on his dark *physognomy ;*
I 'm too much agitated to give a proper statement,
      Or correctly publicate poor Michael Butterly.

" ' I wonder Father Murphy or the respectable parishioners
      Permit so base a *vagabone* to manage their affairs :
But I know it is through charity and magnificent benevolence
      That they support such puppies as plainly it appears.
He wears a Barcelona like an estated gentleman,
      Although by all appearance he 's of mean posterity ;
With his black and hairy face he 's a shame to any place,
      And to Ireland a disgrace, big-mouthed Butterly !'

"There was as much more, but it was so scurrilous
that you 'd have no pleasure in listening to it. This Mr.
Lonergan was a dreadfully passionate man. He used the
rod like fun, and indeed I am sorry to say that he 'd as
soon strike a child with his fist or a stick as the rod.
He had one pet question for every one he 'd be arguing
with, and had a drawling cranky way of talking. He
was going up one day to the Kennedy's place there above,
and a roguish boy that was safe behind the big ditch,
roared out in the master's own cross voice, 'Misther
Lundhrigan, how would *you* find the centhre of a cercle?'
'Ah, well enough', said he, 'and when I ketch you, me
poulterer, I 'll find the centhre of your back with the
birch in less than no time'.

"Ah, what a passion poor Matt Foley was in, one day
that I met him with a well-seasoned blackthorn in his fist,
going to the school to give *Misther Plundhergun,* as he
called him, a lambasting for too severe a throuncing his
son, poor Mick, was after receiving at his hands. A
master ought to guard against passion, of all things ; for
I have observed that the longer he holds beating a child,
the angrier he grows".

"You are quite right, Mr. Lennon", said Edward,
" and a naturally tender-hearted person more than another.
When passion gets head at all, his good feelings make
him displeased with himself for his severity ; and this

makes him the more angry with the offender for being
the cause; and the punishment gets sharper; and his own
mind loses its proper balance; and when all is over he is
afflicted with a galling remorse for days".

"I have not heard many complaints of your getting
into passions, master; but a great deal of your earnestness and good methods with the children".

"I have met so much good nature, both from children
and parents, that I would be a bad man, if I did not
exert myself to some purpose for them. Instead of one
home, I have half a dozen at least, where I feel that
there is a real cordial welcome always before me".

"You do n't get a better welcome than you deserve, I
am very sure", said Mrs. Hogan. "Instead of smoking,
or sitting idle in your chair, or guzzling in the sheebeen,
and when you come back, giving a sweep of your rod
round the poor children's bare shins, you do n't find the
long summer's day long enough for your wishes; and
when you come home with your pupils, you will still be
anxious to do more for them, or turn your hand to some
other useful thing. And instead of going on Sunday
afternoon to an orchard with other boys and girls, you
assemble all that you can, for catechism for a couple of
hours. There would not be justice nor good feeling
among the people if they were not fond of you".

"Yes", said Paddy; "and in addition to his other
cares, he spent hours on hours cudgelling that divel of a
sum into my stupid noggin—

'There was a man that bought a horse', etc.

I had it in my head as clear as a whistle about a week
ago; but because I have not the sight, and can't see it
plain on the slate before me, there I am as dark as bags
about it now. If I was n't ready to eat the head of that
stupid ass of a Stephen Keating yesterday! I was sitting
on one side of the fire, and John *(Paddy's son)* and
himself at the other; and there he began to propose very
hard sums to me across the fire, ay, and ingenious ones
too. Well, 1 answered one or two, and the bosthoon,

though I knew him to be as flat as a fluke, still held
on. 'Arrah, Stephen! you ignoramus', says I at last,
'where did you sort out these questions?' After a pause
he blurted out, 'Ah, sure! I got them of the *Gosther*'.
Would you believe it! John was reading out the sums
under his breath to the thief, and at last he was n't able
to catch the word *Voster* rightly, and so I detected him.
But all this won't get the 'man and the horse' to fit
into my brain again, botheration to it !"

"Bah !" said Mr. Hogan; "it 's all for want of good
will and resolution that you do n't succeed. My father
and myself were one day in the high field over the river,
with a steep bank thick with furze bushes right under
us; and there was a whole dozen of cattle breaking into
the field of young wheat on the other side. 'Och, father',
says I, 'the field will be destroyed before I get round by
the stepping stones'. 'Do n't go round: down with
you, and across the river like an arrow'. 'But how will
I do it, father?' says I. 'Look at the thick knoc, and
the depth of the water'. 'Fly across, you dog', says
he. Well, now, you may believe me or not as you like,
but I felt so with the sight of the damage, and the fear I
had of the old man, that I opened my coat, stretched my
arms, spread out my fingers, and on the honour of a
miller, down I flew *skeow ways* across the river. It
would have done you good to see the fright I put the
thieves in. 'That 's well, Mick', says my father: 'always do the right thing whatever be the consequence'.
A wonderful old gentleman he was to be sure! He
planted an acorn in the sluice of the mill when we lived
in Kildavin; and how many years do you think it took
before it sprouted?"

"Seventeen exactly", said Edward. "Well, that was
a wonderful guess: how in the world did you find it
out? It 's a favourite number with me since I read
O'Keeffe's play of the *Wicklow Gold Mines*. *Billy
O'Rorke* wants a favour from the schoolmaster, which the
old rascal won't grant till Billy, who is yet unmarried,
engages to send his seventeen small children to school.

"Still it was a wonderful guess. Ah! I have seen few men with my father's gumption. One day our servant, who stuttered terribly, ran in with his face in a blaze, and his eyes ready to start out of his head, and he striving to get out some dreadful news; but the blacker his face got, and the greater his offers, the farther he was from being relieved. Well, he held on stuttering, and flinging his arms about; and my father gave him a shake or two, and it was not a bit of use. 'Put an air to it, you tinker', says he at last; and with the wind of the word out sung the poor fellow, and sung to a very good air into the bargain:

'*Tol-dher-ollaw, the kil' is afire!*'

"Well now, Mick", said his wife, "don't you think that you told the master some of these things three times already?" "What of that? The little master at all events never heard them. Please goodness, he wont have that story long to tell".

Dinner was over; and Edward, whose seat afforded him a view of the bawn gate, caught sight of Margaret Lucas in her Sunday bonnet, shawl, and gown, returning from Bunclody in company with one of her brothers. No time was to be lost: he was on his legs in a moment, taking leave of his kind hosts, apologising for his haste, and recommending me to their kind consideration. We were on the road when Margaret and her brother were on the other side of the bridge; and by stepping out in earnest, we were all soon side by side, making an exchange of some commonplace ideas.

CHAPTER XIII.

AN AMICABLE DISCUSSION, THE PRIME MOVER BEING SELF-LOVE: EDWARD'S DEPARTURE.

I HAVE seen people embarrassed and miserable while striving to do the agreeable to each other in a nicely furnished drawing-room, chairs and tables, pictures and other incumbrances, adding to their discomfort by the relentless order and symmetry of their arrangement; and every mouth dreading to open, for fear of a frightful discrepancy between the issuing words, and the cast-iron genius of the apartment. But when some adventurous lips hazarded the notion of an out-door walk in the lawn, or the shrubbery, or on the smooth grassy bank of the stream; and when the imprisoned spirits were out in the open air and sunshine, and freed from the surveillance of the rigid furniture, how genial, how unpremeditated, how nonsensical and to the purpose, flowed the interchange of thought and feeling!

Our subject was Edward's approaching departure, and perilous journey to the metropolis, and how regular he would write to us every week or fortnight, and all the strange things he would have to tell; and Margaret supposed that when he returned, his mind would be so full of the delicate complexions of the Dublin ladies, and their silk and muslin dresses, that he would not be able to endure the freckles of the country girls, nor their stuffs and cottons. " Oh, time will tell all that", said he; and as one word borrowed another, either Edward and Margaret walked on slower than Peter and myself, or we walked faster than they, for there was soon a couple of perches between the divisions. However, as we approached our village, the distance was diminished, and when we arrived at our bawn gate, we were altogether. I observed that the longer the conversation held up between them, the more serious it became. It required no great insight to see that the approaching separation was weighing sadly on the hearts of both, though no declaration had yet been made.

At the dismissal of the scholars that evening, Edward addressed a few parting words to his flock. He exhorted them to diligence, enjoined obedience to his substitute, and shook hands with each little friend as they passed out. Mary Kennedy, Anne and Catherine Whitty, Mary Hogan, and Catherine Kehoe, could not restrain their childish tears, and the poor master had some trouble to keep his own from flowing.

In the evening, we were again enjoying Mrs. Lucas's hospitality, and Edward happened to sit next Margaret at table, and afterwards when we assembled round the turf fire. The discourse fell on the next day's journey, and Mr. Lucas, who sometimes relaxed into serious waggery (tall, thin people being generally incapable of brisk fun or humour), exhorted Edward to be of good heart, but yet keep his eyes and wits about him, if he wished to return to Tombrick as safe as he left it. "On the road, you have n't much to dread; but do n't let peddling-looking fellows come too near you in lonesome places. There is a bridge over Poul-a-Phooka waterfall, and if you keep in the middle of the road, you won't fall over the battlements; but if you are fool-hardy enough to look down, I 'll not go bail for you ever seeing the Duffrey again. But after all, the only real danger won't be near, till you get to the city. So if you have any valuable thing to carry from Luke Byrne's, of Francis Street, down towards Stephen's Green or the Bank, take a couple of men with you out of Luke's house, and let one go before, and the other behind. Keep your parcel tightly tucked up under your left arm, and a pistol cocked in the right hand. I forgot to say, that if you could not borrow one at Luke's, it would be good economy after all, to buy a cheap one, no matter whether it would go off or not; for the town thieves are a cowardly set, and the sight is quite enough for them. Keep a sharp look out at the corners of Hanover Lane, Drury Lane, and Goat Alley, and when you find yourself safe as far as William Street, or Stephen's Green, you may put your pistol up, or send it back by one of the men. A shilling a piece is quite enough to throw away on your attendants; they will be grumbling, but if you give away money to every one that asks for it, you 'll have very little to bring back to us.

"Suppose you have no parcel at all; then I advise you not to venture down Plunket Street, where they sell old

clothes. You 'll see the rogues standing at their doors
in wait for simple country people; keep in the middle of
the street, and look straight before you at nothing at all;
for if you only cast an eye at one side, the man, his wife,
and daughter will pounce on you, and drag you into their
den; and if you do n't make a purchase, down goes your ·
house, and then they 'll follow you half-way down the
street abusing you. Another fellow will pick up a
guinea just at your foot, and ask you if you dropped it;
and then he will take you into a tap-room to treat you
out of his good luck. He 'll make you tipsy if he can,
and win all your money playing cards". "Well, as I
do n't know the value of one card from another, he won't
have much trouble". "Oh! please God, you will escape
all these perils, and have the privilege of seeing the Lord
Lieutenant going in state to church with his battleaxe
guards before and behind him, or maybe the Lord Mayor
and the Corporation riding the '*Fringes*', with the big
sword of state, and return safe and sound to Tombrick.
Beyond everything, take care of country people some time
settled in the city; they are ten times more tricky than
the native townspeople".

Murtagh Horan, who was in the company, and who
without any positive ill-will to Edward, would not be
very sorry if he never returned, began to pity school-
masters for all the time lost in learning their business,
and the poor way most of them lived in after all their
trouble. "I 'm sure I wonder how any decent farmer's
daughter could ever be brought to marry such a person
as my own old teacher, Joe Cody, with one leg cocked
over the other, and one shoe in a sligeen hanging down,
and the poor man himself listening to some little child
making mistakes in her lesson, and he looking up to the
rafters of the cabin, and his rod lying in the hollow of his
elbow. Maybe there is a bad fire down, for it is n't every
day that the children think of bringing turf; and the poor
woman has no better occupation than darning her own or
the master's stockings; and sometimes when the children
scatter home to dinner, there is small sign of a comfortable one for themselves or their children".

"Murtagh", said Edward, "your picture is so true, and so well drawn, that if you have an old book of ballads convenient, you might swear me never to ask any girl to share my fortune, if I had not reasonable hopes of offering her something more comfortable than poor Joe's wife (if he had one), was in possession of".

" Then, master", said Matt, " I 'm sure you would not consider it honourable or decent, suppose you were fond of any girl, and thought she was fond of you, to keep her on and off in expectation of a good time, for years and years, till maybe she 'd lose all chance of another husband, perhaps better fitted for her than yourself, and then there would be no choice for her but to be a lonesome old maid".

" Matthew, you would be a severe father confessor if you took to the trade of a priest, as I think I heard you call it some time ago. But to make your mind easy, I assure you that I have not laid myself out to entrap any one with vows or promises, or declarations of love. I am not yet in a condition to offer a comfortable home to any respectable girl, and I think I can wait for a few years without risk of becoming an old bachelor".

We were sitting round the fire or on the settle bed, the men looking into the burning coals, and the women sewing or knitting. I never saw a pair of female hands unemployed for five minutes through all the evenings I enjoyed at my godmother's, at Donovan's, or the Lucas's. So, as Margaret was thus circumstanced, and the light was not falling on her face, none of us could be aware of the effect of Edward's little speech.

Edward was silent and abstracted for awhile, till he was roused by Matt asking Jane, what she would do if the master's thoughts were occupied about her, while he kept the matter to himself. " Oh, indeed !" said poor Jane, with a laugh, " the master is neither thinking of me, nor I of him. We 'd make a bad match, I think. I recollect one evening when he was reading something for us, an I happened to have neither needle, thread, nor scissors in my hands. I was out of one sleep and into another till he

9

stopped; and I do n't think he 'd take much delight if I
began to talk to him about the rearing of geese or
turkeys, or the feeding of calves.   Please God, if I do n't
die an old maid, some sculloge of a farmer will take compassion on me, and give my hands something to keep
them from mischief, between the bawn and haggart.   I
think my father will give me a good *charec'ther* for
spinning wool for the Rathdrum flannel, any way".   Murtagh, who would have been glad to have made Jane his
wife, only for his infatuation for Margaret, let these
words slip into the store house of his memory, and find a
corner for themselves: they were found and *made a note
of* on a subsequent occasion.

Matt took up the ball.   "Well, indeed, Jane, I think
you and I ought to think the matter over: we are something of the same way of thinking and feeling.   I declare
people make too much of learning, after all.   Do you
see them sort that make most money, and have most
property; big farmers, and big shopkeepers, and cattle
dealers and corn buyers.   I 'm sure I never see one of
them dawdling along the road of a summer's day, reading
a Latin book or a book about astronomy or philosophy,
one foot getting so lazily past the other, and a threadbare
coat hanging loosely from the shoulders; and if you ask
him the time of day, he 'll look at you with a pair of fishy
eyes, and give you an answer after striving to recollect
your question.   That 's not the way with the man of business. He 'll be either looking down and thinking of some
new profitable job, or straight before, seeing his way
through the world, and his hand fumbling with a big
purse in his right breeches pocket; and if you ask him a
question, he 'll have the answer as pat as A B C on the
tip of his tongue.   I suppose some of yez know the
Kennedys of Ballybui, beyond the Slaney.   It would
make you sick to spend an evening with five big geo-
chachs of old bachelors of them, as I did last winter.   No
matter what you wished to talk about, they would go
back to some old history, or invention of some kind.   One
lluny of them was saying that he saw in Dublin a house

lighted by the *smoke* that comes from coal, he called it 'gauze' or 'gaze', or something that way. Much good do him with his invention! would n't it be enough to choke us if we used it! There they held talking all the evening like people that were between asleep and awake; and tired enough I was of their company before bed-hour came".

The discourse did not halt here. Matt, though he argued with zeal worthy of a better cause, made no proselytes to his know-nothing system; for there is inherent in our peasantry an instinctive respect for learning and learned people, and no tendency to feel proud of their own ignorance. "I declare", says Jane, at last, "Matt, you 've taken up so much of our evening with your conthráry arguments, you must give us a song to make up for it". Matt, who had a tolerably good voice, was not sorry to exhibit his accomplishments, and after a decent pressing he thundered out,

Billy O'Rourke.

"In the county of Leitrim I first got my name;
I 'm a native of Connaught, and think it no shame.
The night I was born there was humour and joy
To think that my parents were sent such a boy.

"Och, mavrone! how the midwife did talk to me;
'You 've your daddy's big lips, and your mammy's bluff cheeks'.
'Be the piper', says Paddy, ' he 's a son to his daddy;
We 'll have the boy christened this very night week'.

"The clergy got notice the night 't was to be,
The gossips were sent for to wait upon me;
The people all gathered, the priest got his book,
Says my father, then, 'Call the boy Billy O'Rourke'.

" Och, mavrone! there was all sorts of usage there;
Lashings of whiskey, fat pullets, and pork;
The stuff was so soltening, they all fell a jostling,
To keep up the christening of Billy O'Rourke.

" To make me a scholar my parents agreed,
Before I could spell, faith they 'd have me to read;
But I gathered up all sorts of learning so fast,
That the master cried, ' Billy, you 'll bate me at last'.

"Och, mavrone! how the girls got fond o' me;
My face in their samplers the craythurs would work;
For mendin' their thumb-stalls and writin' their copies,
They all found convaynience in Billy O'Rourke.

" But the mistress as well as her girls got fond o' me,
And after a glass, oh it 's loving she 'd look!
And it 's then she would cry, if ould Baywig would die,
That she 'd soon make a master of Billy O'Rourke".

A good many of the company had the same thoughts
in their minds while the song went on. They were to the
effect that if Matt had the ability, *Billy O'Rourke* could
not match him in selfishness and want of principle. The
song being ended, he called on Jane to gratify the company, and after the ordinary ceremony she gave with a
rich sweet voice.

The Servant Maid that became a Lady.

" The Lord of Oxfordshire was a man of birth and fame;
He killed a man in passion—a man who was but mean.
Five hundred pounds in shining gould was offered for his life,
But this large proffer was refused by the murdered person's wife.

" Some people did persuade her that gold would do her good,
But she being careless of the bribe, she would have blood for
blood,
Saying · As he was so cruel as to send him to his grave,
And as he slew my jewel, it 's blood for blood I 'll *have*.

" This young lord he was pitied by his mother's waiting maid,
Saying, · If I was admitted or permitted now', she said,
'It 's to the court-house I would go in hopes to end all strife,
And both from judge and jury on my knees I 'd beg his life'.

" This maiden she got ready immediately, I 'm tould,
And from a Jew who lived hard by she borrowed a chain of gould;
And in a coach in rich attire straight to the court she came,
Approaching like a lady of honour, birth, and fame.

" And when she came before the judge, she fell all on her knees,
Says, ' My lord, I ask for pardon, and grant it if you please.
Pity a weeping lady, and reprieve a noble lord,
And may the Judge that rules above, grant you a kind reward'.

"'How can we reprieve your love?' the judge and jury cried,
  'For the crime that 's proved against him, it cannot be denied;
  For he has in his passion a fellow-creature slain;
  Dry up your tears, fair lady, your petition is in vain'.

"'Well, since you wont reprieve my love all from the jaws of
    death,
  Before I leave this court-house I will resign my breath.
  Behold this pen knife in my hand; with it my life I 'll take,
  Since one of us must suffer death, I 'll perish for his sake'.

"'That 's most amazing!' cried the judge; 'such love I never
    knew.
  Dry up your tears, fair lady, bid sorrow all adieu.
  I freely do acquit him, fair lady, for your sake;
  His life to you I do bestow, although it lies at stake'.

"She thanked both judge and jury, and prayed long live the king,
  'For sparing of my own true love, God grant you a better thing!'
  She took him in her coach, and she drove along the road,
  Till she came to the spacious court, which was the lord's abode.

" When they sat down, she said, 'Kind sir, to you I must let known,
  I 'm but your mother's waiting maid, these clothes are not my
    own'.
  He kissed her and embraced her, and thanked this handsome
    maid,
  'For ever I 'm bound to love you, my dearest dear', he said.

" ' You 've got my gracious pardon, and have prolonged my days;
  For that my bride I 'll make you, and ever sound your praise'.
  His mother soon gave her consent, the marriage knot was tied,
  The bridegroom was a happy man, and happy was the bride".

Murtagh being called on by Jane, gave what was once
considered in the light of a treason ditty, the lamented
personage being no other than Prince Charles Edward.

The Royal Blackbird.

"It was on a fair morning for soft recreation,
  I heard a fair lady was making sad moan,
  With sighing, and sobbing, and sad lamentation,
    Saying, 'My Blackbird most royal is flown.
  My thoughts they deceive me, reflection does grieve me,
    And I 'm overburthened with sad misery.
  Yet if death should blind me, as true love inclines me,
    My Blackbird I 'll seek out, wherever he be.

"In England my Blackbird and I once did flourish ;
  He was the chief flower that in it did spring.
Prime ladies of honour his person did cherish,
  Because that he was the true son of a king.
But that false fortune that still is uncertain,
  Hath caused this parting between him and me ;
Yet his name I 'll advance in Spain and in France,
  All blessings on my Blackbird wherever he be !

"The birds of the forest they all met together,
  The turtle was chosen to dwell with the dove,
And I am resolvèd in foul or fair weather,
  Once more in the spring for to seek out my love.
He 's all my heart's treasure, my joy and my pleasure,
  And justly, my love, my heart follows thee,
Who art constant, and kind, and noble of mind,
  All blessings on my Blackbird wherever he be".

There was more treasonable stuff, full as bitter as the
above in the full lament given by Murtagh, but we have
probably quoted enough. The last song given that night
was *Willy Reilly*, which may be easily found in modern
collections, or in the cheap edition of Carleton's novel
of that name.

At last Edward arose and pressed every one's hand,
and I suppose an affectionate spirit entered into his
gentle pressure of Margaret's hand: and we set out, and
talked but little till we reached Mr. Donovan's.

Next morning John Donovan and I accompanied
him part of the way to the metropolis. We crossed the
Slaney at Bunclody, and left him on the ridge above it,
from whence there is a gentle descent to Clonegal. He
went on his new path in life, and waved his hat when
about to escape from view. We then returned, John to
attend to his farm occupations, and myself to cultivate as
well as I could, the morals and intelligences of my borrowed flock.

CHAPTER XIV.

EDWARD'S JOURNEY TO DUBLIN. HIS IMPRESSIONS, AND HIS FIRST ACQUAINTANCE WITH "WAVERLEY". THE BATTLE OF BALLINVEGGA.

THE harsh winds and sleet of early spring had been succeeded by milder weather, and we occasionally enjoyed the warm sunshine, as we went to school in the morning by sheltery fences.

I paid a temporary visit to Courtnacuddy on a Saturday afternoon, crossing the wood of Ballinakill, the road where Daniel Jourdan's last fight was achieved, the wood of Moynart, and the Urrin, and by lanes and field-paths, an intricate route. The sun shone in pleasantly on us next day through the windows of the little chapel of Courtnacuddy, and I spent part of a pleasant afternoon with the O'Briens and the Roches, and made them happy with the picture I drew of the useful and pleasant tenor of Edward's life. I learned that Charley was about taking his departure for Dublin, having got an appointment in an extensive nursery in the neighbourhood of the city. This would be a pleasant circumstance in Edward's way. I left Bryan and Theresa thoroughly occupied about their young child, their farm, and each other.

About a fortnight after Edward's departure, we were assembled on a Sunday evening in my godmother's large parlour, sitting on dark oak chairs, round a long dark oak table. There was no annoyance from too diffused a reflection of lights, as except the white-washed walls, all the furniture of the room corresponded to the grave hue of the articles mentioned. The loft was a hurdle. The faces of young and old pleasantly reflected the lights on the table, tea and hot cake being an agreeable variation from our established evening meals. Mr. James K., the younger brother, had been in Dublin more than once, disposing of honey, butter, hams, and other country products; and, apropos to Edward's present residence there,

amused the company with some of his city experiences.
My godmother interrupted his narratives, by inquiring if
I had Edward's letter about me. I happened to be so
provided, and at the general request read out a portion.

In those old backward times of slow coaches and dear
newspapers, I paid eight pence for the pleasure of hearing
from my friend, and if there was a suspicion of the
flimsiest enclosure, the authorities would exact another
eight pence, a sensible loss to me, and very little gain to
the king. So Edward had selected a large sheet of blue
paper, and had written close, and again crossed this close
writing. Good-natured little Molly and Catherine and
Larry opened their eyes, and cocked their ears, while
I proceeded leisurely through the chequers.

"DEAR HARRY,—   *   *   *   *   I will not take up
my space with a description of the fine seats along the
road. I thought, once or twice, how nice a thing it would
be to live in one of the houses, and possess the fertile
lands attached, and walk about on the sunny lawn, instead of trudging along a strange road seeking my fortune, and then I checked these covetous feelings, and
pushed on. I did not feel entirely abandoned, till I lost
sight of Mount Leinster. I cannot furnish you with the
statistics of Clonegal, Tullow, Rathvilly, Baltinglass, or
Blessinton, nor tell whether they are incumbered with
mayors or aldermen. I enjoyed through the clear, calm
day, the view of the Wicklow hills to my right, and met
with our own old river at Baltinglass again. Leaving
Stratford-on-Slaney on my left, I reached Dick Wornall's
carman's stage at the fall of night, and for the first time
in my life, paid for the privilege of being flea-bitten.
Taking Mr. Lucas's advice, I escaped with life at Poul-a-
Phooka. I went down the path, however, and experienced
a sense of the sublime from the descent and roar of the
body of foamy water, and again from the steep rough
sides of the valley above the bridge. After leaving
Blessinton, I had a free view of a waste on my right,
stretching away to the hills, and sat on Tamlacht hill
for a while in company with some chance wayfarers, with

the double object of resting ourselves, and taking in the boundless view on the north side. You must figure to yourself a broad and deep plain lying below you, manor houses, castles, groves, thickets, hedgerows shooting up or stretching along on an emerald green plain. On one side, a few bright specks and dark chimneys, and steeples were overhung by a gray fog; this I was told was Dublin. Beyond was the hill of Howth, seeming as if it was lifted some perches over the drab and green sea; then came Bray Head, somewhat nearer, seemingly connected with our standing place by a chain of hills. Beyond Howth the eye noted a rocky islet, then a flat island, then wandered, till some faint blue hills enclosed the picture. I remember feeling in my desolation a sort of envy for the comfortable state of mind of a young servant in company, who was returning to his mistress's house in Bagot Street. The sea kept possession of my sight, and completely saddened me. Your good godmother will enlighten you on my disrelish of that element".

My godmother and her sister laughed heartily at this point of the reading, and promised when I had done, to tell the cause of Edward's woes. So I proceeded. "We descended, passed through the old town and gateway of Tamlacht; struck across the marshy fields by the old castle of Timon, with the green hills on our left, and got a closer view of the roofs of the city, which we entered through Crumlin and Dolphin's Barn. I was disagreeably struck with the shabby ruinous appearance of the streets in the Liberty; but was nearly terrified by the amazing height of Saint Patrick's steeple, after I had made my way to a clear view of it through the old rag and crockery fair held on the Coombe. Then I added to my stock of knowledge by a glimpse of a soldier with an ordinary hat on his head, and cross belts over a blue coat, standing sentry near the Deanery house. On inquiry, I found he was only a policeman. I gazed with veneration on this old red building, owing to our great interest about its former occupant, Dean Swift. I then began to think when would all the rusty keys, hasps, chains, and dismantled fire-irons that littered the shops in Kevin Street, be sold.   Even in the well-built houses that increased in number as I approached Stephen's Green, I missed the cheerful cut stone of so many of our Ross and Enniscorthy buildings, and looked on the dull red brickwork with little approbation.   I admired the fine square of Stephen's Green, with the massive flights of stone steps by which the doors of the Protestant archbishop's palace, and other great houses were approached.   Alas! on presenting myself at the office in Kildare Place, I found that, owing to some informality, I could not have assurance of admission for a couple of days.

"I returned rather dispirited to the old hotel or carman's stage in Francis Street, kept by Luke Byrne, of whom I had so often heard.   He is old and feeble, but his mistress is a portly, well-looking woman still.   On hearing of my disappointment and the part of the country I came from, they gave me a very kind reception.   I was struck with the affected tones of some young fellows during the evening, while singing some of Moore's Melodies in the big tap-room.   They endeavoured to pass for gentlemen; but their opinions and sentiments were stained by the rust and taint of low breeding in spite of the polish they endeavoured to maintain on the surface.   By the way, Mr. Lucas, I am sure, will be pleased to hear that I have not been put to the extra expense of the second-hand pistol, nor of the two guardians.

"Next morning I heard the seven o'clock Mass in Francis Street chapel, and afterwards took a walk by way of exploring the neighbourhood.   It was a gloomy cold morning, and my low spirits were not much cheered by the squalid and dirty-looking halls, and the appearance of pale, lightly-clad little girls, with long, tangled fair hair, and bare feet, carrying home little jugs of milk, or herrings, or bread and butter, to their poor and probably improvident families.

"I paid a visit to the outsides of St. Patrick's, and Christ Church, and the Castle, and the College, and the old Parliament House, and the Royal Barracks to see the

Highlanders on parade; and when the first impulses of curiosity were satisfied, and not a single known face to be seen, I began to feel the time dreadfully wearisome, and to wonder how I would endure the remainder of that day and the whole of the next. This desolation fell on me at Carlisle Bridge; but looking up the river I bethought me of the Four Courts and the old book stalls. Oh, joy! I find there an odd volume of *Ossian* at one shilling, and, to enhance my good luck, Miss O'Reilly, who keeps a circulating library in the open air in the upper angle of the front, offers to lend me *Waverley* at one penny per night. Eagerly depositing a half-crown, I seize with rapture on the precious volumes—precious despite their greasy marbled covers—put the second and third volumes in my pocket, and regardless of horses, cars, and long beams, read end-long from the quay, with Patrick's steeple as my beacon.

"Oh, Harry, you thief! I nearly forgot my yearning for the looks and tones of my dear Tombrick friends till I got to the end of the third volume, spending the interval among the braes and glens of Perthshire, looking up at the gray walls and turrets of Tullyveolan from the old-fashioned garden, listening to the disquisitions of the kind, pedantic old baron, or crossing the moors at the heels of Waverley and Evan Dhu. Oh! how I love Flora and Rose, and lament poor Fergus in spite of his defects; but I recollect I 'm speaking to you in an unknown tongue. Wait till I reach home, and I 'll give you the substance, and a good deal of the language of the glorious work, into the bargain.

"Next morning, provided with the third volume of *Waverley* and the first two of *Old Mortality*, I strayed to the Park, and spent good part of the day sitting in sunny nooks under old thorn trees, or walking by the sides of its thickets and through its sheltered hollows. I found out on my return an old school fellow, who made me look in on him in the evening. He occupied a couple of rooms in a house in Bride Street, which must have been once a richly-furnished private residence, from the remains of the massive, finely-sculptured staircase, the rich wainscoting of the rooms, and the well-wrought chimney pieces and ceiling. Now, the broad staircase steps were filthy with the mud of the streets, the banisters greasy to the touch, and the room scantily filled with poor furniture.

"The names in this now obscure locality are all redolent of ancient and holy memories. 'Patrick's Street', 'Kevin Street', 'Bride Street', 'Bishop Street', 'Cathedral Lane', 'Canon Street', and 'Mitre Alley'. Even the 'Coombe' (valley) reminds us of the time when a noisy stream gushed down a green glen, and sparkled along the walls of the Cathedral.

"Next day I was formally admitted to the barrack life of Kildare Place. I will give you some particulars of my experience thereof in my next. Tell my dear friends of Tombrick and Coolgarrow that I did not know how dear they were to me, till I came here. God bless you and them!"

"Ah, how desolate the poor master must have felt those two days, except when he was reading his novel!" remarked my godmother. "I have a notion of it from having seen children weaned. A grown person, used to dear relations or kind friends, when he finds himself transplanted, feels I believe like an over-grown child".

"Or a lobster after losing his shell", added Mr. James.

"But what has given my friend such dislike to the sea?" inquired H. W.. and he got this answer.

"Peggy and a couple of the children were at the seaside, near River Chapel, a month or so last summer; and he heard that I was about going down one Saturday evening to bring them home. As he had never been at the sea-side, so he felt a curiosity to try the effect it would have on him. We left here about dusk on a beautiful summer evening, the master sitting on the side-shaft, and myself on the quilt filled with straw in the body. He was in great spirits all the earlier part of the night; and seemed to enjoy the wonderful stillness that was only broken by the creaking of the wheels. We

went through Ferns and past Carric Ruadh; and he made
me tell him the names of all the places we passed through;
but at last there was no variety but the fences on each
side, and the drab-coloured high road before us. Then
he began to look at the different collections of stars, and
mentioned how sorry he was that he knew only the names
of a few, such as the 'Plough' in the north, and the
'Seven Stars', and what he thought was 'Orion's belt'.
Now and then he would turn to have a look at Mount
Leinster, which was in sight a long time, for there was
beautiful moonlight. At last the moon set, and still the
road stretched before us, and we got sleepy, and chilly,
and I am sure he wished he had staid at home. The
morning at last began to appear, and we thought we
smelled the sea. We could see pits where marl was got
from, and the road was sandy, and the walls of the houses
were all of mud, except a little rim of white-wash to every
window; and at last up rose the sun, and troubled our
eyes, and the sea breeze was any thing but agreeable.
Mr. O'Brien fancied the tea we got for breakfast was
made with sea water; and when we set out for Mass along
the high bank of the shore, the dashing of the waves on
the strand, and the wide flat level of blue, and gray, and
green made a most disagreeable impression on him. The
'River Chapel' was so crowded that he had to stand up
most part of the Mass, and he told me that he was hard
set to keep himself awake. A good part of the day was
spent afterwards, walking on the stony strand or the
high bank over it; and the return in the evening and
night was very dreary, the master falling asleep very
often on his dangerous perch. Next day at noon he lay
down on the grass; and without intending it, he fell
asleep, and the sun made free with his face; and he woke
with a headache, and was not thoroughly himself again
for a few days. Since that excursion he could never
think with comfort or pleasure about the 'ocean wide',
and I have often felt annoyed about my own part in the
business".

"What a different feeling he would have of the sea, if

his first view had been got under pleasanter circumstances. I think it would be delightful to walk along the moist sand on a fine summer day; or to sit on a rock or a tuft of grass on that high bank you mention, and look over the great plain with its many colours; but I suppose that a person would take no pleasure in reading *Waverley* for the first time, if he was suffering from tooth-ache. I wonder that he did not make off to Clontarf at once. He will have something to say to that, and Kilmainham, and the Bloody Bridge when he returns. I am sure he would pay a visit to Glendalough if circumstances allowed".

"What a pity", said Mr. K., "that places where great multitudes were killed, or some great calamity happened, are always better remembered than those where people spent quiet and devout lives! Do you think, Mr. W., that any other country was ever so badly off as ours in respect to wars and rebellions?"

"Many a one", answered H. W. "You'd be frightened to hear of all the wars England had, besides the fighting with ourselves; and when she had every thing her own way at home, and there happened to be a dog or a cock-fight on the continent, or in America, she could not keep her hands out of it".

"Any person with Christian feelings", said my godmother, "who witnessed 'Ninety-eight', will never long to see such another year, whatever might be the result. It is a very different thing to read about such things and to see them with your own eyes. I was a young girl at the time, and remember the terror I felt at the sight of a yeoman's helmet or his black gaiters. And yet I used to read with great pleasure an old manuscript that belonged to poor Joe Cody, our schoolmaster, about the battle of Ballinvegga, that was fought in Cromwell's time. Poor Joe was a bad teacher, but he was very devoted to the old traditions of the country. I will repeat as much as I can of the story, which I read over many times. So, if, while I am telling it, any part appears like what you would meet in print, you must suppose that my memory has kept a hold of the very words of poor Joe's copy-book.

The Battle of Ballinvegga.

" The castle of Clonmullin stood on the brink of the Clody, in the hills above Newtownbarry. I am told there is now scarcely a stone left on another, but it was a very different place in the time of Cromwell's wars. There was a square block with strong walls, and a high wall surrounding the yard. Outside the wall again was a deep moat, kept filled from a little race made from a higher point of the stream, and there was a draw-bridge cross-ing this moat. The castle and the lands about it be-longed of old to the noble and royal family of the O'Cavanaghs; but about the time I speak of, the branch that held it were driven out of possession by force or craft, and a well-wisher of Cromwell had a firm hold of the lands, and the strong, square-built castle. Well, the O'Cavanaghs did not take the matter very easy: they attacked the castle once and again, and killed several of Sir Silas Naughton's followers; and he was obliged to have a body of his faction keeping watch, and a sentinel was ever on the look-out, moving along the top of the castle backwards and forwards, or standing up in crevices at the corners, and looking out for the approach of danger through deep slits in the stone-work.

" At last, one hot summer's day, as Sir Silas was sit-ting on the roof of the castle in one of the corner turrets, and looking every now and then, north, east, and south, through a long spy-glass, he saw on the side of the hill out beyond the Slaney,—it is now called Gibbet hill—two men lying asleep under the shadow of an oak tree. He looked again with greater attention, and then starting up he swore a great oath that he had his enemy in his power at last.

" He came down at once; and gathering about a score of his idle followers, he led them down through the valley of the Clody; then across the Slaney and round the hill, still keeping in the shade of rocks and trees;

and before the O'Cavanaghs were aware of their danger, they were surrounded by their deadly enemies. The chance clanking of a scabbard wakened them from their light sleep, and they had out their swords; and standing back to back they cut down seven of their foes before they were overpowered. The elder brother received a spear thrust in his side, while engaged with a man in front, and fell on one knee; and while his brother turning round to his rescue, left himself exposed, they rushed in and bore him to the ground.

"Securing his arms with cords, they threw him across the horse of one of the dead troopers, and set back for the castle, while his brother was expiring from his wounds. Just as the last horseman was turning the brow of the hill, and was out of sight, a man who had seen the fight from a point of the hills more to the side of Carnew, and had run as fast as his legs could carry him to the spot, came up to where the dying man lay; and seeing the state he was in, burst into a fit of rage and lamentation. This was a faithful follower of the family, a foster-brother to the young chief who was now breathing his last. The dying man made a sign to him to cease his wailing; and making the sign of the cross, and joining his hands, he began to pray, and humbly resigned his soul to the mercy of his Creator.

"As his spirit passed away, some others of the tribe who had caught the alarm, were on the spot, and amid sobs and bursts of grief, they prepared to bring the corpse to a stronghold more to the sea side, in the same chain of hills that you may see from Clonegal, stretching into the County Wicklow. What is the use of dwelling on the desolation and misery of the mother of the slain man, or the sorrow of his family and followers! They were at present in a moated rath belonging to a kindred tribe of the O'Byrnes, who had sheltered them on their being driven from their own castle. There was no need of hired caoiners, the stifled sounds of real woe were heard through the summer evening and the night, in and round the apartment where the young chief was laid. Still, one or other whose feelings could not be restrained, approached the couch, and expressed in a fitting kind of verse the sorrow that was uppermost in his mind at the time, the words being in the Irish tongue, which was then, and long after, spoken by the old Irish clans through this part of the country. Towards dawn the poor bereaved mother, with her heart bursting, resumed her seat, which she had given up to one of the caoiners; and looking on the noble features of her son, now stiff and cold, and wringing her hands, and rocking her body, she commenced her caoiné. Slowly and plaintively it went on at first; but the tone and action became soon more wild and affecting, till it changed into a loud and vengeful wail. The meaning of a part of the lamentation is still preserved, but the Irish words and the poetry are lost.

"Oh pulse of my heart, prop of my failing years,
The hope of your house, the right arm of your clan,
Will the sound of your voice never fall on our ear again?
That voice that was low and kind in the hall,
And that rung in battle, loud as the piercing trump.

"The eyes that shone on your people with love,
Or flung dismay among the ranks of our foes,
Are now closed in the leaden sleep of death:
And your limbs, that were fleeter than the wild deer's,
Are cold and powerless as the icicle from the bough.

"When I looked from the Rath, on the gathering of the warriors,
I could see your lofty head over the hundreds around you;
But where is now the chief of the scattered tribe,
To drive the armed robber from the halls of your fathers?

"Woe for your short race, darling of our heart;
Woe for our own hap, bereft of your strong arm!
But while life beats in the hearts of your followers,
Grim terror shall not quit the heart of the Sassenach.

"May he meet his end from a wound that brings no honour,
May his death be unwept by bard or female,
Or even the selfish wail of the hired mourner!
Let the track of the goat be at his bed side;
The green grass spring through the crevices of his hearth-
stone;
And the wood-cock build her nest in the heel of his gate!"

10

"When the mingled chorus of grief and rage that joined and prolonged this lament was silent, a feeling of anxiety began to creep over the crowd, and a troubled whispering went on, for it was said that Eileen O'Byrn, the daughter of the friendly chief, had not been seen since an early hour in the night. A trusty female attendant was also missing, and so was Eogan M'Murrogh, the devoted follower of the surviving O'Cavanagh, now either dead, or lying in the dungeon of Clonmullin. Some ten or a dozen others were also not to be found, but as so many were absent, and were naturally supposed to be together, fright gave way to uneasiness. A little before sunrise, however, the young lady and her servant, and four of the kernes were seen approaching the Rath; and as soon as she was left at liberty from the kissing and hugging that greeted her arrival, she gave an account of her proceedings to her mother and Lady O'Cavanagh.

" She had collected about a dozen followers at the hour mentioned, and set out for a farm-house in the neighbourhood of the castle of Clonmullin. Nothwithstanding the dislike, and want of communication between the dwellers within the castle-wall and the surrounding people, there was an attachment existing between a young woman in this farm-stead and one of the warders of the fortress.

" It was now near midnight; and the young girl being informed of the service expected of her, was approaching a certain point on the border of the fort; and as if by mere chance, the friendly warder was not far off at the moment: Eileen, with her maid and three or four of her guards, were not far behind, to attend the issue of the adventure. Our young damsel had a basket of provisions on her arm; and she requested her faithful squire to get it conveyed to the young chief, as she was sure he must now be hungry, and dejected, and lonesome; and anything from his friends outside would be naturally welcome.

" The lover was more frightened than pleased by the request, but at the end of a long parley, he took charge of the basket. The lucky basket held among other dainties, a roll of butter; and if the guards would inspect this roll, they would find a good file withinside, and all hope would be cut off.

"The conference being over, Eileen and her people went back to the farm-house; and after some little time, returned by safe paths across the Slaney, leaving seven or eight of the followers lying concealed in the neighbourhood, to keep an eye on the point at which O'Cavanagh might attempt an escape under the favour of the ensuing night.

"The day passed dismally and drearily in the rath; and the night saw the glare of torches again, illuminating the dead room. About the third watch, a confused murmur was heard in the wood below the outer mound, and this soon changed to a cheer of joy and triumph, and there was an opening of gates, and rushing of feet, and the poor worn-out mother felt something like a return of sunshine, as she pressed the manly form of her only remaining child to her heart. Alas! the burst of joy was but for a moment; he was soon sobbing and weeping over the remains of his dear companion in war and hunting. You may well suppose that the night did not pass without his fair and heroic deliverer hearing from his lips some words of love and gratitude.

"Next day, the funeral rites were performed over the dead chief; and by an early hour of the following morning, the hills were alive with thousands of armed men, all proceeding down their sides to the river, and all with stern faces turned towards the doomed castle. The loss of the young warrior had spread sorrow and resentment among the neighbouring tribes; all sent reinforcements, and now the earth was darkened with crowds hastening to revenge his death. As they approached the castle, they were surprised to see no flag waving on the turret, nor sign of warder pacing behind the battlements. They were however on their guard, and proceeded with some caution, till those who first came in front of the principal entrance, saw the strong door flung open, and the drawbridge lying

flat across on the moat. Sir Silas expecting a visit
of this kind—from the information of his spies—had
decamped with his garrison on the night before, wound
his way quietly down the valley of the stream that runs
under Rossard; crossed the Glasha at the ford of Ballinacoola; passed round the hill near Shroughmore, and
then turning eastwards, and keeping the hills of Kilachdiarmid and Coolgarrow on his left hand, between himself
and the enemy, passed the Slaney at Ballycarney bridge,
and was now hastening to join Cromwell's forces that
were marching on Wexford, after butchering the garrison
at Drogheda, and beating the Royalists at a place near
Dublin, called since that time, 'the Bloody Fields'.

"It was mostly the fate of the Irish party to meet
treachery among their own people, or bad faith on the
side of the enemy. Through both these causes, a large
number of the inhabitants of Wexford were murdered in
cold blood at the Market-cross. The Cromwellians after
this, proceeded towards Ross, where the Royalists were
in force under Luke Taaffe, a leader of whom his country
has no reason to be proud. The Cromwellian general,
learning that the O'Cavanaghs and other clans were
coming down from the mountains to assist the garrison,
sent Sir Silas Naughton with a considerable force to in-
tercept them; and the two bodies met in the plain of
Ballinvegga, which lies on your left hand when you are
even with the far end of the White Mountain. Nothing
could exceed the eagerness both of Sir Silas and of the
O'Cavanagh to try their swords on one another, and their
followers were equally full of hatred. The O'Cavanagh,
in the beginning of the fight, charged the wing where the
banner of his enemy was seen; and being seconded by
about fifty well-armed horsemen, broke through every
obstacle, and dashed right upon him and on his sup-
porters; and several of the Irish kerns pushed on along
with the troopers, and killed many of the Cromwellians
and their horses with their long skians. O'Cavanagh
attacked Sir Silas with such fierceness, that though a
strong and skilful warrior, he bent him backwards to the

very croupe of his saddle. At the same moment a kern stabbed his horse, and a blow of the young chief's sword coming full on his helmet, would have cloven him to the teeth, but the fall of the steed deprived the stroke of its full effect. Horse and man were, however, in a moment rolling on the moor, for it was a rushy common clear of wood where the fight took place. Sir Silas would have taken his last look of sky and moor, banner and spear; but O'Cavanagh's party having too rashly pushed into the enemy's strength, they were surrounded, and it was with much difficulty, and by dint of hard fighting, that they were able to cut their way back again, their leader being almost beside himself for the escape of his foeman. Many a stout warrior slept his last sleep on the moor, where people now pass on the high-road to Ross on market days, without ever thinking of them, or offering a prayer for their souls. Taaffe surrendered the town, and the English commander was so pleased with Sir Silas Naughton's conduct, that he gave him an additional force, and permission to return home, and resume possession of his castle and lands again: he did it the more readily, as the knight was suffering still from the stunning blow he had received on his head, as well as other hurts received in the combat.

"His followers and allies now amounted to about one hundred and fifty men; and they set out at an easy pace, through the flat country, on the eastern side of the White Mountain. They took good care to keep a sharp look out as they entered the Glounthaan, and passed the fords in the beds of the several streams that run down from the mountains to the Slaney, as you come through Coolbawn, Tomenine, Killane, and Ballinlug. The road lay through moor and wood; and as they cast their eyes about, they could see but little except the boughs of trees, and rising over them on their left hand, the dark ranges of the Cooliagh, Black Stairs, and Mount Leinster.

"Pretty late in the afternoon, the party were crossing the brook that runs through the ancient church yard of Templeshanbo, and while passing, Sir Silas Naughton's horse stopped to drink. The rider leaned forward to give his steed more ease, and as he did so, and stooped his head, the back peak of his helmet was a little raised, leaving his neck bare above the top of the steel back-plate. While the horse was quietly drinking, and the others passing the stream, and splashing the water, the report of a musket came from some furze bushes on the rocky side of the valley, and a bullet entering the un-guarded spot on the back of his neck, doubled him down on the mane of his battle steed.

"On the withdrawal of the tribes homewards after the surrender of Ross, Mac Murrough, the devoted follower of the O'Cavanagh, who had been badly hurt at the fight of Ballinvegga, was unable to get farther than the village that adjoined this old church yard. He was cared for at a friend's house; and having on this evening crept out for the enjoyment of the mild afternoon, and being out of sight in the furze brake as the troop was passing, he recognized the foe of his house, and thus Sir Silas met an ignoble death at his hands. A cavern whose entrance was hidden by brambles and bushes, secured him from the search that immediately took place; and the baffled troopers once more resumed their journey.

"Two of their body riding at each side, supported the dead warrior, and in this state they arrived, weary and dispirited, at the castle gate of Clonmullin. They say that when they lifted the body from the back of the war horse at the gate, he drew out and dashed his head furiously at the wall and fell down dead.

"Sir Silas Naughton having no immediate heirs, the O'Cavanaghs did not endure as close a persecution as they otherwise would. When order was somewhat re-stored, the young chief was married to the fair and brave-hearted Eileen O'Byrn, and through the whole country from Ross to Arklow, a finer couple could not be found. Whatever part of the story may be right, or may be not, the caoiné prophecy came out true any way: not a stone of the old castle now remains on another; the woodcock may make her nest in the hollow of the gate if she likes;

and the goats have every thing in and around the castle
at their will and pleasure".

"Mother", said little Mary, "you have forgotten to tell
us whether the young woman was married to the trooper
or not".

"I am sorry to say that she was, and could not be persuaded from it by all the prayers and advice of her
people. My brave trooper had been used to do nothing
but stand on guard, or fight, or drink; and he took
mighty badly to industry on the land; and when he had
a sup in his eye, he would begin to preach to his wife and
his servants, about the terrible sin of idolatry, as he used
to hear Cromwell himself preach to his soldiers. Once
he took a good hazel switch, and whacked wife and children all round. Well, for all that, he was a good-natured
fellow in the main, and cried bitterly the next morning,
when he saw the welts on his wife's arms. So I think we
have said enough about that happy couple".

"Poor Joe! Poor Joe!" said Mr. K. "*There* was a
man whose thoughts and wishes in his youth were all for
the glory of his country, and her liberation from England.
His chief pleasure lay in reading the old histories or
manuscripts. I am sure he often fancied he would be
called on one time or other, to do some patriotic thing
for which his name would be remembered with honour,
and yet, with his indolent, dreamy disposition, he spent
his life a poor, lazy schoolmaster in little repute. So,
young people, take warning; do n't content yourselves
sitting with your hands across, and building castles in
the air, or 'killing dragons in Arabia'. Work like May-
boys when you are at it, and when you are really at leisure for play, enjoy it like children. Devote every day's
business, work and play, to God's honour; and that reminds me that we have had shanachus enough for one
evening: so to your prayers like Christians. Let us
have our hearts and tongues saying the same thing, and
then there will be no sprawling or yawning".

"Oh, I declare", said my godmother, "it is too early to pray, and we had n't a song yet. To punish you, Billy, for going to scatter us all so early you must sing for us". Mr. K. fought bravely to get off, but was forced to yield, and give the only lay in his recollection, viz:—

Peggy Bawn.

"As I wandered o'er the Highland hills, to a farmer's house I came,
The night being dark and very wet, I ventured into the same.
There I was kindly treated, and a pretty lass I espied,
Who asked me if I had a wife, but marriage I then denied.

"There we conversed the live long night until near the dawn of day,
When frankly she said to me, ' 'T is along with you I 'll gae ;
For Ireland is a fine country, and the Scots unto you are kin ;
So I 'll e'en gae along with you my fortune for to begin'.

"The morn being come and breakfast o'er, to the parlour I was ta'en,
Where the old man kindly asked of me if I 'd marry his daughter
　　Jane
'Five hundred marks I 'll gie to her, and besides a good piece o'
　　land' ;
But scarcely had he spoke these words when I thought of my Peggy
　　Bawn.

" 'Your offer, sir, is very good, and I thank you too'. said I ;
'But I cannot be your son-in-law, and I 'll tell you the reason why.
In my own country there is a maid, who is constant to me and
　　kind,
My very heart lies in her breast, she 's the fairest of womankind.

"Oh, Peggy Bawn, you are my honey, and my heart lies within
　　your breast ;
And although you are at a distance, yet I love you ten times the
　　best.
Although you are at a distance, and the seas do between us roar,
Yet constant, dear Peggy Bawn, I 'll be, now and for ever more !"

My estimable old friend did not select this lay for its superior qualities of poetry or morality, but for the simple reason that no other ballad or song had remained on his mind since his "coortin' days". On the incorrect conduct of the hero neither he nor his audience bestowed a thought, no more than do fathers, mothers, and children, witnessing a pantomime, on Messrs. Clown and Pantaloon's want of principle, even though their evil doings for the most part remain unpunished. We enter our protest against the thoughtless conduct of the wandering Irishman, but retain his ballad, as, for some cause or other, perhaps its fine air, it was exceedingly popular when we were in our boyhood.

CHAPTER XVI.

A PARDONABLE (?) BREACH OF CONFIDENCE: THE USURER'S
GHOST.

In a few evenings' time, I was returning from Castle Dockrell, where I had some business after school hours. I was to spend the night at Mr. Lucas's, and was for the moment enjoying the quiet evening, the sight of the wood fringing the lower side of the hill of Coolgarrow, now getting on its first summer mantle, and the farm house of Mr. Pounder, so snugly situated near the bottom of the hill among the oaks. Every one does not know that the little stream springing somewhere near Glanamoin runs along the southern base of the hill, crosses the road at Ath-bui, and courses still at the edge of the wood towards the Slaney below Mr. Donovan's. As I was coming down towards the ford, I got sight of the straw bonnet, the quiet-coloured shawl, and the stuff gown of Margaret Lucas, coming up the lane from Bally-duff. We joined company, crossed the ford, and proceeded to her father's along the shady wood road.

Despite the absence of training, there was in all Margaret's movements a natural grace and ease, arising from a native dignity of mind, a sweet disposition, and an aptitude for mental improvement. We had been on very good terms from the beginning, both being interested in a common friend, and we found no lack of matter for conversation till we got home. Perhaps I went beyond the proper line of prudence in my communications; but, though having little of the match-making spirit in me, I felt a great desire for a happy union between herself and Edward; for I had reason to think there was a sincere attachment on both sides, and as far as my limited judgment of such things went, I considered that their union would secure whatever happiness usually falls to the lot of worthy people in the married state.

"I have received", said I, "a letter to-day from Edward, and will be happy to read it for all the family in the evening". " I am glad to hear it. Is Mr. O'Brien in good health and spirits? He is not forgetting his absent friends, I hope?" " He is quite well, and very busy, but his mind is not in that happy state which I would desire for him". " What is the cause of his unhappiness? Perhaps I should not ask the question. If so, you know best whether you ought to inform me or not". " Well, though Edward might give me small thanks for what I am going to do, I will read to you a few lines of his letter. I know the high esteem he has for you". I noticed the quick going and coming of her breath as I was speaking, and caught a sudden flush on her cheek. " I am struck with the pale unhealthy looks of the women of this city. However regular the features may be, they make the same impression on me, when I recal some at home, as the faces of statues beside fine portraits. I suppose this arises from my heart being filled by the sweet image of one left behind me. I regret that I am not so well off as to justify me in asking her to share my lot". " I think", said Margaret, " that Mr. O'Brien will not be obliged to you for letting this bit of confidence get abroad. Are you not afraid of telling a woman a secret, especially about a love affair? I wonder who the young girl is? perhaps Alice Donovan?" " I am not certain no more than yourself, but it is not she. Alice has had her mind fixed on the life of a nun a long time". " Well, then, some farmer's daughter near Castleboro?" " You are not a bit nearer the truth. I was thoroughly aware of his likings till he came here". " I am told his people at home are comfortable. Do you know why he would not like to settle in the farming business?   Lord Carew, I believe, holds him in great esteem?"

" He was born with a strong turn for reading and study, and would be altogether out of his element, if you set him down to the rearing and sale of heifers, sheep, or swine of low degree and dirty habits.   Set Matt Horan to study history or philosophy, and see how he 'll enjoy it".

" You say he is not attached to any Bantry girl.   Do you know anything about the little alabaster box, or whether it is as precious in his sight as it used to be?" " There was a disappointment I grant, but from the close of the first year after he settled in Tombrick, there was an end to that fancy of youth".   "Maybe he would not be inclined to feel happy with a person who had not read much, or was not so well informed as himself".   " I dare say he would not think it a compliment, if his wife fell asleep while he was reading to her, or began to knock things about, or cudgel the children, or the dog, or the servant maid, or if she seemed quite out of sorts when any literary subject was introduced, or if she preferred the tittle-tattle of her ignorant neighbours to his favourite subjects.   Further than that, I do not think any squares would be broken".

With conversation such as this, referring more or less to Edward's character and prospects, we reached home, and had to endure various pleasantries from her brothers on the circumstance of Margaret and the little master taking an evening walk together.   If she did not enjoy a succession of pleasant thoughts that evening, I am much mistaken.

When the cows had been looked after, and the horses furnished with hay, and the mankind were enjoying that comfortable state of inaction so dear to labourers at night, and the womenkind, young and old, were exercising their fingers as they plied sewing or knitting needles, I was called on to read Edward's second letter. I obeyed, with those reservations of which the reader is already aware.   The subject matter consisted of the life led by the writer and his companions in the training school, which may be communicated some day to our readers. The narrative being concluded, he thus continued:—

" I expect to be on the road home in a month. Having more to say than would agree with the compass allowed by the post office, I have written this volume bit by bit, and now forward it by hand. My earnest love to my dear friends, the Lucases, the Donovans, the Whittys, the K.s, the Hogans, etc. Let them know that when Sunday evening comes round, I am often seized with a profound sadness; and my heart seems to wish for wings to fly back in a moment, and enjoy communion with them once more.

" I have cheated some of the heavy time, and kept off attacks of home sickness by writing out a story which I have somewhat altered from the fashion in which I heard it some years ago from poor Joanna. I am sending it to you by Nick Bowes, and if you can conscientiously declare in your next letter that the reading of it has given pleasure to any of the dear family groups in Tombrick or Coolgarrow, won't I be pleased!"

A unanimous call being made for the reading out of Edward's tale, I obeyed and gave the assembly the legend of

The Usurer's Ghost.

"Once on a time, and a very hard time it was, for it was only a week before Christmas Eve, and it was snowing, and along the frozen road there was sweeping an east wind, that would dry the marrow in your bones to elder-pith, a poor young man was struggling along the same road, and he had not even the comfort to have the wind in his back. The poor fellow could hardly keep any thing like heat in his inside, for it was many hours since he had eaten his scanty breakfast, and he was nearly ready to drop with fatigue and hunger. At last, at a turn of the road, he came in sight of an old manor house on the ridge of a slope, that lay a little off the road. He hoped to find the entrance gate at the end of a little‘ grove, that stretched on for a bit inside the road-fence, and he got all his strength together to help him on. At last he came to where the road bent round on the grove-side, and there, sure enough, was an open space, and a farm-house, where he expected to find the gate and the gate-lodge.

"He lifted the latch, and found the family seated round the big kitchen table at dinner. The mistress sat at the upper end, the master on her right hand, the hand-some young daughter on her left, and the labourers and servants filled up the lower part. As soon as the door was opened, a blast of wind rushed in, and almost blew the fire about the house. The traveller closed it at once, and made the usual salutation, 'God save all here! Much good do you!' 'Oh! God save you kindly!' answered the mistress: 'that's a hard day to be on the road. Come and join us'. 'Thank you kirdly, ma'am! but with your leave, I'll stay near the fire ti l I feel the blood once more in my hands and feet'. 'Well, do n't go too near it, or you 'll have chilblains; and you may as well be eating a bit while you 're getting the benefit of the heat'.

"So a round stool was settled for him near the fire, and a big plate full of good cup-potatoes, and a noggin of skimmed milk, and a print of good fresh butter were laid on it; and if he did not make a hearty dinner, never believe my word again! As hungry as he was, he could not help looking at the young woman near the top of the table, and thinking he had never seen so good or so well-looking a face on any one. When the master thought he was at leisure to answer questions, he asked him how far he had come since morning. 'Oh', said he, 'I came from beyond the mountains, and I believe I never worked or travelled on such a blowing day'. 'And where, may I ask, are you going?' 'Indeed, I am going no further if you have any employment for me. I have· left an old couple and a little girl behind me, and I want to earn something for them'. 'Well, never say 't twice.

One of my men is in the sickness, and it was God that sent you to fill his place. If he recovers I'll find work enough for you both'. 'God prosper you, sir! I expect you'll never have cause to be sorry for holding out a hand to them that stood badly in need of it'.

"It was a rather late dinner, and there was not much done after it except looking to the wants of the cattle for the night. When the evening's work was over, the whole family sat round a turf fire, the women knitting or sewing, one man making a whip, another mending a horse collar, and others merely resting their backs against the partition wall. The chat and gossip never ceased till the potatoes were turned out on the big table. The conversation at the table was continued afterwards at the fire for a short time, and then all joined in the litanies before separating for the night.

"The boys made a luxurious bed for themselves in the barn;—straw under them, walls of straw round them, and heaps of bedclothes over them. One or two reposed on the stable loft,—a resting place which I do not recommend: Bryan slept in the barn. Next morning all were on their feet betimes; and through the day, the master was struck by the intelligence of his new ally, and the interest he took in every occupation that fell to him. He was particularly handy about the cattle, and the very dogs and cats seemed to take kindly to him from the first.

"At nightfall they assembled again round the hearth, and by this time Bryan looked a different man from the tired and hungry traveller that had lifted the latch on the previous day. Few words had yet passed between himself and the farmer's daughter, but their eyes had met more than once, and probably their thoughts also.

"The night before Christmas Eve, Bryan's new master detained him a little after the rest, and thus addressed him in the presence of his wife and daughter. 'If you please me as well during the rest of the year, as you have to-day, I will give you eight pounds at the end. Perhaps you would like to let your family know what has happened at once: they would spend a happier Christmas I

am sure, if you did. Here is a quarter's hire; and if
you wish, you may go back to-morrow, and spend Christmas at home. I will expect you back the day after St.
Stephen's'.

"Poor Bryan was hardly able to speak for wonder and
joy. The tears started to his eyes, and he grasped the
good man's hand with both his own, and expressed his
gratitude in a very confused manner. 'You need not
wait for breakfast, if you wish to start early. You will
find a square or two of bread on the kitchen table, and
you can begin your journey at daybreak. Good night,
and God speed, and a happy Christmas to yourself and
family!' 'The same to you, sir, and all belonging to you,
and may your heart never know sorrow!' The farmer
gave a great sigh at these words, and the women's faces
looked sad. Bryan longed to know the cause of this sadness, but good manners kept his mouth closed.

"Next day the air was calm, the sun shone, and the
road was pretty clear of the snow, which had been blown
into the dykes; and Bryan's spirits were so good that he
would not have minded drifts, if they lay in his way.
His little family were startled, and glad, and sorry, to
see him back so soon; but joy got the upper hand, when
he told them of his good fortune, and of the kind family
that had engaged him. There was some bustle for the
next two or three hours, providing something better than
they had hoped for, against the next day. They went
to bed with content and gratitude in their hearts; and
were up and in time for the day-break Mass at the
neighbouring chapel next morning.

"Bryan's new mistress did not give much praise to
her husband for his off-hand generosity to the young
stranger. She said it was a chance whether they would
ever see him again or no; but her words did not much
lessen the confidence which both father and daughter felt
in his honesty. There was also a division of opinion on
the same point among the servants and labourers; but
about noon on St. John's Day, there he was again on the
kitchen floor, a strong handsome young fellow, nearly

six feet high, with joy in his face to see the family again.

"He put his little bundle of clothes in the barn, and at once fell to work; and whenever there was nothing particular for him to do, he made out some employment for himself. When others would be sitting with their hands in their breasts or their pockets, around the big fire in the long evenings, his hands would be ever employed at something of greater or less use, mending or making.

"Before he was two weeks in the house, he was struck with an appearance of great sadness in the master's face at times. He sometimes came by chance on the family, when none of the servants were by; and then he could see that the mother and daughter were just as sorrowful as the father. They shook off this feeling when conversing with their neighbours, or joining in the general chat round the fire in the long evenings. Though Bryan felt some curiosity to know the cause of their melancholy, he was gifted with that natural politeness which results from the possession of good blood and a strong Christian spirit: so he never asked a question on the subject from any one employed about the farm-house.

"About three months after his engagement, he happened to be returning from Mass one Sunday in company with the family, and as they were sitting on the grassy side of a fence, and looking at the cattle grazing or chewing the cud, and seeming to enjoy the beautiful sunshiny day, he ventured to broach the subject. 'I have often taken notice, sir', said he, 'of some trouble that you seem to be suffering from at times. Would it be too great a liberty for me to take, if I asked you to let me know the cause? The mouse once was of service to the lion. Who knows but that I might be able to do something in return for the great kindness you all have shown me? I suppose it must have something to do with the deserted house on the hill, for so long as I have been here, I never saw any one going near it, nor heard any of the people talking of it'.

" 'It is not a pleasant subject at all', said the farmer, 'nor one I like to speak about, but as you have asked the question, I will answer it as well as I am able. I spent all my youth, and some part of my married life in that house. My mother died when I was about thirteen years of age, and my father kept but a small household about him. He was not very social in his habits, and, I fear, was more fond of money than a good Christian ought. He gave me but little of his confidence in his private affairs, but I could guess that he was in the habit of lending money at high interest on all kinds of securities. He left the management of the farm pretty much to me, keeping a close look to the receipts and expenses; and when I married at the age of twenty-four, my good woman managed the house concerns, and brought some life and cheerfulness amongst us. My father used a back parlour and an adjoining closet as offices, and continued to transact business with gentlemen, farmers, and shopkeepers, who were continually calling on him. He was a constant attendant at the assizes in the next town, when they were held; and I often remarked mean and suspicious-looking fellows coming and going about the house for a week or two after. I do not say that he was an unkind father to me; but his mind seemed ever dwelling on disagreeable points connected with these law matters, and he was never open in manner, nor seemingly at leisure to enjoy the ordinary comforts of life. If he took pleasure in anything or anybody, it was to sit and look at his new daughter as she would be going about, regulating her household matters; and he was very fond of the little daughter, and paid her more attention than I could have expected. About ten years ago, one evening just as supper was ready, Ellen was sent to call her grandfather. He had been in his office for two hours or more with the door locked. She tapped, but there was no sign of a stir. After a while, she tapped again, and put her ear to the keyhole. She heard something like a sigh, but no one came to open the door. She cried out, 'Grandfather, I am sent to call you to supper', but still

11

there was no step on the floor, nor any other sign that she was heard.

"'She ran back, and told us how she had heard a groan inside, and said she was afraid that something was amiss with grandfather. We all ran to the door; and as there was no other way of opening it, we burst it in, and there we found my poor father lying on his back beside his office-chair. His eyes were open, but except that he still breathed, and could move his eyes, and now and then the ends of his fingers, all the powers of life seemed lost. We raised him up, laid him on a sofa in the next room, and spoke to him, but he was unable to do more than turn his eyes from one to another. After a little time spent in great anxiety, we sent off for the priest and the doctor. The doctor came first, and felt his pulse, and touched him in several places. He looked earnestly at him for a little time; and then taking me aside, he said there was not the slightest chance of his recovering the use of his tongue or of his limbs. Just then the priest arrived, and sent us all out of the room. He opened the door in about twenty minutes, and comforted us very much by saying that he had great confidence in the contrite disposition of the patient. ' I joined his poor hands together', said he, 'and repeated the Confiteor and the act of contrition; and from the earnest and contrite expression of his eyes as he raised them to heaven, I hope that his soul is in a fit disposition to be called away. I expressed aloud, what I supposed from the manner of his life he would have acknowledged if he had the power; and as far as his eyes could show consent, they did. I have given him absolution, and humbly trust that it is ratified by Our Merciful Father'. He then directed us to kneel down and join in the litany for the dying. You may be sure that we all joined devoutly in the prayers recited by the priest. When we were rising from our knees, we found that life had departed.

"'Well, I need not enter into all the particulars of what followed. There was very little money found in the desks or boxes, and no papers of the slightest conse-

quence. I was called on by lawyers to appear in court
to recover various sums due to my departed father; but
I could not produce any documents to strengthen my
claims, nor had I any personal knowledge of the transactions. So the different parties got off free at some
expense to myself. To say truth, I felt very little interest in the cases, and soon washed my hands out of them
altogether.

"'From the very night after the funeral the distur-
bances began, that soon drove us from the big house.
No one could get an hour's rest through the night in
any room, up stairs or down stairs. Steps would be
heard pacing from one room to another, sighs and groans
heard by the bedsides, doors clashed and banged, and
frightful noises heard from the apartments formerly used
as offices. A tenant had quitted this house where we
now live, a week or so before the death of my father.
We could not endure the terrors of the nights beyond
the third: so we removed down here, bag and baggage,
and here we are likely to remain.

"'At different times within the past ten years, four
foolhardy fellows undertook to spend a night in the
deserted house. I never gave them the slightest encouragement, rather did what I could to dissuade them;
but they would see it out, and it was a sorrowful seeing
they had of it. In one point they all followed the same
plan: everyone would take a bottle of whisky with him,
and here is the way they succeeded. The first person
that tried the adventure was seen next morning, making
his way out of the country, and he has never since
returned. The second was found on the parlour floor
next morning, a miserable paralytic: he never spoke
an intelligible word afterwards. The third walked down
here after his night, a helpless, witless idiot; and the
fourth was found lying cold and stiff, lying across the
threshold. No one has made the attempt since then,
and I hope no one ever will.

"'As during my father's lifetime I had always received
from himself whatever sums were necessary to carry on

the farm business, and handed him over the produce, I was left at his death with bare hands; but God has enabled me to be even with the world. The first year or two, several distressed people applied to me for relief, alleging that their distress was owing to my father's hardness in money matters. I was not able to do much for them, besides I could not be sure whether their statements were true, or overcharged, or altogether false'.

"They had got up and proceeded homewards during the narrative, and were arrived at the bawn-gate just as the farmer came to this point, so nobody will be troubled with Bryan's observations, as he had no opportunity for making them. He was very much occupied with the workings of his own mind for the rest of the day, and made some inappropriate answers to questions that were addressed to him. The next day he remained very silent, and Ellen, who was no more stupid than any other country girl, caught him looking very earnestly and lovingly at herself when he supposed no one was taking notice. The same Ellen had discovered within the last two months, that Bryan was of a respectable stock, though his parents had been reduced to poverty, and that he himself had received a fairish education; that he employed his leisure moments in useful reading, and that he was blameless in speech and conduct as well as she could judge. Whether those his good qualities drew her attention to his handsome face and good figure, or these last induced her to search for his good qualities, neither our readers nor ourselves can at this time determine. All we may venture to declare fearlessly is, that if her father had, on any evening after supper, expressed a wish to make Bryan his son-in-law, and if she lost two hours of good sleep that night in consequence, grief would not have to bear the blame. This day she found herself obliged to pass where Bryan was employed in the haggard; and after a word or two she said, 'You have been very thoughtful or very sad since our return from Mass yesterday. I hope you have no intention of imitating these rash people whom my father spoke about'. 'I am sure, ma'am', said Bryan, 'that I am very grateful for your kindness in thinking about it; but would n't it be a very gratifying thing to all your family, if this curse was removed from the old family dwelling? I think it would make my future life happy, if I could have a hand in bringing it about, and restoring gladness to the hearts of your father and mother, and yourself, since I can't help saying it'. 'But you cannot make any attempt without the risk of your life or your reason; and if anything bad happened to you, you may fancy what further affliction it will bring on us all'. 'It would grieve me to the heart to give any trouble to your father, or mother, or yourself, Miss Ellen—but there 's the master calling me. Here I am, sir. If they say anything before you, you may—In a few minutes, sir. God bless your kind heart, ma'am', and Bryan, not sorry for an interruption, which would in other circumstances be very unwelcome, hastened to see what he was wanted for by 'the master'.

"For some time past he had been promoted to the dignity of a sleeping-room under the roof of the dwelling-house; a flight of stone steps led up to it from the yard. To this room he retired at an earlier hour than usual this evening, giving for excuse that he was troubled (as he really was) with a head-ache. Ellen was uneasy till the boys and men had betaken themselves to their slumbers. She then began to look about earnestly for something or other, and at last asked Esther, one of the maids, who was preparing for her well-earned rest in the settle-bed, if she knew what had become of her *Poor Man's Manual*, which she had laid on the dresser after breakfast. 'Musha, faith! myself does n't know what happened it. I saw Bryan looking at it just as we were all after getting up from dinner. Poor boy! how devout he is to be sure! I saw him kissing the picture of OUR SAVIOUR on the cross, with the death's head and the serpent at the foot of it, when he did n't think any one was spying an eye on him. Maybe if it belonged to Judy or myself, it would n't have the same effect on him. Well, if he won't make us proud he won't make us sorry; for all the time he 's in the house I never heard an improper or jibing word out of his mouth, nor oath nor curse'. 'Would you think bad, Hetty, of going up the steps and tapping at his door, and asking him if he recollects where he laid the prayer-book? I want to read my penance'. 'To be sure I will, ma'am; but maybe some of the boys will see me, and goodness knows what a life I'd have to-morrow with their jokes and their gosther!' 'Oh, they are all in bed, and even if they were not, I'll take care that they shall take no liberties of the kind!'

"Esther went out by the back door, and returned in about ten minutes. 'I declare, Hetty, it is too bad! what has delayed you?' 'Oh, ma'am, nothing has delayed me, for I saw nothing and heard nothing'. 'Did he not give you any answer?' 'Not an answer did he make me. I do not think he is in it at all. I did not tap very loud for 'fraid the boys would hear me from the barn or the stable loft, but from that to this I never stopped tapping or calling to him through the keyhole'. 'And you heard no stir?' 'Neither stir nor move, nor whisper—purshuin' to his conçait! But maybe he is away serenadin' at some of the neighbours' houses'. 'No, no; he's fast asleep. You know how hard it is to waken working people, yourself among the number'. 'Ah, Miss Ellen! you'll have your joke. Good night; you may borrow the mistress's *Key of Paradise* to make your *thurish* (penance)".

" I fear that Ellen's devotions were much disturbed that evening. She was morally certain that Bryan had proceeded to the waste house to strive to undo the spell; and she passed the night in terror, lest he might undergo the same fate as befel the other unfortunate adventurers. Still her fears were not without a mixture of hope, as she was conscious of his good intentions, and was certain that he would not resort to the treacherous aid of the whisky bottle. She neither undressed, nor lay down on her bed; she spent part of the time walking about, and part resting in a chair. If she happened to close her eyes through weariness, she soon awoke in a fright, with her heart

beating and her nerves fluttering. Sometimes she had a
thought of rousing her father, and getting him to go up
to the house with two or three of the labourers. But
then, if she was mistaken, it would be hard to let her
father and his assistants suspect that Bryan occupied so
much of her mind and heart; besides (as was hinted before), her hopes of Bryan coming safe out of the trial
were strong. So she endured this harrassing suspense,
one of the hardest of life's trials to be endured, praying,
and thinking, and hoping, and fearing, till the view
through the window changed from dark to uncomfortable
gray. She then took her seat near the window, and never
turned her eyes from the lane that led up to the haunted
dwelling. At first, she could distinguish nothing; then
the fences of the lane appeared of a deeper gray than
the fields; then they became darker and the fields
brighter, and at last different colours came to be distinguished. She began after a while to feel the stupefying
effect that is caused by gazing long on one object. She
occasionally started up, being ignorant for a moment of
the cause of her being in her present position, and in the
wandering of her mind she sometimes fancied that it was
breakfast time, being unable to decide whether she had
been watching the lane for minutes or hours. At last
her wearied eyes closed for a moment, and when they
opened again, she could scarcely trust them for surprise
and joy; for there were the hat and great coat of Bryan,
and the well-made form under them, entering the bawn.
She started back from the window still keeping him in
sight, and she could perceive signs of weariness about him
as he proceeded to the steps that led to his dormitory.
When she lost sight of him she fell on her knees, and
offered up heartfelt thanks to heaven for his preservation.
With the mental relief came a strong inclination to sleep,
and she hardly laid her head on her pillow when she was
wrapped in a blessed forgetfulness.

"When all were sitting down to breakfast, Bryan and
Ellen were missed. 'Where can Bryan be staying!' said
the mistress; 'he is never unpunctual at his work, and

seldom unpunctual at his meals'. 'I called at his door
about a quarter of an hour ago', said one of the boys,
'and he said he was not well, but would get up shortly'.
'I hope', said the master, 'that it is nothing serious.
This is his first complaint since he came to the house.
Why is n't Ellen here?' said he to his wife. 'I hope
there is nothing amiss with her'. 'I do n't think there
is. She seemed in a very sound sleep when I was in her
room, just now. The like so seldom happens, that I did
not disturb her; we can afford to let her sleep one morning of her life'. The odd coincidence struck the attention of every one at table; some looks were exchanged,
but no one gave his thoughts an airing.

"When they had all scattered after their breakfast, the
farmer said to his wife, 'I will go see what is the matter
with Bryan, and you can look after Ellen. I 'll be back
in a few minutes'. They went on their separate errands,
and met in the kitchen in about ten minutes. 'Bryan is
getting up', said the farmer, 'and will be ready for breakfast as soon as it is ready for him. He says he is quite
well now, and makes ever so many apologies for the
trouble he has given'. 'He surely need make none; he
is the most ready and willing boy that ever was on our
floor. Ellen is getting up, too. She complains of a
head-ache, but says it is almost gone'.

"In less than half an hour the four were sitting at the
parlour table, employed in diminishing a pile of buttered
squares of hot wheaten cake. It was a great treat to
Bryan, and not unwelcome to Ellen, for it was only a
Sunday evening luxury. Ellen examined Bryan's countenance as earnestly as opportunity and bashfulness permitted, but could learn nothing of what she wished to
know. The elder folk took a cup of tea to keep them in
countenance. Bryan was sensible of the respect shown
him, but was a little embarrassed. Great was the pleasure with which he received his cup of tea from the young
girl's hand, but he was afraid to show it, and he was
searching for the best mode of beginning his narrative of
the last night's proceedings. The mistress was pressing

him to take another cup of tea, but he thankfully declined it; and seizing his courage with both hands, he
leaned his elbows on the table for better support, and began his tale. His voice was at first unsteady enough,
but it soon acquired strength.

. "'Dear master, yourself and the mistress have been
very kind to me since the day I first entered your door,
and last night I attempted to make some return. I kept
watch in the waste house from after supper till daybreak
this morning; and now, with God's blessing, any one may
eat, drink, and sleep there from New Year's Day to next
New Year's Eve, without hurt or harm; and there is a
little box in the wall with thousands of guineas lying in
it, and the whole is yours without let or dispute'.

"The farmer eagerly grasped Bryan's hand, his wife
would have hugged Bryan's neck only something prevented her, and his daughter had like to burst out crying,
and there was great but pleasant confusion for a while.

"'But how', said the farmer, at last, 'can I repay you
for the terrible risk you have run, and the great, great
service you have done for me? I declare you must share
this money with me. I never expected a farthing of it,
and the half of it will make me as rich as I ever wish to
be: the rest of it must be yours'. 'Not a penny of it
will I take', said Bryan, 'but you can make a present if
you like, and that present I value above anything in the
world'. 'Ah! what can that be?' said he; but just then
he caught sight of Ellen turning away her blushing face.
'Oh, oh! I see how it is. Settle it between you, and if
you please one another, you will please me'. 'And me,
too', added his wife. Bryan in the height of his joy
grasped the hands of father and mother, and then went in
quest of the hand of the daughter, who, in her confusion,
gave him that, and a modest loving look into the bargain.

*   *   *   *   *   *

"'Now', said the farmer, 'let us hear all that happened
to you last night. I am sure that I am glad enough that
I had no suspicion of what you intended'.

So Bryan began his narrative.

"'Since last Sunday, at noon, I could not let the haunted house out of my mind for a moment, and all yesterday I was determined not to allow the night to pass without trying my fortune. I got a couple of candles, a flint, and steel, and tinder, and secured the dark lantern. I also put my old prayer-book in my pocket, and left the house without being suspected immediately after supper. While we were finishing the family prayer, you may be sure that I prayed pretty fervently for a blessing on you all, and protection for myself. When I got to the bawn-gate of the old house, I felt my heart beat a little; the deserted place looked so gloomy and ghostly. There were some gleams of moonlight about the chimneys and the edges of the roof, and the bawn near where I stood was out of the shadow of the building, but everything else under the canopy, and the moon, and stars was all deep shade. I lighted one of my candles, put it into the lantern, and walked to the kitchen door; and you must not think me a coward, if I acknowledge that I was a little daunted by the ring of the nails of my shoes on the pavement. I lifted the latch, and felt some awe, while my eyes were wandering over the dark corners of the big kitchen, half expecting to meet some terrible looking faces glaring at me out of the gloom. The things on the dresser that had any metal in them were all brown with rust; so were the grate and fire-irons; and cobwebs were hanging in all the corners, and from the ceiling.

"'I passed into the hall, and from that into the front parlour, and that was nearly as gloomy as the kitchen. The wall-paper was mildewed, and hanging in big flakes; and the floor had a quarter of an inch of dust on it, and shook with every step I made, for the boards were all rotten. The back parlour had a desk in it, and a form, and some chairs. There were rusty bars to the windows, and the night breeze was blowing through broken panes. Well, there was nothing very cheering in all this, but I saw no reason why I should not make myself as comfortable as I could. I searched about and found the remains of a fagot, and bits of boards, and some turf in the kitchen. I swept the old dust off the hearth under the grate; lighted a few sticks, very few at first, as the chimney was so long out of use, drew a little table towards the fire, set my lantern on it, and then knelt down and said my prayers; first sprinkling round the table with holy water. When my night prayers were finished, I read the litanies and part of the rosary out of the prayer-book. I used to stop and listen every now and then, but nothing could I hear but the wind outside, and the crackling of the sticks in the grate. You may depend that there was an awful lonely feeling all over me, but I felt confident in the power given to my guardian angel against anything that an evil spirit could do.

"'So the time wore on between reading, and thinking, and praying; but at last, when I was getting a little drowsy, and leaning my elbows on the table with my head between my hands, a frightful shiver ran through me, and I knew that something not of this world was in the room. I raised my eyes; and there, with nothing between me and it but the table, was the dim appearance of a man looking at me as intently as if he could see through my solid body. His face and clothes had the appearance as if you were looking at a body through a fine black veil, and his eyes never winked nor turned away, but seemed as if they were fixed on something behind my head. I could not utter a word for a while; but during that short while, I concluded that the appearance was nothing evil, as it seemed to be inside the circle of holy water. So I made an attempt to speak; but the sounds I made were like what I remember hearing long ago from my own lips, when I would be awakening up from a frightful dream, just as if my heart was jumping into my mouth, and I could only utter half words. However, what I intended to say was, "In the Name of the FATHER, SON, and HOLY GHOST! let me know what is disturbing you".

"'Well, there came a mild expression over the face, and I began to get a knowledge of what I am going to tell you now; but I heard no sound, and his lips never moved. How I felt and understood what he communicated, I cannot explain. It seemed as if I was carried out of myself, and that there was a strain on my seeing and hearing, and that my soul was suspended in the air with a feeling of cold and terror on it, and it wishing to get back again into the comfortable home of the body. In that state, I saw people, and things, and places, and could tell what the people thought or wished to say to me, just as I could hear my own whisper; and all the time, what I saw and heard seemed a part of myself, or as if everything was passing within my mind like a moving show. This is the substance of the vision, or whatever it was.

" 'For a week before your father's death he had been very much troubled in his mind. The thought of having beggared so many struggling people was tormenting him, and at last, through God's grace, he formed a strong resolution of restoring all that he had got by too high a rate of interest, and of giving assistance to every one that had come to poverty by his means, or to their children, if themselves had been called away. At the very moment when the fit seized him, he was beginning a list of all the people whom he had injured. For the sincerity of his resolution, and the sincerity of his sorrow, he escaped the torments of the damned, but his soul was not to know rest till all possible reparation should be made to his victims. • Out of this arose the disturbance ten years before at the old house, and its speedy desertion. All that had ventured to sit up were more or less drunk every one, and none had sufficient courage or presence of mind to address the ghost. The hoard was behind the wainscot in a recess in the back parlour, and a book containing the names of his former debtors and his dealings with them in another recess near it. A panel of the woodwork was the door of each, and they were opened by pressing round bits of wood about the size of a small button, and no one could, except by the merest chance, find the spot where they lay, or distinguish them from the woodwork in which they were set.

You are to take possession of the money, and to the best of your ability restore all the ill-got portion to those who have been wronged or treated harshly, or to their children.

"'While these things I have mentioned, and the instructions I got, were revealed to me, I was under no terror from the sight of the apparition after the first few moments. It was as if my sight and hearing were strengthened and strained in some way. At last, just as if a thick veil fell round my eyes and ears, all was dark and silent. I felt the shiver running over me again, and found the candle burned out, and a streak of gray light across the window. Ah! I would not for any possible advantage to myself, go with my own free will through such a trial again, I felt so chilly, and dispirited, and awed, when all was over. However, I fell on my knees, and returned thanks from the bottom of my heart for being allowed to do some good for my dear friends, and for my own preservation through the sharp trial. The beating of my heart ceased by degrees, and I found my courage gradually returning. I stepped into the other room, and found even in the dim light, the knobs of the presses as if I had been using them for years, everything was so clearly laid before me in the vision or whatever it was. The panels opened, and there lay the gold and notes in one, and the book in the other. I closed them after taking a look, hurried out of the house as fast as I could, staggered home some way, and got a three hours' sleep, and never was a sleep so much wanted.

"'You offered to take me as your son-in-law when you thought you were much richer than you will now find yourself to be, after you have returned so much of the hidden treasure to those who have the best right to it; so I must set a greater value on your favour'. 'Richer or poorer, I would select you out of thousands: you have made us happier, I am sure, than we can express. The soul of my poor father is, I hope, at rest, and the curse is removed from the old family place'.

" About half an hour later they were passing through
the rooms of the old house. Where the windows were
not broken, there was a close unhealthy smell; and the
dust disturbed by their feet floated up through the broad
slanting sun rays in white volumes. They opened windows and doors, and of course inspected the secret
recesses, and spread great joy and excitement among
the domestics and labourers on their return. Father
and son were diligently employed for a week or two
inspecting the book, and returning most of the property
found in the recess to the rightful owners or their heirs.
Then it was a work of love to put the old house again
in habitable repair, and to prune trees, clip hedges, clean
walks, and bring the orchard and the flower garden into
a healthy condition. Bryan's family were brought and
settled comfortably on a skirt of the farm. Bryan and
Ellen were married, and if they and their parents met
with after-trials and crosses, it was to prevent them
from looking to find heaven on earth, a place where
it has never yet been found by any of Adam and Eve's
children".

After sundry comments made on the tale, most of them
being of a laudatory character, even Margaret not seeking
to conceal the pleasure she felt, Mrs. Lucas exclaimed:

"The poor master! I knew he would feel lonesome
enough at times. Well, if it is a comfort to him, Mr. W.,
assure him that there's no love lost between him and his
country friends".

"It's all very fine", said Matt, "but now think well
of what I am going to say. As fond as Mr. O'Brien
is of us all, I'll engage he'll strive to get some business
in Dublin, where he'll have novels enough to read, and
novel-reading ladies enough to talk to; and if any girl
here is such a goose as to let her mind run too much on
him, she'll sup sorrow; that's all",

"The Lord be praised!" said Jane, "that when there
are so many different things to be done in the world,

there are just as many different dispositions in people! Think of Murtagh going to Kildare Place, or Mr. O'Brien holding the plough for thirteen cold spring days, or one of them young girls behind a soft-goods counter in Enniscorthy, that you 'd think would be afraid to touch any thing with the tops of her fingers, for fear it would barn her—think of *her* carding, or spinning, or setting potatoes in a drill, or binding after the reapers, and myself behind the counter, with my shoes polished, and a tortoise-shell comb in my hair, and my silk hankecher, and all as fine as hands or pins could make me, and I hardly opening my mouth, but squeezing the words out of the corners. 'Yis, mim, a lovely article that: them is as nice a glove as ever you laid eyes on. Well, young woman, what 's your will?' Och! if I had my will, I 'd whip the *bracket* comb out of her conceited head, and mark her conceited face with it! But that 's not what I wanted to say, but that if the master and myself were fond of one another, which, thank God, we 're not, and if he promised to be faithful and constant to me, I 'd let him go and live among a whole *bilin* of novel-reading girls without suspecting him. Mr. W., do n't mind what Matt says: his bark is worse nor his bite; and do n't put it in your letter. Oh, dear! Where in the world did the master find time to write that long noration that you 're after reading? It would take me a quarter of a year, and then five quarters of it would be badly spelled".

"And that 's just the time", said H. W., " that Edward would require to spin as much wool as you would in a day; and then six quarters of it would be full of lumps. If you and Edward were this moment to change occupations, one of you would be in a mad house in about a twelvemonth".

" Indeed, I think you are right", said Mr. Lucas. " We let very curious things pass by without paying any attention to them. Now, here you, and I, and the boys are without a single ha'porth to keep our hands out of mischief, and see how busy the fingers of the women are! Do you think it is out of a wish to be industrious? Not a bit: they are driven to it in spite of themselves; and we would be quite uncomfortable if we were obliged to keep handling the needles after our ten or twelve hours' labour. But we are getting out of our depth: let some one sing a song".

George Huggins, Paddy Lennon's right hand man with the shuttle and the gears, was that evening in our society, and being asked to contribute to the recreation of the company, sung the following Scottish ballad, naturally substituting *Cashel* for *Cassil* or *Cassilis*. George was a very intelligent man, whose opinion in doubtful matters was in great request among the dwellers of Coollatin, Moyeady, and Tombrick. He was the only person in the country whom I knew to have any part of this ballad. He, as will be seen, had it in an imperfect form. George had been as far as Glasgow in his journeyman-weaver life, and had brought this as well as some other Scotch lays home with him.

The Earl of Cashel's Lady.

"There were seven gipsies in the north,
　　And they were blithe and merry O;
　They sat, and they sang a long summer's day
　　For the Earl of Cashel's lady O.

" ' Come throw off your bonny little pumps', they said,
　　' That are made of the Spanish leather O;
　And get you a pair of hollow-heeled brogues,
　　To gang along the heather O'.

" The Earl of Cashel he came home,
　　Enquiring for his lady O,
　But all the words the servants did say,
　　' She's gone with the gipsy laddies O'.

" ' Come bridle me the milk white steed,
　　Come bridle me the berry O,
　Till I overtake my lady gay,
　　Before she's wet and weary O'.

" He rode all day, and he rode all night,
　　And a part of next morning early O,
　When who did he spy but his love passing by,
　　And she both wet and weary O.

" ' Come back with me, my own wedded love,
    Come back with me my deary O;
And I will swear by the hilt of my sword,
    My hand shall never slave thee O.

" ' And wont you come back to your houses and lands,
    And wont you come back to your children O ?'
' I wont return to you nor to them,
    But I 'll stay with my gipsy laddies O.

" 'They gave to me of the cinnamon sweet,
    They gave to me of the ginger O:
But I gave them a far better thing,
    The seven gold rings from my fingers O.

" ' Last night I lay on a soft bed of down,
    My wedded lord beside me O,
But to-night I 'll lie in the ash corner,
    The gipsies all around me O'.

" These gipsies all he placed in jail,
    Bound down in heavy irons O,
They all were hung on a high gallows tree,
    For the Earl of Cashel's lady O".

Bernard Lucas was next secured, but he stoutly de-
murred till clamour compelled him to yield. "Well",
said he, "you will be no better for your tyranny unless you
relish a nice bit of balderdash. Here is a description of

Sweet Castle Hyde.

" As I roved out on a summer's morning,
    Down by the banks of Blackwater side,
To view the groves and the meadows charming,
    And the pleasant gardens of Castle Hyde.
'Tis there you 'll hear the thrushes warbling,
    The dove and partridge I now describe,
And lambkins sporting every morning,
    All to adorn sweet Castle Hyde.

"There are fine walks in those pleasant gardens,
    And seats most charming in shady bowers,
The gladiator who is bold and daring.
    Each night and morning does watch the flowers..

12

There 's a road for service to this fine arbour,
  Where nobles in their coaches ride,
To view the groves and pleasant gardens,
  That front the palace of Castle Hyde.

" If noble princes from foreign places
  Should chance to sail to our Irish shore,
'T is in this valley they should be feasted,
  Where often heroes had been before.
The wholesome air of this habitation
  Would recreate your heart with pride:
There is no valley throughout this nation
  In beauty equal to Castle Hyde.

" There are fine horses and stall-fed oxes,
  A den for foxes to play and hide,
Fine mares for breeding, and foreign sheep in
  With snowy fleeces in Castle Hyde.
The grand improvements that there are making,
  The trees all drooping with fruit beside,
The bees are humming the fields with music,
  Which yields more beauty to Castle Hyde.

" The richest groves throughout this nation,
  And fine plantations you will see there,
The rose, the tulip, and the sweet briar,
  All vieing with the lily fair.
The buck and doe, the fox and eagle,
  They skip and play by the river side,
The trout and salmon are always sporting
  In the clear streamlets of Castle Hyde".

CHAPTER XVI.

A VERY LONG DAY, FOLLOWED BY AN EXPERIMENT IN THE
"BLACK ART".

IT was early summer; and the lately arid-looking wide
ridges and drills of the fields were now pleasant to look
on, with the brown clods and gray stones concealed by
the green blades of tender corn, or the spreading leaves
of the potatoe. The bishop was soon expected to administer confirmation in the chapel at the Cross of Kilmeashil; and the children were requested to attend at the

chapel of Marshalstown at ten in the morning on a certain Thursday, to be examined by Father Cullen. This parish chapel is approached from our neighbourhood by a path across the fields, from the Scarawalsh or Slaney side by a lane, and from the Enniscorthy side by lanes and paths dovetailing into one another. The site is low, the position lonesome, and it would seem as if the object of the original founder was to select a spot that would escape the notice of *Shan-a-Sagarth* and his class.

It was as pleasant a morning as sunshine and shade could make, as I walked into the town, enjoying the view of Vinegar Hill, the straggling streets of the old burgh sprawling up the eminence on the western bank, the fine old castle and its garden, the bridge, the green island, and the river itself with its rich meadows. Then back to the chapel, along lanes and paths shaded by trees or high fences, I sauntered contentedly; and there I found the little building occupied by several little classes from different parts of the parish. I set to, and by means of monitors and my own exertions, strove to keep the young populace occupied. It did pretty well for an hour or so; but the priest did not come to our relief, and we began to feel wearied. No use in giving way; "Courage, my lads! let us commence the catechism again: may be Father Cullen will be here by the time it 's gone through". Great humming and buzzing for another hour: then scouting out and craning on styles for a long sight of the priest's horse and the priest himself: all in vain. Once more we buckled at our now sapless task; and with many distractions, yawns, and inappropriate accompaniments, it was got through. Not willing to inflict on the reader a lengthened description of the utter weariness we suffered on that day from sheer fatigue of standing, want of refreshment, desperate efforts on my part to keep the attention of the pupils awake, and my own spirits above the desponding point, I will only add that when we were on our last legs about half-past four o'clock, we were relieved by good Father Cullen, who had been prevented by some urgent sick calls from keeping his appointment. If any reader of the present melancholy occurrence can really present to his mind the misery of suspense, on a hot day, in a standing position, aggravated by want of refreshment and the necessity of endeavouring to keep up the spirits of a hundred little boys and girls, let him register a vow, never wilfully to inflict such punishment on a fellow-creature, but punctually keep his time engagements like a "man of feeling".

About sunset, after measuring the distance from Marshalstown to Coolgarrow, through the pass of Glanamoin, refreshment, rest, and the absence of present responsibility restored my exhausted powers, and I listened with interest to such conversation as was kept up.

The talk round the fire rolled on fortune-telling, tricks on All-Hallow Eve, attending to omens, etc. Mr. K. seeing a greater tendency in the minds of the youngsters to put faith in these superstitious practices than to despise them, directed their attention to the Catechism, where they would be informed that consulting fortune-tellers, or depending on dreams or omens for knowledge of future events, or for the discovery of hidden or lost things, was strictly forbidden. "If it was desirable", said he, "that we should know beforehand things to come, God would not leave us in ignorance of them".

"It is generally believed", said Owen, "that ravens knows what's happenin' in far off places. There was a fairy man cutting wood up there in Ryland long ago, and he heard an old raven that came flying down from the hill, rcoak out,

'The King of Spain is dead'.

And as he understood the language of the bird, he answered,

'It 's treason you said',

and frightened him a bit, I 'll be bail".

"I wish", said Larry, "somebody would tell us a fine long story where there would be magic or witchcraft. I do n't think the little master told us any one since he came, and Mr. O'Brien told us ever so many".

"Well, Larry", quoth H. W., "it is only fair that I should take my turn. People of a certain name beyond the Slaney believe that what I am going to tell you really happened among their own ancestors, about a hundred years since. The first of this family came from Limerick or Tipperary in some of the old troubles. They did not arrive empty-handed, for many of the race about fifty years since were very well to do. This is the tradition".

The Young Prophet.

"A gentleman farmer of that family was very much looked up to by his neighbours: for along with being the proprietor of a few townlands, he enjoyed the reputation of being a man of learning. He was also suspected to have in his possession books that treated of sorcery, and that he paid great attention to omens, lucky and unlucky days, etc.; and would not allow the green enclosure of an old rath to be tilled for a king's ransom. I 'm not the one to blame him for this particular prejudice.

"He had a herd who was as wrong-headed as himself on these points; and on this account he enjoyed more of his confidence and favour than any other of his servants or labourers. One morning this man entered the parlour where his master happened to be alone reading, and addressed him with a mysterious air, first carefully closing the door, and looking out through the window for fear of an intrusion from abroad. 'Master, master, do n't you believe that ravens, scald-crows, and sea-gulls, and them kind of fowl have the gift of prophecy? To be sure you do'. 'Well, well, tell me what you have to say'. 'I think, master, you won't be sorry for my news. Look out for the next calf that Browney will have, for as sure as the hearth-money, the father of it is a sea gull'. 'If that be the case, you have brought me the best news for yourself, that you ever told in your life. Now mind what I tell you, and you 'll never see a poor day. When she calves, be sure to bring me the *beestings* before a drop of it enters the mouth of any living thing; and between this and that, take every possible care of her'.

"The herd did his duty well, and sure enough, the first milking was brought without mistake or accident to the master. His wife had brought an increase to the family about a quarter of a year before—a fine healthy boy; and on this morning, she was much surprised to see her husband bringing a cup of beestings into her bed-room, and making the infant swallow as much as he could.

"Mr. * * * had read in his books of magic that a child so treated would be endowed with a power of know-ing what was passing in any place that he thought on, or what was doing by any person mentioned to him; but that if he was asked any question concerning those hidden or absent things till he was fourteen years of age, this power would be lost, and some dreadful thing happen to him. In order to guard against such a misfortune, the father was obliged to reveal the secret to his wife, to his herd, and to one or two domestics of long tried fidelity.

"Little Anthony took very kindly to his studies, especially the Latin and Greek languages, and grammar, and philosophy. He had no great relish for field sports or out-of-door exercises at all; and unless some one obliged him to accompany him abroad, he was sure to be found at his books in a room set apart for his own use.

"His father had not been at confession for years, for the clergy would not admit him to communion in con-sequence of his attention to forbidden studies; and this so affected his mother, a simple-minded and devout woman, that she lost all enjoyment of life. The constant, anxious watch, that she and his father had to keep, in order to guard the boy from being questioned, added to her unhappiness. Her health failed; and after a twelve-month of suffering and anxiety, she was released from her worldly trials. She was in some degree comforted during her illness by remarking the devout disposition of her son; but do what she could, her spirit passed away without witnessing the reconciliation of her husband to a well-ordered religious state. Though the father's heart still remained disobedient to the call of religion, the death of his gentle partner plunged him into the deepest grief. The sorrow of the boy for the loving mother, who could never be replaced, added to his sufferings; and at times, he would be subject to the most bitter remorse. Still he could not prevail on himself to relinquish his forbidden studies, nor forego the advantages he hoped to obtain from his son's powers.

"According as the natural faculties of the child's mind strengthened, the acquired gift, assisting his imagination, frequently brought before him visions of things that were to happen people that he knew or chanced to hear or read about; and when he began to study geography, he became aware of his faculty of seeing what was taking place in any locality on which his attention was fixed. For some time he supposed that those about him were equally gifted; and he frequently spoke of what was occurring to the public characters of the day, wherever they might be at the time, as if his company were as clear-sighted as he himself. As he advanced a little in age, he found out his mistake from remarking the wonder on the faces round him, and from the trouble which he saw his parents suffering. He became reserved in consequence, and melancholy began to steal over him, on finding that he was in some way separated from those around him, and that he could not enjoy a free and loving intercourse with them.

"So year followed year, Anthony's knowledge was hourly increasing, and in another week he would be fourteen years of age.

"The herd before mentioned had a son now full grown. He assisted him in his business, and was a well-dispositioned young fellow; but he was not proof against the weakness to which the youth about Slieve Buie were liable. He loved, and was beloved by, the daughter of a little farmer in the neighbourhood; and the house they were to occupy, and the little farm to be taken, were more than once a favourite subject with them.

"Within a week of Anthony's coming to his prophetic majority, the brave young herd was looking after his charge at some distance from the house, in a pleasant-lying meadow. There was a stream on one side, the remains of a former wood on another, a rising ground at the back, and a well-worn path by the fences, followed by the cattle in their coming to, or returning from pasture. The young girl lived about a quarter of a mile to the north of this locality, and on this particular morning she had business which called her to a neighbour's house, about half a mile to the west of her father's place; but from thoughtlessness or some other circumstance not worth dwelling on, she took this very pasture on the line of her journey. Of course she was quite surprised to find the cows and their guardian at that particular place, and was besides in rather a hurry to get her business done; but an hour and a half went by, and she was still sitting on the trunk of an old tree, and her future husband also sitting at a little distance, and fully under the impression that he would not find it tiresome to sit there till sunset, provided that she would keep her place also.

"Their discourse was not very intellectual; but still it interested themselves very much. 'Did you like the ribbons Kitty Cassidy had on her bonnet last Sunday in the chapel?' 'Faith, if you made me knight of the shire, I could not tell you what colour was on her ribbons'. 'I thought I saw you on one knee, and looking rather earnestly at her, just before the last gospel'. 'Well, for my sins I must own that I looked at some one three or four times, when I ought to be looking at my prayer book, but it was n't at Kitty Cassidy'. 'Well, sure, if you let me know who the girl is, I can tell her to go kneel for the future in some corner where she won't disturb you'. 'Ah, you will do no such ill-natured thing. * * * * * There is one thing that puzzles me now and then, Mary. You have seen as well as *me*, husbands and wives so cold or so cross with one another, and not seeming to care if they did n't see one another for a whole day. Do you think they were ever as fond of one another before marriage as I am of you, or as I hope you are of me?' 'Oh, how conceited we are! How do you know that I care anything for you at all?' Here the poor youth looked a little annoyed, and she relented at once, and cried out, 'Ah! do n't mind what I say. I care more for you than I do for myself; but about the cross people, I do n't know what to say. I declare that when I look at old peevish couples that way, I can't fancy they were ever young, or pleasant, or loved anything but their own four bones. I do n't mind a body being in a passion now and then. You were sitting by Miss Kitty at *Shan Gar's* wake, and yez were skitting and laughing together; and I declare only for the people that were by, and the poor corpse under the sheet, and that I would n't let her see I cared so much for you, I 'd have left the marks of my ten fingers on her cheeks or yours, so I would. But what 's the matter? Is there anything amiss among the cattle?' ·The "amiss" is that I do n't see young Browney. The master had a remarkable cow about fourteen years ago, and this is her grand-daughter. She is about calving, and I got particular charges to keep an eye on her, and the *sarra* bit of her I can see now, high or low'. 'Oh, musha! what a sad girl I was to come this way, this morning, above all days in the year!' 'Do n't say a word to yourself, my darling. We 'll find her. She is either under that bank, or got *beyant* the thicket'.

"It was all in vain that they separated, and explored every spot in the neighbourhood likely to attract Browney. When they were meeting after the ineffectual quest, she heard him mutter to himself, 'Oh, if I could speak to Mr. Antony! but I wont if I was to be set adrift to-morrow'. 'What 's that you 're saying about Mr. Antony?' 'Oh, nothing; only that he 'll be very vexed too, if anything goes wrong with the young cow. He is mighty watchful about the ways of birds and beasts; and there is n't a nest on the farm that he does not know; and *pursuin'* to the bird ever stirs off of her nest when he 's going by, nor flies away—I mean any of them that frequents the garden or the fields about the house, even if he 's going within a yard of them. ˙ And the same with the cows, and horses, and sheep, and goats. When he is passing one of them in the fields, it will stop grazing and rub its head again him, and *lue* or bleat after him when he's going away'.

"'I do n't think', said she to herself, 'that Garrett is letting me know the whole truth about Mr. Antony: though they keep him so close, they can't help reports and suspicions from flying about. (*aloud*) Well, Garrett, I must go now, at any rate. May be God would put me on Browney's track; and if it happens, I 'll come or send while a cat would be licking her ear. Do n't let it trouble you so much: she 'll be found, never fear'.

"So with a loving pressure of hands they parted; and she, as soon as she was fairly out of sight, turned her steps to the farm-house, looking in all directions for the cow, and fearing that she might not succeed in gaining access to the 'young master', and devising the form in which she might make up her question, if she did succeed.

"On approaching the house, she was relieved from one of her anxieties, for she saw Anthony walking along the side of the paddock fence, and reading. To add to her luck, no watchful guardian was in sight, and so she approached him with a throbbing heart, and a blush and smile on her comely face. On seeing her come near, he stopped his walk in a little surprise; for though he knew her appearance, he had never spoken to her: indeed the intercourse between himself and the neighbouring farmers and cottiers was very slight. This reception added to the poor girl's embarrassment; but she thought on Garrett's trouble, and put on the boldest face she could.

"'I 'm sure I beg pardon, Master Antony; but the neighbours does be all talking of your great knowledge about cattle; and there last night what should happen, but a neighbour's cow that was drivin' home with my mother's, gives her a puck of her horn near the right shoulder, and cut her, and damaged her very much; and one person says, some *diaculum* should be put to it, and another that *bowl almanac* was the thing, and another, that it was but wash it, and keep out the air with a rag.

So I made bowld to come and tell you about it, sir'.
While she was speaking, he closed his eyes, and leaned
against an ash tree, beside which he was standing.
When she had finished her invented story, he said in
a dreamy sort of way, as if the words had no connection
with his thoughts, while the position of his head showed
he was looking towards some very far-off object: 'Is the
tip of your cow's left horn broken, and has she a reddish
brown blotch just behind her right shoulder?' 'Yes,
sir', said the girl much surprised; 'but where did you
see her? I do n't think you were ever at our little
place?' 'I never saw her till just now; but if that is
she, her cure has been very quick, or you are telling me
a falsehood; there is not the smallest sign of a wound or
bruise on her whole right side'. 'Oh! sir, honey, forgive
me; it was n't that I wanted to say at all. I was just now
coming by the field where Garrett Moore is minding
your father's cattle; and there the poor boy was in
the greatest distress looking after Browney, that 's soon
expected to calve; and the master gave him all sorts
of charges about her. I had such pity for him—we 're
neighbours' children, and used to be playing together,
when we were small: and so—may be I 'm doing wrong—
but if you could tell us, where he 's likely to find
Browney, the Lord may bless you!'

"Here the poor girl got a fright, that sobered her for
many a day. The boy's eyes that had been closed for
some time, opened with a fearful stare, and his whole
figure and the expression of his features betrayed an
intense terror. He once or twice attempted to speak,
and then these words came, interrupted and uttered with
difficulty. 'The cow is lying dead in the byre. Oh,
unhappy father! Unhappy son! Oh, you wretched girl!
Mother, mother, you are spared this trial. VIRGIN MOST
MERCIFUL, pray for me!' His powers now left him altogether. He attempted to catch the stem of the tree,
but there was no strength in arm or hand; and he would
have fallen heavily on the path, but for the quickness of
the terrified girl. She caught him; and his head with

the long hair fell helplessly over her supporting arm.
She laid him gently on a bank, still supporting him, and
was about crying out for help, but there was no need.
One or two of the family passing in the neighbourhood
of the spot, witnessed the strange sight of the young
master talking with Mary; and immediately after observed his wild gestures and the fall. They ran to the
spot, asked a hurried question or two of the girl, and
one of them, a strong labourer, taking him in his arms,
carried him into the house.

"Poor Mary followed into the farm-yard; but anxious
as she was about the state of the poor child, she had not
courage to enter the kitchen. Happening to see a younger
brother of Garrett's running past, she caught him, and
requested him to go as fast as he could to the pasture,
and tell his brother, that his cow was in the byre,
and that Master Anthony was taken ill, and that if
he could call over to her mother's in the evening, she
would be much obliged to him; and then she burst
out crying, and wrung her hands, and exclaimed, 'Oh!
what a bad unhappy creature I am, to have done all this
mischief, when I would n't do hurt or harm knowingly
to any human being! Pat, if you 'd stroll over along
the lane in about an hour or so, I 'll meet you to
hear about poor Master Antony. Lord forgive me
for not going about my business when I had it to
do!' So the little boy went on to the pasture, and she
resumed her interrupted journey with a distracted head
and a sore heart.

"The misery of the father on being called home from
a distant part of the farm, and beholding his beloved
child lying without consciousness, was great. The body
was still warm, and the breathing generally slow, but at
times it was disturbed with sudden jerks. The fingers
were occasionally subject to slight twitchings, and so were
the muscles of the mouth, and in this state he continued
for twenty-four hours. The unhappy father dispatched
a messenger for a doctor who lived about a couple of
miles away, as soon as he recovered from the stupor into

which he had been thrown by the sight of the insensible boy. He continued to watch him; but as the doctor was long of coming, he began to make inquiries as to the cause or the origin of the trance.

" All he could learn was that, Mary Lacy had been speaking to the young master by the paddock-hedge, and that he was seen suddenly grasping at the stem of the tree, and then falling heavily on the ground. Garrett entered the room just as the incensed father was sending off for the young woman, in order to learn the full particulars of the case. There was no one of the household afflicted with such bitter sorrow as poor Moore, for from what his brother had told him, he guessed that his own negligence was in some way the cause of the affliction. He cried like a woman or a child, as he knelt by the side of the gentle young boy, and pressed and kissed his senseless hands. The master waited till his passion of grief was a little appeased, and then requested him to walk over to the young woman's house, and either learn the exact truth of what had happened, or bring her over.

" He set off, and met her in the lane that led from the farm-house to the high road, and for half an hour as confused a scene went on as could be expected, where pride, tenderness, remorse, resentment, sorrow, and deep love, were all at strife with one another. However, the stormy passions gained the upper hand, and Garrett's last words were, ' If you were as handsome as *Diania*, and as rich as Damer himself, and if I loved you ten times as much as I do, I 'll never put a ring on your finger'. ' You will when I let you, you ungrateful boy', was the answer, and in a quarter of an hour more, the poor girl was stretched on her humble bed, passing from one hysterical fit of crying to another, and her poor mother vainly endeavouring to give her comfort.

" Before Garrett had turned back a score of perches, his heart reproached him for his harshness; and only for pride, he would have returned and asked pardon. However, when he presented himself before his master, he:

did all that mother wit and remorseful fondness could
suggest to avert blame from the young girl.   His efforts
were useless.   The self-opinionated and loving father
broke out into such a violent passion against himself, his
unfortunate betrothed, and those who had neglected their
watch, as no one in that house had ever before witnessed.

   " Conscious of his superior intelligence when compared with what he witnessed in the society in which he
moved, and proud of the royal blood of the Munster
kings, which he was certain of inheriting, his demeanour
hitherto among his dependants, was marked by the courtesy and dignified bearing of a chief of the old times;
but now he burst into a storm of lamentations and re-
proaches.

   " The door of the room in which his son lay insensible,
happening to open, and his eye catching a sight of a
couple of the women on their knees beside the bed, and
sobbing and praying, he was brought to a sense of what
was so unbecoming.   He walked in, sat down by the bed
side, and grimly restrained speech and gesture, till he
became comparatively calm.

   " The doctor arrived.   He was a man of no great skill
in his profession, but he never resorted to quackery.   He
saw that nothing could be done for the moment, and
that they must have patience.   So twenty-four hours
passed, and poor Anthony awoke under the influence of
a crazed intellect.   It is probable that his death would
have brought less sorrow on the indevout proud spirit of
his father, than what he now endured, looking on the
unreasoning, helpless, poor being ever before his eyes.
He never called him ' Father', but ' Man, man', and he
had completely forgotten the names of every individual
of the family.   He continued to enjoy good health in
general, but nothing like a smile was ever seen on his
face.   He still resorted to books, but such only as contained descriptive or narrative passages.   He was often
heard talking to himself of distant persons or events;
and would join into conversations, and utter a broken

sentence or two concerning what might be taking place in Dublin, London, or on the Continent; but he was never able to complete the sentence, or relate an incident in full, however short or simple. He was once thrown into convulsions at the sight of poor Mary Lacy, and remained more or less ill for two days.

" The loss of his beloved partner, and the melancholy condition of his only child, proved instruments under Providence for the conversion of the stiff-necked father. From the fatal hour of the accident, he never opened one of his baneful volumes. On a certain day, he collected the entire number of books of that class in his possession, and threw them into the large kitchen fire. He began to pray, to read pious books, to attend Mass diligently, and finally he commenced a general confession.

" About a year and a half had elapsed, and a large congregation was assembled on Easter Sunday morning in the neighbouring little straw-thatched chapel. There were many communicants, and among the number was the now humble and devout Mr. * * *. Anthony, during his bereavement, still retained vestiges of his early pious habits, and always kept his old seat in the gallery of the little chapel. He would stand and kneel at the appropriate times, repeat fragments of prayers, and continue more steady and collected than he could when outside the building. On this particular day, as the comparatively happy father went up to the gallery after the Mass was concluded, judge of his rapture on feeling his hand grasped by the two hands of his son, and on seeing tears of happiness course down his cheeks, recovered intellect beaming from his eyes, and grateful acknowledgments of God's mercies on his lips.

" That and the succeeding days were days of happiness in the big house and its neighbourhood. As time wore on, it was understood in the country, that Anthony had determined on entering the church. His father would probably have preferred seeing him willing to manage his large farm after his death, but he never said a word to dissuade him from obeying the holy call. In time he became the greatest blessing a people can receive—a prudent, devout, and zealous parish priest.

" It was with much complacency and satisfaction that Garrett and Mary presented their third infant to receive holy baptism at his hands. Either through a Christian or human motive, they had not found themselves able to keep up their anger beyond the prescribed limit, the setting of the sun over Mount Leinster".

After the society had discoursed for a while on the probability or improbability of the story, some one expressed a desire for a song, but my godmother said any thing nonsensical would not do well after so serious a narrative. However, she would sing a piece that had no balderdash of love or nonsensical description in it, for them.

When my Old Hat was New.

"When my old hat was new, now thirty-six long years,
I was at the review of the Dublin volunteers.
There have been brought to pass with us a change or two,
They 're altered times, alas, since my old hat was new.

" Our parliament did sit then in our native land:
What good came of the loss of it I cannot understand,
Although full plain I see, that changes not a few
Have fallen on the country since my old hat was new.
  *   *   *   *   *   *

" The nobles of our country were then our neighbours near,
And our old squires and gentry made always jolly cheer.
Ah! every night at some one's house or other's was a crew
Of merry lords and commoners, when my old hat was new.

" They 're altered times entirely, as plainly now appears,
Our landlord's face we barely see, past once in seven years.
And now the man meets scorn as his coat is green or blue,
We had no need our coats to turn when my old hat was new".

This song aroused a political discussion, and there were many things said that night by the company then assembled, which would have been worth listening to by the rulers of the country for the time being, but would be sadly in the way of our story if here given in detail.

CHAPTER XVII.

EDWARD'S RETURN.

IF the reader of this narrative recollects the race of Charley Redmond from Rathphelim to the wood of Kilaughrim as related in the *Banks of the Boro*, he will please to suppose Edward and myself going quietly along the same route on a fine summer Sunday evening, and making our way to Tombrick. He had returned by Friday's coach, and spent the intervening time at Castleboro, and was now giving me the particulars of his Dublin life and future prospects. The superintendent, unsolicited, had procured him a respectable situation, in which the duties required were entirely to his own taste; and the salary was settled at a liberal scale, if his employers were satisfied with his diligence and capacity. He had exhibited his certificate and premiums on the previous day to Lord Carew, who expressed great pleasure on examining them, and hearing of the promotion offered. He also was pleased to confirm my own appointment to Edward's vacated chair. So our progress through the wood, and across the country to the little ridge of Ballinakill, with the sunlight gladdening the meadows and the corn fields and the trees and the road-side hedges, was exceedingly pleasant. How earnestly did my friend gaze on the hill-side of Coolgarrow sloping down to the wood of Tombrick, and it was natural he should do so, as near the edge of the same wood was the residence of Mr. Lucas and his family. A flush passed over his face more than once, as the south-east side of the hill became wrapped in shade, and the tops of the trees merely caught the last rays of the sun, and we were in the wood-road near our journey's end.

13

There was a lively and joyful bustle as we enteied the
bawn at Lucas's; wonderful shaking of hands, and mingling of questions and answers; and if the words were few
and disjointed, when his hand met Margaret's, there was
an unmistakable expression of tenderness in the eyes and
about the lips, and very eloquent language in the diffident
though eager looks that each gave the other. There
was a pretty piece of confusion for a time, as questions continued to come from more quarters than one
at once, and answers given to one party were appropriated by another. However, Edward's approaching
departure, and my succession, came to be under¬tood.
They excited a mass of mingled feelings, regretful for the
most part. Matt and Murtagh Horan were on the spot;
they were seldom absent on holiday evenings. Murtagh
scarcely knew whether to lament or rejoice; he expected
something decisive at all events. Whatever Margaret
felt, her features showed nothing beyond the friendly
regret visible in the countenances of nearly the whole
company. Mrs. Murphy was loud in her lamentations,
which, as she was honest enough to acknowledge, were
chiefly caused by the fear of her son conquering the little
master. "Never fear, ma'am", said Edward, "I 'll leave
him my receipt; and if he allows Garrett to gain the
upper hand, I 'll give him a tiouncing for his want of
energy on my return". "Ah! I 'm afraid we 'll never
see you again when you leave us. You 'll live in fine
rooms in Dul lin, wear nothing but the best of broad
cloth and Wellington boots, and marry some nice Dublin
girl, who 'll never let you come back to see your rough
country friends. And may be you 'll drink wine every
day, and get the gout at last; and won't know one of us
if we rap at your hall-door". Edward burst out a laughing, and bade Mrs. Murphy be of good heart; for he
hoped never to get attached to drink of any sort, nor to
be visited by the gout. "Moreovei", said he, "my kind,
good friend, whenever I find myself privileged to look for
a wife, I give you my word before the present company,
that I will come all the way fiom Dublin, and consult

with your own self on the sub'ect". "It 's a bargain", said she, taking his outstretched hand, and giving it a hearty squeeze; "and mind you keep it, if I do n't send you word beforehand that you may spare yourself the trouble".

Now, it happened that Margaret was a special favourite with the good-natured widow, and she had scarcely spoken when the young lady was obliged to go into the parlour (we were all sitting in the kitchen), to look for some article or another; and indeed I strongly suspected at the time, that she did not find it.

"Faith, Mrs. Murphy", said Matt, "if I was a girl waiting for my sweetheart to come home from Dublin to marry me, I 'd look twice over my shoulder before I 'd put my neck in the yoke. We all know the number of ale-houses, and gambling houses, and houses of a worse kind again, that are scattered through the city, and the sort of people that walks Sackville Street and Grafton Street after night fall; and it 's my notion that you should be a hermit if you wished to lead a correct life there".

"Well, Matt", said Mr. Lucas, "I can't go the whole length of what you say. I visited Dublin a few times in my life; and I had some acquaintance with a few of the steady householders, and I can safely say, that thousands are reared up as innocent from the knowledge of vice, as the best-conducted country people you know. Those that are well-disposed to be devout, can be so more easily than in the country. They can attend Mass every day, be present at sermons and benediction every Sunday, and go to confession and communion as often as they like. The same people hinted to me, that some countrymen have seen and joined in more wickedness in the course of a day or two in the city, than citizens bred and born have witnessed during the course of a long life. One of them, in order to take the conceit out of me, said that he once spent a week in a country house, and heard more indecent language there in one single day, than it was his misfortune to hear during his whole life in Dublin. All depends on our early training, on our natural dispositions, and, above all, seizing on God's grace or not when offered to us".

"Just so", said Mrs. Murphy, "I know a youth who would n't be a day in the city, without bedivelling himself in bad company. But, please God, the master will have his business to attend to, some innocent good girl at home to think about, and some care on his mind about making preparations for her comfort, when he brings her to himself".

"Well, Mr. O'Brien", quoth Jane, "do n't lose your time fitting up a nice room with carpets, and big looking-glasses, and settees for me. You know, you must spend a part of the day from home; and I should sit there, or go asleep on the *sofia*, striving to read the *Academy of Compliments*, or *Valentine and Orson*, or looking at my back in the glass. I 'd be about making my will in three weeks, or crossing *Tallow Hill* to get back to the sheep, and ducks, and cows, and the spinning wheel; and some day you 'd find yourself a desolate widower when you 'd come to your dinner at twelve".

"Well now, it is very cruel in you to refuse me before so many, and may be prevent any other one from taking my case into consideration. I may address you in the words of the ballad—

"'Fie on you, ladies (*Jenny*. I mean)! do n't be so hard hearted,
But pity the case of a poor single man'.

And to punish you, Miss Jenny, I 'll expose your ignorance before the same assembly. In Dublin the earliest dinner hour is about two, and then you have your choice of any time from that to sunset". "And how do the poor creatures endure the hunger from early breakfast to sunset?" "Pretty well, considering. When you are saying your morning prayers, people that go to balls are *not* saying their evening prayers, but getting into their beds". "Oh, Vuya, Vuya! it 's no wonder that there should be a blast on the wheat, and the potatoes eight pence a stone. Where do they expect to go to?"

"Many of them are not thinking of taking the journey at all. While some are occupied bringing up their families in industrious habits, and in the fear of God, others have no concern of a morning, but how to get through the weary day by paying visits to people they care nothing about, buying costly clothes, ornaments, and furniture that they do not want, or going to entertainments, or giving entertainments, which afford themselves no pleasure. We that must employ most part of the day in useful occupation, ought to be very thankful, for if the time was left at our own disposal, I fear we would hardly have the good sense and resolution to devote it to good works, but employ ourselves sauntering about, or looking after some pleasure or excitement, merely to get through the long hours".

"And I believe", said Mr. Lucas, "that many young gentlemen are obliged to spend heavy sums to help them through the heavy work. One will lay money down on the gambling table, another on the race course, and another let himself be plundered in evil company. So great estates slip away from old families, and their descendants sink into poverty, while others struggle up by industry and economy, into the possession of lands and riches, to let all slip away again through the extravagance or ill conduct of their own children".

It here occurred to some one that Mrs. Murphy had not given them a song for ever so long, and that frank-spoken and good-natured woman did not keep them long in suspense. She apologised for giving a love song, as she had experience enough to know how nonsensical was most of what is said about it, but if she had time, she'd read a love story now just as if forty years were taken off her life.

The Soldier Lady.

"As Polly lay musing on her soft downy bed,
  Some comical notions came into her head;
  For father nor mother she'd never false prove,
  She'd list in the army along with her love.

"She went to the stable, and viewed the beasts round;
She viewed the best hero that e'er went the ground;
With her case of good pistols, and sword by her side,
On her father's black steed like a trooper she 'd ride.

"She rode till she came to the bridge of renown,
And there she set up at the sign of the Crown.
The first that she met was a brave English lord,
And the next was the captain, the man she adored.

"She gave a letter just out of her glove,
Saying here is a letter from Polly your love,
In the seal of the letter a guinea was found,
For the soldiers on duty to drink her health round.

"The first line he read, he bitterly cried;
Little thought he that Polly was just at his side.
Pretty Polly being weary, she hung down her head,
And called for a candle to light her to bed.

"'Upstairs', says the captain, 'we live at our ease;
As you 're Polly's friend, live with me if you please'.
'To live with the captain would be a strange thing
For a soldier just listed to fight for the king'.

"'T was early next morning pretty Polly arose,
And dressed herself out in her own woman's clothes;
Down stairs to the captain she gently did move,
Saying, 'Here 's pretty Polly, your loyal true love'.

"He took her in his arms, and called her his dear,
And on her he settled ten hundred a year;
Pretty Polly is married, and lives at her ease,
She may go where she will, and return when she please".

CHAPTER XVIII.

DONOGHA RUA AND HIS PAMPHLET; MICKEY CONNERS
AND HIS POETRY: A HURLING SONG.

Mrs. Murphy having finished her song, insisted that the
relater of these reminiscences should entertain the company. He stoutly resisted the call, urging his being
born without a lark's heel, and the other cut and dry

excuses current in those far-off times. "Well, then",
said she, " I know what you are able to do, and what
you must do. Repeat Dhonogha's Pamphlet for us".
" Well, well", said he, " I suppose I must".

" One of the earliest things that have dwelt on my
mind is seeing my mother helping a very feeble old pedlar
to rise from a stool on which he was resting himself without taking off his pack, and that was poor Denis O'Brien,
or Donogha Rua. That man was an example of what
may be done in the gathering of money by industry, perseverance, and thrift, and the little value of it without God's
blessing. I never saw the pamphlet in print, but I was
obliged to write it out from manuscript copies more than
five times. Denis used to travel to Dublin, and fill his
pack with soft goods, and then set out by easy stages,
till he would get as far as Waterford, selling his ware at
a large profit, as he used to give time in most cases for
the payment. Well, he sometimes missed the payment;
but still his profit was so great on other dealings, that he
would occasionally have from two to eight hundred pounds
in his possession. This money he would then lend to
country gentlemen at high interest; but he had to go to
law in most cases for repayment, and often lost principal
and all. After a long law suit with one gentleman that
lived in Kilbride, in the County Carlow, for about £800,
he got an execution against his property, and walked up
to his house with the officers one morning to take possession; but his debtor had paid all debts by walking out
of this life the evening before, and Denis never recovered
a penny of his money. He never let himself be dis-
heartened by a check of this kind. His pack was on his
back again, and himself trudging from one strong farmer's
house to another, sleeping at certain houses and paying
nothing for food or lodging. He had read a great deal,
and had so much poetry by heart, chiefly from *Paradise
Lost*, that he was a welcome guest where there was any
taste for literature. He had a wonderful memory, and
would repeat pieces of history and poetry for two or three
hours at a time; but could not endure to be interrupted,

or asked any idle questions on the subject. He disliked women and children, and would never commence his recitations till the young folk were sent to bed. He never (by his own account) saw more than three good women in his life. He always wore the broad skirted coat, and the wig and the cocked hat, that were the common dress when he was young (his wig at the time of purchase was always second hand), but though a person of great information, his manners were most disagreeable. He never lost time: while he rested himself by the side of the road, he was writing ballads, and he even composed the music of many of them. You may suppose that his knowledge of law was very great for a person in his rank. He used to be consulted by the country people on law points, and law terms were constantly on his tongue.

" He went to confession once in the year; and people said that he used to write it out, and hand it to the clergyman. This we all know was not the case; but at all events, if he was asked on these occasions where he was going, his answer was, 'I am going to throw out my yearly indictments'.

" He always remained a Catholic, a rather lukewarm one, indeed, as his church at the time was far from being well endowed, and he was a very sincere worshipper of riches and respectability. In the principal piece of his composition, the pamphlet, he makes it an objection to the Catholic clergy, that in spite their of efforts and prayers for two hundred and fifty years, the Church was still in so lowly a state in these islands. He was continually cheated and plundered of his darling treasures. A shee-been-house couple in Ballindaggin owed him half a guinea, and gave him an opportunity of visiting them several times to demand repayment. At every visit Denis was pressed to take a pint of beer or a glass of whisky to refresh himself after his walk; but when law proceedings were spoken of at last, they presented their little bill for drink, had and delivered, to the amount of fifteen shillings. The ill-treated poet took his revenge by publishing this verse,

" A travelling chapman whose name was Denny,
    Was once deceived by Joe and Jenny,
  Spent three crowns to recover half a guinea;
    And that 's the way they paid poor Denny'.

" He had a dispute with a schoolmaster of the name of
Duffy, above Ballychristal; and the master being sacked
at the tongue wished to restore the balance by an appeal
to the fists. However, Michael Brooks, whose house
was one of Denis's stages, interposed; and as usual a
ballad on the subject was soon popular in the Duffrey. I
recollect only two verses:

    " ' 'T was early on an April morning,
        At the house of brave Mick Brooks,
      Treacherous Duffy without warning,
        Thought to slay O'Brien in the nook,
              CHORUS: *Twi, Twaddum, Twoudam,* etc., etc.

    " ' Brave Mick Brooks profound and solid,
        Justice James, prince of honesty,
      Travellers preserve from designs that are horrid,
        Or Duffy and his mob would him bully.
              CHORUS'.

" He made several ballads on his various law suits,
several of which were tried in Dublin. I remember only
a few verses, here is one —

    " ' At Hilary term I played the puck:
        When they ran down I ran up,
      With an injunction rough and raw ;
        Then I did these raps outlaw, law, law'.

" A Duffrey woman well known to myself, was one of
Donogha's three good women, she always had a good fire
before him on winter nights. She made the children go
to bed early, and paid the most marked attention, and
kept strict silence round the hearth, during his recitals.
I have heard her repeat many passages from *Paradise
Lost,* his favourite poem.

" After composing, and printing, and publishing many
ballads, he at last got out his great poem in a pamphlet
shape, price an English sixpence; and sold a heavy edi-

tion through the country. I suppose it saw the light about the year 1773 or '4, for on some one's information, the poor author was taken into custody somewhere about Scollagh, in ' '75', and conveyed to Wexford jail by Vesey Colclough, brother to Adam Colclough, of Duffrey Hall, and, at the time, sheriff of the county. When he was about handing the unlucky man of genius over to the care of the jailer, he reminded him how kindly he had done the disagreeable duty, conducting him on a saddled horse between himself and his son, and in fact consulting the delicacy of his feelings in all respects. 'There is some thing in it', answered the insensible patient; 'but when a man is going to be hung, it's little he minds whether he does the journey on foot or on horseback'.

"One day as the celebrated George Ogle was passing through the gaol, he remarked to a gentleman in his company, pointing at the same time to Donogha; 'There is a man, damned by his genius'. The poet, raising his head, cried out, 'I hope I'll never be damned till your honour signs my death warrant'. 'That, I swear, I'll never do, Denis', said he. The day of trial came, and there was hard swearing; but Ogle made such exertions, that poor Denis was allowed to retain his three-cornered hat with the head that was in it. He often afterwards related the reception he got from a gentleman who resided not far from Enniscorthy, on occasion of a visit he paid him. 'He took me out, and showed me the tower on the top of Vinegar Hill, and says he, 'I am a college-bred man and a philosopher; and I could as soon eat every stick and stone in that tower as write your pamphlet. It was the devil himself that both rammed it and crammed it into your head. But if I ever catch you scribbling another line of such villiany, I'll take and hang you on the first tree I meet, without troubling judge or jury'. 'Lord save us, sir', said I; 'Squire Ogle and the judge and jury read it attentively, and did not find any such harm in it at all'. 'I'll not argue with you', says he, 'lay what I said to the pit of your stomach, and be wise'".

"You may be sure that he glorified Mr. Ogle in a bran-new ballad. This is all that remains in my recollection.

"'Summer assizes, "seventy-five",
The prisoners in Wexford could not thrive;
But Dhonogha's friend remains alive,
Squire Ogle, the Apollo of Wexford'.

"About 1806 I must have seen him: he was very feeble at the time, and died shortly after, at the house of Jack Hughes of Shroughmore. He arrived on a winter evening; and as he seemed very feeble Jack asked him if he wished to have the priest sent for. Denis not thinking himself in danger of death, gave him no encouragement. However, the message was sent very soon after, but poor Denis was no more when the clergyman arrived. Whether he left much money in the pack, or what was done with it remains a mystery to this hour".

"A very humorous gentleman was Mr. Ogle, by all accounts", said Mr. Lucas. "He overtook a beggar one day some miles out of the town of Wexford, and would not be satisfied, if the poor man did not get up behind him for a lift, till they would come near the town. When they did get near it, the beggarman asked to be let down, giving many thanks for the accommodation, but Mr. Ogle deferred it till they would get nearer. When they approached the first cabins in the outskirts, the poor man made another request for leave to descend from his perch; but the squire gave the spur to his steed, and he broke into a trot. The next request for a stop was followed by a canter, and then a gallop through thick and thin; the meal bags flapping about, the meal flying in all directions, the two horsemen as white as flour could make them, Mr. Ogle enjoying the fun, the beggar bawling, and the whole town running after them with cheers and laughter. When they alighted at the Market Cross, the beggar looked very disconsolately at his empty wallets, but the squire slipped a crown-piece into his hand, and all his wounds were healed. So the proverb about 'setting a beggar on horseback' was a liar in his case".

"So", said Edward, "was the other proverb about 'black care sitting behind the rider'. Care in this instance mourned in white".

"Perhaps Mr. Whitney will now oblige us with what he recollects of *Dhonoyha's Pamphlet*, till we see the sort of thing that was considered treason forty-five years ago", said Mr. Lucas.

"I may as well begin at the beginning. Here is the title, the preface, and as much of the poem as I can relect.

"*A Poetical Description of the Downfall of the Roman Catholics of Ireland.*

"*Preface.*

"The author being a travelling man, universally acquainted with the nature, situation, and circumstances of the inhabitants of England, Ireland, and Scotland, these thirty years past; and from the aforesaid opportunities, having collected together a nice fund or treasure of pure delicious remarks on the privileges, promotions, and encouragements, conferred by law on the Protestants, and the hardships, precautions, and discouragements by law enjoined on the Catholics of the said three kingdoms of England, Ireland, and Scotland, begs to enlarge on the same in the manner following; and hopes that as his work shows no prejudice to either party, but rather serves to edify and amuse them, it will be received as a benefit, and not as an injury, from their humble servant,

"DENIS O'BRIEN".

"CATHOLICS of Ireland, weep and mourn all;
Visibly I see your hardship as well as your downfall,
Which began at Aughrim, at the Boyne also,
Eighty circling years and some odds ago.
The fact was, Oliver Cromwell, years before but few,
Directed General Ginckell where to strike the blow;
Nor could Strongbonian valour nor proud Milesian hate

Frustrate Gods' design nor dark decree of fate,
Nor Louis XIV.'s care in succouring them in war
The razor edge of destiny could hinder or debar;
Nor was it Cromwell, Ginckell, nor the Orange Prince's bloom
Ever defeated the Irish, but the mighty sovereign doom,
A curse from their demerits which rose above the clouds,
And fell in time from heaven for humbling of the proud.
Were not that the case, as authors wrote before,
The Irish would be conquerors against as many more;
They having bold commanders who war-affairs well knew,
And none of them were treacherous excepting very few.—
Like Luttrell at Aughrim,—a Judas, no other thing;
James Stuart at the Boyne, a cowardly foolish king;
Talbot at Limerick, who bled to death his veins,
And wrought his own perdition through thirst of sinful gains.
These, of the Irish leaders, were traitors, yet we knew
How many more of them proved loyal and true.
Like the hero of Tyrone, named warlike Owen O'Neil,
Whose death encouraged Cromwell, Irish walls to scale;
And the brave Lord Lucan, who, true at heart as steel,
Often caused his enemies in time of war to kneel;
Likewise Clare, and Dungan, and the magnanimous youth,
Named Berwick, son to James, and the French hero, St. Ruth;
And a great many others, whom loyalty ne'er forsook,
But all could not avail, the people had no luck.
Fulfilling Solomon's proverbs, never speaking wrong,
But wisely intimating, the battle not to the strong,
Nor to the swift the race, when the Almighty on them frowns,
Whose omnipotent hand has pulled the Irish down.
From degree to degree descending to their doom,
Especially each creature professing faith of Rome
By parliamentary projects,—new inventions all,
Which once in each three years make Popish tribes to fall.
Which whetting, screwing, grinding, has rendered them half dead,
Rescinded from promotion and all good earthly bread,
Like tradesmen's tools entitled to no profit,
For each must do the work which is fitting for it.

England, like Esop's fox, makes them, at its desire,
Recover the roasted apple,—cat's foot in the fire.
In fires of affliction, labouring for a straw,
Are all Papists of Ireland compelled by English law.
Which squeezes dire destruction on them by a screw;
What they forgot on yesterday to-morrow will renew;
Violating the acts of Limerick made at the capitulation
Lest the Popish tribe should flourish in the Irish Nation,
Which cherished design they so wisely brought to pass,
I defy the man in Ireland to thrive who goes to Mass,

Except Papists by the funds living, or by sea trading,
Otherwise in cities living by large dealing.

Promotion in Ireland from Papists stands so far,
That higher than a constable they will none prefer.
Captivating culprits being a dangerous snare,
Employment for a Papist that berth they did prepare.
So that Papists for a livelihood must all turn knaves,
Otherwise be craftsmen, or downright black slaves,
Except he of lofty learning degrees above the rest,
Who by studying in Rome may return home a priest.
Yet after such industry English law disowns
Himself or his flock to be aught but vagabonds,
And blackens them daily in that very plight,
Blacker than the jet, but never never white.

One question I ask Papists, having read the above truth,
Which way can they provide for their growing youth?
Had they mountains of gold, beyond their power 't is past,
Any of Irish earth by leases to hold fast,
Penal laws of England to such rules giving birth
As made a Protestant sky over Irish earth.
Papists I entitle mere numsculls by their names,
Who expect to flourish between these two extremes.

Frenchmen and Spaniards, rigid Papists you,
Would you suffer for it as Irish Papists do?
No, you would soon submit, nor further bear the scourge
Of martyrdom which England on Irish Papists urge.
If Popery be a means heaven for to merit,
More chance stand Irish Papists that kingdom to inherit.
Do not Irish Papists adverse kneel to their king
And so are branded vagabonds for that very thing,
Stripped of all liberties, likewise every power,
Scourged by the lash of government top like every hour,
Crucified daily, like Christ between thieves,
While Frenchmen and Spaniards wear honour on their sleeves.
They and their sovereign one way kneel and bow,
In regard to faith, therefore does he allow
Them liberty and property without being sidelanged,
While Irish Papists by starved honesty are banged,
Doomed to live thereby, otherwise be hanged.
Sidelanged, spancelled, and fettered, they must draw a trace—
Burthened, while Protestants both gallop, trot, and pace.
Like the miller's boy named Unfortunate Jack,
Compelled beyond his strength to carry both miller and sack,
Ever without wages until he broke his back.

So by Irish Papists, and such is their way
Since the Battle of Aughrim and the Boyne Day;
Ne'er possessed of joy but it shall end in tears
Their glory being no longer than one-and-thirty years;
Allowed no longer title to any spot of ground,
But afterwards transplanted and to beggary bound;
Going on bad errands like bulrushes on water
Or as butchers drive cattle to the house of slaughter.
Thus fare Irish Papists by the nose led,
Except he whose friends at Limerick secured him better bread,
At the capitulation when matters then were new,
In Ireland of that kind there are but very few.

From valuable truths no matter if I speak again,
A Papist that lives in Ireland is the man of men,
Bearing of the yoke his credit only save,
Holding up Popery from the cradle to the grave.
England pronouncing hardships against the Papists all
He dies as great a martyr as ever did St. Paul.
Preferable to Paul, Paul's time being a new age
When Peter denied Christ in dread of the same usage.
Who but Irish Papists could hold this resolution,
One century to withstand a violent persecution?
A tree hewing each day and the tree to stand
Against a whetted age and a strong fal'er's hand,
Four score some odd years, a miracle wrought on Irish land.
Which tedious persecution so closely Papists touched
That they look in appearance now like things bewitched,
Without colour of life, by Protestancy hacked,
As if every Papist out of a gibbet dropped;
Groaning under yokes 'neath oppression weeping,
Protestants flying, and poor Papists creeping,
As unable to resist wrongs on them imposed,
As if hornless cattle horny beasts opposed.
Like toothless, nail-less, cold-perished cats,
All *stigmatized* and murdered by an invasion of rats.

Stripped of all liberties that mortals should enjoy,
Every Papist in Ireland must both live and die;
And if a Papist's father save anything by wit,
The son will be a beggar and hold none of it.
Robbers may deprive him with a quick surprise,
Not being allowed fire-arms for to secure the prize.
Nor could the father's prudence by his wit ensnare
One bit of lasting bread for the growing heir;
Forbid of lasting holds by established law,

At each thirty years end they become all men of straw.
Plants set on rocks can neither spring nor shoot,
No more can any Papist in Ireland take root.
Law encouraging daily before the poor Papists,
Barbarians, Turks, Jews, and the very Atheists.

Observe, Papist youth, what must be your fate
If under these discouragements you wed or procreate.
And if you unwisely wed, remember for certain
Your sons will be tools to Protestants of fortune.
He that has no inclination Protestant seed to raise,
From marriage indulgences modestly should cease.
But if Papists marry their fortune to augment,
They and their posterity that folly will repent.
In furnaces of misery he and they will boil
As the martyrs of old did in cauldrons of oil,
Or as naked Bezonians stripped like Esop's daw
By Protestants who ride triumphant by law
To churches on Sundays, all like wealthy men,
While Papists at chapels look like Adam leaving Eden.

Popish clergy led by interest's halter
These matters ne'er discuss standing on an altar,
But like all worldly wits seldom recommends
Any thing in life but what best suits their ends.
Therefore they treat not of your national misery,
But read the other leaf which draws to them the money.

Poor Papist laity in Ireland ever crawling,
Doomed to live by slavery, some poor trade or calling,
Otherwise begging from door to door,
Or sheltering in cottages living very poor,
Expect no relief but from the Most High,
Who sees your abuses with an ever-open eye.
Once He delivered you from the Danish tyrant's hand;
Far worse the situation in which you now stand.
Dogs engaged with wolves were the Irish then,
Now they 're naked lambs near the lion's den.
Danes disturbed your peace for a long time 't is true,
But knew not like England, your hardship how to screw.
England has you environed like partridges in a cage,
Without condition of liberty during time or age.
Danes did not do so, nor were they so acute,
None of their institutions were ever absolute;
Therefore when opposed in downright earnest,
Suddenly were banished, and made of but a jest;

Nor could their fortifications, nor earthen ramparts stand,
Irishmen defeated them both by sea and land.
But expect not England ever to serve so,
Out of your power they put it long ago.
Danes had you hamstringed, but to their own loss,
They did not know, like England, how to cut your reins across,
Nor cripple you judiciously with a proper wound,
For their own service always to be found,
Nor fix you with a straddle your shoulders to scald,
Which your disobedience will make be deeper galled.
Therefore bear it patiently over the liver,—
You must, Irish Papists, and no thanks, for ever.
England has bound you with fetters of steel,
Think not to leave them, but learn to kneel.

And all your humility, merits, and good grace,
Shall never advance you to to sit in a high place.
To be a lawyer, attorney, or justice of the peace ;
Nor to two pounds a-year which *quality* allows
To Protestant tenants for votes and vows
To swear them into the law-making house ;
Nor to any advancement higher than a trade—
Bailiff, constable, or working with a spade ;
Nor to hold Irish earth by a long chain of time,
For fear your posterity should grow up sublime.
Only for a spurt as hounds with their prey,
Until the huntsman's lash disperse them all away,
That the fruits of the chase may feed themselves next day.

Thus fare Irish Papists, carrying the double load,
Without any inheritance till the grave is their abode.
Dwelling in some cottage, cavern, or cell,
Far from life's feast, but near this world's hell,
Labouring like moles, they seem still decreed
To keep in slate houses Oliver Cromwell's breed ;—
Like the useful dog that turns the spit,
Roasting meat for others, not for himself one bit.
No tongue professing Christ but may purchase and renew
In Ireland except Papists who are dealt with like a Jew ;
And he 's respected more—who nailed Christ to the cross—
In Ireland, than the Papist seen going to Mass.

Those facts concerning Papists let no mortal doubt ;
They are twice worse dealt with than here is given out,

14

Each day augmenting hardships on them falling down,
Past hopes of ever mending under the English crown.
Papist and cobbler's lap-stone in Ireland one fate draw—
One 's reduced by hammer, the other damned by law.
Against them what can your talents ever more contrive?
Unless you gibbet them in chains alive.
Much more welcome would that death be to them all,
Five to one than the way ye with them deal.

The world is a staff, which men pull from each other;
In this iron age one brother would from th' other.
When Papist and Protestant come to this point,
At once does the Protestant the Papist disjoint,
Having staff or most part out all behind,
And poor Papist holding but a scrap of the front end.
Had Papist abilities more than enough, }
Protestant maketh of him but a scoff, }
And by small industry shaketh him off. }
Were thousands to join Papist, this staff for to haul,
By virtue lodged in Protestant he 'd take the staff from all.
The one grass path of life where sun or moon appears,
Thereof Papist from Protestant gets but a few years.
When these few years are out, as I hinted before,
Never will poor Papist that farm get more,
Except by undergoing destruction and harm
In the case of rack rents which they never can perform.
Quakers are not so, who baptism reject,
They leases for ever can both take and perfect.
The soldier who refuses in Christ's service to enlist,
English law promotes before the poor Papist.
Thus fare Irish Papists, excepting a few,
In Ireland are chances for all men but you.
Abounding in starved honesty you daily draw breath,
Expecting life eternal by a most shameful death.

No more let genealogies trouble your head,
For paltry is that honour that 's borrowed from the dead.
Nor ancient coats of arms, once esteemed great—
Them—Cromwell and Ginckell have blotted out of date.
Where Papists stand in need of either sword or shield,
English law forbids them even to hedge their fields;
To each designing foe exposed to be undone,
Like soldiers environed without sword or gun.
The law which by long leases sets Protestants quite right,
Reduces Papists' interest by short ones to a mite.

Thus Papists in Ireland stand no chance of bread, ⎫
Sooner than the day they all become dead, ⎬
Unless they imitate their own Church's Head : ⎭
Which is to live childless, and raise no more tools
To work for Protestants, or be their footstools ;
Or to fill their ranks where bullets do fly ;
Or their men-of-war when sea dangers draw nigh ;
Or their charter schools with your indigent breed,
Strengthening their factions in time of their need.
Avoid matrimony, and if yon do,
You 'll stint them of helps which daily oppress you.
By marriage you raise issue, which you cannot support ;
Therefore, to your oppressors for bread they must resort.
There bound to obey for getting such bread,
Against their inclinations, they will after break your head.

Poor Denis was very worldly-minded, so though he outwardly lived as a Catholic, and went once a year to confession, he was far from being resigned to the social position then held by his co-religionists and himself, and would have gladly exchanged it for the well-being and respectability enjoyed by Protestants. He had conceived a spite either of a personal or political nature against his clergy, and often gave vent to this ill-feeling in verse. A specimen was quoted above, and here is the compliment he paid them at the end, because they had not obtained riches nor political equality for their flocks by their prayers :—

Clergymen of Rome, two hundred and fifty years,
God seems to have been deaf to your continual prayers.
What time since first this malady Popery did seize,
Your ever greeting God yet renders it no ease.
Wonderful be it, if what you say be real,
With God in shorter time your prayer could not avail.
The uprise of your church you oft request of Heaven,
Contrary to your wish, a downfall is what 's given.
Sovereignty and power from Heaven being a lift,
Odd if you be favourites, but you hold the gift.
But England, in opposition, argues against you bold,
And makes Irish Papists know themselves that virtue hold".

"Well, Harry", observed Edward, "whatever merit

lies in the poem, there was no labour spent in laying out the plan. If you remove all the similes and excursions, the whole consists in declaring that the Papists were in a wretched condition, social and political, in Denis's day, and that the only cure was, to allow the race to come naturally or unnaturally to an end. It is odd that I have never seen a copy in print".

"Neither have I", observed H. W. "I suppose he left none on sale with booksellers in the towns, but distributed them at full prices through the country houses. An unbound pamphlet is soon torn and lost: perhaps all his unsold stock at the time of his arrest was taken and destroyed. At all events, I never saw but one complete copy, even in manuscript; but I was obliged to write out four or five from that, when I was a boy, and that 's the reason I recollect so much of it. It is probable that there are several deficiencies in my repetition. I left out some lines, not being able to shape any sense out of them.

"I have not read of any Talbot, a traitor, who put himself to death. There were, however, complaints against Talbot, Earl of Tyrconnel, but he was faithful to James to the last, and died at Limerick during the siege".

"The Duffrey people seem to have paid more attention to the preservation of the pamphlet than we of Bantry. This is only the second time I have heard it at any length. Mr. Harry Keeffe, of Poulpaisty, is the other reciter, and it was through Duffrey friends he had secured his copy. I think neither Duffrey nor Bantry have produced many good poets. Mr. Lucas, have you retained any thing from very early days worth repeating?"

"I do n't know whether you will think it worth repeating or not, but I retain most of the song made about the hurling in Moghurry before the Rebellion. The match was between the counties of Carlow and Wexford, and the bard was an O'Cavanagh, a smith, who had got the surname of Bacchus, from a love he bore to the quart and glass. These great matches made a great stir among the people, and more than once the defeated party shed tears of shame going home after their defeat. The Wicklow women once seeing their men losing the game, crowded to the goal and stopped the ball from getting through. One of our poets made a song about it, but I recollect only one verse:

> "They stopped up the goal with their mantles and plaids,
> And it's with their enchantments they foiled our brave lads,
> And it's oh, bold braggers!"

"The gentlemen of the two counties used to attend, and so there were no fights. Sir Simon Butler and other Carlow gentlemen met, with our own Carews and Colcloughs and Fitzhenrys. Every hurler did his best to win honour in the eyes of his own landlord, and the presence of the great people kept good order. Here is brave Bacchus's attempt at describing the field-day he witnessed.

The Hurling at Moghurry.

All you that court fortune and her fond smiles,
A jade that is giddy and made up of wiles,
Beware, lest, like Carlow men, you get a fall,
That hurled against Duffrey at Duffrey Hall.

Themselves are to to blame; they're lately grown bold,
For they knew that the Duffrey was famous of old.
Their sires and grandsires the same story could tell,
That the brave county Wexford bore always the bell.

As I sat in my chair in a sycamore tree—
A place which the hurlers appointed for me;
I was struck with surprise when I saw Carlow men
Appearing in stature like the great *Anakim*.

I then invoked Pallas the goddess by prayer,
Beseeching that she might the Duffrey men spare.
Said the goddess to Cavanagh, "Be not in dread;
David though little, Goliath left dead.

Though they have the advantage of ground, sun, and wind,
Our brave Duffrey heroes will goal them, you'll find.
Like bulwarks they stand in a thick fearful host,
But those Hectors, we'll make them all pay for the roast".

Squire Colclough, our patriot, threw up the ball,
And Dick Doyle from Marshalstown gave the first fall.
Our men being well trained in the hurling school—
Like a shot from a cannon they sent the ball *cool*.

When Carlow men 'tempted to force back the play,
Pat Byrne, like Ajax, stood much in their way.
Mick Murphy, from Bantry, performed great deeds,
And men stood before him as feeble as weeds.

Thumkin and Mullet did manfully play;
Those were to be pitied who came in their way.
Dick Doyle and Art Murphy like thunderbolts played
Brave Sullivan and Ryan made numbers afraid.

Bob and Mick Fitzhenry stood counterscarp;
Thumkin and Mullet and hardy Jack Tarp,
Nick Cowman, Pat Connor, and Ned played that day;
Without them we never had carried the sway.

Once at a time when the ball it came down
Unknown to the heroes of brave Marshalstown,
Pursued by brave fellows who drove home the play,
Our counterscarp heroes obstructed the play.

Jack Tarp, Bob, and Mickey, great valour displayed,
Like Achilles' myrmidons manfully played.
They kept up the ball like the hurlers of old;
Poor goal-keeper, Kelly, had like to get cold.

Dillon and Nolan played well in their turn,
And sent up the ball to the gallant Pat Byrne.
Pat with his thunderbolt ran like a roe,
Brought with him the ball, and drove it through the bow

So let not the Carlow men ever pretend,
Though they 're surely brave fellows, with us to contend.
Were they not defeated the Sunday before?
Mick Murphy of Oulart had his collar-bone sore.   .

Now. since we have won this Olympian prize,
Let us drink till the liquor flows out at our eyes;
And toast the brave offspring of Cæsar the bold,
Who means to establish the customs of old".

———————

" Really, there are stirring lines in that poem, and
what a number of genuine English surnames! Do you

think, Mr. Lucas, you recollect any other about the same age and merit?"

"We were not left trusting to Bacchus alone. Mickey Conners, a weaver of the Crosses, made a book full of songs, but they are all gone out of my head except one or two. He took a tour into Munster, and after he came home he used to entertain his ale-house friends with the 'New song of the Munster Lass'. However, he let it out of his mind as soon as Father Stafford proposed to take him down to Tagoat in the Barony Forth to see if he could please a cousin of his. Mickey was so glad that he fell in love with the girl off-hand, and made a song about the journey they were going to take, and the reception they'd get.

Ellen of Tagoat.

What signifies the Munster lass? I'll think on her no more,
Sweet limpid Slaney I will cross, and leave the Suir and Nore,
A few pleasant nights to spend, and sing some songs by rote,
Along with Father Stafford's friends, and Ellen of Tagoat.

When Wexford's craggy cliffs appear, the glass must motion know—
A cordial th' optic nerves to cheer to view the expanse below.
Th' experienced eye will easy find where dwells, perhaps, my doat;
We'll spend the night in great delight, with Ellen of Tagoat.

"I believe the journey was made, but happily for Ellen no marriage took place.

"Scores of Mick's songs were popular between Bunclody and Enniscorthy during his life, and for some years later. I have only one entire one in my memory.

"A poor, honest goose-plucker, once happening (in punishment for some sin) to entertain the poet at Molly Finn's *public*, he composed an ode in his honour on the spot; and so pleased was the poor, simple, vain creature, that he took the manuscript to Wexford town, got some quires printed, and employed himself singing it at fair and market till he became a thorough tinker, shoeless,

stockingless, and coatless.   Here is the entire song except
one indecent verse :—

A new Song in praise of the Great Mr. Breen.

On Erin's wide plains, in the town of Kilmeashil,
   If inquiry be made, there is yet to be seen,
Of the race of Lord Lucan, one bright in his station,
   If you 'd know his name, he is called Mister Breen.
He 's in the line of traffic, of commerce, and dealing,
   In honour and honesty he plays his part ;
And may these three things that I say never fail him—
   Money, a bottle, and a friend to his heart!

He deals in the apple, the skin, and the feather,
   And for what I know, in the plum and the pear,
In brass, gold, and silver, and all sorts of metal,
   No dealer 's so knowing in hard and soft ware.
The fair ones unto him are constant and kind,
   From a stingy old maid to a lass of sixteen ;
And the housewife,—'t is she would be troubled in mind,
   If she 'd sell off her wares till she 'd see Mr. Breen.

His transcendent merits exceed all expression,
   Were I to the impulse to give but a loose ;
The feathers he makes fly in geometrical progression,
   As he pulls them off from the neck of the goose.
The poor creature ne'er pines, but seems well contented,
   Although perhaps burning with an inward spleen.
His absence is by the whole country lamented,
   May Jove grant us peace and success, Mister Breen!

" Father Stafford once said in a joke, in Mickey's hearing, that he would win fame and fortune as a Methodist
preacher.   In time the poet emigrated to America, and
news came home, after some years, that he had really become a preacher, and was held in great estimation by his
flock.   The priest was struck with surprise and sorrow,
too, when he recollected what he had himself said in jest.
He followed in his steps, and died from fatigue and illness
before he could reach Mickey Conners".

" Poor Mick ! poor Father Stafford !" said Edward.
" Well, Mr. Lucas, you have proved that you had a poet
or two in old times in the Duffrey ; but we have had a
great deal of recitation and no melody.   Jane, will you

oblige us with a song, and if possible let it be on some
Duffrey subject, and made by a Duffrey poet".

Jane's voice was sweet, and as she had but little vanity,
and was very obliging, she sung the following local ditty
undisturbed, by fear of criticism : —

The Banks of Clody.

Down by the banks of Clody I heard a maid complain,
Making sad lamentations for her false-hearted swain.
She says, " I 'm deeply wounded, bound in the chains of love,
By a false-hearted young man who does inconstant prove".
I straightway stepped up to her, and put her in surprise;
I own she did not know me, I being in disguise.
I said, " My dearest jewel, my joy, and heart's delight,
How far have you to travel this dark and rainy night ?"

Said she, " 'T is too much freedom for to accost me so,
But as you heard my secret, I 'll also let you know,—
I seek a faithless young man—young Johnny is his name—
And it 's on the banks of Clody I 'm told he does remain".
"This is the bank of Clody, fair maid, whereon you stand,
But don't depend on Johnny, he is a false young man.
Do not depend on Johnny, he will not meet you here;
But come with me to yon green wood, no danger need you fear".

" If Johnny he was here this night, he 'd keep me from all harm;
He 's in the field of battle all in his uniform.
He 's in the field of battle, and his foes he does defy,
Like the *rolling* king of honour, going to the wars of Troy.
Bould Sarsfield was not braver when Erin he did guard,
And when the wars is over his king will him reward;
He 's crossing the main ocean for honour and for fame".
" No, no, fair maid, his ship was wrecked going by the coast of Spain".

When she heard that dreadful news she fell into despair,
A wringing of her hands, and a tearing of her hair;
"Since Johnny he is *drownded*, no man alive I 'll take,
Through woods and lonesome valleys I 'll wander for his sake".
So when he saw her loyalty, he could no longer stand,
He flew into her arms, saying, " Bessy, I 'm the man.
Bessy, I 'm the young man—the cause of all your pain,
And since we met on Clody's banks, we 'll never part again".

An ill-natured critic will have no great trouble in detecting some incongruity in this ballad, but let him not

blame Jane nor the present chronicler. One sung and the other copied what she and he had heard more than once.

The remaining business of the evening consisted of conversations which interested the various personages of the company, but could not possibly interest our readers. The feelings of the four young folk whose loves were returned or unreturned, were of a mixed nature,—happy in the presence of the loved ones, unhappy at the restraint imposed on them. At last, happy, unhappy, and indifferent, all bade each other good-night.

CHAPTER XIX.

THE FIGHT OF SHROUGHMORE.

NEXT evening found us at my godmother's, Owen Jourdan occupying his usual nook and enjoying well earned repose. I had often heard of the bravery of an ancestor of his, who had fought under Sarsfield, and on this evening I asked him to tell us all that was remembered of the gallant trooper. "Ah!" said he, "if you want me to tell any of my great grandfather's actions, I'd rather not. I'd a great deal rather hear one of them from the mistress. She had the advantage of getting the *edication* in her young days; and parts of what she tells is like what they put in books. So if you please, mistress, will you tell us about the fight that held from Shroughmore to the Bloody Bridge, and how Enniscorthy would be burned down only for the bishop?"

My godmother, who was at this time busily knitting, pulled an additional length from the worsted ball in her side pocket; my godmother's husband placed more turf on the fire; Hetty stopped the noise she was making among the pots; Larry let go the cat, who was getting cross under his caresses; the little people got into the laps of the big people; and my godmother began this traditionary tale.

" After the escape of King James to France, and the flight of the Wild Geese"—

" Is it Shemus a Choka (*ch.* guttural) you mane, ma'am ?" asked Owen.

" Yes, to be sure".

" And did yez never hear the answer he gave to the King of France, when he came to his coort ?"

" No ; let us hear it".

" 'James', says Lewis, says he, 'what sort of people is the Irish ?' 'Be me word, your Majesty', says James, ' they are the finest people in the world for baskin' in the sun, and combin' one another's heads *(Owen here entered into particulars connected with this exercise, more graphic than genteel);* the finest people they are', says he, ' for havin' house-fulls of childher; an' for thinkin' it a riches to have 'em, an' a grate poverty to be without 'em'. Sir Pathrick Sarchfield, who was standin' by, pulled out his soord, and would have run him through, but well becomes Lewis, ' Stop', says he, ' what ever he is', says he, ' he 's a crowned head any how'".

Owen's malapropos interruption meeting with no particular comment, my godmother resumed.

" Daniel Jourdan was one of Lord Lucan's best troopers ; he wore a suit of armour, and was so strong that he could twist a horse-shoe like a gad. He came back to his farm, on the slope of Rossard, there beyond the Glasha, after the siege of Limerick ; and though so great a warrior, he was as quiet as a child, and so cordial and obliging that the bitterest Williamite that knew him would not hurt a hair of his head. He minded his farm; but would sometimes sit sorrowfully by the bank of the stream that runs under the bridge of Thuar, and look down on it for hours. The wall of one of his rooms was covered with a lion or tiger's skin, and over this hung his armour. The priest could not show himself in public, or go through his parishioners, as they do now ; and many an unjust thing would be done, only for the dread the bad people felt at the name of Daniel Jourdan. Wicked laws were in force against priests, and schoolmasters, and chapels, but the

Protestants in the Duffrey were not disposed to molest their Catholic neighbours. The people wore wigs, broad-skirted coats, and three-cocked hats; and every gentle-man had a sword sticking out under the flap of his coat.

" To make a long story short, there lived on Daniel Jourdan's land a poor widow with a son and daughter; the name of the widow was Farrell, and her daughter was Monica. They had three or four acres of land, and the women spun wool and flax, when they had no out work to do. Flax was spun in those days on *coigeals*, and it was much slower work than it is now. No one could work harder than poor Monica all the week; and no girl had on a cleaner gown, cap, or kerchief at Mass, at the little old thatched chapel that stood near the cross of Shroughmore.

" Well, there was a young farmer that held about forty acres of land there above in Ballinacoola, and nothing could hinder him from taking a liking to Monica. He was a brave, strapping, good-natured young fellow; and Miss Monica had no objection to the match, but she was afraid she would be looked down upon by his mother and sisters, if she married into their family, and herself so poor.

" There was a strong iron-monger at that time in the main street of Enniscorthy, and this iron-monger's wife,—his own name was Ellis, I believe he was one of the old Palentines,—had a knowledge of Mrs. Farrell, and often when she would see Monica passing the door on a market day, she would make her come in, and rest herself, and take a bit of dinner before starting for home. She was very badly in want of a trustworthy girl to look after her young children, and used to press Monica to come and live with her. Monica was very unwilling to leave her mother, and indeed, I believe, would be sorry to miss seeing Barry O'Carroll on Sundays and odd times; but when he began to press her to marry him, she took the notion of going to Mrs. Ellis for two or three years, to enable her to help her mother, and to provide a good chest of linen for the *hauling home* day.

" So she took service with Mrs. Ellis in spite of her
own family and of O'Carroll; but rather to the pleasure
of O'Carroll's mother, who, though she had a great respect for Monica, would rather see her son take his blackman along with him, and ride into the county Carlow,
and bring home an ignorant slob of a girl that did not
know B from a bull's foot, so that she had the stocking
full of guineas with her.

" Well, as I said before, Monica being a headstrong
little lamb, took this step, though her own heart ached
for the pain it gave her people, and for the loneliness she
knew herself would feel, day and night, while her service
lasted.

" She was not long in her situation till her master and
mistress looked on her as if she was their own daughter;
and the young children she was minding did not seem to
know whether they were fonder of her or of their mother.
She was dismal now and then, but she knew that she
could change her state when she pleased; and, besides,
there was sure to be a Thursday once at least in every
week; and so sure as the market cars were heard creaking
down the street, and the market stalls a setting up, so
sure was Barry to be seen on his bay horse, slowly passing by the house, his three-cocked hat on one side of his
head, and his eye examining every window.

" Mrs. Ellis, who had heard all from Monica, was often
on the watch to ask the lively young farmer in; and then
there was scrambling, and whimpering, and striving
among the little people to see which would first get into
Barry's arms or lap, to examine his big flapped pockets
for apples, or nuts, or other country rarities. Then one
or other would get into the saddle, and ride down to the
old castle and back, till a dispute would arise if he would
not be allowed to use the whip. Then, of course after his
seven miles ride, Mr. O'Carroll would not be the worse
for lunch: then Mrs. Ellis's business would call her out
of the room, and somehow or other, the children and
Monica and Barry would not seem to mind how the time
went by.

"If the evening was fine, Barry, after clearing Duffrey-gate, would perhaps find Monica and her young friends taking the air on the side of the fine high road; and then the youngsters, in turn, would enjoy their jaunt on the bay horse while our lovers talked on subjects very important to people in their situation. Many a look would Monica cast across the valley and the woods, to the hill above this house, and from that to the ridge of Mount Leinster.

"The dearest company must part—there would be hugging and kissing of the children, a grasp of the hands between him and Monica, and a loving look into each other's faces, a jump into the saddle, and off he would be, slowly however at first, till the children and their guardian were shut out from his sight by the first bend of the road. Sometimes on their return they would be met by George, the eldest son, a young man about twenty-three years old; but his compliments and remarks were always very coldly received by Monica, and he would then vent his ill humour on the children; and this only adding to the coolness of her manner, there would be a good deal of discomfort on every side by the time they returned home.

"Our young gentleman thought he was very condescending, in addressing a few civil words to Monica on her first living with his mother; then being taken by her comeliness, and modesty, and good manners, he began by degrees to take opportunities of conversing with her. Seeing that she purposely avoided him, he began to be more in earnest, but found that she now gave him no opportunity of speaking to her at all.

"He began to notice the visits of O'Carroll; and though she never spent a minute with the young farmer, except in the presence of his mother or the children, he contrived to make a good guess at the truth; and being worked on by jealousy and a desire to cut out his rival, he managed an occasion of speaking alone to Monica for a minute or so; and proposed to marry her whether his parents liked or not. She gave him of course a flat

refusal, and as he did not even then cease to annoy her
with his offers, she thought it best to quit her kind protectors and return home. However, when she made the
proposal, there was such a storm of questions on Mrs.
Ellis's side, such a shower of tears and lamentations among
the children, and so much consternation in the house,
that she was obliged to reveal all to her kind mistress.
Mrs. Ellis spoke to Mr. Ellis, Mr. and Mrs. Ellis spoke
together to Mr. George, and there was a regular storm.
However, it ended in the young gentleman keeping himself to himself, and not exchanging a word with Monica,
good or bad.

"Well, the woods were after shedding their green
coat three times, Monica's chest was nearly full, O'Carroll was urgent for the long trial to be over, herself was
pining for the society of mother, brother, and lover, and
longing to be once more by the sides of the green hills
and the noisy streams of the Duffrey, and to enjoy the
sunny, sheltery side of Mount Leinster. So one day in
winter, Mrs. O'Carroll and her daughter paid the long-
expected visit to town. They came in their grand block-
wheeled car filled with straw, which was covered with a
new quilt, worked with three times as many colours as
you could see in the rainbow. When they stopped in
the main street, there was Barry, ready to lift them out,
there were Mrs. Ellis and the children, and there was
Monica so pretty, and a fine roaring fire in the parlour
(it was a clear dry winter's day), and the tea-pot on the
hob, and a pile of hot buttered cakes all ready. Her new
relations kissed Monica, and had to be pressed very much
to eat and drink hearty, they were so very genteel; and
there were great praises given to Monica for her good
nature and her good conduct; and by-and-by, there was
great roaring among the children, and shedding of tears
by Mrs. Ellis and Monica, and great scrambling into the
block-wheeled car by the young folks, who could not be
consoled without getting up into that vehicle of little
ease, and sitting on the quilt of many colours, till they
were drawn outside the Duffrey-gate. Their kind nurse

promised over and over again, that she would send for
them for a whole week next summer or harvest, when
they might milk the cows and goats with their own
hands, and eat delicious pap made on sheep's milk, and
gather strawberries by the hedges, or fraughans in the
woods, or mushrooms in the sheep-walks; and they
would roast the mushrooms with a pinch of salt, and
may be they would go to the great bog of Cummor,
and see the turf in clamps, and scramble to the top of
Mount Leinster, where they could see four counties
and the far-away sea, from the top of the great cairn.
These pleasing visions partly dried their tears; at last
they got off, and with many a wave of the hand, they
watched the slow-moving car till it was lost among the
boughs that overhung the road.

"You may believe that it was a long evening in the
widow Farrell's cabin, waiting for Monica's return. The
floor was swept as clean as a plate, the turf fire burned
briskly, and the dishes and plates on the dresser shone
bright and cheerful in the blaze—her brother went a part
of the way to meet the car; and the poor mother was in
a fever of hope, and fear, and pleasure, listening for every
sound. At last the creaking of the wheels was heard at
the end of the stony lane; and out she ran, and was
pressed in her daughter's arms.

"After some bustle, mother, son, and daughter were
left together; and though Monica was somewhat dis-
heartened at first at the small and poor appearance of
every thing round her, compared to what she had just
left, this soon wore off, and many were the happy plans
that passed in their discourse, till it was more than time
for rest.

"Next morning, Monica and her mother paid a visit
to their kind landlord, Daniel Jourdan, whom they found
scrubbing one of the pieces of his armour. He received
them most kindly, gave Monica a fatherly kiss on the
cheek; and a *housewife* with the pasteboard leaves covered
with the richest silk; and inquired about the wedding,
which he promised to attend on next Thursday, at early
dawn, at the little chapel of Shioughmore.

" A great many officers in King William's army, as I suppose you all have heard, got grants of land here and there through the country. Some got pensions, and many of them after the war, having no fighting to do, and not liking any other work, took to drinking, and soon ran through their little property, such as it was. There was a man of this kind in Enniscorthy; his name was Jacob Hunter; and whenever his money was spent he would work for a spell in Mr. Ellis's forges. He was very skilful in iron-work; but would often lay down his tools, and say how much pleasanter it would be to be hammering on a Jacobite's helmet or breast-plate. Indeed, like the great Daniel Jourdan, he had preserved all the pieces of his armour. I have heard people say that the officers of the time wore strong, three-cocked hats, buff coats that would bear a heavy blow of a sword or a thrust of a pike, and high jack-boots.

" This very evening, as one of the lads that worked about Mr. Ellis's premises, went late into the workshop to look for something he had forgotten there in the day, he saw a light shining through the door of an office that lay on one side, and heard persons speaking. He distinguished young George's voice, and would have drawn back, but that he thought he heard something about Monica, and a wedding, and taking the priest prisoner. So, being fond of Monica, like every other one about the house, and very sorry for her leaving, he drew near the door, and overheard a plot laid out between George and Jacob and two or three others. They had found out that the wedding was to take place next Thursday morning before day, at early Mass, as I told you before; and they settled that they would get a warrant to seize on the priest and as many of the congregation as they wished, by taking oath before the next magistrate that the assembly at the chapel was for a treasonable purpose. Indeed, I believe that it was against the laws of the time even to assemble to hear Mass.

" The five men present were to collect all their acquaintances that had been out in the wars, and join these to

15

the force granted by the magistrate; they would leave Enniscorthy early in the night by three different roads; and then, all meeting at the little chapel, they might seize on the clergyman, on the bridegroom, and on Daniel Jourdan, whom they were most anxious to secure, and clap them all in prison. George could carry off the bride, and afterwards make her his wife if he thought well of doing so.

" Poor Shamus was so frightened at the villany he was listening to, that he broke out into a cold perspiration; his teeth chattered, and his hand trembled so much that a hammer which he had grasped, without minding what he was doing, clattered against a bar of iron, and the noise was heard in the next room. Out rushed two or three of the plotters, and found him stretched on the forge-hearth and snoring. He saw them through his half-closed eyelids, hold a candle over him, and look at each other, and then Jacob taking the candle moved it across within an inch of his eyes. He was expecting nothing less than death; but had sufficient endurance to lie still, breathe regularly, and keep his eyes closed. After some whispering and signs, he felt a handkerchief tied across his eyes, his mouth secured with a gag, and his hands and feet strapped together. He now found himself lifted up, and carried through passages and lanes for about ten minutes, and at last laid down on the ground. The bandages were then removed, but as the place was thoroughly dark, he had nothing for it but to wait till light would come; so after an hour or two, he thought he might as well sleep till the morning light would make its way to him somehow. On awaking he found a few glimpses of light oozing in through doors and shutters, into the bare room that was his prison for the time. By this very faint twilight he found out a loaf and a bottle of milk in the corner. He ate and drank, and thought with sorrow of the fate that was awaiting poor Monica and her friends; and so the tedious day passed off slowly, and darkness once more spread over the bare room, and the miserable Shamus dropped asleep again. Next day, after lying, sitting, and walking about the room till his very life seemed a burthen, he cried out, and asked for what cause he was treated in that manner: much to his fright, he saw the open mouth of a gun pushed in through a chink, and staring him in the face by way of an answer.

" He shifted about, but found he could not get away from the gun's inspection; so he doggedly sat down and held his tongue, finding life much more endurable than it appeared to be a few minutes before. Next morning he found a change of provisions, and hour after hour he longed for liberty to warn his friends of the storm waiting for them; but night came and still there was nothing but the bare walls and the floor, twilight fading into night, a sleep disturbed with frightful dreams, a gray twilight again, the awful muzzle of the gun for the only variety; and Wednesday morning was now breaking.

" About midnight of this day, three parties of horsemen left different parts of the town by different roads, endeavouring to make as little clatter, and draw as little attention as possible. One took the road that leads near the Slaney till they came to the cross of Ballycarney, and then turned up by Castle Dockrell and the back of the hill here above: another troop made their way to Moghurry, and then turned down by Ballindaggin: the third held on at a slower rate through the hollow of Ballinure, and the three parties met on the high road of Shroughmore just before dawn. They then went on quietly in a body down an opening, with trees scattered here and there on each hand, towards a light which they guessed was coming from the little chapel they were in search of.

" As they approached, the men at each side spread out, so as to surround the chapel and let no one escape.

" While they were widening out, the word of command to halt was passed in a whisper from the centre where Jacob and George stood; and hardly was the order given, when a long blaze of light flashed out in their front, stretching to the right and left of the building, the report of a score of muskets broke the dark stillness, and the boughs of the scattered trees crashed and dropped:

about them. Not liking their situation, they drew back with as little confusion as they could, till they gained the cross road at their back, and then they wheeled round, and formed a long line. They were about sixty in number, well mounted, and armed with swords and large horse-pistols or blunderbusses, and they were all dressed as I mentioned before, except Jacob, who sat proudly on a trained war-horse, and was covered with armour".

"But, mother", said Larry, "how did the country people hear of the coming of the army, and how is it that they were so well prepared for them?"

"A little after dawn on Wednesday morning, Shamus heard a light knock at one of the shutters; he peeped at the hole where the musket used to be looking at him, and not seeing it he asked in a whisper, 'Who is there?' 'It is Biddy Walsh that is in it', said the voice; 'I found out where you were, though the young master said you were gone away to see your people for a few days; but I never could get a way of speaking to you till this morning: what are you here for, and what can I do for you?' So he up and told her the whole business, and begged her to get leave for a day, and be off home (her people lived there beyond the Glasha, up in Gurteen, and she was servant in the house next to Mr. Ellis's), and warn O'Carroll and Monica of their danger, and consult the priest and Daniel Jourdan what was best to be done. So Biddy returned to warn Mr. and Mrs. Ellis of the plot; for she knew their goodness, and the goodness of the mayor, and their friendship for the bishop, and that they would put a stop to the wickedness as soon as they heard of it; but both mistress and master had gone on a visit to a friend's place down at St. John's; and so feeling that no time was to be lost, she made some excuse, and *magh-go-bragh* with her for the Duffrey. She never drew rein till she crossed the hill above Shronghmore, nor tasted bit nor sup till she entered Daniel Jourdan's parlour a little after mid-day.

"He was sitting dismal enough at a table, looking at a map, but according as she got on in her story, a new

life seemed to come into his eyes. He began to stride
up and down the room, and at last taking down his
sword that hung by the wall, he cried out, 'I 'm glad I
did not die before this happened!' Calling his housekeeper, he gave her strict charge to entertain his visitor
with the best the house could afford, and sent off two
or three farm servants to summon the priest, his own
brother, Barry O'Carroll, Monica's brother, and one
or two others: a council was held, and now you know
why the party got a warmer reception than they expected.

"Jourdan now advanced with his troop of horse and
foot after the enemy. The first volley had been fired on
purpose over their heads, for he wished by all means to
drive the marauders back without bloodshed, and to
save his friends from present harm, and keep the peace.
The light of the clear winter's morning began to show,
and Jourdan's forces were seen by the other party moving
on them steadily, in the form of a half moon, outlapping
them on either side. Jacob seeing that there was nothing
to be hoped for in an immediate battle, made the men
next his centre wheel round, and set out at a steady
canter along the straight road that led towards the town;
and the two wings then drew in to this track, one man
after another, till all had quitted the cross road. George
and Jacob last of all, followed their men leisurely, casting a look back from time to time at the pursuing party.
The road lay for the most part through a wood; there
was scarcely any fence, and the growth being very open
near the road, six men could ride side by side in some
places.

"On they went. Jacob and his party were vexed
enough that they could not come to blows; but they
found the number of their opponents increasing every
moment; a long column of horsemen with Daniel Jourdan
in his armour at their head, filling the road behind, and
more footmen than they could count, pressing on through
the woods at each side. In this way they went down
Ballyhumbledon, and along by the Friar's bush, and

through the hollow of Ballinure; till on gaining the brow of the little hill beyond, the retreating party caught sight of the uniforms of a large body of military marching from Enniscorthy down the slope of the hill that leads towards the hollow of the Bloody Bridge. They set up a shout, and forgetting that they were far enough off from any help, they halted and fired a volley backwards, and on each side. A few were levelled by the discharge; and the pursuers, roused into fury at the sight of their comrades wounded or struggling in pain, dashed forward, and discharged their guns on their assailants.

"Ten or twelve were dismounted, and the rest repenting their hasty exploit, gave spurs to their steeds to shorten the distance between themselves and their friends. They reloaded as well as their flight would allow, and in about ten minutes they halted and again fired, but this time the Duffrey men were ready, and gave them a welcome as good as they brought.

"Some fell on either side, and as the smoke cleared off, they saw Jourdan and O'Carroll in advance of their party, thundering down on them with the light of the rising sun flashing from their swords; nor were Hunter and George backward in meeting them; and the sight of the fierce encounter of the four men, especially of the two fully-armed troopers, deprived the others on either side of the power to do more than gaze on the combat.

"They met, and the swords clashed on each other, striking out a shower of sparks; the well-trained horses stopped, and the strokes of the two troopers rung on the helmets and breastplates, and the swords of each other, like the din coming from a smith's forge. Nor were O'Carroll and Ellis much behind them in force and skill, for one had been made an expert swordsman by Daniel Jourdan, and the other had practised from his boyhood among the military stationed in the town.

"Jourdan was in a silent rage at the beginning of the struggle, at the sight of the friends that had dropped; but as the strife went on, he regained his usual coolness, and seemed to mind nothing but to guard his horse against a cut, and observe how his scholar was behaving. His calmness enraged Jacob, but his furious blows might as well have fallen on a stone pillar. All at once, while O'Carroll was parrying a blow, a shot struck his horse in the hind quarter, and giving a violent rear he fell backwards, and brought his rider under him. Daniel seeing what happened, shook off his sloth in a moment, and rising in his stirrups, and shouting in a voice of thunder, 'Sarsfield and Ireland', he brought down his heavy blade with such force on Jacob's helmet, that it shore away the crest, and drove through the solid steel cap to the very skull. The wounded man threw up his arms, and fell heavily on one side, the fury of the blow and his heavy weight bringing his horse down along with him.

"Jourdan instantly wheeling round, encountered George, who crossed swords with him manfully, though much awed by the fame of his great force, and the terrible proof just given. They had not exchanged three strokes, before his sword was sent spinning into the boughs of a neighbouring tree, and Jourdan changing his blade into the left hand, and edging his steed sideways, dealt him such a blow with his iron glove on the side of the head, that he fell senseless to the ground and rolled over.

"The foremost men on both sides, who had drawn near to look on the fight between the four chiefs, dismounted in haste, without thinking of the risk they ran, and got their disabled leaders freed from the stirrups, and bore them gently to the banks on either side. O'Carroll and Ellis were much bruised, and both were bleeding from wounds they had given each other; and Jacob was lying without a stir. They unclasped his helmet, and Jourdan stooping down, bent a searching look at his head. After a little, he gave a sigh of relief, and smiling grimly, he cried out, 'Hunter, you terrible whig, I am glad that your death can't be laid at my door after all. At Aughrim or the Boyne it would have done well enough, but here, by our very hearthstones! ugh! I would n't sleep for a month after it'.

"The assistants, after the first hurry was over, now began sulkily to draw off to their steeds, not knowing the moment they might be charged by the opposite party; and swords were grasped, and reins tightened, when a shout and a blast of a trumpet came up the road; and the horsemen opening their line on that side, they saw beyond, at a quarter of a mile's distance, the front of a column of cavalry; but still nearer, and riding side by side, the colonel of the regiment, the mayor of Enniscorthy, the Catholic bishop, and the elder Mr. Ellis, were seen hurrying on. Any notions of further strife were now at an end, and hurried greetings were exchanged with the four gentlemen. Mr. Ellis's anxious eye soon discovered his son: throwing himself from his horse, and stooping over him, and striving to check his tears, he fervently prayed that the sufferings he was most deservedly enduring, might become an instrument in the hand of God for a change in his ill regulated heart. He then arose, and addressed the Duffrey men that were standing around. 'Brave neighbours! do not lay the blame of the blood spilled here on the authorities of Enniscorthy either civil or military. The good creature who warned your brave leader, was not able to get back to the town till very late, on account of a hurt she received in one of her feet on her return, and so with one delay or other, notwithstanding all our eagerness to stop mischief, I see, to my deep sorrow, that some of my old acquaintances are wounded or killed outright'.

"'I consider that any intervention on my part would be unnecessary here', said the bishop, 'as both parties seem so well disposed to understand each other; but there beyond', said he, pointing to one of the wounded, 'my services may be useful. Brave and good man', he continued, addressing Daniel Jourdan, 'yourself and those with you will meet in a good spirit the friendly advances of my kind protectors, the mayor and Mr. Ellis, who have ever done all in their power to soften the rigour of the laws that oppress us': so, grasping his hand, he passed on to where his spiritual assistance was needed.

" ' I am happy to assure you, Mr. Ellis', said Jourdan, ' that neither the hurts of your son nor of mine, as I may call O'Carroll, are mortal. I hope that this morning's work may have a salutary effect on the future behaviour of one of them, and that neither may feel it necessary to get into another strife in a hurry, to show his courage or skill in arms, as there are enough here present to be witnesses of both for a score of years to come.

" ' And now', said he, raising his voice, and addressing all the opposite party within hearing, ' forget this morning's strife if you can, and lend your hands to relieve the sufferings of the wounded. I could still enjoy the excitement of a charge in an open battle field, where I knew nothing of the faces or persons who met me in manly fight; but this deadly strife among neighbours who should only contend with each other in deeds of kindness, is horrible. Do not like us the less for being constant to our forefathers' faith, and let not differences in belief or politics lead to hatred or unkindness. Life is sorrowful enough at best; and if we cannot relieve each other's burthens, let us at least not aggravate them'.

" It is time to bring my story to an end: the wounded were removed to the nearest farm-houses, and attended by surgeons who had come along with the army: the few that fell were brought home; and loud were the lamentations of their friends; and deep was George's regret to his dying day for the misery he had caused.

" Monica got a fine shock, I promise you, at the sight of poor O'Carroll brought back wounded; you may be assured that she had suffered finely all that morning from the firing of the first shot; but for a reward she had the pleasure of a fortnight's nursing on the wounded man. The marriage took place in due course, and they *say* that her mother-in-law never had a dispute with Monica. They also say that Monica found the marriage state a very serious business, and not at all the end of a fairy tale; and that though her kind mistress's children came to visit her at times, she afterwards was fonder of other children; and that though she had trouble enough with her new relations, her farm, her children, her husband, and her pigs, she would not exchange these troubles for any other pleasures in the world.

"Daniel Jourdan continued to be much more cheerful afterwards. The excitement of that day roused his spirits, and made him take more interest in the things about him, and he diligently exerted himself to keep up a good feeling between both parties.

"His means were ever at the service of all who were in need; when he died at a good old age, his funeral reached from Kilmeashil to the bridge of Thuar; and his remains are lying before the church door of Templeshanbo, dressed in the same armour he wore at the Boyne, at Aughrim, and at the fight of Shroughmore".

Owen, who had begun to listen to the tradition with his pipe well filled, forgot in his engrossing attention to pull at the shank, and so it went out: there he sat, pipe in mouth, eyes fixed on my godmother's face, hands on knees, and in a state of blissful attention.

When the narrative ended, he began to draw the pipe without meeting the usual recompense; and between the state of ecstacy in which he was wrapped, and the consciousness that something was wrong, his features presented a most ludicrous expression. Larry, casting his eyes on his meagre figure, long gray coat, and bewildered brown face, exclaimed: "And can it be possible that Owen here is a descendant of the great noble Daniel Jourdan?"

They were not a very musical family at my godmother's. She herself had the chambers of her brain furnished with no end of prose and poetic legends, at least as many as were current in the Duffrey. That evening at the general request, Bess, the fat servant girl already mentioned, sung the old lay of Lord Bateman, at least as much as she recollected, the names and circumstances in the ballad, illustrated by George Cruikshank, being varied somewhat for the worse. But we feel it part of our self-assumed duty to present the minstrelsy of the Duffrey half a century old, as it was, not as it ought to have been.

Lord Bakeham and the Turkish Lady.

Lord Bakeham was a gentleman,
  A gentleman by birth was he;
He put his foot on yon ship-board,
  And vowed strange countries he would see.
He had a hole in his right arm,
  And in that hole a planted tree,
When he was taken and put in prison,
  Where he could neither hear nor see.

The Turkish man had one fair daughter;—
  A fair and beauteous maid was she;
She stole the keys of her father's prison,
  And vowed Lord Bakeham she 'd set free.
"Oh, have you houses, or have you lands,
  Or livings of a high degree?
What would you give to a lady fair,
  That out of prison would set you free?"

Oh! I have houses and I have lands,
  And I have livings of a high degree;
And I 'd give them all to a lady fair,
  That out of prison would set me free".
"Then if you live for seven years,
  For seven years without more ado,
And if you wed no other woman,
  No other man shall I wed but you".

When seven years were past and over,—
  Seven years and a little more,
She packed up all her fine attendance,
  And she sailed over to the Irish shore.
When she came to Lord Bakeham's castle,
  She jingled boldly at the ring;
" Who 's there, who 's there", says the brave old porter,
  " That knocks so bold, and would fain get in ?"

"Good man, is this Lord Bakeham's castle,
  Or is Lord Bakeham himself within?"
" Oh yes, oh yes", says the brave old porter ;
  " This morning he fetched a new bride in".
" A cut of bread, pray bid him send me,
  And a bottle of his wine so free,
And not forget the foreign lady,
  That out of prison did set him free" !

Into the hall went the brave old porter,
   And at the table he knelt lowly;
"Rise up, rise up! thou good old porter,
   And what you 've done, come tell to me!"
"I 'm at your door these seven long years,
   These seven years and a little more,
The finest lady I e'er laid eyes on,
   I do declare is at your door.

"She has a ring on every finger,
   And on the middle one she has three,
And the rich gold chains that 's on her neck,
   Would buy your house and your lands from thee".

He rapped his hand down on the table,
   Till he broke it into splinters three,
Saying, "I will wage all my lands and livings,
   That *Shuzy Pilate* is come for me.
You may take home your daughter Bessy,
   For she is nothing the worse of me,
She came here on her side saddle,
   She may go home in her coach so free".

The songstress had never heard more, and her audience were left very uncomfortable, both as to the future fates of *Lord Bakeham and Shuzy Pilate*, and the mystification about the lady's name. Their natural shrewdness inclined them to suppose that the ballad maker never gave a Turkish lady so vulgar a name, but the least ignorant of the company were as much in the dark as the rest, Bess having only once heard it from a Palatine girl near Gorey, and no other one in company having ever heard it any where or from any body.

⋆⋆⋆

CHAPTER XX.

EDWARD'S ATTEMPT AT A ROMANCE.   KING ART O'CAVANAGH.

An evening or two later, when we were assembled round the fire at Mr. Donovan's, I happened to ask Edward what was in the roll which he had laid on the dresser as

ɪe came in. He seemed not well inclined to answer the
ʒuestion, so I let the matter rest. But we were all soon
ʒtartled by an exclamation from young Pat, who, unper-
ʒeived by the company, had laid hold on the article, and
ɔpened it. "Oh, faith!" said he, "the master has been
writing a romance or copying one. I thought first it was
Dhonogha's Pamphlet". "Only my authority is at an end",
ʒaid Edward, " I'd make your ears hot for prying into
ɪny secrets". It would waste too much marketable paper
to detail the conversation that ensued. O'Brien finally
acknowledged that the name of the Bloody Bridge, the
highest one in the city, and the Bloody Ford above it,
had set him on searching out particulars concerning King
Art MacMurroch, and that the roll contained a story
about him, which he had put together at odd times. At
the general request, and after a decent quantity of pressing, he read out his story of

The Moat of Cromogue.

" There are few Irish readers, young or old, who have
not heard of Dermod MacMurroch, the infamous tyrant
of Leinster. This Dermod, nicknamed *Na nGall* (of
the strangers), died at the end of a long and wicked
reign at Ferns, leaving no legitimate heir. His son,
Donald the Handsome, surnamed 'O'Cavanagh' from the
place of his birth, Kilcavan near Gorey, succeeded to the
throne of Leinster. He was patriotic in his way, brave,
and generous. His illegitimate birth did not stand in
the way of his succession, for it was an old usage in Ireland, to select whatever relative of the deceased sovereign·
appeared best qualified to rule the territory.

"The O'Niallans, or O'Nowlans, had the privilege of
nominating the kings of Leinster; and the O'Dorans,
who were the brehons or hereditary councillors of the
province, crowned them on the hill of *Cnoc an Bogha*. I
wish that some one with leisure at his disposal, would
search the hill of Slieve Bui for the stone chair, on which
Donald the Handsome first felt the weight of his uneasy
crown. Three years later he was slain by an O'Nowlan,

a near relative, probably, of the man that had nominated him.

"The ancestor of this family was a certain Cahir Mhor; his descendants ruled in a direct line to near the days of Henry the Eighth; and so well did they manage with the aid of the O'Byrns and O'Tuathals of the Wicklow glens, that in 1335, nearly two hundred years after the conquest, Edward the Third of England covenanted to pay them eighty marks per annum for their tolerance of their Anglo-Norman neighbours; and this arrangement continued till the reign of the eighth Henry just mentioned. Their chief places of abode were Ballyloughan, now called Ballyāne, Polmonty near the southern extremity of the White Mountain, and Ballymoon with its great bawn, at the back of Mount Leinster.

"Art, son of Art, was born in 1357, and when he was about ten years old, his father fought a battle with Lionel, Duke of Clarence, near Dublin. About the same time were passed the statutes of Kilkenny, denouncing all of English descent, who dared to adopt Irish usages, appeal to Irish laws, or form connections with Irish families. Every one knows what little effect these severe regulations produced in the end. The foreigners, when opportunity offered for living on neighbourly terms with the natives, not only acquired their generous character and their enjoyment of social intercourse, but pushed these good qualities to the extreme, and became prodigal in expenditure, and negligent in the discharge of needful duties, in fact, ' more Irish than the Irish themselves'.

"When Art was sixteen years of age, the brave old king, his father, was borne to his last resting place in the cemetery of St. Moling's in the southern angle of Carlow, and the young hero was crowned on the side of *Cnoc an Bogha*, and his standard, a silver harp on a green field, floated from the flag-staffs of thirty castles in Wicklow and Carlow on the same day. He kept down the power of the chiefs of the Pale so effectually, that the vain and gallant young king of England, Richard the Second, came across the channel to humble his pride. He landed in Water-

ford, and laying aside the standard on which the three
leopards showed their teeth and claws, he raised the
banner of St. Edward, and advanced through Hy-Kinsalach in the direction of Dublin.

"The first halting place would probably have been
New Ross, which was, at the time, a fortress of great
strength; but the wild-looking troops of King Art,
pouring down from each side of Mount Leinster and the
Cooliagh, fell on all the gates at once, not even sparing
the one dedicated to the ladies, broke them down, demolished the walls, and scarcely left a roof to shelter the
royal head of Richard, if he felt disposed to make it his
resting place.

"At the close of the previous century, this town was
undefended by gate or wall; and it happened that on a
market day, a country man, mounted on a small shaggy
garron, and unencumbered with housing, saddle, or
stirrup, was making a hard bargain with an honest
citizen for a piece of frieze. This simple rustic not only
tried the good mercer's temper and abused his time, but
when he saw no chance of a mutual agreement as to the
exact value of the article, carried it off without taking the
trouble of handing its value to the owner. Striking the
heel of his brogue into his charger's flank, and throwing
the web over his neck, he was many perches beyond
where walls ought to stand, before the injured man could
take any effective step for his detention. This was a case
in which it is no sin to reveal our neighbour's faults, and
the whole town was soon in possession of the ugly exploit.

"A rich and generous widow, who is named in books
'Rose Mac Bruin', but whom, following country tradition, I will call Rose McCroy, showered her gold into the
common purse, and roused the citizens to raise defences
to their insulted town. All generously contributed money
or labour, and set to the work like people in earnest.
The sea-faring men began to work on Monday; they were
relieved by the soft-goods men on Tuesday; the curriers
worked on Wednesday; fishers and huxters on Thursday;

carpenters on Friday; and men of iron and stone on Saturday: even the Sunday was not spent in idleness. On that day the women carried the stones to where they would be wanted for Monday's work, after they had been at Mass, and prayed for a blessing on their labours.

"A fosse, twelve feet in depth, and three miles in circuit, was excavated; and within was raised the strong wall with towers and gates, the remains of some of which are still to be seen. One of these was most justly entitled the Ladies' Gate, and well they deserved the compliment. They helped with their hands, they cheered the workers by their presence; and to the sound of musical instruments, were ditch sunk and wall raised. Most of these brave men and good women were of foreign descent, and they are at rest more than five hundred years: nevertheless let their memory be kept in honour.

"King Richard being disappointed of his expected resting place, and unable to pass through the territory of the Leinster chief without losing many of his warriors by the long heavy darts of the enemy, invited him to a conference in Idrone in Carlow; and terms were agreed to, and Art invited to share the king's hospitality in the Castle of Dublin.

"Passing over his return to his mountain fastness, and Richard's departure for England, we find him invited to a banquet in one of the strongholds of the Pale, either Carlow or Castle Dermot, and saved from assassination by the zeal and acuteness of his harper and his own terrible appearance, when on finding the hall invested by armed men, he snatched his casque and shield, and flashing his heavy sword around, he rushed out on the treacherous foe. He afterwards battered down the strong walls of Carlow, and was instrumental in gaining the victory on the king's river beyond the Nore, where Roger Mortimer and the flower of his army perished.

"When Richard returned again to check his unceasing and successful efforts, and was making way from Kilkenny to the sea coast at Arklow, the forces of Art hung on his skirts, cleared the country of provisions;

and many who escaped the javelins and war-hatchets of the galloglachs, met their fate from fatigue and hunger. Against the sweep of an Irish battle-axe, or the flight of a long heavy lance, the best tempered mail of the Anglo-Norman knights was of no more avail than a linen jerkin.

"At a conference held with the Earl of Gloucester in Glen-Art, near the stream of Avoca, an English eye-witness described the wild, martial appearance of the Leinster chief, as, mounted on a horse of great value, he dashed down a hill at full speed, and as he approached the English party, flung his spear to a great distance. No stable conditions could be agreed to. The king soon after crossed the channel to meet imprisonment and death at the hands of unkind relatives and disloyal subjects.

"King Art having strengthened his hands on every side, joined his forces to those of Murroch O'Connor, the brave ruler of- Offaley, and outside of the walls of Dublin, fought the greatest and most glorious of his conflicts against the united powers of the citizens and all the Anglo-Norman forces that could be collected to do battle with him. This was in September 1408: the occurrences about to be related took place in the following month.

*　　*　　*　　*　　*　　*

"On a pleasant evening in the year and month above-mentioned, a petty chief of Mac Murroch's, Donoch O'Brien by name, and probably a descendant of the serpent slayer of the legend, was sitting near the entrance (north-east side) of his double moated strong rath of Cromoge. Whoever has seen the remains of this rath can judge of its great size and probable strength in that day. On the south side it could only be approached through the bog, above the level of which it rose to a considerable height, and on the other sides the fosses were deep, and the fortifications very strong.

"Our chief appeared to have no more absorbing care. on his mind, than to look out for a belated wayfarer, make him tarry for the night, and enliven the stillness of the little fortress with news of what was passing at a

16

distance. A rough road, partly paved, partly of tough clay, and in marshy spots eked out with logs laid side by side, ran in nearly the same direction as the present one from Ross of the long bridge to the town of Bunclody. The extreme boundary of the fort was a very deep trench supplied from a spring, and inside of this rose a mound of stones and earth bristling with stakes. Within this again, and separated from it by another trench, sprung a still loftier barricade inclosing the wide, level bawn and the dwellings of the chief and his immediate relatives and retainers. There was also accommodation for the cattle, when unsettled times obliged them to be driven into the rath, and suitable granaries for provisions. The chief's own dwelling consisted of a spacious kitchen and hall on the ground floor, nearly capable of entertaining the entire population on any festival, of a floor overhead containing private apartments and dormitories, and above this again, of a long suite of attics intended for holding dried provisions and lumber, and provided with narrow windows widening inwards, and overlooking the approaches on the northern side. From these windows missiles could be effectively launched against enemies attacking the fort on that quarter.

"The appearance of the fortress from the clear ground outside, was not so raw or uncomfortable as might be supposed. The sides of the mound were overgrown with long grass; and weeds and bushes, and little russet-coloured paths made by the feet of children, might be seen sloping in and out through these small thickets. The buildings on the summit were made of stone in the lower story, and of wood in the two upper, being of a very irregular conformation, and marked with many weather-stains; the whole thing, with Mount Leinster in the back ground, would form a pleasing picture under the hands of a good artist, who possessed the power of bringing things that exist only in tradition freshly and distinctly before his mental sight.

"From the general size of these raths, it may be judged that they were not calculated for sustaining a siege by a strong power, or for a protracted period. But it is to be remembered that the clans or tribes of an entire province, being under the same rule, and on amicable terms with each other (generally speaking), none but those on the borders were in danger of an unexpected attack; and the standing custom was to meet the danger in the open battle field, and not wait a leaguer in their separate holds. The same spirit led to the neglect of armour, and to the contempt of discipline and military tactics by our forefathers. They manifested great personal prowess with axe, sword, and lance; but lost many a battle to the skill and discipline of the Anglo-Normans, after displaying surprising bravery in combats fought hand to hand.

"Our chief was a man in the decline of life, but still vigorous, and his hair of a healthy iron-gray tinge. His broad open countenance, with its strong dark eyebrows and moustache, would probably assume a terrible appearance in fight, but was now expressive of mere good humour, and a slight tinge of curiosity, while examining the line of road between marsh and hill as it went on towards the old church of Kil-Mihail.

"He was sitting near the upper gate, and by his side stood a young girl of exceeding beauty of countenance and grace of form. Her dress was simple in style, a gown fitting her well-formed figure, and confined by a silken sash, and a short cloak fastened below her white throat with a curiously carved brooch of gold. Her abundant dark hair was gracefully wound round her head, and fastened at the top with a rich bodkin.

"She was now by his side, playing with the long hair that lay on his shoulders after escaping from the conical birredh; in a moment she was chasing some laughing children into the fort, or through the low tufts just mentioned; and, finally, their gambols brought them to the edge of the moat. A sign from the chief brought them up in a hurry, and following his looks they became aware of the approach of a cavalier. The dress of this knight was in the Norman fashion, and there was an appearance of weariness about himself and his steed, as if they had come a considerable distance that day.

"At a sign from the chief, an inmate of the rath, a *Duine Uasal*, *i.e.*, one of gentle blood, crossed the moats, stood and bowed before the wayfarer, and expressed the desire of the chief, that he would, if not very near his journey's end, deign to share the hospitality of his home for that night. 'I am in search of the rath of Sir Donoch O'Brien', said the stranger. 'If this is the one I seek, I am glad that my journey is over. If not, I have no hesitation in asking your services to put me on the direct route'. 'You are at your journey's end, sir knight. This is the rath you seek, and there is the lord on the look-out for tired wayfarers: enter and gladden his heart by sharing his hospitality'.

"The pleased traveller alighted, and proceeded to the upper entrance, his horse quietly following him up the pass. Sir Donoch meeting him in the gate, cordially grasped his hand, and bade him welcome. The handsome and stately stranger returned thanks in good set terms, but his eyes were in haste to take an earnest, though very respectful survey of the young lady who for the time was as serious as could be desired.

"'Before I accept your kind offer, I suppose you would have no objection to learn my rank, name, and business with yourself?' 'By no means', interrupted the host. 'We have quarrels enough on our hands already; but if your offer was generally accepted, many a wearied knight would have the wood, the heath, or the cavern for his bed, instead of a welcome to food, and rest, and a cordial God-speed in the morning. When we have taken bread and salt together, use your will. I hold some of your race in my heart, and have personal feud with none: so receive our welcome with easy mind'. They then directed their steps to the entrance of the principal building, which seemed no way calculated to resist an attack from the inner bawn: all care for that purpose was expended on the outer walls, which approached the verge of the upper mound. As they retired the drawbridges were raised, for the shade of evening was thickening in the valley.

"Our traveller was conducted to a dormitory to refresh his appearance a little, and then into the great hall on the ground floor, and seated between the matron of the family and her granddaughter near the head of the upper table. The chief presided, and near him on either hand, sat his next relatives, the Duine Uasals. Then followed some bronzed and moustached galloglachs, and the lower part was filled with the domestics and some wild-looking followers. To one of our times, the walls would have a rough and uncomfortable look, but now from bronze cressets or candlesticks, fastened in the pannels, twisted rushes well dipped, or pine bogwood, cast a cheerful light on the table, which groaned under dishes of various kinds of game, and the flesh of swine, piles of flat cakes, and plates of water-cress, and vessels of mead, and wine, and diluted usquebaugh, and medhers of many forms and of every substance,—silver, pewter, and carved wood. Towards the conclusion of the meal, the family bard taking a small harp on his lap, and accompanying his wild verse at intervals with appropriate chords, sung :—

" *The Legend of Conrigh, son of Dairé.*

" Black lay the Druidic fog on the strong fortress,
   In the rocky isle of the sea vexed Dun Scatach:
   And in the bay rocked the galleys of Banbha;
   While the warriors whom they bore from proud Emania,
   Emania, the stronghold of the Red Branch warriors,
   With their fierce chief, Cuchullain of the heavy shield,
   Stood silent and sad before the darksome fort ;
   The sunbeams burned on their dark helms,
   And a fly's wing could be heard across the plain.
   Within was heard the whirling of a mighty wheel,
   A wheel worked by the dark spirits of the mist,
   And sadness was in the hearts of the armed leaguers.

"But the clash of a warrior's arms was heard behind;
   And out from a pass came Conrigh of the south;
   Who accosted the chief of the Red Branch knights,
   And asked, for guerdon, his choice of the spoils of war,
   For stopping the charmed wheel and scattering the fog,

And putting the foe at the feet of Clan Concobhair.
Cuchullain hailed the offer with joy;
And Conrigh spoke in whispers to the unseen spirits,
Of the hills, the waves, the rocks, and tumbling cataracts,
As he turned to the four faces of the sky.

" Then was stilled the buzzing of the magic wheel;
And the dark fog rose up to the soaring clouds ;
The walls of the fort lay before them unguarded,
Shrieks were heard from women and weak children;
And the men of Uladh were masters of the rich stronghold.
* * * * *

" Across the rough waves of the Northern waters,
Went the barks of Uladh in the calm day;
Bright Baal flung his rays from above the giant pillars;
And the wave tops caught them as they danced round the skiffs.
Which now held priceless spoils from the rocky island,
And the pearl of all, Blanaid the beautiful.

" The halls of Emania, the palace of the red Conor,
Were heaped with riches brought in the swift galleys ;
And the chief taking the right hand of Conrigh,
Showed the rich treasures as they lay in piles:
And bade him welcome to his heart's choice.

" Then answered Conrigh ot the undaunted breast—
Conrigh who swayed the spirits of earth and sea,
' I value not skiaghs plated with gold,
Strong-linked luirechs, nor mantles with sleek fur,
But if I have merit at the hand of Cuchulainn,
Let Blanaid of the fair cheeks be my recompense,
And gladden my mountain fort in the far south.

" Then shook with rage and sorrow the Ulster hero,
And he said: ' Not so, valiant but grasping chief:
All else that thy heart may covet shall be thine;
But Blanaid I resign not, neither for thy great service,
Nor for the ransom of the five Kings of Erinn'.
' Then shall the chief of the Red Branch be forsworn,
And humbled in the sight of his northern warriors:
Conrigh takes not the value of a wooden brooch.
Watch well thy captive, thankless Dog of Uladh !'
His shadow darkened the sunbeam streaming through the door,
And shame and trouble gnawed the heart of Cuchulainn.
* * * * *

" The spirits obeyed the wishes of the strong man,
And he went onwards over plains and hills ;
And his journey was one long trance of delight,
For by his side went Blanaid the beautiful.

" But as they traveised the marshy side of Almhuin,
   A baleful cloud seemed rushing along the waste ;
   And the dark-armed Cuchulainn closed the narrow path.
   Small was the time given to taunt or parley :
   Like thunder claps rung blows on shield and helm;
   The stony ground trodden by their strong limbs,
   Became as the soft quaking bog :
   And the marshy surface of the field,
   Was trod to the hardness of the slaty rock.

   At last, powerless lay the bold hound of Culann;
   And with tough withes Conrigh bound his limbs,
   He took the sharp sword from his failing grasp,
   He shore the long waving locks from his head,
   And left him to the scornful pity of the strayed hunter,
   Or the milder pangs of death-causing famine.

   *   *   *   *   *   *

" The bright red moon large as the shield of Conrigh,
   Was rising on the rocky vale of the roaring Finglaisse ;
   And a circling year had noiselessly passed,
   As Blanaid looked from the strong ramparts,
   And the tears fell bitter down her fair smooth cheeks.
   As she thought on the brave, dishonoured knight of Uladh.
   But he, tall and strong as she first beheld him,
   And as if her wish possessed life giving power,
   Stood pale and sad below the high rampart;
   The curls of his hair danced again on his shoulders,
   And the fire of passion burned in his dark orbs.

" ' Beautiful Blanaid, hear and fly not.
   For you I 've suffered agony beyond death ;
   For thirteen moons I 've shunned the eye of man,
   My food wild roots, my couch the damp cavern.
   Your love is yet as strong in my constant heart,
   As waves rushing from the swell of ocean.
   Quit these rude walls for the fair palaces of Emania ;
   And let me bask in the bright sunshine of your face.
   If not, this hard unfeeling rock
   Is the last bed of the once foremost knight of Uladh'.

" The eyes that should have turned away,
   Were fixed in pity on the earnest upturned gaze ;
   The mantle swelled over her heaving breast,
   And her words fell on the chief like dew on the parched herbs.

" ' I have not forgotten, true and constant hero;
   And your wrongs have rankled in my bosom
   As ears of spiked corn in a fresh wound.
   By the eve of the joyous festival of Samhain

Collect a band of true and brave followers;
And lie unseen in the narrow vale,
Where the noisy Finglaisse rushes through its rocky arch;
And when the level pool is white as boiling surf,
Take the path that winds upwards to the gates'.

" Then weariness brooded on the waveless life of Blanaid;
And she would be attended by gay-dressed crowds
Of knights and ladies of noble rank;
And courts and halls should be enlarged.
Her fond lord sent forth his following,
To gather wise artificers from fort and city;
And stone, and wood, and cement of the best.
So when the eve of Samhain sunk in mist,
And few the shields resting on the walls,
The anxious watchers in the rocky vale,
Beheld a white flood issue from the gorge;
For the milk of a hundred cows,   .
Pressed by the skilled handmaids of the *Bean a Tigh*,
Had changed the hue of the black tumbling torrent.
   *   *   *   *   *   •

" And the yet unconquered son of Dairé,
Careless, at ease beside his father's hearth,
Was in a moment hemmed by armed crowds.
But ere his form fell powerless on the flagstones,
Flags slippery with the blood of his enemies,
His never failing sword sent many a fierce foeman
To the low mansions of the shadowy Tir na-n-'Og.
   *   *   *   *   *   •

" There were sounds of joy on the cliffs of the north sea,
And glad were the sunbeams on the lofty rocks,
As the fairest dames in the thick-wooded isle of Banbha
And noble *flaiths* of gentle mood
Trod the narrow paths of the beetling cliffs;
Now looking south over woods and green lawns,
Now o'er the boundless plain of the blue waters.
Below, the white-crested waves broke on the beach,
But the crash reached not the ears of the joyous groups.

" Who are the loving pair with arms entwined,
And hearts and senses steeped in happiness,
As slow they move apart from the gay concourse?
Who but Cuchulainn and his long-sought love !

" But while words and thoughts were instinct with rapture,
A baleful cloud saddened the bright morning,
Fearcheirtne came, the bard of the murdered Conrigh;
But his face was laden with humble sorrow,
And hands outstretched like those of a supplicant.

With troubled look false Blanaid scanned his figure.
And turned her step as filled with sudden fright,
But swift as thought his arms were round her form;
And the hollow rocks rung with the name of Conrigh!
He sprung from the dizzy ledge of Rinkan Barra,
And swift they sank a hundred fathoms down;
And the loveliest form within the encircling seas,
Lay mangled on the sharp stones of the strand,
A prey to vultures and the grisly sea-birds".

"After the minstrel had received due plaudits from the company, and a bracing draught of wine from the chief's own cup, Sir Donoch intimated to his guest that he was at liberty to reveal his name, station, and business in that lonesome district; and that it would be very agreeable to all the dwellers of the fort if he could prolong his stay, and enjoy some days' hunting in their company.

"The stranger at once declared his name, and the circumstances from which arose his visit; but he touched lightly on incidents already known to his audience. So the commencement of his narrative shall be given more in detail till we come to the point where his information began to be altogether new to the assembly in the rath, and then let him speak for himself.

"It has been already mentioned that a battle was fought near Dublin, between Lionel, Duke of Clarence, and the father of King Art. There was a young squire attached to the service of the Earl of Ormond, present at that fight. The Leinster chief finding himself outnumbered, ordered a retreat; and our squire, whose name as given by Froissart was Henry Castide, following the fugitives with more zeal than discretion, outstripped his own party; and when he bethought him of returning, his unmanageable steed would not agree, but carried him headlong into the rear of the Irish force, who were clearing the ground in nearly as good a style as himself. He expected nothing better than a lance through his neck or side from one moment to another, when he found his restive steed quiver and bend under the weight of a tall, strong warrior, who had sprung up behind, and who

now pinioning his arms, and clapping his heels to the
flanks of the astonished beast, made him rush forward at
tremendous speed.

"In a short time they arrived at a temporary camp in
the hills near Tamlacht, and the captor springing lightly
to the ground, politely requested his prisoner to dis-
mount, making use of the Norman-French tongue with
tolerable success. 'You are my captive', said he, with a
smile on his massive, pleasant countenance. 'My position behind you, though not at all so pleasant to myself,
has spared your ribs from the visit of an arrow or Leinster
pike. Will you give knight's parole not to attempt to
escape, and you may remain among us unmolested and
unwatched?' 'I am no knight', said Castal, in a sorrowful tone. 'Had fortune smiled on me this morning, I
would be master of knight's rank at sunset'. 'Not yet
knighted! what have you been about till now? I had
my spurs at the age of twelve. Well! well! so many
races, so many customs. I do not think you will be
much longer a simple squire. Give me your word as a
Christian gentleman, that you remain true prisoner, rescue or no rescue, till I return your engagement'. The
word was readily given, so much was the stranger won
by the brusque courtesy of the Leinster chief, Sir Donogh
O'Brien.

"The campaign being over, the captive set out with
the native forces southwards, through woods, along
mountain sides, and in the depths of valleys. Their progress was a leisurely one. They hunted, and otherwise
amused themselves, and renewed or made acquaintance
at various hill-forts on their way. They arrived at last
at the rath of Cromoge, and the young gentleman was
soon domesticated, and began to feel as much enthusiasm
for deer and wolf hunting as the inmates themselves;
and as the chief's only daughter was very lovely and
gentle in manner, he found the interior life of the rath as
interesting as the exterior exercises in military sports
and the chase. Within a twelvemonth from his capture,
he was the chief's son-in-law.

"In time the union was blessed with two fair daughters, and there was as happy a household of three generations within the rough mounds of the fortress, as could be found in Leinster; but still the times were unsettled, and few were the intervals of ease enjoyed by the young king, whose coronation on the rough stone chair of Cnoc an Bogha, was witnessed by Sir Henry Castel. Sir Donogh with sixty armed followers, crossed the draw-bridge one morning, to join an expedition of his young prince, and in the ensuing fight, was separated from his followers by his own rashness, taken prisoner, and carried to the head-quarters of the Duke of Gloucester. The horse he rode on that luckless day, was the same that had borne Sir Henry on the occasion of his capture. It was recognised by some of the veterans, and the chief questioned as to the fate of its former master. On hearing his explanation, there were loud cries of wonder and disbelief, but the upshot was, that Sir Donogh was offered his liberty, on condition of pledging his knightly word, that Sir Henry, and whoever chose to accompany him, should be rendered in safety to the present camp within ten days from his own liberation.

"Very severe was the struggle in the father's heart, but at last he yielded on obtaining permission to retain one of his grand-children. On reaching his fort on a fine evening, he did not damp his people's joy by mentioning the conditions on which he had obtained his release; but next day there was a renewal of grief, when they learned the terms fixed by his captors.

"Finally the places of the young knight, his wife, and elder daughter were vacant, and gloom fell on the rath, and many a sorrowful look was cast westwards from the banks of the distant Severn, by Sir Henry and his family, as they recalled the happy days and nights spent in the sheltered vale of the Duffrey.

"In those unsettled times of war, few were the opportunities of communication between the divided families. As may be supposed, they were always eagerly seized on, but for the last four months no intelligence had arrived from the exiles.

"At this point of the narrative, the lady of the mansion with her voice affected by tearful emotion, interrupted the speaker. 'Oh! my dear children, and my loving little darling! are they alive and in health, and shall my eyes ever again behold their dear faces!' The young lady also joined her voice: 'Dear, dear mother, and father, and sister! Oh! speak, sir, and relieve our anxiety'. Eager inquiry was on the intent countenances of every one in the hall, but the speaker, Sir Eustace Raymond, set their minds at ease in a moment.

"'Be of good cheer, my kind hosts! All are in the best health, and your daughter and son are at this hour on their way to your hold, with intent of never quitting this neighbourhood again'. Here he could obtain no opportunity of proceeding with his narrative, so many and so various were the questions, which were showered on him. Having done his best to meet the immediate demands, he was allowed to continue.

"'You scarcely need expect to behold your granddaughter again. Her husband is my eldest brother, and the happiness of the united families would have been complete, only for the home sickness suffered by Sir Henry and his lady. So strong did this become at last, that they sailed about two months since to Dublin, and through great interest and a good deal of trouble, Prince Thomas of Lancaster, the lord deputy, has been induced to permit Sir Henry under these peculiar circumstances to reside in Ireland, on conditions of never bearing arms against the Pale.

"'He would not send you any information till he had got the express sanction, and made safe provision for the management of his estates on the borders of Cumbria, for fear of inflicting sorrow. At last when he had all settled to his satisfaction, and was preparing to commence his southern journey, the whole city and the surrounding country were dismayed by the rushing of the forces of Murrogh O'Connor from the western plains, and those of King Art from the hills of Kinsalach to try the strength of the Pale at the very gates of their strongest hold.

"'About a month since, we witnessed from the summit of a tower near the walls, a struggle between two fierce powers, such as I would not behold again for the wealth of Britain, nor the highest honour I could receive from my sovereign, if I were obliged to look on and remain inactive. I was the whole time quivering with excitement, and my blood boiling in my veins, and I uttering maledictions on the chance that bound my hands from assisting either party. The knights and men-at-arms, together with the equally warlike citizens, under the command of Prince Thomas, Sir Jenicho D'Artois, Sir Nicholas Ferrers, and Sir Thomas Butler, the lame Prior of Kilmainham, issued forth in two bodies, one through the western gates, and the other along the northern bank of the Liffey. The uneven ground, especially on the farther bank of the river, was studded at intervals with clumps of large trees throwing broad shadows on the smooth sod. The warm morning rays were resting on the vapours rising from the river and the dewy turf, and bringing out the orange, red, and dusky-green tints of the foliage of the large trees, which covered the ground at intervals wherever our eyes wandered. But the rough fighting men, as they passed along, noted not the fine landscape under the influence of the lovely morning; they were intent alone on shedding the blood of their opponents, or selling their own at the dearest rate.

"'The towers and spires of the hospital of St. John seemed enjoying the warm sunshine, but the warlike Prior, instead of observing the peaceful duties of his state within its walls, was now marshalling his division of the gallant Palesmen.

"'By some oversight, the coppices that border the rivulet running between the Priory and the city, had been neglected, as well as some other coverts; and as the archers proudly stepped in front to pour their deadly hail on the foe when they came in sight, out from the coverts sprung, with the most terrific cries, hundreds of wild-looking infantry, with no arms but long sharp double-edged knives and slings, and falling on the startled bow-

men, who had scarcely time to draw their short swords,
they massacred them like unresisting sheep.

"'The cries were answered by a rolling and prolonged
shout from the slope between the Priory and the river,
and bodies of the Irish horse were immediately seen
rushing on with the speed of wild deer. Dashing through
the dead and dying archers, they cast their long heavy
lances before them, and neither shield, helm, nor mail-
jack, sufficed for defence against these deadly missiles,
nor against the crushing sweep of the battle-axes, as
they fell on the Anglo-Norman warriors.   We soon remarked a gigantic knight, distinguished by a crimson
mantle, and wherever his steed ploughed his way, a lane
of levelled foes marked his passage.   Prince Thomas
observing the devastation spreading round this champion,
spurred to meet him; but ere they could come to a personal struggle, a javelin from the hand of King Art (for
the knight of the red cloak was your terrible Leinster
chief) transpierced his arm.   The sword fell from his
valiant grasp, and he only kept his seat by a great effort.
He was forcibly removed from the combat, but his place
was efficiently filled by D'Artois the *Lawless*.

"'The foot-kerns were in the hottest of the strife, and
in danger (only for their wonderful agility) of being
trodden down at every moment.   They seemed not to
bestow the slightest care on their own safety, but continued to plunge their sharp skenes into steed or rider
according as opportunity came.

"'But these were only the vanguard of the native
troops, and few in comparison to the multitude that still
continued to stream out from the city.   The chief with
the red mantle, staying his hand for a moment, and looking over the agitated sea of conflict, blew a piercing blast
on his bugle horn, and the strife ceased as by magic.
Wounded men were caught up, and laid across the horses,
the foot-men seized the manes of the steeds, or sprung
behind the riders; almost before you could breathe, there
were perches between the lately mingled combatants;
and in a few seconds the Leinster men joined the

heavy armed galloglachs of the main body, that had been steadily advancing during the skirmish.

"'The city forces on the northern bank, under the command of Sir Thomas Butler, whose care it would have been to oppose an attack in that direction, finding no movement attempted on their side, and supposing from the swift retreat of the vanguard, that the main body would be immediately in rout, rushed down to a ford, and pushed across to share in the anticipated victory. But they found themselves opposed by the spears and short, heavy swords of a portion of the galloglachs under the direction of two young chiefs of the O'Dorans and O'Niallans of Wexford. Fierce and deadly was the conflict on the bank and in the shallows, and the waters below the ford were soon reddened with the blood of heroic men; and their bodies, just now full of life and vigour, were seen floating onward to the city, as valueless as the foam that crested the currents, or the weeds that fringed the banks.

"'The main body of the Anglo-Normans were now engaged hand to hand with the heavy armed infantry of Leinster. O'Connor shouting his war cry of '*Offaley Aboo*', led on his troops, and then ensued a series of single combats between individuals of the two races, marked by the dismal clang of the well-tempered weapons, shouts of encouragement, and yells of rage. The Norman horse frequently charged detached portions of the galloglachs, but they were always met by a hedge of bristling spear points; and from behind this defence, axes or heavy lances, flung with all the strength and skill of practised fighters, lightened the burthen of many a gallant war-horse.

"'The King of Leinster, who, as I believe, would have found it impossible to keep in the one place, and direct the operations of a scattered fight, was to be seen in every part of the field. I saw him charge an opposing squadron of horse, headed by Sir Jenicho D'Artois; and though his steeds were not so strong nor his men so well fenced by armour, such was their activity, lightness of movement, and speed, that they broke through them, and left several on the bloody ground, being seconded as before by their light equipped kerns. When need required, they disentangled themselves from the opposing cavalry, and in a few minutes a new charge ensued, the Leinster chivalry continuing to be reinforced with fresh auxiliaries. When they saw a prospect of success, they rushed on the men-at-arms; and in several instances broke their ranks by the suddenness and agility of their attacks, and the fatal aid of the footmen.

" ' Were an equal number of horse and foot selected from each side, equally armed, and arrayed against each other in a level-listed plain, I would place a high stake on the success of my own countrymen; but here, with diversity of surface in the field, and a want of unity in the command and movements, and the other advantages on the Irish side, I saw there was on that day no hope of victory for the Pale. At every separation of the combatants, the Leinster forces, both of the plains and hills, returned to the charge with increased fury: and ranks were broken, and at every shock the gory tide of battle rolled backwards still nearer to the walls. The deadly charges and partial retreats of King Art's troops seemed like the flow and ebb of a furious tide, at every turn driving the foe before them, as blocks of wood or loose stones would be impelled still further on the beach by each augmenting rush of the waves.

" ' Whatever could be effected by stubborn valour and discipline, was done to make the retreat as damageless as might be, and as the sun was declining over the wooded height of Kilmainham, all that escaped from the bloody field were safe within the walls. After the fight, the victors were observed collecting the swords and spears that had served the Palesmen, bending or breaking them across their knees, and then throwing them into a pit.

" ' The victory could not be pushed beyond the outer defences, as there were no means of storming the strong walls, but the terrific shouts and yells that pursued those getting last under shelter, must have struck terror into the hearts of the unwarlike portion of the citizens. The shallow where the conflict raged, and from which the river ran blood, has since been, and will, I suppose continue to be called, ' *Ath cru*', or the Ford of Blood.

" ' Loud and deep were the lamentations and sorrow of thousands within the walls that evening; and if the Irish chiefs could have effectively followed up their advantages, the Anglo-Norman power in this country would be as helpless at this hour as the pebbles by the way-side against the iron shoe of a war-horse.

" ' We paid a visit to the hospitals where the disabled of our own people were settled, and also to the wards where the wounded Irish had their hurts looked to, for the Christian kindness due to open and honourable foes was exercised. In passing through, my eye fell on the figure of a tall, strong young knight, who bore a striking likeness to Lady Sybilla Castal. I managed to bring her in full view of the wounded youth, and in a moment she was on her knees by his bedside, and his head encircled in her arms'.

" Here the course of the narrative was stopped, and the narrator obliged to assure his eager auditory, that their young chief, Sir Turlogh, was at that moment, as far as he could judge, nearly as strong and in as good health as when he last quitted home.

" ' He had been disabled in the early part of the day by his steed falling, and was carried prisoner into the city. His hurts had been since attended to, and he was at the time of our visit in a fair way of recovery. Sir Henry was rejoiced at the opportunity of doing his young relative a kindness; and by the influence of his friends he got leave to have Sir Turlogh removed to his own quarters.

" ' Next day at an early hour, white flags were hoisted over the western gates, and at the nearest point of the Leinster camp, and they set to work at each side to give Christian interment to the slain. A great portion of the large cemetery near the Priory, together with the burial grounds inside the walls, were put in requisition;

17

and Masses were unceasingly celebrated till an early
hour in the afternoon in the city churches, the Priory,
and at temporary altars in the camp of King Art.

"'It is the general opinion of all those whom I have
heard discussing the matter, that since the fight at Clontarf, no such remarkable conflict has occurred within this
kingdom, yet the only results seem to be, a greater respect for the talents of your king, and a greater awe of
his power. Before the Leinster army turned its course
southwards, we had joined it for greater security in our
journey hither, a brave knight of Monmouth having been
passed over to Prince Thomas in exchange for Sir Turlogh. It must have increased affection to the king in
the hearts of all who saw him embracing your son, and
kissing him on each cheek, when he was restored to the
camp, just as if he was a young child of his own. But
the same cordial spirit influences his every action: I believe he knows the name of the meanest kern in his following. A frown on his face or a slight reproach from
his tongue strikes dismay; and it is little wonder that
his people are such devoted subjects and soldiers, for his
accommodation both at bed and board is the same as
theirs, and he is as solicitous for the well-being of every
individual, as if he was a member of his own proper
household. Now if this was the result of skilful or selfish
calculation, it would be laudable and judicious enough,
but every one feels that his actions are the mere mani-
festations of an unselfish, loving, generous, and heroic
nature.

"'We set out homewards along the borders of the Pale,
confirming the confidence of the fortresses of Castledermot and Catherlogh; and a strong body has just gone
across from Idrone to invest the strong fortress of Ferns.
Art is determined to reduce the garrison by famine, if
they will not capitulate, and then capture in succession the chain of fortresses from Ball'athcairn, somewhere here on the Slaney, till he reaches Loch Carmain.
Your young chief, as might be expected, has accompanied
his king, but Sir Henry and lady Sybilla are coming

here, having parted from the main body at Catherloch. They have a sufficient retinue, as their progress is through a friendly country, and so as I had become tired of slow marches, I sped on before by way of avant-courier. I judge that you will have them all to yourselves at an early hour to-morrow'. (The cunning and restless young knight omitted to mention his own wish, to have an early sight of the young beauty of the rath, as a very strong element in the cause of his speedy movements.)

"The speaker ceased, and there was a lively conversation kept up for some time, and the young knight and the young lady soon let it escape from their minds, that till this day they had been strangers. Neither they, nor the old chief nor his wife, enjoyed profound sleep on that night, but still their waking hours were not tiresome. At noon next day they met son, and daughter, and train, near the church of Kil-Mihail, and joyous was the return, and the crossing of the drawbridge, and every-one felt a touch of sadness at seeing some traces of time's yellow fingers on the restored relatives. But this soon wore away, and lady Sybilla shed tears of chastened joy on again taking possession of her bridal chamber for the rest of her days as she hoped. She hugged and kissed her father, and mother, and daughter, in an ecstasy of joy, which soon lapsed into sadness, as she thought of her other child beyond the sea. All walked round the fortress, and explored the recesses of the neighbouring woods, and once more gazed on the steep face of the neighbouring mountain, and the day of excitement was closed by a happy evening, and a night of rest and quiet.

"On the third day after the return of the exiles, the united members of the family were conversing within the parapet on the roof of the principal building, and enjoying the view on every side. Beyond the rivulet on the west, spread the broad face of the mountain, with the wing sweeping off towards Clonmullin and Bunclody. The patches cleared for cultivation or pasture, the rough, drab-coloured road winding through the landscape, the many-coloured, decaying foliage of the trees, and the reddish-purple or gray tints of the upper part of the hill, and all seen under the effect of a floating soft vapour, and the mild October sunlight, gave an additional charm to the domestic happiness that ruled the rath at that hour.

"The prospect on the south, embraced the marsh, on the upper edge of which the fortress stood, the Glasha rushing eastwards, and beyond it, the range of hills extending from Temple-Shanbo on the south side of the stream, the chief being Kilachdiarmuidh and Coolgarrow, separated by the defile of Glanamoin. A faithful kern had brought them intelligence of the expected speedy surrender of Ferns, and now another was descried skirting the marsh, and approaching at a rapid pace.

"When he came before them, he delivered his message in this wise: 'I bring you pleasant tidings, chief of Cromoge, from the young hope of the clan, Sir Turlogh. I left him at the ford of Moyeadha, attended by Cormac Dhu and Ruighri Bawn, for he had something of moment to say to his loving foster-mother: they took the hill side to her house near the pass (of Glanamoin, to wit), and I came on to bring the acceptable news. The young chief sends you word that the garrison of Ferns has surrendered, and that King Art is determined to reduce the whole river chain of forts to the very bay of Loch Carmain. Then will the country to the sea-washed lands of the O'Niallans in the south, once more obey the descendant of Cathair Mhor'.

"Sir Donogh smiled, and turning to Sir Henry and his lady, he said: 'You have not forgotten the brave governor of Bal'athcairn, nor his fair young girl, who is now a lovely young woman. I suspect that the visit to the foster mother has something to do with an inquiry after lady Isabella. Being a delicate child when deprived of her mother at an early age, and Sir Reginald being advised to send her to be nursed among the hills, he addressed a courteous request to me, and I secured the services of Turlogh's foster-mother for the little Norman lady.

"'Often during your absence have we sadly dwelt on

the many pleasant visits we used to pay to the little rath when lady Isabella was yet a baby, coursing about on the green turf under the care of Turlogh, her senior by a few years. As this immediate neighbourhood has not witnessed actual hostilities for several years, and as Sir Reginald took the kindness shown to his child in very good part, there has been as good an understanding between the castle on the river and this rath of ours, as could consist with the circumstances of border forts. You may judge that nothing beyond mutual civility could be shown by Sir Reginald and myself, but it has been no secret to us for some time that our children are attached. I am far from being delighted with the matter, but am waiting till some circumstance occurs to break off the correspondence of the young people, or afford a good and 'sufficient sanction of their union. Now if King Art drives Sir Reginald Aylmer from his fortress, and if the brave old knight loses his command or possessions, his daughter shall find a heart's welcome here. But if he choose to hold out, and the castle be stormed, how are we sure that the dear young lady will escape harm in the confusion? *Cead milé Cuirh!* I will send this very day to the castle, and implore Sir Reginald to entrust the young chatellaine to us till the present warfare comes to a close. I scarcely knew till just now, when I reflected on the risk she may run, how dear the lovely good-hearted creature was to me'.

"'I scarcely think', said Sybil, 'that lady Isabella would quit her father in this strait. At all events, we had better wait till the return of my brother, whose knowledge of the intended movements of King Art will help us to a correct judgment of what is best to be done'.

"So nothing was done for the time, and the conversation continued; but when a couple of hours passed without the expected arrival of Sir Turlogh, and the sun was sinking lower and lower, a feeling of inquietude and alarm began to prevail. No appearance of knight or follower on the route which went along the western border of the marsh to the ford leading to Moyaidh's residence;

so messengers were dispatched thither, and about sunset one of them returned. He brought intelligence that lady Isabella had paid a visit to her nurse that day, a little before noon; that she had staid about an hour, and then departed with two of her own retainers, and her foster-brother, who was to see her safe in sight of the castle, but had not since returned; that Sir Turlogh had been seen by none of the household; and that the other messengers with some of the people of the hill farm-house were now gone in the direction of the river for further information.

"We must now leave our family, a prey to severe anxiety, and wait on the young chief and his followers from their passage of the Slainge at the still practicable ford of the big meadow of Tombrick. The young knight was in a cheerful mood; he had a prospect of rest for a day or two: he was soon to see his loved and loving relatives, and his affectionate foster-mother, and perhaps hear some interesting news of Lady Isabella; and moreover he had received the promise of his sovereign, that Sir Reginald's castle should remain unmolested till he would have reduced those to the south. Something might occur in the interim to avert disagreeable proceedings; at all events he was resolved not to anticipate an evil which might never occur.

"Ruighri was to the full as lively and energetic as his young chief, and as eager to reach the rath, as pretty Siobhan was either counting the hours of his absence, or (oh, misery!) bestowing a stray smile on one of the lazy stay-at-homes. The supreme wish of the other follower, who was tall and of a shambling configuration, seemed a speedy enjoyment of refreshment, and repose from his marches, watches, and skirmishes. As they breasted the hill, he frequently seized the mane of the war-steed to aid his lazy limbs; and when they reached the little eminence at the near side of the present village of Coolgarrow, and had the wide breast of Slieve Lainge, and the intervening valley of the Glasha, and the marsh, and the high rath of Cromoge, all lying so calm and varied in character before them, Cormac cried out: 'By your black head, Turlogh of the swift foot, I long for the wings of one of the eagles of that hill—and talking of the eagle, may his mate soon be deprived of his company, the black thief! for robbing us of so many lambs and bonnives as he does—I say, if I had his wings, and could use them without too much trouble to myself, would n't I fly in three reaches over this wood below us, and that bog beyond, to my comfortable bed of heath and dry leaves in the old rath! If I do n't sleep two days and two nights without stirring, my sorrow on the meddler that will disturb me! Let us sit down to get a little rest after that tiresome reach of a hill. I wonder what were hills first invented for! But is n't your foster-mother's just at hand? I see the wattled chimney through the opening. Sure when we call, won't they ask us to stay till to-morrow with them, and for your sake I think I ought to accept. They surely won't attempt to disturb me till I choose to rise. But *milé molachd!* Art of the fifty fights —may he soon be sitting on the necks of the strangers, and give us a little rest—will be gathering us to smash another stone house; and then what eye will dare to wink? And with watching, and climbing walls, and tumbling into trenches, and getting knocks from the heavy maces of the Clan-London, the oil of our joints and the marrow of our bones will be as dry as elder pith. O Diarmuidh na n-Gall, you devil, was there no handsome woman nearer to you than Orgial? Let no one bless your memory! You have left us now, for three hundred years or so, sleeping with our heads on our skiaghs, and eating our hurried meals with the naked sword lying by the side of the trencher'.

"'I would be glad to know, Cormac', said his master, 'how it is that no one in a surprise, is sooner on the enemy than yourself, or farther away from him when there is a retreat, if you are really as lazy as you appear'. 'Och! it 's easy seen; the quicker I attack the iron-shirted bodachs, the sooner I will have my time for rest and quiet; and the faster I fly, the sooner I will put it out of their power to disturb me. Besides, the heavier and lazier a stone tumbling down a hill-side, the harder it finds to stop itself, and the sooner it will be in a comfortable bunch of dry fern at the bottom. But if I am not dreaming with my eyes open, there is the fair-haired heiress of the castle. There between the trees I see a piece of her horse and the skirt of her kirtle. Is it at Moyaidh's she has been? Thsu! thsu! what luck some people are born to! Do n't stir, son of the O'Brien: she will soon be at the brow of the pass. I see Rupert and Hubert and Humphrey, sitting on the big stone; they are big and ugly enough to guard her to the ford of the cairn'.

"But Turlogh had already covered half the distance that intervened between the lady and himself. She was advancing at a slow pace, and in a rather pensive mood when she first heard the sound of his horse's feet among the uneven ground, partially covered with trees. She was in the act of encouraging her palfry to a canter to come up with her trusty attendants; but a second or two made her aware of the presence of her early friend; and in a moment their hands were joined, and the colour in their cheeks heightened, and unanswered questions were exchanged, and broken remarks made, and the mind and heart of each was filled with the other's presence, and all in the world beside forgotten. The features of the young lady were set off by hair of a chestnut hue, and better adapted to express archness than melancholy. Her dark-gray eyes and well-defined eyebrows, and short upper lip, and the healthy-coloured cheek, gave her countenance an expression, the reverse of the faded washy effect, that mostly accompanies a pale face and hair of a light tinge of yellowish red.

"In answer to his eager inquiries as to her being at such a distance from the keep, she explained that she had been a close housekeeper for some days; and having felt a troublesome headache that morning, she had crossed the ford, and ridden to the top of the ridge on the near side of the river; that she could not prevail on herself

then to return, but continued her excursion to the old
beloved abode of her childhood; that she had left her
attendants at the summit of the pass, for fear she should
be suspected of distrust by Moyaidh or her family; and
that just as they met, her mind had been disturbed by
the thoughtlessness of the whole proceeding, for she
feared her father was at that moment in trouble about
her absence, the times being so unsettled.

"'And how is the dear old mother?' said Turlogh,
grasping the hand of his foster-brother, who had come on
with the lady as she left the house, but was now following at a convenient distance. 'When I crossed the
ford, I could not prevail on myself to go straight home,
but took this round for the pleasure of seeing her, and
of showing her her "Paustheen Dhu", as she still calls
me'. A satisfactory answer was got, and Lady Isabella
detailed part of the sayings and doings of the morning;
and however guarded her statements, Turlogh, if he was
disposed to be critical, might easily discover that one of
the objects of her visit was to hear some tidings of his
own whereabouts, and that the 'Paustheen Dhu' was the
subject of three-fourths of the conversation between herself and the foster-mother.

"By this time the two followers had come up; and
with the foster-brother they joined the Norman men-at-
and exchanged greetings as with old acquaintances. The
descent being steep, Sir Turlogh dismounted, and assisted the lady to do the same; and they walked down
the pass leisurely, leaving the horses to be brought after
by their followers.

"The dress of the Norman lady differed in some respects from the Irish fashion, in a greater attention to
the covering of the throat, and in its closely following
the outlines of the figure. She had adopted the native
cloak, the hood of which was brought over the beautifully formed head.

" She inquired about the siege of the great stronghold
of Ferns, and felt not a little frightened at the news of
its being captured. 'Oh! what a thoughtless act I have

committed this day !' said she.   'I intended merely to gain
the first height on this side the ford; and now the castle,
perhaps, is already invested'.   Turlogh eased her mind
on this point by mentioning King Art's general design
in the ensuing operations, but he omitted to mention his
own agency in the arrangement.   Though she felt relieved by this information, she could not conceal her
anxiety to hasten home.   Being placed on her palfrey at
the bottom of the pass, she thanked the knight for his
escort so far, but expressed her desire to push forward to
put an end to her father's anxiety.   'I cannot see you
attend me further without uneasiness, for it is probable
that we shall soon meet some party sent out in quest of
me, and perhaps you might be insulted, or your life endangered.

"'Surely I would receive neither insult nor injury
from any knight or follower of Sir Reginald Aylmer's'.
'Assuredly you would not, but a certain Simon Fitzstephen of some fortress to the south, has been for the
last week, staying with about a score of his followers at
the castle, and if they happen to be out on the search, I
cannot answer for their good manners or forbearance'.
'May I without intrusion ask the object of the visit of
this Sir Simon Fitzstephen, who has, on one occasion at
least, acted the part of a dishonourable and treacherous
enemy towards my sovereign?'   'My father has not yet
spoken openly to me concerning his business.   I can
only say that I wish himself and followers good health in
his own fortress far off'.   'By my hopes of your regard,
lady Isabella, his wishes are to obtain your hand in
marriage.   Dear Isabella, you scarcely need a declaration from me, to know that you possess my undivided,
first, and only love.   Return not to the castle.   This
forsworn knight will get yourself or your father into
some cunningly-contrived snare.   Repair to my mother
under the charge of our united escort, and remain with
her and my sister.   I pledge my word as a true knight,
not to approach the hold, till you are once more in safety
in your father's hall: but even if I were to bring my

king and his countless followers—yes to the last man, round wherever that dishonourable partisan has taken refuge, I will have him shamefully expelled from the companionship of Sir Reginald and of every honourable knight that holds with him. I will depart for the camp of King Art this moment: let me entreat you to accept my counsel. Hubert will bear tidings of your safety to your father without delay'.

"The lady had kept her head averted during this appeal, and though when she turned her eyes on her lover, there was an expression of resentment on her fine features, the traces of tears could be seen, and her tones were far from well seconding the sterness of her words. 'How can you propose such an unseemly proceeding, especially under the circumstances of my present absence? What would be said but that I deliberately quitted home this morning to take refuge in the rath of a chief of King Art, between whom and Sir Reginald's sovereign open warfare prevails at this moment? Besides you must have little confidence in the resolution of my father or myself, if you think we are likely to be overawed by a stranger guest even with forty men at his back'.

"The young chief looked down abashed, and appeared so affected by this show of resentment, that the lady stretched over her delicate hand to be treated according to his will, and said nothing more about his immediate return.

"The knight and lady continued their conversation in Norman-French or Irish, and the followers were intelligible to each other in a mixture of the tongues prevalent among the borderers of the Pale and the native territories. They had got some distance from the bottom of the pass along a stony and broken way, and were proceeding through a partially-cultivated piece of forest land, till they came on a tolerably commodious road, occupying the same, or nearly the same position as the present highway to Ferns. The lazy Cormac had been requested to remain on the brow of the pass till Sir Turlogh's return, but he asserted that, 'he could not sit still for five minutes without falling asleep, and then perhaps he would catch a rheumatism. Besides, a red-haired woman was the first person he laid eyes on after awaking that morning, and a hare skipped across his path as he was going to wash his face. Sixthly, if anything happened to his young chief through his neglect, they would never let him have a real good long night's sleep at the rath again; lastly, he was so put about by this delay, that out of vexation, he would give himself a thorough tiring, and to conclude, he had made up his mind to do nothing else.

"They were proceeding at a steady pace along the road mentioned, and between her hints for his return, and his entreaties for a prolonging of his happiness, they at last came to the brow, from which were visible below them, at the farther side of the river, the large keep and offices, the embattled wall surrounding the court yard, and the wide fosse supplied by a cut from a higher point up the water. Just as this view met their eyes, their troubled but happy discussion was brought to a close by the swift approach of about a dozen of horsemen from the direction of the ford, and of the same number from the wood on each side. The followers of our party drew in close to the chief and the lady, while the new comers were forming a circle round them, and the leader, whom Turlogh rightly guessed to be the treacherous Sir Simon Fitzstephen, was approaching and paying his respects to the chatellaine.

"'Welcome from your rambles, lady Isabella. Your absence has left terror and sorrow in your home. Sir Reginald is nearly beside himself, troubled at once by your unaccountable absence, and the expected attack on the castle by Mac Murrogh's savages. Will you vouchsafe an explanation, and why you are now escorted by this wild-looking youth and his wilder-looking kerns?'

"Turlogh was about uttering some wrathful words, but Isabella interposed, her features expressing high disdain, as she replied: 'Sir Simon, no other but my father should feel authorised to put such a question; but I do not choose to make a mystery of having ridden to this spot in the morning for the sake of air and exercise, and then of having thoughtlessly extended the excursion to my foster-mother's at yonder pass in the hills. Returning, I met this gentleman, Sir Turlogh, son of Sir Donogh O'Brien, tanist of several cantreds of land in this neighbourhood, and a much-valued acquaintance of Sir Reginald's. He has kindly given me the protection of himself and followers, as he knows the disturbed state of things. If he were not anxious to reach home after prolonged absence, I would entreat him to pay a friendly visit to our castle'.

"'His presence at the castle shall not only be requested, but enforced', thundered Sir Simon. 'Is it befitting that the daughter of Sir Reginald Aylmer should be found wandering abroad on the eve of her father's fortress being assailed, and under the escort of a foe to her family and her family's sovereign, an obscure and unnurtured son of the bogs and woods, one who would be honoured by doing duty as a horse-boy in her father's offices?'

"'And, dare you, insolent and treacherous recreant, and all unworthy of the name of knight, thus speak of the son of a chief of the land's best blood? Your past treachery to my king would justify my driving my lance through your foul throat this instant, but let our strife be on equal terms, though you little deserve the courtesy due to an honourable foeman'.

" His ordinarily pleasant and noble features assumed the terrible expression given by hate and excitement. Dashing his heavy lance into the road-side turf, seizing the handle of the ponderous war-axe, that hung by his thigh, waving it round his head, and pressing the side of his steed, he rushed on the Norman, who with drawn sword, prepared to abide the shock as he best could.

" Lady Isabella had signed to those of the troop in whom she had most confidence, while Sir Simon was yet speaking; so a press of horsemen now interposed between the rivals before the disloyal knight could make nearer acquaintance with the battle axe of the fiery young chief. They glared on each other across the barrier; but after a few moments, Sir Simon, striving to suppress his rage, addressed his own and Sir Reginald's mingled followers: ' My friends, you are aware that the present is no time of truce; and that there is every prospect of the castle being invested before to-morrow by the chief of these Leinster clans. Would I then do the duty of friend and ally to the master of that threatened hold, in letting this haughty young chief to go at large? No! and if he is of the noble blood he boasts, and if we are obliged to capitulate to MacMurrogh's multitude of woodmen, our possession of this prisoner will obtain better conditions from his master. In so doing we are guilty of no breach of the laws of warfare. An avowed enemy is found on our lands in time of war, with all his arms offensive and defensive on his person. Conduct him then unharmed to the keep, if he offer no useless resistance. Otherwise use your weapons, and if he suffer harm, let him thank his own insolent folly'.

" Turlogh had received his spear from the hand of Cormac, who with the two others were now standing by the side of their young chief's steed, with their dangerous-looking skenes ready bared for conflict. The horsemen were in no hurry for an attack, for they neither liked the look of the spear, nor of the sharp knives, nor indeed the business itself; and at the moment, Lady Isabella pushing her palfrey within a convenient distance of her lover, addressed him in a low tone. ' Dear Turlogh, if your heart spoke through your lips half an hour since, will it be any consolation to you, when expiring under overpowering odds, that I am left to the persecution of yonder tiger? Submit to me; and once under the protection of my father's roof, you will rejoice at having yielded your own rash will to my cooler judgment. Sheathe your swords', said she, addressing the cavaliers. 'Sir Turlogh O'Brien accompanies me to my father's presence. Sir Reginald is the

best judge of what is required of him by the present condition of the war, and by the chivalric courtesy due to an
honourable foeman, and by the circumstances of the present rencontre'.

"The young knight seeing the horsemen sheathe their
weapons, set his lance upright in the stirrup-stay. The
words so softly and sweetly addressed to him by Lady
Isabella, had so enthralled him, that he would have sub-
mitted to any thing short of dishonour for a prolonged
enjoyment of her presence. His followers put up their
weapons, and moved on beside their chief, who with Lady
Isabella on one side, rode in front of the cavalcade down
to the ford, the rear being brought up by the irritated
and gloomy Sir Simon and his immediate partisans.

"A little above that part of the river opposite the castle,
somewhere about the present site of the bridge, was a ford,
defended by a rude strong building on the western bank.
Below this ford the water formed a deep pool which was
separated from the ditch of the fort by a strong dam:
this ditch was supplied as before stated, and could be
emptied into the river by a flood-gate.

"Many anxious eyes were gazing from the upper floor
of the keep and from the walls, and as soon as the
vision of the fair truant appeared on the opposite slope,
there ensued joyful bustle, and exclamations of pleasure,
and hurrying to and fro. As they approached the little
fortalice of the ford, Sir Simon beckoned to his side one
of his trustiest men, and gave him a few directions in a
low earnest tone. The man immediately quitted the
party, and spurred southwards through forest and meadow, keeping at some distance from the bank of the
river.

"The poor lady's heart was throbbing, and her cheek
burning, as she met her father in the gateway. Though
his joy was great on being released from the mortal
anxiety he had been enduring some minutes before, he
put on a frown, and would have striven to give his
daughter an awfully severe reception; but she sprang to
the ground, and rushing into his arms cried out, 'Do not

chide me, dear father. I have suffered much already for my foolish excursion, which at setting out, I intended to be no further than the brow above the ford. The wish to see my dear old nurse drew me on; and while I was talking with her, and running over the old rooms and garden, I completely forgot every thing outside. When I bethought myself, and was returning frightened enough, I accidentally met our neighbour and friend, Sir Turlogh O'Brien, returning from the siege of Ferns. As he feared some danger to be possible, owing to the smallness of my retinue, he would see me in safety to the outer works. Whatever blame you give me you will not withhold gratitude from him'.

" ' Ah, you inconsiderate damsel!' said the hasty but affectionate father, 'you little know how much I have suffered from your unaccountable absence. Thanks from the heart, my brave kind neighbour, though my king's foeman—not foeman, however, while voluntarily within our walls. Eh! it strikes me that in the present state of actual warfare, and you not invested with the sacred office of herald, I cannot let you freely depart, and at the same time discharge my devoir to my sovereign Henry the Fourth. Sir Turlogh O'Brien, if my daughter in her ignorance or inattention, gave you permission to accompany her thus far, were you not thoroughly aware yourself of the risk incurred by being found in a hostile territory, completely armed, and not commissioned to treat on terms or peace or war by your king? Perhaps, after all, you are the bearer of conditions: if so, produce them, and relieve me of my present annoyance'. Here Lady Isabella was obliged to lean against her father for support. She hung down her head to conceal the bitter tears that remorse for her heedlessness was drawing from her eyes. The young knight was so disturbed by this, and the position in which his imprudence had placed him, that he hesitated to make a reply. He was saved any trouble in that respect, by his watchful enemy, who had by this time made his way from the rear of the party.

" ' Sir Reginald, I have already signified to this young man the necessity of putting him, for the present at least, under corporal restraint, my reasons being the same as those so correctly given by yourself. He seemed, not unnaturally, to object to the arrangement, and only for Lady Isabella's interference, some lives might have been forfeit. There is still a stronger necessity for the measure, as it is now beyond doubt that Ferns is in the possession of MacMurrogh, and that from hour to hour, we may expect to see his wild kerns pouring out of yonder wood to invest this stronghold. I have already dispatched a trusty messenger to the captain of Prendergast's fortress, to Sir Miles Furlong of Castleboro, and others of our trusty castellans; and I hope to see the forces of our allies crossing the river at an early hour tomorrow morning, to help us to check the further progress of the deadly enemy of our sovereign and ourselves. Were you to set O'Brien at liberty, it would be at once a disloyal act, and a neglect of a powerful instrument of our safety. I believe that few stand so high in the favour of MacMurrogh as he does; and if we are hard pressed in this hold, his presence will bring better terms from his dangerous master'.

"Sir Reginald's attitude and countenance exhibited the greatest perplexity and indecision while Sir Simon was speaking; but his daughter now interposed, and her words brought relief. 'Dear father, it will probably save you the necessity of resorting to the strict usages of warfare, when you hear that it is not the intention of the King of Leinster to invest our castle till he has attacked the other strongholds of the south. If he had any design in this quarter, you would have seen the approach of his forces before this, so rapid are his movements'. She added in a whisper, 'you scarcely need to be told the name of the friend by whose counsels King Art has been influenced in this proceeding'. 'Ah! you dear mischief!' answered the gratified father, 'see what a turmoil you have brought us into by your silliness! Oh, why did our mother Eve set such an example of gadding to her

18

daughters! Sir Simon', he added aloud, 'this proceeding on the part of the Leinster king, relieves us from the
necessity of detaining my friendly young neighbour
longer than he voluntarily chooses to partake our hospitality. Sir Turlogh, you will not refuse to share our
afternoon meal, and meantime, one of your attendants
may proceed to the rath to set the minds of your family
at ease'.

" Fitzstephen here interposed. ' Sir Reginald, before
you decide anything, perhaps it might be expedient to
ascertain whether these same attendants are present.
One at least, a shambling lazy-looking fellow I do not
see, though he was certainly in the barbican outside the
moat'. So it was. The foster-brother and Ruaighri were
on the spot, but Cormac the lazy was not to be found.
One of the soldiers said that he had seen him lying on a
bench in the barbican, and was sent at once to bring him
forward or get information. There was an undecided and
unquiet air among the chief personages till his return,
and his report changed their inquietude into unmistake-
able trouble. The wearied Cormac had stretched himself on a bench, and after a while had modestly requested
the sentinel to hand him a cup of water. The man's
duty not including the relief of hungry or thirsty visitors,
hinted that his business was to keep watch with pike on
shoulder, compliance with the request would subject the
same shoulders to the discipline of the stirrup leathers
and that the applicant might resort to the moat if he was
too weary to enter the court-yard, and make application
at the buttery. ' Then', said Cormac, 'if you ever visit
me at the rath of Cromoge, you will be ashamed of your
disobligingness to-day. I will not be under a compliment to your buttery for a drink: I will follow that cut
till I come to the clean river'. The sentinel not having
received orders concerning the strangers, Cormac sauntered up the water course, complaining of pains in his
bones, and of his present whereabouts the warder knew
nothing.

" ' What think you of the proceeding of your follower?'

said the Castellan. 'My opinion', said the young knight, 'is, that at this moment he is half way to the camp of King Art. Remarking the unfriendly demeanour of your ally towards me when we met beyond the river, and at present judging my life or freedom endangered, he has taken what he considers the surest steps for my safety. After he has delivered his tidings to the king, he will be found within an hour at the rath; and it is all but certain that by an early hour of the morning the castle will be invested by three thousand armed men'.

" ' And how', said the enraged Sir Simon, 'can you take such interest in a foeman, who scruples not to display such arrogance within your walls? Is it come to that pass, that a knight of the noble Norman lineage will allow himself to be bearded by an obscure Irish hobbiler within his own gates, and in presence of his knights, retainers, and allies? Your chivalric young friend, after prompting his wily knave to execute this treacherous move, now glories in its success'. The lady commented on this virtuous outbreak in a low tone to her perplexed sire. 'The morals of the age are improving: Sir Simon Fitzstephen declaims against the crime of treachery'.

" ' A truce to irritating remarks', said Sir Reginald to his ally. 'I ask you, Sir Turlogh, on the word of a knight, did you give instruction by word or sign to your follower to act as he has done?' 'On my knightly faith, I did not, Sir Reginald'. 'Even if you had done it, I do not see that under the circumstances you would be blamable. Ah, my daughter! whatever ensues, you will not escape censure. If we let Sir Turlogh depart, his king and people will impute it to fear; if we detain him, they will cry out on our dishonourable conduct, taking the circumstances of his arrival into account. Well, let the result be what it may, we will do the honourable and just duty of Christian knights. My young friend, whatever your king or your family may think of our motives, here you shall not abide longer, unless with your own free will'.

" The decision was hailed with pleasure, except by the

allies; and their chief immediately expressed his dissent.
'I am here, Sir Reginald, only as your guest, but you
must allow me the consideration due to an upholder of
the rule of our sovereign lord, Henry the Fourth, over
this conquered district; and this rule I will maintain
with sword and tongue while action or speech is left me.
If I am overpowered be it so; but it shall be under protest that in proper time and place I must denounce your
proceeding as foolish and disloyal'.

" The face of the stout castellan flushed at this threat,
and a serious quarrel might have ensued, but the Irish
knight interposed. ' Sir Reginald, I am deeply sensible
of your generous treatment, but I will not avail myself of
it.   I can best prevent mischief by remaining; and I will
remain, unless you resort to inhospitality, and thrust me
out.   If you permit, I will dispatch my followers to the
camp and the rath to calm any fears entertained for my
safety'.

" So Sir Reginald, not at all displeased by the offer,
found himself relieved of some anxiety, and as the hour
of the afternoon meal was at hand, a corteous invitation
was given to Turlogh, to partake of the hospitality of
the fortress.

" In a short time they were all seated in the great hall
of the castle, at two long tables, running nearly the
length of the apartment. Sir Turlogh could perceive
some difference from the native customs; for here the
master of the castle, his daughter, Sir Turlogh himself,
Sir Simon, and all those who had received the knights'
spurs, exclusively occupied the upper seats. Next came
the young squires or candidates for knighthood, and
below them sat the men-at-arms.   In his own rath, or
even at the court of his king, something like this order
was observed, but not with the same degree of strictness.
King or chief, bard and galloglach, frequently had their
places side by side; and among the ordinary viands common to rath and castle, the new guest had to endure the
smell of roast crane, peculiar to the Anglo-Norman
feasts. Though the Normans were comparatively a sober

race, he saw more wine and ale consumed than at a native entertainment. The brewing of ale and beer, called by the Irish 'bior' and 'gurm' was in practice among the natives. It was learned, according to tradition from the Danes, who, as was believed, extracted such beverages even from heath: but our forefathers were more partial to mead, wine, and usquebagh.

" The discourse at table was of a constrained character. The hospitable old-knight, however well-disposed to his guest, was in some awe of his evil-minded ally; and the lady kept silent, except on necessary occasions, for she felt that by her imprudence she had brought those most dear to her into peril. At a suitable hour it was hinted to sir Turlogh that he was at liberty to retire to his bed-chamber when he felt disposed, the castellan himself not looking for much rest, while any thing remained to be looked after, connected with the defence of the fortress against the expected attack.

" Turlogh was conducted to a square tower on the S. E. angle of the castle, on the ground floor, the passage that led to it and other chambers, the narrow flights of steps, and the corkscrew staircases, lying in the thickness of the exterior walls, or in the angle towers.

" Though the apartment was bare and bleak enough, the new occupant found no lack of comfort. Light came from a narrow and very deep window, high in the southern wall; the wainscot concealed the bare unplastered stones about four feet from the floor; and a massive bed, a few seats, and a small table composed the furniture. Our young hero, unlike some modern chevaliers, spent fifteen minutes at least at his devotions; and after devoting twice that time to rumination on the present tangled state of his fortunes, on the probable issue of the war, and his own chance of gaining or not gaining the hand of his adored Isabella, fatigue, youth, and nature put in their claims, and sleep seized on his faculties.

" After his withdrawal, an eager discussion was held, and high words were exchanged between the host and his haughty guest; and their partisans kept the controversy

at an unhealthy and feverish point. The wine flasks were
not spared, and while every one was occupied either in
violent declamation or violent rejoinder, Sir Simon took
the opportunity of letting a few drops of dark liquid fall
from a small vial into a goblet which stood near Sir
Reginald's right hand. He then took an opportunity of
considerably allaying the bitterness of the discussion;
spoke of the common cause, and of the common foe, and
of the necessity of unity of feeling and purpose among all
the friendly and loyal subjects of Henry the Fourth, whom
God preserve; finally proposing that the sovereign's health
should be honoured in full cups. All the goblets on the
table were filled and emptied with a good will; and Sir
Reginald rose to his legs with intent to address the knights
and squires around him. All at once, his countenance assumed a stupid and at the same time, startled expression,
and the few words that he succeeded in pronouncing were
destitute of connection. He turned an appealing look to
one or two of those in whom he was known to have confidence, gradually sunk into his chair, and leaning his
head backwards, lapsed into unconsciousness.

"The attention of his knights and trusty followers,
was now painfully fixed on their beloved chief; they expressed their surprise at the sudden prostration, for which
they considered the quantity he had drunk insufficient;
and they bitterly lamented, that such an infliction should
take place, when the full vigorous use of his faculties
was needed. After a few unsuccessful attempts to rouse
him, attempts seconded in the most friendly manner by
Sir Simon, the proper attendants were summoned, and
he was conveyed to his bedchamber on the next floor.

*　　*　　*　　*　　*　　*

"As the day was slowly brightening through the soft
vapours of a fine October morning, the warder on the
tower over the north-eastern gate, discerned the movement of a strong body of men on the skirt of the forest
eastwards, where it approached nearest to the fortress.
His bugle was soon at his lips, and with the first blast,
numbers of the garrison men thronged from every part of
the keep and court to the adjoining wall, and mounting

the steps placed at intervals, filled the platform immediately behind the crenelated parapet; and there they silently stood with their spears upright, and their shields resting in the embrasures.

"Sir Simon, with some of his immediate adherents, and Sir Walter Devereux, lieutenant of the garrison, took their places on the wall beside the gate tower; and in a few minutes, a gathering of about ten horsemen appeared in front of the strange forces; a bugle was heard from the same quarter, and a white flag was hoisted. A corresponding signal was given from the tower; and at once the cavaliers came forward at full speed, headed by a tall, strong warrior. The horse stopped within a few yards of the outer edge of the moat without any apparent hint from their riders, and without disturbing their (the riders') posture in the slightest degree. The leader would have been an object of attention at any time, but under the spectators' circumstances, scarce a movement or gesture of limb or feature but was closely scanned.

"He was above the ordinary height, and proportionately stout; and his limbs seemed possessed by the greatest strength and pliancy. Under the heavy plume of black eagles' feathers shadowing the four-ridged conical helmet, appeared the handsome but massive features which in battle assumed such a terrible and fierce expression, that the boldest knight scarce ever ever met him in the melée without a feeling of involuntary terror. His long dark hair escaping in heavy masses, from under the helm, fell to his shoulders, which with his body and arms, were defended by a finely wrought coat of linked mail, fitting over a jerkin of soft leather. When he walked, this hauberk fell to his knees, leaving his finely formed legs to the native chequered trews and untanned buskins. The red mantle which had spread terror among the Palesmen at the figh of Ath cru fell behind or round him in broad folds, and was secured over the gorget by a brooch, which I hope is still to be seen at Borris, or in Trinity College or the Royal Irish Academy.

.. "As they paused with looks fixed on the foreigners, a herald, whose place was next the chief, cried out: 'On the part of Art, Prince of Kinsalach, I request speech with Sir Reginald Aylmer, castellan of this fortress of *Ball'ath-Cairn*, presently held for the behoof of the King of England'.

"As he spoke, another bugle-blast was heard from the western bank of the river, and hundreds of armed men were seen crowding down the slope. A flag of truce was waved in front, and three horsemen, on seeing the signal answered, rode under the fortalice, dashed through the ford, and were presently beside the other party. There were warm salutations and embraces between Sir Donogh, Sir Henry Castal, Sir Eustace Raymond the young English guest at Cromoge, and King Art's small retinue; but the attention of all was soon directed to the wall, from which came the harsh voice of Sir Simon Fitzstephen, who with folded arms and scowling face, gave this uncourteous reply to the summons of the herald.

"'Sir Reginald Aylmer, commander of this fortress for the puissant Henry the Fourth, King of France and England, and Lord of Ireland, is at this moment helpless on his bed from an attack of sudden illness. The command of the garrison meanwhile lies with his lieutenant, Sir Walter Devereux, and myself, Simon Fitzstephen, military commander of Taghmon. We are prepared to treat with Sir Arthur Mac Murrogh, who, we believe, is chief of Ballylaughan and Ballymoon, in Catherlogh, knight by favour of Richard, second of that name, King of England, and now in revolt against his liege lord, Henry, King of England, whom God preserve!'

"A shout from the walls on either hand, greeted this speech, but the herald's ready reply was given the moment it ceased. 'Before the cause for which we came is announced, I must rectify your false statements, Sir Simon Fitzstephen. He, whose style and title you wilfully demean, is, by descent in right line from Cathair Mhor, by nomination of the O'Niallan, and proclamation of the Brehon of Lagenia, O'Doran of the true speech—true-

born King of Leinster, from Inver Colpa, to the fair
harbour of Port-Lairge, and was crowned on the royal
stone on Cnoc-an-Bocha with acclamation of the entire
tribes of Hy-Kinsalach. He received knighthood at the
age of ten from the sword of his royal father, to whose
soul be happiness! He is therefore under no tie of duty
or gratitude to the king of the strangers, and will continue to break their power in this land, and exact mail for
right of residence, from every holder of territory of the
race of the Galls. These being declared, Art, King of
Leinster, demands that the younger Flaith, Turlogh, son
of Donogh O'Brien, chief of Cromoge and other cantreds,
made prisoner and brought into this fortress, when doing
the devoir of a courteous knight, be presently delivered
up unharmed, and with his armour and weapons as he
entered this gate on yesterday'.

"Sir Simon hastened to reply: 'The youngster whose
deliverance you claim, was arrested on the seignorial
lands pertaining to this castle, and will be detained till a
stronger reason be given for his release, than the insolent demand of a rebel vassal found in arms against his
sovereign'.

"Then spoke King Art for the first time, and his clear
and powerful voice was audible in the still morning, to
the remotest part of the great court yard. 'Simon Fitzstephen, your base proceedings towards me forbid that I
should give you any honourable title. I was once invited
to a social meeting of the chiefs of the Pale, and but for
the wariness of my bard and foster-brother, who struck
the Rosg-Catha instead of the festal ode on his clair-
seach as we entered the hall at Castledermot, my body
would be now mouldering in its moat, and my people
under foreign bondage. In that hour of extreme peril
you were the evil-inspiring genius of the knot of assassins;
and with thee, unworthy of the gorget or gold spurs of
knight, I hold no parley. Sir Walter Devereux, I give
respectful greeting to the brave and honourable master of
this fortress, and request him in all courtesy to set
at liberty my trusty lieutenant, Turlogh, son of Sir

Donogh O'Brien, here present, who, I understand, has had
friendly intercourse with him for many years. If you
take the trouble of dispatching a messenger to his chamber, I reckon on a favourable reply'.

"Fitzstephen had so wrought on the fears and prejudices of the garrison, and had so well impressed them
with a sense of his own influence among the other chiefs
of the Pale, and of the speedy succour from the southern
castles, that all regarded him for the time as paramount
in the fortress. Sir Walter cast a wistful and inquiring
look towards his gloomy associate, and he soon spoke his
mind in accents of wrath and defiance.

"'Whatever annoyance it may cause you, I command
this fortress, till its master is in a fit condition to resume
his authority. To such as you, who scarcely know what
knighthood means, I give no explanation of my conduct.
To you forsooth! whose treacherous and cowardly followers never meet us in a fair fighting field, if they can
find rocks or trees to shelter them while they fling their
missiles. I grant them fleetness in their unexpected
charges from defiles and thickets, and tenfold fleetness
when seeking safety from our weapons. Is the leader
of such a crew to be appointed judge of the rules of war
and of its lawful stratagems!'

"The king, who had kept his eyes sternly fixed on the
speaker, now directed his looks with a respectful expression to the knights and men-at-arms who were standing
near Sir Simon, and thus addressed them: 'Brave foemen,
to you I will speak a few words in explanation of our
policy. To my hands is entrusted the defence of the
tribes of this portion of Eiré—tribes hemmed in by a
race of the most skilful and determined warriors known
in Christendom. I make no aggression that can be
avoided, but I will defend my kin and my native clans,
while brain can think, heart beat, or arm wield the sword.
All lawful helps in the strife we will continue to use;
and while you shelter your bodies by strong armour and
stone walls, we will not disdain the aid of rock, tree, or
morass. Little we reck of your mounds of granite. Let

Leinster of the blue spears decay when she prefers your piles of stone and cement to the bulwarks formed by the bodies of brave and patriot warriors. If, as I suspect, some foul work has been practised on the noble-souled commander of the fortress by yonder treacherous partisan; and if the fort is really under his orders; and if the young knight be not forthwith set at liberty, I will have the moat filled, and if Sir Reginald or the lady Isabella meet with evil treatment from those new allies, I will have them put to death without mercy. Let their blood fall on the head of their recreant leader!'

"'Enough of bravado', said Fitzstephen, whose features and speech exhibited bitter, intense hate. 'On the casting of the first fagot in the trench, or the hurling of the first lance against the defenders of the walls, the neck of your lieutenant shall feel the headsman's axe, as sure as the sun is shining on us at this moment. Ho there! Rupert Coniston, take four men, and conduct the prisoner with hands tied and neck bare to the heading block. If the chaplain of the fortress be not on leave of absence, let him discharge his functions; and when the headsman sees this scarf fall from my hand into the court-yard, let him strike. In a quarter of the sand-glass, let the white flag be replaced by the broad banner of England, and God defend the right!'

" He met the stern looks of the king with equal sternness of feature, and a stillness like death fell on the thronged walls, and the party outside the moat. The sun shone on the vapour that lay in the hollows, and pleasantly brightened up the gray walls, and battlements, and the projections of the keep, and brought out the orange and red tints in the woods beyond the river, and cast shadows from the large trees across the glades. And the calm, unclouded sky over the purplish-gray summit of Mount Leinster smiled down on the varied landscape, and perhaps the sanctity of this scene of quiet natural beauty will be profaned in a few minutes by the groans, imprecations, and agonies of men dying by the hands of their fellow-creatures.

"King Art was deeply affected and chagrined by the turn which the conference had taken, and by the deep anxiety in the faces of the old chief and his son-in-law, and some minutes went by, heavy with anxious alarm to the small party outside. Sir Donogh was beginning to suggest to his chief, something in a low tone, but the re-opening of the conference was very annoying to Art after the exchange of so many taunts. Still the desire to save his young favourite was so intense, that he was on the point of once more addressing his bitter enemy; but just then he perceived one of the five, sent to bring out the captive, approach and deliver a message to him with signs of affright and trouble in his countenance. At the same time, there was a hurried movement, and some exclamations among the men on the walls to the left, as the looks of all were directed to a small clump of old thorn trees, some perches in the rear of the party outside the moat. These turned round to learn the cause of the commotion, which cannot be explained without going back some hours in the story.

"Our young knight found himself reduced from the condition of guest to that of prisoner in about an hour after retiring to rest, for he heard the approach of footsteps, the shooting of a heavy bolt, and then the regular pacing of a sentinel. Fitzstephen taking advantage of the state of the chatellan, had, by skilfully aggravating the imminence of the common peril, got himself invested with the direction of the garrison, conjointly with the lieutenant, a brave, but easily-influenced soldier.

"He had not been able to succeed in administering a strong dose of the opiate to Sir Reginald, and this circumstance in connection with the anxious state of his mind, prevented the utter prostration of his faculties. While seeming thoroughly unconscious, his powers were feebly battling the enemy, and some hours before the ordinary period of being relieved, he succeeded in getting his confused thoughts and feelings into some sort of order. Casting his still over-laden eyes around, his glance fell on the sorrowful face of his daughter, who at

once joyfully hastened to his bed-side, and tenderly inquired how he felt. 'Dear child', said he, 'I feel as if a
weighty helmet was crushing my brain, and a thick fog
floating before my sight. Perhaps some clearness will
come over my mind in a short time. Call my trusty
Hubert hither, and we will consult as to what is best to
to done'.

" The faithful follower was not far away, and as soon
as he could give vent to an outburst of pleasure at the
change in Sir Reginald's state, he explained the present
condition of affairs outside, and the approach of the
Leinster forces.

" 'Attend strictly to the directions which I hope this
thick mist on my brain will suffer me to give', said the
poor knight; and rousing himself as well as he could, he
spoke for a few moments with clearness and energy. He
then began to repeat his instructions in a confused manner, and finally his features became expressive of bitter
chagrin at his want of command over his thoughts and
utterance; and he fell back into the troubled lethargy,
from which he had been roused by a strong effort of will
and sharp anxiety.

" Lady Isabella left the apartment for a little to give
directions to the trustiest of the domestics as to the care
of her father. Then leaving two of them at his bedside,
and embracing the insensible knight, with bitter tears
streaming from her eyes, she handed a small bunch of
keys to her faithful attendant, and they went into a
secret passage cut in the thickness of the wall, the lady
as she left the room casting a sorrowful look on the helpless condition of her loving father. They descended til
they came to the level of the room in which the young
knight lay in durance, but on a different side from that
where the sentinel was on duty, the two passages approaching the tower being separated by massive stone
work. Hubert, after examining for a moment the surface
of the wall, removed a small stone; and applying a key
to the interior of the cavity, and giving it a peculiar
turn, an irregular upright piece of the apparently solid

structure, secured by strong hinges on the other side, gave way, and admitted them to a narrow passage within. Hubert, replacing the stone, closed the door, which was constructed of a strong wooden frame-work, the outer surface being of stone and cement. They were now in the end of a narrow passage, at some distance in which there was a descent by a flight of stone steps. Isabella seemed much agitated at this point of their progress, while Hubert was examining the wall on the opposite side, and undoing a piece of latchwork. The door being of the same construction as the one they had passed through, gave way, and they were in the entrance of the captive's apartment. The light from Hubert's raised torch revealed the visitors to the knight, who being aroused by the outer noise, was found standing in the centre of the room. The naked sword was at once sheathed, and the captive kissed with joy the proffered hand of his fair deliverer. Mrs. Radcliffe would have dwelt with pleasure on this scene: Hubert's raised torch casting a yellowish red light, on himself as he stood in the door-way, streaming round the lady's head and the upper part of her person as she timidly stepped into the apartment, and falling on the young knight as he bent the knee, and touched her fair hand with his lips.

"Hubert softly advancing into the room, prevented the knight from speaking aloud, by making a significant sign, and addressed him in a whisper. 'Sir, my lady has been permitted by Sir Reginald to make this visit, in order that you may conduct her to your father's rath and place her under the guardianship of the ladies of your family. You will be informed of his motives as we go along; but first give me your word, that you will never use your knowledge of the outlet to the prejudice of himself or his cause'. Turlogh readily gave the required promise, and was about addressing the lady, but she pointed towards the passage where the watchman was placed, and all proceeded into the lobby, Hubert quietly fastening the door behind them.

"They now began to descend the steps, Hubert going before and lighting the way, the lady following, and the knight closing the procession, and addressing words of encouragement to her. After a descent of about twenty-five broken and slippery steps, they came on a level passage partly paved with flags, the roof and sides in a very mildewed state, and the air unpleasant and heavy. It was not entirely cut off from the upper air however, for little openings were observed at intervals, sloping upwards. After a few perches they found themselves gradually ascending.

" We left Sir Simon listening anxiously to the report of his messenger. This report was, that they had found the room in which the knight had gone to rest, undisturbed, but no appearance of the knight himself. While he listened anxiously to the unwelcome tidings, with his eyes fixed all the while on the outside group, he heard the cries and sudden movements among the defenders of the wall, and was struck with dismay at the sight of the young chief, advancing towards the king from the thorn thicket that lay at some distance on the east side.

" Cormac Dhu, who was standing near the old chief, was the first to catch sight of his young master. He ran towards him, and doing so, he looked back to the walls with an instinctive dread of Sir Simon. At the moment he saw him raise a bent bow, which lay within his reach, fit an arrow to the string, and draw it with a practised hand to his right ear. With the instinct of the faithful wolf-dog, he made a few rapid bounds and flung his arms round Turlogh. At the same instant, the dart striking him under the right shoulder, he loosed his hold, and would have fallen powerless on the turf, but for the grasp of his afflicted chief. Maddened at the sight, Turlogh laid the body gently on the grass, and poising his heavy spear he rushed towards the gate tower.

" The eyes of the king had wandered from the felon knight for a moment, and so he was prevented from anticipating the discharge of the arrow; but as it was on the point of taking flight, his left hand drew tighter the bridle-rein, his body swayed a little backwards, and the heavy spear, whirled as with the force of a catapult from.

his raised right arm, crashed through the strong cuirass of the treacherous knight. Such was the force of the stroke, that he was hurled into the court-yard, his death-groan and the clang of the armour falling dismally on the ears of the appalled bystanders.

"The defenders of the wall were ready to discharge their darts and javelins on the small band outside, but Sir Walter Devereux blew a shrill blast on his bugle, and shouted to them to hold their hands. He pointed to where the master of the fortress with uncertain steps, and supported by a couple of his faithful followers, was crossing the court in the direction of the gate. He was startled by the sight of the corpse of his late guest, and as he gained the platform, his features had a scared and perplexed expression.

" The Leinster chief bowed his stately head, and courteously waved his hand to the castellan as he hailed him. ' Sir Reginald Aylmer, true friend or honourable foe, the object for which we came hither is attained, and we depart, standing still in the same relation towards you and yours as on yesterday morning. Your unworthy guest has fallen by my hand, but it was only meet return for his treacherous and nearly fatal attempt on the life of the young lord of Cromoge. On my return from my southern campaign, I will pay you a hostile or friendly visit at your own option; but whether friends or honourable foes, our personal esteem shall continue unchanged. I fear that my young lieutenant has only escaped a temporay confinement to exchange it for a permanent yoke; and as I am aware of his wishes in this matter, and have small time for parley, I request that you make him happy by the gift of the hand of the Lady Isabella'.

" ' Generous prince', said Sir Reginald, ' your words fill me with sincere pleasure and satisfaction. I give my hearty consent to the proposed union, if it can be done without prejudice to the allegiance I owe my sovereign. But for the kindness of my always good neighbour of the rath, I would most probably be childless at this mement. As there are to be no immediate hostilities, I request-yourself and chiefs to honour our hold with your presence at as good an entertainment as hurried circumstances admit'.

"The Lady Isabella and Hubert had stayed in the shelter of the thicket on emerging from the subterranean passage, but when the dull sound of the arrow as it struck the poor kern, and the groan of the wounded man met her ear, she rushed out and flew to the spot, fearing that the victim was her betrothed; but on finding him untouched, the sudden relief from agonized feeling had such an effect, that she sank powerless on the turf.

"A skilful surgeon who formed part of King Art's immediate staff, was immediately on the spot. He at once cut away the protruding head from the arrow, and gently drew back the shaft, the blood welling out in abundance as it was extracted. He bound up the wound, and gave hopes to the bystanders, that the vital parts had escaped, and that with care the man might be saved. It turned out according to his opinion, but owing to his tedious recovery from the fever that ensued, poor Cormac enjoyed a longer interval of idleness than was agreeable, even to him.

"The king, on receiving the friendly summons, sprung from his steed without further ceremony, and giving directions that his forces should set about cooking their morning meal, he took the blushing lady by the hand, and conducted her across the now lowered drawbridge to the arms of her joyful father. He was the chief object of attention to all within view, and they acknowledged, while he was proceeding across the court to the door of the keep, with the joyful, confused young lady hanging on his arm, that they had never before witnessed such a powerful form, such nobility of feature, such ease and manly grace of movement, or such urbanity of manner.

"As many of the Leinster Duine Uasals and Tanists as could be well accommodated, were pressed into the hospitable banquet-room, and for a couple of hours, many who had erewhile met in the conflict, and perhaps might

19

so meet again, were engaged in agreeable conversation, and doing the civilities of the table to each other.

"The sun was declining from his mid-day elevation, when the numerous forces of King Art were beginning their southward march, and at short periods there capitulated or fell before them, the forts of Killybeg below Scarawalsh, of Iniscortha, of Ballyboro, of Adamstown, of Sigansagar, of Ross-Mac-Treon, and, finally, of Loch Carmain itself, till the whole Contha Riavach recognized the sway of Art. Ah! what country on the habitable globe could match with ours, if the Almighty had granted us a succession of rulers such as Brian, Art Mac Murrogh, and the unconquerable Hugh O'Nial!

"No more remains to be done than to invite our readers to the wedding of Turlogh and Isabella, which took place on the same day with that of Sir Eustace and the young lady of the rath. To give a suitable description of the double solemnity would require a dozen pages. It needs only to be said that the 'newly-married' found themselves more comfortable a month afterwards than on the wedding day, and that no one looking on the capers of the arrow-stricken giolla for the first time, would ever think of calling him 'Cormac the Lazy' ".

"Eight years after the period of our tale, King Art, then in his sixtieth year, kept Christmas in royal state in Ross of the long bridge, and before the last of the holidays, himself and his chief Brehon were found on the same morning, lifeless in their beds. If we can credit tradition, poison had been administered to both. When he was being borne to St. Moling's ancient cemetery, where rest the ashes of so many saints and kings of Leinster, there was wailing among the tribes through the length and breadth of Hy-Kinsalach. He was succeeded by a son not unworthy of his fame, and to him and his successors, was paid tribute by the Pale for one hundred and fifty years after the fight of the 'Bloody Ford' ".

CHAPTER XXI.

A DAY AT DUFFREY HALL.

EDWARD did not again resume the penknife, ruler, nor rod, but spent the interval before setting out for the city, in winding up his concerns among the parents of his pupils, and paying his rounds of farewell visits. A great deal of concern was felt or shown by his different patrons, Father Cullen among the number, and at last the day of departure was approaching with the usual fatal steadiness which human hopes or fears can neither delay nor hurry.

Nothing during this time could be more cordial than the demeanour of Mr. and Mrs. Lucas to him; but he found that unless he contrived to appoint a private meeting, he had not the slightest chance of an unheard conversation with Margaret. Owing to his resolve in the matter, it may be supposed that he did not directly seek an interview, but he would not have been at all sorry if it would occur without contrivance. He was frequently at her father's, and enjoyed the very chequered pleasure of hearing her sweet tones, and delighting his eyes with the graceful and modest, but now saddened lines of her features; and finally we were at the last day of his sojourn among us.

That evening I dismissed my pupils at a rather earlier hour than usual, after Edward had paid his farewell visit to his now deserted flock, and he and I indulged in a walk towards the wood. We came upon our young friends the Lucases, who were occupied at the useful, but unpoetical task of weeding a fine plot of potatoes sowed in drill. They were soon to give up their labours for the evening, and we fell to work with them heart and hand. The conversation among six or seven young people engaged in a mere mockery of labour, could not be otherwise than of a sprightly character, and I suppose Margaret and Edward were not sorry for the opportunity of exchanging some words even on subjects that were not

otherwise interesting. Good-natured Jane managed to
draw him a perch or so away from the group, and to keep
that distance between themselves and the rest, so that
they might converse unheard. Edward afterwards gave
me the substance of the conversation.

"Well, Mr. O'Brien, you are leaving us for good and
all. I suppose, at any rate, you'll pay a visit to Castleboro every year. Ovoch! no one ever finds his friends
or acquaintance the same way he left them a twelvemonth before". "True enough, Jane; I left my friends
near Old Ross one time, and Susan Williams among the
rest, just after being married, and she as blooming as
one of these potato-flowers. You can't believe what
a shock I got when I saw her again in a year and
a-half, with a thin and anxious-looking face". "Well, I
suppose there will be some marriages among ourselves
before you come back. Matt is acting the black man
like vengeance with my mother and father for Murtagh,
though I suppose he would n't, if he had any chance for
himself, or if it was n't to spite some other body".
"Well, and are you so set against poor Murtagh, that
you give all this bother to Matt?" "Ah! what fools we
are! Murtagh does not care a pin for me (*a sigh*), but
he seems to doat on the track of Margaret's foot in the
dust". "And I suppose it will not be hard to persuade
her to make him happy?" "Throth, I do n't know;
anyhow, I won't tell you. Do you think in your heart
and soul, he is good enough for her?" Edward was
struck on a weak point of his armour, and answered
hurriedly: "He is not good enough for her; nor do
I think any one in the neighbourhood good enough for
her?" "Not even yourself?" "Now, do n't be cruel to
a friend. I need not tell you how uncertain my prospects are; and even if I was owner of Munfin, I would
not think myself worthy of your sister". "Well, well, I
won't ask you to make me your father confessor. But
suppose (it will only be a suppose), that you were very
fond of Margaret, and that you are going off to Dublin
to-morrow, without saying one word to her about it, and

that she is bothered out of her life by every one to have Murtagh, and that she would rather a million of times wait for you, if she thought you were fond of her, and that she is shamed at last out of waiting for one that never asked her, and that you find everything looking well in a year or two, and fly home here some fine day, and get a cool shake hands from Mrs. Peggy Horan, instead of a heart's welcome from the same Margaret that you find just as you left her. What do you say to that?" "I say", said poor Edward, with his heart beating, and he almost ready to drop, "that I love Margaret beyond anything in the world; and that I would wait for her twenty years if it was necessary; and that I think I 'll go mad, if I find her married, when God enables me to ask her". Being very near each other, and the drills deep, Jane, unperceived by the rest, took Edward's clayey fingers in her clayey fingers, and never was a more cordial grasp exchanged. "Well", Edward, said she, "whatever one friend can do for another, I 'll do for you. If Peggy is worthy of you, she 'll wait: if she does not, you 'll have a lucky miss; but unless Harry and myself lose the little senses God gave us, you shan't be left one day in doubt, if the worst comes to the worst".

The evening's work was done and we returned home. Edward and Margaret were occasionally at liberty to speak to each other without being overheard, but neither seemed ready to use the fleeting opportunity. There was too much to be said; and the hearts were too full to be relieved by the outpouring of feelings for a few moments. So these few moments witnessed nothing but sadness and restraint. - Meanwhile Peter Lucas mentioned how he envied Edward his good fortune in getting into city life; and how himself, if it was his luck, would enjoy his tumbler of punch every day, and be at a dance-house every night he could, and go to the play, and listen to the fine singers, and keep a horse, and canter about on the Circular Road. Peter, though a steady young fellow, generally took a latitude in his discourse, which he never intended his actions to fill; so no one took him at his own valuation.

When we were at leisure in the evening, some allusion was made to the subjects of the previous evening, but Jane and the youngsters clamoured against the introduction of any more old chronicles of sufferings and dismalities. Mr. Lucas relieved their fears by saying that he would give them the substance of what took place at Duffrey Hall a short time after Denis's imprisonment, but there should be nothing very dismal about it. The gentleman who occupied the old seat at the time was Adam Colclough, brother of the Vesey whose disagreeable duty it had been to take Denis into custody. "The most ancient seat of the family is Tintern Abbey where our member, Cæsar Colclough, now lives. It was founded about seven hundred years ago, and called after Tintern in Wales. A knight built it in consequence of a vow he made when in danger of his life at sea. The Colcloughs got possession in Elizabeth's time, but they remained Catholics till within the memory of some old people I have talked with. The change of religion was made to prevent the estate from passing out of the family. The first Protestant of the name often served Mass when a boy; and before he changed, he tormented the poor old priest to allow him to conform outwardly, while he still heard Mass and went to the sacraments in private. The clergyman, as willing as he was to do any thing in reason, told him that what he wanted was beyond the power of the Pope himself to grant. So worldly honour got the victory at last, but the old influence of the name remained nearly as great as ever among the people. I do not remember to have ever hard of a tyrannical thing done by the family; and I have heard of numbers of kind and generous ones".

"I would not", said Edward, "desire a pleasanter occupation on a fine morning than a walk through Kilaughrim and Moynart wood, past Duffrey Hall, and up the gap of Scollagh, with glimpses of Black Stairs on the left and Mount Leinster on the right, marking the variety formed by the gray rocks and purple heath above, and the green patches lying like islands among them, and the

cultivated fields stretching down with their stone fences,
till they meet the clumps of big trees about Wood Brook,
and the noisy Urrin as it tears down the pass that's cut
out for it".

"I dare say", hinted H. W., "a person going the
same road up to Carlow on a disagreeable business, would
be affected very differently from another to whom it was
a mere pleasure excursion in agreeable company". A
look which the speaker received from Edward gave him
no encouragement to proceed, and Mr. Lucas commenced.
"Yes, I would recommend every one that wishes to enjoy
a thing of the kind, to choose a fine day, to have all his
debts paid before hand, to possess a decent little circle of
friends, if married, to have a wife of good temper, tract-
able children, a few guineas laid by, and a conscience at
peace.

"An old neighbour who was at Duffrey Hall the day
the things I am going to tell about, happened, gave me the
account. It was a little after the time of Donogha's affair.

"The master of the house was taking his ease in a
rustic chair in his garden; his three-cornered hat hung
on the back of this seat, and the curls of his wig were
falling on his shoulders. The features were expressive
of good nature, with a dash of testiness; two or three
neighbouring squires and some farmers were standing or
sitting; and the conversation embraced hurling matches,
hunting, and farming.

"A tall, muscular, high-featured farmer was seen
coming in at the gate: his lower lip had a habit of hanging, his brogues were innocent of grease, the straw with
which they were lined was looking out dismally over the
quarters, and through an odd hole in the uppers; his
gray stockings were not sound at the heels; it would be
a difficult problem to find the moon's age at the last
washing of his feet, and a needle and thread would find
useful employment through his garments generally. Still
there was no appearance of poverty about him; snuff had
left a fine brown colour in the neighbourhood of his nose,
but to mark his respect to his landlord, the dirt was

washed away into the caverns that lay in and about his countenance, and a strong yellow pin was doing its best to keep the collar of his coarse shirt fastened.

"There was a general smile on the faces of the company, two of the farmers exchanged a grin that had a shade of fright on it, and *Mihal-na-Raheen* made his salutation, clapping his greasy hat under his arm.

"'Well, Myles', said the squire, 'how is the vanithee? No complaint on any of the neighbours this morning, I hope?'

"'Indeed is there, your honour; my plough-irons were stole yesterday in the middle of the noon-day, and I 'm come to trouble you, sir, for a search warrant to look after them'.

"'How and where was the theft committed? This is abominable: I have not heard of a thing of the kind in the neighbourhood for seven years'.

"'And to make the matter worse, your honour, it was committed, as you are pleased to express it, in the open field, and the horses yoked at the same time'.

"'And yourself between the handles, I suppose; this is very unaccountable, Myles, to say the least of it'.

"'Indeed your honour may safely say so: I was ploughing away, and whistling to amuse the poor beasts, when I bethought how I forgot to tell little Jem, when he 'd be buying my pen'orth of snuff, to be sure to get it in two separate ha'porths, they way he 'd have the two tillies. So what could I do but run home, to see if he was gone, and finding that it was so, off with myself after him. Well, as I was hurrying on, who should I see but my brave boy picking blackberries on the side of the hill. As soon as he spied me, he laid leg to ground, but after a smart run, I *cotch* him, and maybe I did not give him a flay in his ear for miching. I then took the penny myself, and as it was only three or four fields farther off to Matty Doyle's, thinks I, I 'll go myself for the snuff, and be sure to get my tillies.

"'Well, as I was going in, I heard great talking and laughing, and I was n't much surprised at it, as I found

Jack Drooghan, and Simon Behan that I see here now, and Watt Forrestall that I do n't see, drinking hand to fist; a *point* o' beer before each man, and a full half gallon of it in the middle of the table.

"'Sith ye merry, genteels', says I. 'Your health, Myles', says Jack; 'here 's to the vanithee at home', says Simon; 'come Myles, take a drink', says Watt; and though I did not care to sit down so early, nor know that I had any money about me, they bothered me so much, and swore so, that they would not let me pay a penny more than I done already; I 'm sure I do n't know to this moment what they meant (here Mr. Drooghan winked at Mr. Behan, who twisted his mouth by way of answer), that I was obliged to give way; and so with their jokes, and jibing, and gosther, they made me swally more nor was good for me; and when it got into my head, what did I do, but like an ould ass, I pulled out a *thirteen*, and got in the worth of it; and, maybe, Cauth did not make the same thirteen ring on both sides of my head ever since. Well, your honour, the long and the short of it was, that my brother Peter found me in the *bocheen* staggering home, with both sides of the road under me, about sundown; and Shamus the cottier got the horses grazing at the end of the field, with the plough lying on its side behind them, and the irons gone; and with the drink and the balragging the old woman gave me, my head is splitting ever since; and now, will your honour be good enough to tell me what to do? I 'm sure that Jack and Simon there, with their grinning and winking they 're at *unknownst* to me, could tell us something about the articles if they chose'.

"Just as Myles got to the end of his grievance, a stout farm servant came into the grounds, carrying Myles's sock and coulter like a musket on his shoulder, and Myles, at the sight, stepped behind a couple of the by standers.

"'Plase your honour', said the boy, 'them tools were pledged yesterday with my mistress for two gallons of drink (here he got a glimpse of Myles's long nose and fer-

ret eyes); and as she heard this morning, that Mial-
na-Raheen was making a pullalu about them, she took
the liberty of sending them to your honour, for he 's
so conthráry, that she expected nothing but the hoith of
bad thanks from him; and she won't ax for the price of
the drink, as she hears he is hard set'. (*Says he then
in a low tone to Mr. Colclough, and looking at Drooghan*),
'Some one paid for the beer last night'. Then he spoke
up. 'And besides he spent a whole English shilling
yesterday when he got hearty, and lost a testher, poor
fellow! rowling home, and got a lambāsting from the
mistress besides.

"'And, you foul-mouthed vulgarian', says Myles, 'who
told you or your mistress that I am hard set? did I ever
ask her in my life for a naggin or a pint in score? If it
was n't for the presence you 're in, I 'd beat you within an
inch of your life, so I would; and see if I do n't get the
law of *her* for taking my goods in pledge'.

"'I 'm sorry to see you in a passion, Mr. Myles', said
the lad. 'Here is your irons; cool yourself carrying
them home. I wish good morning to your honour and
the other gentlemen'. He made a bow to the gentry,
and then turned to Myles. 'Better luck, sir, next time
you let yourself be overtaken. Ah, that was mortial
sthrong liquor you were looking at yesterday! My compliments to the mistress, and I hope she 'll throw no
more wather on a dhrownded rot, and that she 'll send
some one to mind you, the next time she lets you out'.
So off went the boy, closely followed by Myles, who was
encumbered with the ploughgear, and so angry that he
almost forgot to salute the gentlemen: he shook his fist
angrily at Drooghan and Behan, who could hardly keep
from roaring out.

"Mr. Colclough being obliged to preserve his dignity,
could not relieve his feelings by a laugh, but he seemed
no way disposed to prevent the rest from doing so.
'Here', said he, 'is a fine instance of exchanging a sheep
for a pennyworth of tar; yet I do not think that the
lesson will be of the slightest service to our departed
friend'.

" ' Not the least, sir', said Jack Drooghan. ' Have n't I seen him as often as I have fingers and toes, riding into town, on the old gray, of a summer afternoon, when I 'm sure his chief business was to buy two-pence worth of snuff in four separate ha'porths'.

" ' For all that, Myles can be generous', said Simon, ' when the maggot bites him. I saw him treating the congregation, last Sunday was three weeks, at least all of them that were too lazy to go inside the chapel before Mass, to a whole halfpenny leaf of fraughans'.

" ' I wonder àt it,' said Drooghan, 'after the hobble he got into the Sunday before. The day was hot, and Myles, out of laziness, or for sake of the cool, knelt outside the chapel doors. He was after walking on the Thursday, Friday, and Saturday before, all the way from the County Limerick, where his brother, Father John, has a parish; and you may believe, the poor man was tired. He fell asleep on his knees, with his head resting against the door-jamb, and Watt Forrestall, the thief of the world, slipped off his brogues, and hung them on the nails that were stuck in the wall, to fasten up advertisements.

" ' Well, when the people began to come out after Mass, the clatter woke him up, and there was his poor bare soles on the cold flags. Myles was n't inclined to keep his grievance to himself, and there was a purty commotion, every one helping in the search, and playing Job's comforter, but taking good care not to lift an eye towards the wall. It was only when they saw Father Stafford coming down off the altar, that some one pointed to the brogues; and *Magh go bra* with the whole bilin' of them before the priest got to the door'.

" ' With all this', said Mr. Colclough, ' Myles has many good points. He is a most obliging neighbour; you are welcome, not to his purse indeed, but what comes to the same thing, his time, his horses' labour, or his own; and when did ever a hungry traveller enter his house at meal times, without a hearty welcome to the potatoes' and milk? moreover he is strictly conscientious, and faith-ful to his promise'.

" ' All as true as the Gospel, sir', answered Jack, ' but by my *faicks*, I 'd rather, any day, have to do with a brisk lively rogue, than your hard honest man'.

" ' Well, Mr. Drooghan', said the squire, ' I promise you that your lively rogue will trick you out of a pound, for every shilling you gain by him: but if I do not mistake, here comes the Poet Laureate of the Duffrey, with his nose in the air, and composing one of his extraordinary ranns'.

" While he was speaking a tall ungainly man, with his big coat fastened like a cloak, and the sleeves dangling down, came sauntering up, his forehead and eyes showed the poet, but the lower part of the face was of a weakly character. His whole air and appearance showed he was fonder of wool-gathering and dreaming on his two legs than tailoring or working in his little field'.

" ' I wish your honour, and the other gentlemen', said Peter, ' enjoyment of this salubrious morning and soul-delighting view: may prosperity wait in your walks, and health sit at your tables: may your honoured, virtuous, and lovely ladies——'

" ' Thank you, Peter', answered the squire. ' Any new sacrifice to the Muses of late? Oh, confound it', said he then to himself, ' what have I done? I mean are the needles and shears kept busy?' The poet was the tailor of the townland, and a very bad one. ' How does the potatoe garden flourish?'

" ' Glorious, your honour, with thousands of thanks for your kind inquiries. I 'll have such a crop this year, please goodness, that I think I 'll put up a beam and scales, and sell to all the neighbours that come short'. His potatoe field extended to one half acre, Irish measure. ' May be the *Bhan a shrōn mhor*' (he meant Mrs. Fitzhenry of Ashgrove), ' won 't have all the selling to herself this season, any way. But in the central fountain of delights, as I heard Father Stafford read from a Latin book, something bitter arises; and I must complain to your honour, whose educated and lofty soul can sympathise with a poet's sorrows, that my neighbours are more apt to scold when a coat or breeches won't sit neatly on their clumsy limbs, than to listen to the effusions of my muse; and when one of the seams happens to rip——'

"'I hope, Peter, that our pleasure at seeing you is not to be disturbed by any complaints against your neighbours'.

"'Oh, make your mind easy, sir! Deuce a charge have I against man, woman, or child, if they would not be breaking in on my verses, when I do be repeating them aloud, for fear they would go out of my head. But there's Squire Jones of Achasallach; what does your honour think his mean menial of a bailiff does, when I went to draw home my little turf that I cut, or rather that I did not cut, but that my good neighbours cut for me, about a month before, while I was composing one of my best *ranns*, lying on the warm grass. Well, what does this despic'able hireling do, but stop the car and creel of the good friend that came to draw home the turf till the master's dues were paid. And what a *purty* squire and estated gentleman we are *inya*, and warn't we waxing our ends in a stall in *Ball' a Cliagh* when the Carews, and Hays, and the Fitzhenrys, and the Colcloughs, and the other ancient families of Wexford, were eating white bread, and the best of beef and mutton, and drinking claret and *usquebuidh*, and keeping open house for high and low!

"'Well, well, may be I did n't take satisfaction on the *naygur* in a few verses that I made, as I came home sitting in the empty creel. I composed them in Irish, but of course, I was then forced to find out English words. My sorrow on it for English, for thoughts do n't look the same in it all, at all; and the music instead of moving with fine free strides, seems as if it was a horse striving to get on with his two fore legs spancelled. Howandever, if your honour has no objection, I'll repeat them before the present honourable and learned assembly.

A New song in honour of Adam Colclough.

"Good neighbours, and the nine Muses, I pray you pay attention,
. While I sing of the scare-crow that keeps us in subjection:

Though he dresses fine and grand, the real blood of the county
Look on him with contempt for they 're all gentlemen of bounty.

" Can he compare his bogs and heaths to the woods of Moghurry,
Where the bugles were a soundin' and the huntsman a runnin'?
He thinks himself a lord, when he kills a black-nosed sheep,
While three ox-beefs are slaughtered in Moghurry, every week.

" No, but when he 'll go to Dublin to finish the old law-shuit,
He 'll put into his budget his ends and his awls;
He 'll lay them on his back, and carry 'em very *sausty*,
He 'll step into his bulk, an' he 'll folly his ould callin'.

" Now this Jones of Achasallach is a monkey-faced rascal:
He 's swarthy in the face, and admi'rable yalla;
Not so by Adam Colclough, he 's both white and red;
He 's handsome when he 's dressed, and much handsomer in bed.

" And Miss Kitty and Miss Mary, they 're both fair and tall,
They 're as courteous in behaviour as a fleet 'o man o' war.
When they walk in crimson mantles under the old trees,
'T 's Venus and Diana you fancy that you sees.

" ' You need not be grinning, Simon; if I did not
end the two last lines with the same letter, it 's yourselves would be the first with your stupid jokes and remarks, as you always are, when I only mind to have the
same vowels in the end.   Well, I 'm afraid I won't think
of the other verses with your bother.

" If you go to Achasallach, and stay but half a day,
You 'll surely have a belly-ache before you come away :
If you go to Moghurry in the beginning of the week,
You 'll get beer, ale, and brandy till Saturday night.

" Now may our Duffrey heroes, and the *Yellow Bellies* all,
For ever beat the Wicklow boys at hurling and football;
May Jones of Achasallach be banished over say,
And Colclough reign at Duffrey Hall for ever and a day".

" All began to roar out laughing, and Mr. Colclough,
whose sides were aching, cried out, ' That will do, Peter:
I really feel unworthy of praise, wrapped up, moreover, in
such sublime poetry.   No matter; I will speak to Mr.
Jones, and I venture to promise that you will see your

turf safely stacked in your bawn, before the week is out. Mr. Jones does not know an atom about your grievance, or he would have righted it long since, and I am not at all pleased with a part of your poem. Now here comes a gentleman much more deserving of your poetic homage than I am'.

"As he spoke, a tall, shambling, near-sighted, mild-looking gentleman, dressed in a clerical suit, a little the worse for wear, sauntered up, and shook the gentlemen and farmers by the hands, inquiring after their concerns, and the health of their families. 'Oh, Mr. Drooghan', said he, 'how is my good friend Father Stafford, to-day? Tell him that the money is scarce with me; and that I will not be sorry to receive these odd half crowns that come to my share from his late marriages. Remind him that I have a wife and children to keep up, while he has only his old housekeeper to provide for; and all his parishioners only too happy to come to his help. Indeed, I think he ought to make me compensation for the wear and tear of my watch-chain and waistband, every Sunday when I 'm riding to church, pulling out the old turnip every perch, either to quicken the pace of the loiterers going to Mass, or to calm the fears of the old people who are afraid of being late. As I can't succeed in making them good Protestants, I 'll make them good Catholics if I can'.

"'God bless you, sir', said Simon. 'It 's yourself that 's the good warrant to do that. I 'm sure, next to Father Stafford, and Mr. Colclough here, you 're the best-liked gentleman in the parish, and the most welcome sight, yourself and the little black horse, to the people going to Mass on Sunday mornings. But how is Paudheen, sir? Ah, that is a curious slip of a boy you have; would n't he strive, the other evening, to persuade a parcel of us, that you can work miracles?'

"'Surely that 's a privilege I lay no claim to', said Mr. Lowe.

"'Well, sir, I 'll only repeat his own words'. Says Paudheen: 'Myself and my master, were riding the other evening up by the old church-yard of Kilmcashil, when a cur of a dog ran out of one of the bawns, and kept barking, barking, barking, and would not let the master's horse alone. 'Confound you, you dirty *divel!*' says the master, 'lie down, and beg pardon'. With that, the unfortunate animal threw himself on the flat of his back, and put up his four paws, and began yowling, for all the world, as if he was doin' what he was bid. After the master looked at him for a minute or so, says he: 'Get up, you nasty cur out of that, and away with you!' and the poor brute only waited for the wind of the word, till he was off like shot, with his tail between his legs; and now, neighbours', said Paudh, 'what do you say to that?'

"'Well, whatever *they* said, *I* can say of Paudh, that he is the greatest tyrant of a boy that ever fell to the lot of a poor minister. It was only the other day, that Mrs. Lowe, taking it into her head that my company was not particularly entertaining, gave me a broad hint to leave the parlour; so, going into the kitchen where Pat was threshing, as the roof of the barn is not in good order; 'Arrah, master', says he, 'there is room little enough here without you'. 'Why, you terrible tinker', said I, for I was a little nettled, 'are you going to turn me out of my own kitchen?' 'It 's not a bit your kitchen, sir', said he, 'I insist that it is my barn'. But this nonsense has put the business that brought me here, out of my head. Poor young James Deacon will be buried to-morrow, and as his family got engaged with Mr. Wesley when he was through the country last year, and have never attended church regularly since, I hear that there are to be a couple of Methodist preachers at the funeral, and that they intend to take more on themselves about the funeral service than I can allow. I trust that you will all attend at the burial to-morrow, and in a quiet way, support the rights of your old clergyman'.

"'Oh, your reverence may make your mind easy!' said Drooghan, 'sorrow go with the swaddler we 'll let open his

mouth and your Reverence by; and we 'll neither beat
nor abuse him, nor say an uncivil word to him for all
that. Oh, sir! here is Jemmy Shanach, one of your precious lambs, that I 'm sure you would not grudge to
any meeting or Mass-house in the kingdom, although
by all accounts he is a dear bargain to you'.

"The honest fellow that was just after catching Jack's
eye, was a compound of laziness, indevotion, selfishness,
ignorance, and cunning. There was every appearance of
humility and respect about him, but he had a keen and
unquiet eye; and the leer at the corner of his mouth,
changed to a droop every now and then, and left a very
unpleasant impression on his hearers. Mr. Colclough
asked rather smartly what was his business.

"Shanach bowed awkwardly, and went on drawling.
'Heaven bless an' save de honourable master of Duffrey
Hall, an' de oder respectable gentlemen, an' de pious
clargyman, an' de good naybours. I 'm sure I ought
to ax pardon for presumin' to show myself in such an
assembly, but as 'umble as I am, me nor mine won't be
let alone by dem scruff o' de world; an' dat 's de rason
I 'm obleeged to intrude on de honourable company.

"'Mr. Shanach, I 'll be obliged by your explaining
your business in as few words as possible'.

"'An' dat 's de very ting I 'm strivin' to do, your
honour. I 'm sure dat me nor mine never wor known to
be sittin' in de naybours' houses, backbitin' nor havin'
disputes about Prodestin nor Catolic, nor anyting else
dat does not consarn us, nor envyin' de favour dat any
ov de tenants gets from de master, nor tellin' him tales
about dis body nor dat, nor picktanking, nor currying
favour'.

"'This is really too bad; you will keep us all day occupied, listening to your rigmarole'.

"'Traut, an' I wish I had n't any ting worse nor rig-
marowl to occupy your honor wud; but dough I 'm to de
fore, I have hardly courage after all to tell me story.
Well, well, as I see your honour is gettin' onpatient,
I 'll go on. D' oder evenin', Titty an' de choild, and

20

meself wor out takin' a walk; an' gettin' a little tursty,
we called into Matty Doyle's, and sot down, and got in a
pot o' beer. Well, while we wor takin' a sup, and talkin'
of one ting an' anoder, and not meddlin' wud cat or dog,
a parcel of dem fellas bowled in after us, an' sot down at
de oder table, an' dey had in a pot o' beer too; an' dere
dey could light on no cup o' discoorse but de consarns of
me an' me little family'.

" 'Well, what was the nature of the discourse? Be
brisk for mercy's sake: was it treason, or what was it?'

" 'Why, really, your honour, I 'm ashamed o' me life
to mention de goster de dirty divels wor goin' on wid: it
'ud be enough to make de very hair o' your honour's wig
to stand ov an end'.

" 'Well, if your modesty does not allow you to repeat
their talk, it can't be helped: I dare say it was no great
harm after all. Go into the kitchen, and get your dinner, and perhaps you will be in a better state of mind
towards your tormentors after it'.

" 'Bless your honour for your goodness! I 'm sure, only
I tink it my duty, I would n't demane meself nor your
honour, be repatin' deir abominable talk'.

" 'I am sure no one cares to hear it: go and do as you
are told'.

" 'Well, as your honour insists on de naked troot,
what de wor sayin' was, 'dat Jemmy Shanach's choild
was Mr. Colclough's choild'.

" There was a roar of merriment on all sides, in which
the squire joined from the teeth out. What was more to
the poor fellow's taste, he threw him a half crown, and
exhorted him not to let his comfort be disturbed by the
idle talk of Matthew Doyle's customers.

" 'May all sorts of prosperity light on your honour',
says Jemmy; 'I 'm sure I would n't care a farden for all
deir impedence to meself: what hurt me feelins was, dat
dey should take de liberty of bringin' de name o' your
honour widin a hen's race o' deir dirty mouts'.

" 'You have full permission to retire now, unless Mr.
Lowe here has any thing to say to you'.

"'Traut, an' its glad an' sorry I am to see his Reverence: glad to see his healty looks, an' sorry for losin' his
good opinion. Your honour must know dat de wordy
gentleman used to be axin' me de rason dat I did n't
attend church regularly; an' I laid de blame, as good
right I had, on me ragged clothes. 'Well, Jemmy', says
his Reverence, 'rader dan you should have dat excuse,
I 'll give you a coat meself'. Den, was n't I settin' off
to prayers next Sunday, as proud of me new coat as
a paycock, when castin' down me eyes, dere was de
breeches, all full of holes an' patches; an' Titty says
to me: 'Jemmy', says she, 'is it goin' to church you are
wud dat small clothes, like a gazabo, before de good
clargyman, an' de dasent 'congregation? Av coorse I
could n't do so despi'sable a ting as dat; an' his Reverence
findin' out, next week, where de shoe was pinchin', gave
me his own second-best pair of small clothes. Well,
den, de oul' caubeen an de brogues matched so bad wud
de coat and de oder wareable, · dat still I did not ventur
to show me nose inside o' de church, till at last, de kind
gentleman had me fitted out, from de new caroline on me
head to de pumps on me feet. 'An' now, Jemmy, your
sowl', says I to meself, 'won't you look respectable in de
pew next Sunday'. Well de sun was hardly as high as
dat big ash tree, when I was up; and de minnet I
done my breakfast, I sot down an' laddered meself for
a rale clane shave. As bad luck 'ud have it, Titty was
cuttin' her nails an' corns de day before (saven de company's presence) wud de razhur; an' when I tought
to shave meself, I might as well be raspin' me poor jaws
wud de billuke. Well, I runs wud de ladder on me face
to Tom Lamb's. I suppose your honour knows Tom: he
does be shavin' de naybours dere every Sunday mornin';
dey find it so hard to keep deir own. razhurs in order,
an' de poor hands o' dem does be so onsteady after
de week's work: but de room was so full, dat de divel
a shave could poor Jemmy get, till de people wor comin'
out o' de church. Well to be sure, I was so lude o'
meself, dat I took care to keep out ov his Reverence's

sight till next Sunday, bein' cock-sure of makin' me appearance den widout fail. So on Saturday evenin', just as I was fasnin' up de pig, and seein' de cocks an' hens safe on de roost, who should walk in but de divel himself in de clothes of Jack Drooghan dere, an' a bottle o' puttheen in de pocket of his big coat. He did not lave us till after de dead hour; and was n't Titty and meself a nice lookin' pair de next mornin', when we woke wud our heads splittin', about eleven o'clock. Well, next week dere was no soap to wash de shirt, nor no grase to put on de pumps, an' so wud one ting and anoder, I trew up de notion altogeder of bein' a spectacle among de good Christians; an' I 'm ever sense obleeged to spend de hours o' sarvice, sleepin' on de sunny side of a sheltery ditch'.

"'I suppose', says Mr. Lowe, 'you will allow us to believe as much of this true history as we choose.'

"'Deed, sir, an' if it was all as true as de prayer book, I 'd give your reverence lave to believe every word of it; see there now, an' why should n't I?'

"'Sir', says Jack to the clergyman, 'with your permission, I 'd like to ask Mr. Shanach a question or two out of his catechism'.

"'You have my full permission, but I own I 'll be rather surprised, if the answer you get be an edifying one'.

"'Well, Mr. Shanach, will you put yourself to the trouble of letting us know how many sacraments you have in your church?'

"Jemmy was evidently taken at a loss. He first took a peep at his questioner, then a look at the company in general; by and by his eyes took in several square miles of the mountain side: last of all he inspected his own brogues and Jack Drooghan's small clothes, and then relieved his mind.

"'Traut, an' Mr. Drooghan, you ought to be ashamed o' yourself for axin' de same question: you know well enough dat it 's seven years sense I saw de inside of a church; an' so dere may be more or less o' dem dere for any ting I know to de contrary: an' even when I was dere, I 'm sure I never took de trouble o' countin' 'em'.

"Shanach evidently considered that the question was about fixtures of some kind in the parish church, and gave his answer accordingly; however he was spared further queries on this unwelcome subject, by the entrance of a tall stout man accompanied by his three sons.

"The new comers were all respectably dressed according to the fashion of the time; and even a stranger would guess from their chestnut hair, blue eyes, and fresh complexions that they were one of the *Palentine* families scattered through the country. Being well known and respected by most of the company present, they received a cordial welcome and took seats at the request of the squire, who expressed his hopes that they would spend the rest of the day at the hall.

"'I wish, sir', said the father, 'that our visit was of so pleasant a nature: we are now returning from the church-yard of Templeshanbo, after interring the deceased aunt of these boys for the third time'.

"'Interred for the third time! only for your serious looks, I would suppose this to be a joke'.

"'I'd be very far from joking on such a subject, sir. The poor old woman was first interred about a month since: a few days after, there was a funeral which came from beyond the Slaney; and, next morning, the coffin in which the remains of my poor sister lay, was found perched up against the church door. Word was sent to us, and we laid it in the earth again, and set a night watch. All was useless, and this is the third time of performing the sorrowful duty. What can be the cause? We cannot possibly suspect Protestants for doing it, and I ask our Catholic friends present, whether we deserve a turn of the kind from any of our neighbours or acquaintances of their persuasion'.

"'I would take my oath', said Simon, 'that not a Catholic, great or small, that knows your family would do such a thing; but why any one at all should do it is as great a mystery to us as to you; especially as you are noted for kind and friendly acts to every one, without minding what persuasion they are'.

" ' Seldom', said Mr. Colclough, 'have I a case arising out of religious difference brought before me, and so this matter is the more annoying: but rather than you should be so disturbed again, I am sure that every family in the three parishes will take turn to watch; and I warrant that before one round is gone through, we will find out the sore spot and have it healed. There goes the dinner bell, and I think I see Myles passing by, stooping down to escape notice; his wounds are still open. Be after him', said he to a servant, 'and tell him to turn back and take dinner with us, or never see my face again. Come, friends, you are all my prisoners to-day; perhaps before we see the bottom of a decanter, some light may be thrown on this dark business'.

" The dinner passed off in the usual manner. The farmers felt shy and awkward in the beginning, but they were soon set at ease by the good nature and politeness of their entertainer and his family; and by the time they began to try the quality of the liquors the poet felt either the spirit of poetry or whiskey punch move him to enlighten the assembly on the antiquities of the church-yard, where the poor old lady was not allowed to repose.

" ' With submission', said he, 'I beg to drink to the strength and endurance of the roof-tree of Duffrey Hall. May it endure as long as grass grows, or water runs, and while a tomb-stone stands in Templeshanbo. Perhaps all of this honourable company have not heard of the first founding of that old burial ground. So, with permission, I 'll give a slight sketch of it, taken from an Irish poem that I have by heart. People do be telling me that I am no great things in English verse myself : may be so, but here I hope for luck, as I will give the sense only of the old poem, one word after another'.

" But you all know about the serpent of Lough na Peisthe, so I need not repeat Peter's poem. Indeed I could n't if I tried. All I know of it is that he made a knight in armour kill the serpent. When the poem was over he went on:—

" ' I 'm sure that most of this well-born assembly know

how this faithful warrior, in thanks for the victory, intended to build a church at the old rath of Cromoge (you may still see its trench and bank, as you go towards the cross of Kilmeashil); but getting up one morning, after a dream he had the night before, he followed a duck and mallard that flew before him, till they lit, one on each side of the mountain stream that flows through the rocky and bushy glen where the churchyard of Templeshanbo lies now. So he built a house for monks where the drake alighted, and one for nuns on the other side. This passed about eight hundred years ago; and of course, the nuns' burying-place was on one side of the stream, and the monks kept to the side next the rising of the sun. Well and good, long after both buildings went to decay, or were destroyed, the country people still kept laying their dead in the old way, and no womankind ever attempted to bury herself on the men's side'. 'That's true anyhow', said Mr. Drooghan. 'At last and at long, the great trooper, Daniel Jourdan (heaven be his bed), that fought under the brave Sarsfield at Aughrim and Limerick, and who, after he returned from the wars, hunted the army from the old chapel of Shroughmore to the Bloody Bridge;—this brave and devout warrior, when he was dying, ordered himself to be buried before the church door, with his sword by his side, his cuirass on his breast, and the crested helmet on his head'. Here one of the young Ballinlugg boys cried out, 'Father, my aunt is laid close beside the tomb of this famous warrior, and as sure as you live, some one or other has taken offence that a woman should be buried on the men's side, and so near this great trooper, and she a Protestant too, and has got her removed'.

"Mr. Colclough struck the table with such a good will that the glasses danced, and then cried out, 'By the old ruins of Tintern, the boy is right. Why did you bury your sister in that forbidden place? is it possible that you never heard before of the tradition?'

"'Sir', answered the Palentine, 'we live a good way from the church-yard, and besides our people do not heed or pay much attention to these old legends. If I was aware of the custom, you may be sure that I would not attempt to offend my neighbours by violating it: but why did not my friends, Drooghan, and Behan, and Forrestall give me some information before the matter went so far?'

" ' Why', says Jack, ' you must recollect surely, that the three of us were at the fair of Rathdrum, on the day of the burial, with our cloth'. And says Mr. Colclough, ' I was in Dublin'. 'And I at my relatives in Old Ross', said Mr. Lowe. ' We could have enlightened you as well as any, if we had heard of the matter sooner'. ' Well', continued Drooghan, ' I suppose that many others, thinking you knew the custom well enough, and broke through it in a devil-may-care way, would take no trouble about it one way or other'.

" ' You will never lose any thing', said Mr. Colclough, ' by making yourselves well acquainted with the popular traditions, and prejudices, and customs of your neighbours, and paying ordinary attention and respect to them, whenever by so doing you need not offend against morality or religion; but talk is cheap; we must set out to undo the mischief. I think we 'll have day enough for a walk to the church-yard, to remove the body from its unfortunate neighbourhood'.

" No sooner said than done: the whole dinner party proceeded on foot or horseback, to Templeshanbo, the procession swelling as it went, as it was joined by the roadside people, and those who were at work in the adjoining fields. Father Stafford met them and turned back, holding a brisk conversation with the minister. The good-natured dispositions of these gentlemen attached them in the beginning to each other; and there was always some unsettled subject, either in learning or divinity, on which they wished to hold further discussion. The grave was soon opened, and the coffin borne across the brook, and a new grave prepared. All being ready, it was lowered into its last resting place, and the clay thrown in, and the grassy ridge nicely arranged in respectful silence.

" Mr. Colclough, standing on a green hillock with the

two clergymen on each side of him, made a motion as if he wished to say a few words.

"A deep silence fell on the crowd, while their landlord briefly mentioned his friend's previous ignorance of the legend connected with the burial place, and his sorrow for having unintentionally broken through one of their old customs, and hoped they would receive the apology in as good a spirit as it was given.

"He then jokingly mentioned his surprise, how long the custom should have held out, separating those in death who had been so fondly attached to each other through life; and in conclusion he expressed his hopes, that the only strife among the Protestants and Catholics under his jurisdiction would be a strife of friendly actions towards each other. The sacred character of the place prevented any noisy sense of the satisfaction given by the speech, but there was a general waving of hats and handkerchiefs, and an agreeable murmur of pleasure and approbation.

"Myles was in such good humour, that he actually expended a full halfpenny-worth of snuff in promiskis pinches among those who surrounded him, and which at going to bed he regr—— no, this was only a report: Myles would not regret even a full pennyworth of snuff spent on such an occasion. Indeed, so little did he profit by yesterday's lesson, that when Mr. Colclough was quitting the church-yard, he saw him in the clutches of Drooghan, Behan, and Forrestall, led off like a lamb to the next beer-house.

"However, catching a sight of Mr. Colclough's clenched hand, they reluctantly let go the prize; and Myles being called up by that gentleman, went home in safety; and Cauth ignorantly congratulated herself on the good effects of her late curtain lectures. As the crowd was dispersing, the poet was seen lying on his back, his head resting against an old gray stone, his hands clasped under his head, and his eyes enjoying the glorious scene formed by the sun, the clouds, the mountain ridge, the cool rays, and the unsteady shadow beneath them.

"I have often thought of the uncomfortable and useless life of a person who takes pleasure in nothing but reading, or studying, or talking with others that have a taste like himself, if he is obliged to labour for his support, and has no one about him to whom he can let himself out on those things that give himself any real delight".

The collector of these country records has only a dim recollection of the old church-yard, having been within it only once in his life. The impression left on his mind is that of two banks of broken ground, with a brawling stream between, the rich verdure studded in thousands of places with moss-covered, gray monumental stones both on the upper levels and the sloping sides, the little church pleasantly perched on the left bank, with some trees scattered round, and the great purplish expanse of Mount Leinster's sides at the rear. A funeral, furnishing red, yellow, and green tints in the women's dresses, and a gigantic fan of cool rays flung over the wide, undefined, purple back-ground, combining with the normal appearance of the picturesque cemetery, would produce a very fine landscape.

The last adieus were given by Edward to my godmother's family, Mrs. Hogan and her family, and to the Donovans. He left the Lucases to the last. He made no attempt to speak to Margaret alone. So the parting between them was of a constrained character. Indeed some of the juniors, Jane included, did not seek to check their tears; and whether with or without consent, they came to the eyes of Margaret and Edward. Finally, his place at the few firesides where he had found a friendly home, was vacant; but we were not left without intelligence from him, more than a fortnight at a time. Sometimes the letters were cheerful in complexion; sometimes they spoke of obstacles arising from the ill-feeling of an officer in the establishment; but from all, it was evident that he was making incessant struggles to give satisfaction to his employers, and secure an independent position

for himself. Margaret's parents spoke to her on several
occasions on Murtagh's behalf; but though most respectful and affectionate in her demeanour, she remained firm
in her determination not to marry yet, and she assured
them that it was not at all probable that she would
ever feel disposed to accept Murtagh as her husband.
He bore this coldness with a reasonable share of philosophy. To say truth, Jane's partiality for him began to
make him endure Margaret's indifference with some composure. He often took occasion to speak to her about
his grievance, and seemed the less affected the more he
complained.

CHAPTER XXII.

CASTLE DOCKRELL CHAPEL: SUNDAY EVENING: AND A WHITEBOY TRAGEDY.

IT was pleasant on a fine autumn morning, to sit on the
southern brow of Coolgarrow Hill among the heath and
rocks, and gaze east and south over the valley through
which the Slaney rolls, and let the gladdened eyes
repose on fields of ripe corn and green potatoes, on the
shorn meadows, the furze-clad edges of hill-slopes, and
the varied tones of the foliage of the oak wood at your
feet. The charm of all these, either seen distinctly, or
through the silver haze arising from the streams, and
low-lying inches, and the impressive silence of the morning of rest, stilled mental trouble, and enthralled the
senses, so that nothing seemed wanting for perfect enjoyment, but rest for the body, while the eye drank in
enjoyment from the balmy air, the sunshine, the mellow-
coloured spots where the light fell freely, and the cool
shadows thrown from the trees and hedges. But we
must put a limit to this dreamy enjoyment: the cloaks
and bonnets of the young girls descending to Mass
through the pass of Glanamoin, come into sight; and
people are seen in the doors of the farm-houses, looking

up lazily at the sun to make an approximate guess at the hour. It is near eleven o'clock, and if we wish not to be late at the chapel, let us join one of the little streams of wayfarers, all converging to the cross-roads of Castle Dockrell. As we advance, the numbers thicken; and when we approach the chapel-gate, a crowd is seen spelling out the following poetical advertisement fastened on one of the posts:—

"Let youths of true merit, and perfection neat,
Repair to Rossard, with books so replete,
To embellish their minds with mathematical lore,
And lay up a lasting, and valuable store.
K—— will teach with attention true,
And show them a ready and unerring clue.
The sacred departments his scholars now fill,
To his friends and the public, do evince his skill.
With the following branches he means to make known,
With accuracy and attention, he 'll teach every one.
Reading and writing he means to explore;
Arithmetic, the theory and practice, by way of lecture:
Mensuration with rule and compass expound,
Gunnery and fortification criterionly found, etc., etc., etc.'.

Mr. K——'s mathematical powers need not be guaged by the quality of this composition. He was really a good mathematical scholar, but took more complacency out of his supposed poetical talents, than out of his knowledge of number and magnitude.

Our little chapel was provided with comfortable grassy divans on the inside of the yard-wall, which were appropriated by the early visitors when they had performed some preparatory devotions inside the cool building; and there they lay or sat, lazily discussing the gossip of the parish. As many of the young children as could be collected, were arranged in one class within the chapel, and taught from Father Devereux's catechism till Mass would commence. On this particular Sunday, two shame-faced young fellows were lounging at the chapel-gate, ornamented with handkerchiefs slung round their necks in the style of slings. These appendages supported a pair of good-sized cannon balls, which they had been convicted of bowling along the highway on that day fortnight, to

the supposable danger of wayfarers who, happily for themselves, were on some other road at the time. Thus, though
no one was hurt, some one might have been, or some
malicious informer might throw a slur on the moral
government of the parish; and therefore the offenders
were ordered by poor Father Cullen to attend there on
that identical day with the 'corpus delicti' exhibited in
the manner aforesaid by way of public penance. The
cunning penitents were rather chary of exhibiting their
symbols of woe, till the time at which they expected the
approach of the priest: but as soon as his hat, his snuff-
coloured surtout, his corduroy-breeches, and top-boots
came into sight, there they were at each side of the gate,
as stiff as sentinels, and as sheepish as public penitents
ought to be. The good father was little gratified by the
spectacle, for it was probable that he had forgotten his
order. "Well, boys, I hope you are sensible of the im-
propriety of your behaviour, and the danger you might
have caused, and the scandal you gave to the neighbours
and the Protestants of the parish, by breaking the Sab-
bath with such dangerous sport". Here some additional
misery was pumped into their faces by the two rogues, as
they well knew that their lecturer could not endure the
sight of dejection or sorrow for ten seconds when it was
in his power to relieve it. The muscles of his face began
to relax, and his words to lose their coherence as he continued, "Well, well, I see you are penitent; and you
have attended punctually as you were directed; and so,
as I am afraid that if you came inside with these ornaments, there would be a few of the congregation paying
more attention to you than to their prayers, take them
into one of the houses till Mass is over, and let me have
no more work of this sort".
    The vestments and sacred utensils, which were carried
behind the saddle, carefully packed in a kind of gigantic
purse with a slit in the middle, being now arranged
on the altar, and the candles lighted, the good Father
began to assume the priestly garb, interrupting the
operation from time to time with some uncomplimentary

remarks on the dilatoriness of some of his people. So keenly did he feel for any one losing Mass, that I believe he would have waited for a dawdler coming down Cran Rua Hill at more than half a mile distance, if he could catch a sight of him through the window over the entrance.

All being now ready, and the people on their knees, Mass commences, and the faces vacant a few minutes since, are now mantled with a devout and earnest expression, and following in their manuals the progress of the rite, and thir owners uniting their prayers and intentions to those of the priest; or, if unable to read, repeating the Lord's Prayer and Hail Mary, and the Acts and Litanies. In the chapel of Castle Dockrell, as well as in many another chapel in country and city, there were many instances of distraction at prayer, of gaping about, and yawning; but during the consecration and elevation every one seemed under the full influence of devotional awe. After the communion, our clergyman turned round, and taking some parish topic for his text, either a sudden death or the fall of a house by which some family was injured, or some scandal, such as the one mentioned, held forth in a style more energetic and apposite than flowery. How hopeless soever the affair might seem at the beginning, or how sharp the rebuke he was forced to give, his heart would not allow him to leave his audience under such dejection at the close. The bowlers would surely cease their dangerous exercise; if any family had been dilatory about sending for him on a sick call, surely the like would never happen again; and if any poor needed relief, a subscription was set on foot. At this juncture an incipient smile might be seen creeping over many faces in expectation of the standing joke at which they had laughed ten years in succession.

After Paddy Doyle, Jemmy Whitty, Bill Henrick, Tom Neil, Jem Kehoe, and others had signified their intention of giving a shilling each, there would be a pause while all looked towards a giant with a wooden face at the bottom of the chapel. At last a squeaking voice (the owner not visible) would be heard announcing "Michael Short will give a shilling"; and then the giant's mouth would expand, and out come as from a barrel, "And Michael Long will give another". This concluded the collection; the priest turning round resumed the prayers, and soon came the last Gospel, the prayers for the faithful departed, and the sprinkling of the holy water previous to the dispersion.

The inhabitants of the House of Commons are liable to catch colds in their heads in consequence of the wonderful skill and care of their domestic architect, and the fabulous amount of money expended on his plans; but the congregation of Castle Dockrell were exempt from this inconvenience. If any perverse individual was minded to throw a draft of air on himself or his neighbours, he could not manage it without breaking a pane, as the provident architect had so constructed the windows, that they would not open either by rope, pulley, and weight, or by easy working hinge. No state of things, however, being perfectly comfortable in this vale, we suffered a trifle in summer, from the collective breaths of so many people; and welcome was the cool air in the shadows of the trees by the road side. as we afterwards wended our way homewards in groups. How sweetly did the sunlight and the shadows fall on the meadows, and the woods, and the hill-side fields, and the road that led through all, as we leisurely returned home, and conversed on the subject of the exhortation. Youths and maidens who read these recollections of past days, do not wish too eagerly for manhood or womanhood, and their cares and duties; and let not ambitious longings prevent you from enjoying the fresh bubbling day-spring of early life and innocence. Remain young as long as you can; take an interest in your common, every-day duties, and preserve your innocence, and the favour of your Creator, for nothing in after years can compensate for their loss. Strolling along bye-paths through the fields, we take a look at the browzing sheep and cattle, and inspect the crops; and soon after getting home, the dinner of bacon and cabbage, and newly-dug potatoes is laid on the table. I meet the careful portion of my pupils in the school, for a couple of hours' catechetical instruction in the afternoon; and when we return, we find a vigorous match of football going on in my godmother's paddock.

Now and then, a dance took place on the top of Bullān a Rinka, but in general this amusement was discouraged by the priest and the fathers and mothers of the parish. Yet, if countenanced by the presence of the senior branches of families, what amusement is more genial, innocent, and interesting than a hearty jig, or reel, or country dance! but, just as in other things, the abuse has banished the moderate use of this healthy recreation.

Our present business however is with the little paddock lying below, or on the north side of my godmother's kitchen garden. A furze knoc spread below this again, towards the Glasha, and a little stream ran below its western fence into the same river, a stoney lane interposing between stream and paddock. So if you sat in the shelter of the grassy mound that served for fence on the higher eastern side of the field, you had a delightful view over the side of the neighbouring hill and the lower wide valley of the Duffrey. It is evening in autumn, and the sun is fast descending towards the mountain; and the outlines of the ridges are nearly lost in a flood of hazy light which covers the sides of the hills, but leaves the nearer objects in the valley visible. All these objects harmonise in the hazy warm evening. You enjoy the sight of the farm-houses with their bawns surrounded by elder bushes, the cattle passing home along the stoney lanes, and the blue smoke arising from the chimneys, and announcing the welcome supper.

The young boys of the village and those of the neighbouring houses in Ballinahallin are kicking football in the paddock, as if the evening was not warm enough without the exercise; and the young girls are playing at *high gates* and *thread the needle,* assisted by the lads not grown enough for the other exercise.

James K., Owen Jourdan, and other serious-looking

individuals are sitting along with the writer of this chronicle on the sunny slope of the higher fence, enjoying the
warmth of the evening sun, the view of valley and mountain, and the rough pastime of the juniors.   H. W. gives
the latest intelligence from Edward, and mentions the
sketch of old times at Duffrey Hall, as given by Mr.
Lucas; and Mr. James K., coupling the narrative with
the action going on before us, asks if Mr Lucas had said
any thing about a great hurling match that took place in
the time of the same Adam Colclough.   We mentioned
that he had told us of it, and of bearded men going home
crying after their defeat, and had repeated the hurling
song composed by Bacchus O'Cavanagh in his sycamore
tree.   This gave occasion to Owen Jourdan to show the
contempt in which he held poets and poetry.   His speech
included matter already known to the reader, but there
can be no harm in presenting it again in the light in
which brave Owen contemplated it.

"I think", said he, "the ould race of poets have died
out, and indeed it 's no great loss.   I never see one of
the trade that had good sense like other people.   Mr.
James, you might have seen Micky Conners the weaver;
and a blessed weaver he was.   He sometimes put a trifle
of money together; and then sat down in one of the
sheebeens at the *Crosses*, and never crack-cried till he
see the last halfpenny melted in the beer pot.   One time,
they say, he drank his coat, waistcoat, and small clothes;
and had to stay in the straw till some neighbours *ruz*
the other *shute* for him.   And that was n't the only
nishthif he done.   Poor Paddy Breen the goose-plucker
was as industhrus a gandher-dagger as you 'd see from
Killanne to Cloghamon, till his brains wor blew out by a
song that Micky made for him.   He never put gandher
nor goose betune his legs after the Sunday evening that
he thief of a poet sung the lampoon for him at Paddy
Connolly's over a quart of mulled beer; but got it printed,
and kept singing it at fairs all through the country, till
he became a holy show and a gazabo to the entire world.
I 'm sure he got reason to curse poets and poetry, when

21

he found himself trusting at last to a caubeen, a threheen, and a sligeen, on his unfortunate head and feet".

"Do you recollect the verses, Owen?' "No indeed, I do not. I have not three verses of any thing one after another in my mind. I remember ould raimshoges of stories well enough, but I have no retention for poetry".

As Mr. James K. had the goose-plucker's song by heart, he repeated it for Owen, not being aware that some of the company had heard it so lately.

"Thank you, Mr K. Micky was once in Munster, and made a song about the ' Munster Lass' when he came back. Indeed, I never admired that same song much. I think he thought more about fixing hard words in the verses, than of showing how sorry he was for parting from her. In one line he talked about a ' lachrymal *duck* (duct) distilling tears'; and though I'm sure I do n't know the meaning of it no more than a crow knows when a holiday comes, it 's the only thing of the song that remains on my mind".

"Mick", said Mr. James, "was certainly no example of a man's morals being much bettered by his genius. Once when there was a pleasant company assembled and something good before them, Mick got a sup in his head, made a speech, and got great applause; and poor Father Stafford said in a jest, 'Mick, it 's a thousand pities you are not in the back settlements of America. You 'd make out a capital living, going about as a preacher', The thing passed, and in the turning of the wheel of Mick's life, he really was pitched out among the American woods. What was the surprise of the whole Duffrey, when news came at last, that he was really going about preaching, and was doing very well by it as far as this world goes. The priest now recollected what was said in joke; and he could neither get ease nor peace of mind till he put the salt water under him once more, and made off to find out the scapegrace and undo the mischief if he could. He went from town to town, and from post to pillar; and at last when he was tired of his life, he met his death from cold and hardship without meeting Mick;

and the poor countryman in whose log-house he breathed
his last, laid the dead body of poor Father Stafford in
the car as decently as he could, and trudged on for a score
of miles to get him buried in consecrated ground. Heaven
be his bed!"

*   *   *   *   *   *

The cows are driven home, and milked, and our old
friends are sitting or lying on stools, or chairs, or
the settle-bed turned up, and Owen Jourdan expatiates
on the advantage, in general, of having nothing to lean
or loll against at Mass, but to be obliged to kneel upright;
for he acknowledged that he had dropped asleep for half
a minute or so that day, as he unluckily found himself
within lolling distance of a form. "I am often thinking", said he, "how badly off poor Protestant ladies and
gentlemen must be, with their comfortable pews, and seats,
and cushions, for I know that I could not keep my own
eyes open a minute with such conveniencies about me".

"But Owen", said my godmother, "you ought to consider that people easy in their circumstances do n't feel
any way strange in their pews, so they have no trouble in
keeping awake, unless some imp is plotting to make
them fall asleep. I heard of an abbot, and he was
so devout that it was allowed him to see spirits, and
he frightened some of his lazy monks once, by letting
them know that he saw the devil going about bodily
among them when they were saying their office, and
striving to close their eyelids. I believe the nearest
things to pews in Catholic churches or chapels are forms
with backs, and indeed I think there is very little good in
people penning themselves up in the house of God, as if
they thought they were made of better clay than the
poorer part of the congregation. It is now many a year
since a whole family left the church, and two men were
put to death, and all for carrying family pride and
pretension into the house of prayer.

The Whiteboy Tragedy of "Seventy-five".

" At the old chapel of Bunclody there were some seats

allowed near the altar: the family of the F.'s had one, and the R.'s had another. There came ill blood between the women of the two families, and it went so far, that Mrs. F. said that she would not allow the other family to have a seat between her and the altar, and if they did not remove it, she would soon make it fly. Well became the R.'s, they were as stiff as she was stout; and one ill thing brought on another, till some of the faction of the F.'s got into the chapel of a Saturday evening, tore up the seat of the R.'s, and flung it out into the chapel yard. Next Sunday, the other party were vexed enough to find themselves treated so, and some very smart words passed; but early on Monday they got the seat fixed in its place again, and kept a sharp look out through the rest of the week. When people are bent on mischief, it is very hard to watch them close enough, so one fine Sunday morning the seat was found outside once more. The priest did his best to make peace, but all was in vain. The seat was once more fastened down firmer than ever, and the chapel was so well watched, that the devil put it into the heads of the F.'s to send for the White-boys, to come and give a lesson to their enemies as they chose to consider them.

"So one evening as Mrs. R. was sitting quietly in her comfortable chair, knitting, in walked four or five rough fellows in white shirts, and with masks on their faces; and without a word spoken, they seized on the poor lady, and prepared to crop her ears. Somehow they could not bring themselves to lay violent hands on her at her own hearth, and so they carried her out into the road. A little girl, about eight or nine years old, was in the next room going to bed at the time, and seeing what was going on, she got out through a back window, and ran for life to the next house, and told what she had seen, as well as the screaming and crying would let her. Well, just as the Whiteboys had cut off one of the poor woman's ears, the mask fell from one of the fellows' faces, and she knew him for a boy who had been a servant of her own, some time back.

"'Oh, John Daggan', said she, 'how can you be so wicked as to disfigure your old mistress! What did I ever do to you?' 'Oh, by this and that', said the ruffian, 'I'll not stop at your ears now: I'd be a fool to leave it in your power to hang me, so out comes your tongue'. The poor lady gave a scream that would split a rock, and just at the moment, who should come riding by but Owen Carroll, body servant to Adam Colclough of Moghurry. 'Boys', said he 'what are you going to do? Will you put it out of the poor woman's power ever to offer up a prayer for her soul?' The others stopped, on the thing being put in this light before them; but Daggan swore that they should go through with it; and in spite of Carroll's intreaties, it is very likely that he would have had his way, but a crowd of the neighbours that had got the news through the little girl's means, were by this time hurrying to the spot.

"Carroll made no attempt to escape, and Daggan got confused, and was easily secured; but the other fellows took the road in time, and all of them got off in different directions. Indeed, as every one had a sword or pistol, and the new-comers were not overwell furnished with arms, they escaped with little trouble. In spite of all that poor Carroll could say or do, he was taken along with the other, before the next magistrate, and both himself and Daggan were sent off next day, with a guard of soldiers to Wexford jail. Before, and on the day of trial, Mr. Colclough and Carroll's father worked might and main to save the poor innocent boy. But Mrs. R. swore to the words he used, and the counsellor twisted them to show that he must be one of the gang, and with some authority, or he would not be on the spot, and make use of the expression.

"Both were condemned to be hung at the old churchyard of Kilmeashil; and so great was the dread of the whiteboys, and the wish to make an example, that they got very little time to prepare for death. Poor old Carroll hardly ate or slept, till he got a petition signed by every person of weight in the barony; and then he

was off to Dublin with it, mounted on the best horse in
Mr. Colclough's stables.

"He rode day and night, and never closed an eye, nor
ceased going and coming till he had the reprieve in his
pocket, and was once more on his good horse, and shorten-
ing the road home. The day was breaking as he was
rising Tallaght hill, but the execution was to be at one
o'clock that very same day.

"To make his son's situation more sorrowful, he was
attached to a young woman, a farmer's daughter that
lived on the other side of the Slaney. She thought to
get speaking to him while he was in prison, but was not
allowed; and now it was heart-breaking to see the two
poor creatures looking at one another across the files of
soldiers that guarded the cart. She followed the procession from Wexford, the whole way till it reached the appointed place of execution, outside the church-yard. You
may fancy yourself in either of their places, if you like,
for I won't try to explain what they suffered during this
miserable journey. Clergymen were in attendance constantly, both while they were in confinement, and on the
road; and after some natural pangs on Carroll's part in
the earlier part of the day, and disturbance from the remaining hopes of a reprieve, and from the sight of his
intended bride, he turned his thoughts completely to the
object of his soul's salvation.

"Daggan did not lose his courage entirely, till the
procession got through the woods of Munfin and Tombrick, as he was in hopes that the band to which he belonged would be there to rescue him. Many an anxious
look did he cast through the trees, as they came along;
but when the wood was cleared, his head fell on his breast,
and he resigned himself to his deserved fate.

"All this time, the poor father, in a half distracted
state, was pressing on; and short and few were the pauses
his brave animal got to snatch a mouthful or a drink. So
the miles that ever seemed getting longer and longer,
were diminishing before them; and the stones, and purple
heath, and the turf clamps on the back of Mount Leinster,
were coming into sight plainer and plainer.

" Between Tullow and Bunclody he felt his brain so
confused and wild at one time, and at another as if he
had forgotten every thing, that he began to fear his reason
was gone. The poor horse's strength was nearly spent
by this time, but a kind woman that lived by the road-
side, brought out a mash to the beast, and a drink to
himself, and again he took to the road, and swept along
the beautiful edge of the Slaney, and through the fine
old trees on either hand. Little he minded mountain,
wood, or river; and he was soon pushing through the
paved street of Bunclody with many an earnest prayer
from those that stayed at home, that he might be still
in time.

" When he reached the cross near Cloghamon bridge,
and looked up to the right, there were thousands of people all around the old church-yard; and as he strained up
the hill he saw two miserable objects dangling over the
people's heads. He was still supported between hope and
despair, and kept waving the reprieve over his head.
The guards gave way to the rush of the people, the body
of the innocent man was cut down, and the poor young
sweetheart, Judith Gates, was the first to open a vein in
Carroll's neck with a penknife. All attempts to restore
life were vain; and the distracted father seeing the failure
of all their endeavours, went from one faint into another,
and lost feeling and memory for many a day.

" So the guilty and innocent met the same doom on
this side of the grave, and Mrs. R. nor any of her family
ever entered a chapel door afterwards. It all fell out in
the year " seventy-five"; and my father, a young boy at
the time, remembers being pushed under the gallows, and
feeling one of the men's feet touching his head".

"Thank God", said Mr. K., " that we have done with
whiteboys, penal laws, and rebellions: there is too much
ill blood still between Irish people, but nothing like what
it was in those old times; and there is a great deal less
of it in reality than in appearance. Many and many a
person who writes and speaks very violently, acts kindly
and liberally in his common intercourse with his neigh-

bours and acquaintance. Indeed I am sure that any one who deals spitefully or uncharitably with a person of another persuasion, is not a good Christian, whether he calls himself Catholic or Protestant".

"People do be talking", said Owen, "a great deal about the mischief that rises from conthroversy. Now I know that when people have a friendship and esteem for each other, 'arguing Scripture' never brings a real falling out between them. There is two neighbours that I know, living there beyant in Thuar, and dickens a day passes without a shilloo about religion betune 'em; and sometimes you 'll see one of 'em run out of the other's house, and swear he 'll never darken his door again. *Sha gu dhein*, half a day wont pass till they 're as thick again as three in a bed. Well there is another sort of people I like just as little as the *convarthers*. I once heard a person that wished to pass himself off for a liberal-minded Prodestin, say that he did n't care a pinch of snuff what religion any one professed; that he 'd let every one go to the divel his own way: and I 'm sure if I was in hardship, or wanted a compliment, I give you my word, I 'd rather apply to the bitterest arguer I know, than to that liberal-minded gentleman. And indeed I think it a very ill-natured thing to let any one go to the divel at all if you can hinder him: ar' n't we all the children of one man and woman? But at any rate, if people will argue, let them do it for the sake of saving their neighbour's soul, and first get their own catechism by heart, and then read the other person's catechism and prayer book, and not throw any thing in his teeth if he denies it himself, or if it is not in them books".

"All right, Owen", said H. W., "I lately heard from Edward that Sir Harcourt Lees, who writes so furiously in the newspapers, is one of the most good-natured men to his Catholic neighbours, and that all his servants are Catholics. The other day, a man offered himself to him as butler; and just as he was taking up his hat to go out after the engagement was made, he bethought himself of saying, 'I 'm sure, Sir Harcourt, that we will agree very

well, for I am a True Blue myself'. 'Ah, ha', said Sir
Harcourt, 'you are a True Blue, are you? In that case
I cannot engage you, for most of my servants are all
papists, and you and they would make a hell of the house
before a week would be over'. So the butler that was to
be, lost his engagement by not knowing when he had
said enough".

"After all", said James K., "we are not to blame religious discord alone for our national troubles. The Irish
and English races hated one another when all were of the
same faith; and if there was not a Protestant nor an
Englishman in Ireland to-morrow, we would be in no
want of pretences for quarrelling. With the continual
outward and inward struggles, and wars of our island,
sure it is a wonder that she is so well off. And whatever evils we suffer from the strife of the two religious
parties, they are preferable to the state of a country where
the spirit of religion is lukewarm, and the people think
of nothing but enriching themselves, and enjoying the
luxuries of this life. However, you youngsters can't be
too grateful that you were n't alive in ' 98' ''.

CHAPTER XXIII.

"NINETY-EIGHT", AS SEEN FROM THE BAWN-DITCH.

"THANK God", observed H. W., "that the most of us
know nothing of it only by hearsay. There is a very
conscientiously written book, of which I hate the very
sight, I was so often taken from my sports and stories to
read it for the neighbours on winter-nights, when I was
about ten years old; and there is such a quantity of sorrowful matter in it: I mean Edward Hay's account of the
Insurrection. Then after the reading, one body or another
that had been *out*, would begin and tell his adventures. I
do not so well recollect these, as I used to be so tired of
the whole thing that I would be asleep with my head in
my mother's lap. Our own family had not lived through

the time without a fright or two. I often heard my
mother say that during the entire summer, she was not
thoroughly in her right mind, but went about her business in a mechanical sort of way, like a person walking,
and working, and dreaming all the time. A person who
had been a simpleton and chiefly resorted Ballychristal
and the mountain villages, recovered the possession of
sound reason during 1798, and fell into his old state
when all was over. Mrs. Fitzhenry of Ashgrove asked
him one day after the insurgents had won a battle, what
he thought would be the upshot. His answer was, ' Make
your mind easy, ma'am, they must all *simmit* to royalty'.

" Our family being related by marriage to the Ralphs
in Bunclody, were not in so much danger as others; but
on one occasion, my mother and two or three children
were at a little distance from the house, the youngest of
all being within and asleep, when three mounted yeomen
rode into the bawn. These individuals had no knowledge
of our connection with the Ralphs. One of them dismounted and entered the house; but finding no one within,
he soon returned with a lighted sod in his hand, and was
about to apply it to the eave of the thatch. My mother
seeing what was going to be done, and thinking of the
infant within, came out of the hiding place, and was rushing up to them; but she saw one of the other yeomen
knock the turf out of his comrade's hand, and the three
rode off.

" Another time as my father was a field or two from
home, in a knoc of furze, he saw a couple of mounted
yeomen making their approach. He concealed himself
as well as he could; and when they were near enough, he
heard one of them asking the other for a charge of powder. Curious enough, neither was owner of a charge,
but this gave the hiding man very little comfort, as he
could hear the clank of the metal scabbards. On a sudden he saw them stop, and look very earnestly towards
the bog of Kennystown just at hand. A man was walking very leisurely on the stony way by the edge with a
musket on his shoulder, and he seeing how things were,

shouted out, ' Ah, you cowardly dogs, wait till I exchange a word or two with you'. Whether they were cowards or not, neither of them liked to stand to be shot, especially as they had no ammunition; and even if they had, their carbines would be no match for the long musket: so they turned, and forgot to look back till they got a respectable distance between themselves and the gun; and after all, the man of the gun was not possessed of a single charge of powder no more than themselves".

" I believe", said Owen, your father was a rebel, and shouldered his pike like many another good fellow in his day".

" He could not avoid being a United-Man, unless he wished to be killed or outlawed by his neighbours; but, thank God, he gave up his pike when all was over, with its blade as bright as the first day he got it. He felt more inclined to look after the safety of his wife and children, than to meet, at push of pike, some well-known face, or person who had never done him hurt or harm. However, he once attended at Vinegar Hill on some grand occasion, and found poor Mr. S——, an Enniscorthy citizen, with whom he often had dealings, a prisoner left at the mercy of some wicked old hags and thoughtless children. The poor man was wounded, and his tormentors were giving him a prod with a pike every now and then, and otherwise adding to his discomfort. My father, with the assistance of a comrade, got him out of their clutches, and saved him from further molestation; and when better times came round, you may suppose their former friendly intercourse was renewed with additional pleasure to each other".

" If it is agreeable to the company", said Mr. James, " I 'll repeat one of the rebel songs that I used to hear sung, scores of times. Some people are mighty curious about collecting old ballads and things of that sort, because they show what the people of the time were much interested about; and besides they preserve things that historians do n't think worth notice. Talking of histories there is no history of *Ninety-Eight* worth reading, or de-

serving of credit, but the one that was written by Edward
Hay of Ballinkeel, below Enniscorthy, and the one by
the Rev. James Bentley Gordon, Rector of Killegny, up
there in Bantry. Hay, of course was somewhat partial
to the insurgents, and the minister to the loyalists, but
both were truth-speaking writers, as far as they could
get over their prejudices".

"Often and often I pulled my hat or my hair", observed
H. W., "to the same Rev. Mr. Gordon, when going
to Lord Carew's school at Cloughbawn. We often met
him jogging quietly along on his mare, and his somewhat swarthy countenance looking so good-natured and
happy, and himself so careful to touch his hat to the
smallest or most ragged child that made an offer to salute
him.

"He wrote the History of the British Islands, an Account of British America, and also a General Account of
the Earth".

"Mr. W.", remarked Owen, "I hope you 'll now let
Mr. James repeat his treason song for us; and you may
as well write it down some day yourself: you need not
fear it will bring about another rising". So Mr. K. repeated to his attentive audience the lay of

The Wexford Heroes.

" Come all you warriors and renowned nobles,
    Give ear I pray to my warlike theme;
And I will sing how Father Murphy
    Lately aroused from his sleepy dream.

"Sure Julius Cæsar, nor Alexander,
    Nor brave king Arthur ever equalled him;
For armies formidable he did conquer,
    Though with two gunsmen he did begin.
Camolin cavalry he did unhorse them;
    Their first lieutenant he cut him down:
With shattered ranks, and with broken columns,
    They retreated home to Camolin town.

" On the hill of Oulart, he displayed his valour,
    Where a hundred Corkmen lay on the plain;
At Enniscorthy his sword he wielded,
    And I hope he 'll do it once more again.

The loyal townsmen gave their assistance;
   'We 'll die or conquer', they all did say:
The yeoman cavalry made no resistance,
   For on the pavement their corpses lay.

"When Enniscorthy became subject to him,
   'T was then to Wexford we marched our men,
It 's on the Three Rocks we took up our quarters,
   Waiting for daylight the town to win:
With drums a-beating the town did echo,
   And acclamations from door to door:
On the Windmill hill we pitched our tents,
   And we drank like heroes, but paid no score.

"On Corrig-Rua for some time we waited,
   And next for Gorey we did repair;
At Tubberneering, we thought no harm,
   The bloody army was waiting there.
The issue of it was a close engagement,
   While on the soldiers we played warlike pranks:
Through sheep-walks, hedge-rows, and shady thickets,
   There were mangled bodies and broken ranks.

"The shuddering cavalry, I can't forget them ;
   We raised the brushes on their helmets straight;
They turned about, and they bid for Dublin,
   As if they ran for a ten pound plate.
Some crossed Donnybrook, and more through Blackrock,
   And some up Shank-hill without wound or flaw,
And if Barry Lawless be not a liar,
   There 's more went grousing up Luggelaw.

"The streets of England were left quite naked
   Of all its army both foot and horse;
The Highlands of Scotland were left unguarded,
   Likewise the Hessians, the seas they crossed.
To the Windmill-hill of Enniscorthy,
   The British fencibles they flew like deers;
And our ranks were tattered and sorely scattered,
   By the loss of Kyan and the Shelmaliers.

"But if the Frenchmen they had reinforced us,
   Landed their transports in Bagenbun,
Father John Murphy would be their seconder,
   And sixteen thousand along with him come:
Success attend the sweet county Wexford,
   Threw off its yoke, and to battle run:
Let them not think we gave up our arms,
   For every man has a pike or gun".

Success attend the sweet County Wexford! we repeat, though not in the sense of our nameless bard, whose vigorous though ungrammatical verses we have preserved as we received them, for a literary curiosity, and a slight help to any future historian of that terrible time.   Owen now added an illustration.

"I heard one of the men that were at Ross say, that when the battle was lost by the drunkenness and folly of the Croppies, after they drove the king's men over the wooden bridge twice, and the commander of the English was reviewing his forces in a field, one side of the Three-Bullet Gate, they were all surprised to see a country boy with a long pike on his shoulder, come out of one of the burning houses, and walk very *promiskisly* across the far end of the field.   Several of the soldiers levelled their pieces to blow him into geomethry; but one conceited trooper bawled out, 'Stop, and I 'll show you a little sport', and with that he dashed across the field to a gap which the Croppy was making for.   Well becomes my brave pike-man; he turned neither right nor left, but charged the *sidier rua,* pike in hand; and as pretty a scrimmage went on for about seven or eight minutes, as you 'd desire to see.   The trooper at every blow aimed to cut the head from the pike, but the other was as watchful not to gratify him, and he soon found he had enough to do to save his own ribs from the cold iron.   At last the rebel took his opportunity to give the horse a prod in the shoulder; the poor animal reared, and while the soldier was knocked off his guard, he dashed the pike right into his side, and flung him out of the saddle.   There was a terrible shout among his comrades, but my brave, bare-footed boy did not let himself be hurried.   He stooped down, and took off the dead man's cartridge box, threw it over his shoulder, passed out through the gap, and went his way.   Well, you may be sure that the soldiers were in a pretty way, looking on while this happened, but the commander in a stern tone, gave orders that no one should meddle, as their companion had given the challenge, and only lost the game he was so eager to play.   'Now', said he, 'if the croppy had touched a single ha'porth of the man's property, except the ammunition, which is lawful plunder, you might make mince meat of him: but he has behaved like a regular soldier, and I would give twenty pounds this moment, to have him for a true and loyal servant of King George, but there is no use trying; if I sent any one after him, there would be another death or two, so let him go about his business'.

"I fear, Owen", said my godmother, "that your story is too good to be true, but ah! was not the burning of the poor Protestants in the barn of Scullabogue a fearful thing! how could they expect luck or grace after such a piece of inhuman butchery?"

"The brave fellows that fought at Ross", observed Mr. K., "and that beat the king's forces, as Owen says, twice through the town, and across the bridge,—they or the like of them had no hand in the murder.   It was the cowardly scoundrels that ran away, early in the morning, at the very first volley, and just as their comrades were dislodging the soldiers from the ditches outside the town—it was these beggars that fled through the country, crying out that the battle was lost, and the army was after them.   They overpowered the guards that were watching the barn, and set it on fire:—so about a hundred human creatures were sacrificed, and fifteen or sixteen of them were Catholics, including poor Pat Cox the piper: may the memory of their murderers be accursed!   Oh, it is the companionship of such villains that damns many a good cause.

"I saw two such rascals as these, in the heat of the rebellion, sitting one hot day so comfortable at a plentiful loin of mutton, which they had come by, not very honestly you may suppose.   Says one of them, looking across at his comrade, and his mouth nearly filled with a piece of fat, 'Thummaus, if this be war, may we never have peace!' and his worthy comrade made answer: 'Amān, Michael, oh!'

"I am sorry to say that many good-hearted poor fellows were hanged after all was over, merely because they had been the means of saving Protestants during the rebellion. In most cases, the people that were saved were not ungrateful, and did their best to get their deliverers safe off; but just as in the instance of poor Carroll, the counsellors against them used the evidence to make out that they were ring-leaders. Most sensible people that have a right to know something of the matter, agree, that only for the cruelty of the North Cork Militia, with their pitch caps, and the bitterness of a magistrate or two, and the burning of poor Father Murphy's chapel, there would not have been a blow struck in Wexford.

"It is a curious circumstance, that though the brave and honest portion that really fought and suffered, thought they were doing so in defence of their religion; the first contrivers of the insurrection were either men without a spark of any religion, or Presbyterians at the best. I only know one Presbyterian, Jemmy Cook of Thuar, and never had the curiosity to ask him what sort of religion he practised. The English government were so frightened at the devilish acts and cruelties committed by the Paris mob and their leaders, that they did not mind what treatment the yeomen gave to those they suspected to be United Irishmen. If they had thought over the difference between us who hold fast by our early faith, and the French who had hardly any faith at all, or if they had ever considered it worth their while to study the true character of the people, they would have acted with Christian judgment and discretion, and the after cruelties of the yeomen and insurgents towards each other would never have occurred.

"I am glad I can mention one agreeable thing that took place to my own knowledge. At the battle of Tubberneering, where the Ancient Britons were nearly all cut off, an English officer, who was wounded, was going to be shot at the end of the fight. A brave young fellow interceded for his life so vigorously, that he got him off, had his wounds attended to, and sheltered him till he could get away to his own people.

"Well, when the rising was at an end, this young fellow contrived to escape out of the country; and after a good deal of shifting and searching, he got employment in a factory of some kind or other in London. He was cheerful and industrious, and gave great satisfaction to his comrades and employers. As he was working away, one day, in a large yard, and singing to himself, he saw a party of ladies and gentlemen coming round to look at the works: he did not pay any attention till they came up to where he was, but seeing that one of the party was looking rather earnestly at him, he lifted up his eyes, and the moment he did, he dropped the tool he had in his hand, and cried out, 'Oh Lord! I'm done for now at last', he had heard of so many having lost their lives in this way. 'My poor fellow', said the gentleman, 'why do you say so? My dear', said he to the lady that was leaning on his arm, 'this is the brave, good-hearted Irishman that saved your husband's life: I am sure I have mentioned him often enough to you'. Well, the lady caught the rough hand of the poor fellow, and shook it with the tears standing in her eyes; and, however it happened with others, his goodness turned out well for him in the end; for this officer and his lady never ceased till they secured him in a comfortable situation, and they never withdrew their friendship: may be they are all alive and well at this very day".

"My personal recollections of the good old times", interposed H. W., "is connected with a review of the Enniscorthy yeomen, which I attended on the Slaney bank one evening about six years ago. My brave old nailer, Mr. Sly, broadsword in hand, put them through their facings; but such uniforms, such gaps between waistcoat and trousers, such paddings between the forehead and the headpiece to keep it from falling down over the nose, such awkward movements! The standers by were laughing outrageously, and as many of themselves as had a turn for fun joined in the merriment. At last a sudden shower came, and it was a strife between the warriors and civilians to see who would be first in the shelter of an

22

archway. Such a mingling and pressing, and such clattering of guns and bayonets, and all in the best good humour".

CHAPTER XXIV.

CHARLEY REDMOND OFFERING HIS NECK TO THE YOKE. THE TRAGI-COMEDY OF THE THREE GEESE.

WHILE the harvest work was in full operation, our seminary was badly attended; but when it was over, there was a crowding again for a while. Bathing in the mornings and evenings in the deep pools of the Slaney under Mr. Derinzy's house was delightful; so was a walk in the big meadow by the river opposite Srehearth; so was a search through the lower wood for fraughans on Sunday evenings; so was our usual social chat after night-fall, when our worldly cares were stilled for a time. I was occasionally a guest at Lucas's, but not so frequently as at Donovan's, or my godmother's, or at the mill. I succeeded to Edward in the everlasting solution of *There was a man that bought a horse,* for our worthy friend Paddy Lennon; so it could not be said, when I visited him, that we were in want of a subject. It may readily be supposed why there should be a coolness towards me at the Lucas's, though Murtagh was really not so much in earnest as of old. He was wearied of Margaret's indifference to him, and had begun to take considerable interest in detailing his grievances to Jane; but the father and mother went a trifle beyond what parental privileges warranted in too urgently pressing on Margaret the propriety and wisdom of giving the wooer reasonable encouragement. Judging that unreserved communication between the two girls and myself would not serve to forward their views, we found few opportunities of conversing unheard. However, it may be reasonably supposed that Margaret was confident of being uppermost in the mind and heart of Edward, from the surprised avowal which she had heard from Jane, and from chance snatches of conversation with myself.

However coldly disposed they might feel towards Edward's success in his protracted suit, or however unwilling that any lengthened communication concerning him might be made in the hearing of their daughter, I got an opportunity from time to time of reading his letters, which came every week or fortnight. There were threads of thought through the tissue of these letters, which indicated her influence on his heart, and which I am sure afforded her sincere pleasure and mental occupation for days afterwards.

The fine weather ended at last in the frosts and snows of the Christmas holidays, and we that were young, kept up a brisk circulation of the blood by chasing hares along the sides of the hills, by sliding when the ice could be trusted, and by thrashing vigorously when the labourer trusted us with his flail. No day school. I taught at their own homes, for a few hours in the day, and a few more at night, the Donovans, the K.'s, and the Hogans, and when the evening's lessons were dispatched, we conversed and told stories as usual.

It was one of these same frosty evenings at my godmother's. Our business was over, and we ourselves enjoying the genial warmth of the big turf fire. In the present instance, the fuel did not lie directly on the hearthstone, but on a grating like a harrow, that came within about six inches of it. By this arrangement the fire burned brisker and clearer, and as the vacancy under the grating was so shallow, there was not present that curse of our city fires, an icy wind running along the floor, and freezing the backs of our legs. I had received from the regular carrier a bulky letter from Edward, and I now proceeded to amuse the group with extracts.

"DEAR H.,

" * * * Our old school-fellow, Charley, has been employed for some time at the College Botanic Garden near Ball's Bridge, and is, I believe, as great a favourite there, as he was at Castleboro. You may re-

collect that I mentioned paying a visit to an old acquaintance in Bride Street in a house, the remains of old
grandeur. The best apartments of this house were occupied by a small family that had come from below Oulart,
and the men kind had thriving occupations in offices through
the city. The mother and daughter had sent a pressing
invitation to a cousin of theirs to pay them a visit, and
get a glimpse of town life. So she and a young brother
came up. Charley being a distant relative of the family,
and on cordial terms with them, was invited about a
month since, to a little party. So was I myself as his
shadow, and a very social evening we enjoyed. I have
been at little city parties, where foolish people had
gathered certain of their acquaintance, who were unknown,
or nearly so to each other; and I have spent the evening
pitying the hosts striving to provide for their hard-to-be-
entertained guests, subjects of discourse in which they
would take a common interest. I dare say these guests
were entertained after a way of their own, but it was
in measuring, weighing, and noting the dresses, manners, and complexions of their neighbours, criticising the
materials and the serving of the feast, and cutting and
shaping their own discourse so as best to exhibit their
consequence, and leave as little as possible of themselves
to be taken hold of when they turned their backs. I
bethought of the profitless outlay of the entertainers, and
sighed for the socialities of Castleboro and Tombrick.
  "There was none of that miserable affectation of high
life here. Everything was as genial and amusing as in
our own festivals of old times. The manner was more
polished, but the matter was as hearty and genuine.
Charley rattled away, carried on by that animal vivacity
at full tide that seems never to know an ebb. The only
pause was, when he was occupied making a mental picture
of the young woman that was on the visit. I have seldom seen a face more faultless, nor of a more composed
and gentle expression. She said but little through, the
evening, but if she did not drink in at eyes and ears,
Charley's humorous face and humorous discourse, I am

much mistaken. There being no reasonable grounds to prevent their seeing each other, they have since seen each other to some purpose, and here in the attachment that has sprung up is a fine instance of the mutual attraction of opposite dispositions. The lady having a fair little fortune, and the gentleman having good hands, a clear head at his business, and a facility of giving sound views on his profession through the agricultural journals, there seems no reasonable obstacle to our facetious friend settling down as the happy and useful married citizen. I wish the future Mrs. Redmond had a deeper country hue on her cheeks; but we can't have every thing we wish for in this world, as Joanna used to say. When I am in one of my waking dreams, I see my friend and his wife, my own wife, if I am fated to win her, and myself, all sitting at a small table, and talking of past doubts and trials.

"If I do not deceive myself, I may perhaps enjoy next Christmas in a more agreeable and happy mood than the present. When I can speak with any certainty, I will not keep the good news from you for one day. Meanwhile I pass my evenings either writing such stuff as the present, or reading the best works of biography, history, essays, or fiction that I can procure from Mr. Mac Gauran's, of Patrick Street.

"If my friend, Larry K., was only to be with Mr. Mac Gauran in his library one day, and could see the purgatory he endures from the whims of his subscribers, he would hardly think the inside of a shop full of story-books the paradise he fancies it. I got a fine shower of abuse on my head one day from a gaudily-dressed young damsel who came in to look for a dream book or *Boney's Araclon* (Buonaparte's Oraculum). I hinted to her that we are forbidden to search for knowledge of future events by such means; but I think my worst Bantry or Duffrey ill-willer would pity me after the torrent of abuse she poured on my humbled head. "Swaddler, hypocrite, and souper, were the mildest epithets she applied to me".

*　　　*　　　*　　　*　　　*　　　*

Here I stopped, and here Owen took up the discourse, and related the household legend of

The Three Geese.

"O, dear! O, dear! what headstrong crathers the womankind is! The more you want them to do any thing that's right, the surer they are not to do it, unless the advice is given to a young girl by a gay deludher of a young man something above her station, or to a mistress of a family by some tay-dhrinking, gossiping, cabin-hunting, idle sthra that does nothing but go about pretending to knit a stocking, and she does knit it at the rate of four rounds in the day. It reminds me of the tailor and his wife that were not satisfied without bringing trouble into their cabin, when it pleased Providence not to be sending any. The poor man was sitting content-edly on his board stitching away (I'm sure I wish I knew how a tailor manages to keep his thraneens of legs the way he does for so long), and his wife that was cabin-hunting may be, bawled out, just as she was darkening the door, 'Ah, you idle sthronshuch! there you are sitting at your aise, and a hundred geese trampling down our little oats; get up, you lazy drone, and drive them away'. 'Musha, I think', says he, 'you're more at leisure your-self; but rather than have a scolding match, here we go'. So getting up, he went out, and when he looked to the field, 'Arrah, woman,' says he, 'what's on your eyes at all? I see but two geese'. 'Two geese, inagh! purshuin' to the goose less than fifty there, any way'. 'Fifty! I wish I was as sure of fifty guineas as that there is only two in it'. 'Ah! goodness help poor creatures of women with their tyrants of husbands! I tell you up to your teeth, there is forty geese there destroying the oats, as sure as there is one'. 'Well, well, two, or forty, or a hundred, I had better drive them off'.

"When dinner came she poured out the potatoes, and laid his noggin of milk and plate of butter out for him; but went and sat in the corner herself, and threw her apron over her head, and began to sob. 'Arrah, Judy

acushla', says he, ' what 's this for ? come over and take
your dinner, and let us be thankful, instead of flying in
God's face'. ' N-n-n-no indeed, I w-w-w-will not. To
say such a thing as that there was only two ge-ge-ge-
geese there when I reckoned a whole score !' ' Oh! to
Halifax with them for geese : let them go and be shot,
woman, and come over to the table'. ' Indeed and I will
not till you own to the truth'. Well not a bit did she eat :
and when night came, she made a shake down for herself,
and would not gratify the poor tailor by sleeping in her
own good high-standing bed. Next morning she did not
rise ; but when her husband spoke kindly, and brought
some breakfast to the bedside, she asked him to go for
her mother and relations till she 'd take leave of them
before she 'd die, as there was no use living any more,
when all love was gone from him. ' But, Judy dear, why
do you go on in this way ? what have I done ?' ' Do n't
you say there was only two geese there, and at the very
lowest there could not be less than a dozen. Can't you
acknowledge the truth, you obstinate pig of a man, and
let us be at peace again ?'

" Instead of making any answer, he walked over to her
mother's house, and brought her over, with two or three
of her family; and they laid siege to the wife, but they
might as well be preachin' to a stone wall; and she
almost persuaded them that her husband was to blame.
' Now call him', says she, ' and I 'll insense you who
is wrong. Darby, on the nick of your soul, and if you
do n't intend to send me to my grave, speak the truth
like a Christian, and do n't be heapin' sins on your miserable head. I 'll leave you no back door, for I 'll only
insist on three geese, though I 'm sure there was six
at the very least; was n't there three geese in the field
when I called you out?' ' Och, Judy asthore! never mind :
let there be three-and-thirty if you like, but do n't let us
be idlin' and tormentin' our people here. Get up in the
name of Goodness, and eat a bit'. ' But was n't there
three geese there, I say, Darby?' ' Ah, dickens a one
but two if you go to that'. ' Oh, Vuya, Vuya! is n't this

a purty story? Go home, go home, all of yez, and bid
Tommy Mulligan prepare my coffin, and bring it over
about sun-down, and just give me one night's dacent
waking: I won't ax the two, for I do n't wish to give so
much trouble to the neighbours, and indeed I think I
could n't stand the ungratitude and conthráriness of them
that ought to know better, and feel for a body; and after
all that I done and slaved for him, and gave up Neddy
Brophy for him, that was six inches taller, and a carpenter besides'.

"Well, thinking it might give her a fright, they went
and brought a coffin that was ready made at the time,
and some fresh shavings in the bottom; and the women of
the town that gathered as soon as the coffin came, ordered
out the men till they 'd wash the corpse.

"She said nothing till the men were outside; but then
she gave tongue, and asked how dare they think that she
wanted washing! It might do well enough for a real
dead body, but she was thankful it had n't come to that
with her yet, and if she chose to die it was no concern of
theirs; and if any one attempted to lay a drop of water
on her skin, she 'd lay the marks of her ten nails on their
face. Well, she was got some way into the coffin, and a
clean cap and frill put round her face; and, as she was
not pale enough, a little girl shook some flour on her
cheeks. Before the men and boys were let in, she asked
for a looking-glass, and when she saw what a fright she
looked with the flour, she got a towel and rubbed every
bit of it off again.

"She bid her husband be called in, and gave her sister
and mother charge, in his hearing, to be kind and attentive to the poor *angashore* after she was gone: at any rate
till he 'd get a new wife, which she supposed would not be
very far off; for though he was unkind and conthráry,
thank Goodness she knew her duty, and she supposed he
could not help his nature, and it was better as it was,
before they 'd grow old, and she might get peevish and
lose her temper, and they might become a gaza'bo to the
neighbours by fightin' and scouldin'. 'I 'll engage now,

after all is said and done, he won't give way an inch, nor
acknowledge the three geese'. Well, the moment the
geese were mentioned, he put on his hat without a word,
and walked out.

"So evenin' came and the candles were lighted, and the
tobacco and pipes were all laid out, and the poor dead
woman had to listen to a good deal of discourse not at
all to her liking; and the talk went on in this way.
'Musha, neighbour, does n't the corpse look mighty well?
When did she die, poor woman? What ailed her, did you
hear?' 'Indeed I believe it was *Gusopathy*, as Tom K.
the schoolmaster called it just now, something with
'goose' in it any way: you know the way the skin does be
in a sudden cold with little white risings on it, they call
it a goose's skin. May be she had it very bad, and her
husband could not bear it, and so she died of grief'.
'Poor man, he'll feel her loss for a week or two: she was
a careful woman'. 'Ah, but had n't she a bitter tongue
of her own?' 'Troth I think Darby will bear her loss
with Christian patience. He is a young man for his
years; he does n't look forty, he'll be getting his choice
of wives. I think poor Judy was careful and laid by a
few guineas: won't the new wife feel comfortable, and
may be soon put wind under the money!' 'To my notion,
Judy was in too great a hurry to die. From her looks
there, she might bury two tailors yet, and may be get a
big bodagh of a farmer for her third husband. Well, it
can't be helped, but I would not like to be warming a bed
for the best woman in the townland if I was Judy. She
is at peace at last, poor woman; and mighty hard she
found it to keep the peace with her neighbours while she
was alive. Who is that you said used to be walking with
Darby of odd Sunday evenings before his marriage? If
ghosts are allowed to take the air on Sunday evenings,
poor Judy's will have something to fret her in a few
weeks'.

"Well, all this time, the poor dead woman's blood
was rushing like mad through her veins; and something
was swelling in her throat as if she was going to be

choked, but still the divel was so strong in her that she never opened her eyes nor her mouth. The poor broken-hearted husband came up after some time, and leaning over her face he whispered, ' Judy, acushla, is n't it time to be done with this foolery? Say but one reasonable word, and I 'll send all these people about their business'. ' Ah, you little-good-for crather, you have n't the spirit of a man, or you would never bear all they have been saying of your poor neglected wife these two hours past. Are the three geese there?' ' Not a goose but two if you were to be waked for a twelvemonth'; and off he went, and sat in a dark part of the room till daylight.

" He made another offer next morning, just as the _led_ was puttin' on the coffin, and the men were goin' to hoise it on their shoulders; but not a foot she 'd move unless he 'd give in to the three geese.

" So they came to the churchyard, and the coffin was let down in the grave, and just as they were preparing to fill all up, poor Darby went down, and stooping to where he had left some auger holes in the lid, he begged of her even after the holy show she made of himself and herself, to give up the point, and come home. ' Is the three geese there?' was all he could get out of her, and this time his patience got so thread-bare, and he was so bothered by want of sleep, and torment of mind, that he got beside himself, and jumped up, and began to shovel the clay like mad, down on the coffin.

" The first rattle it made, however, had like to frighten the life out of the buried woman, and she shouted out, ' Oh, let me up ! I 'm not dead at all : let there be only two geese, Darby asthore, if you like '. ' Oh, be this and be that ', said Darby, ' it is too late : people have come far and near to the funeral, and we can't let them lose their day for nothing : so for the credit of the family, don't stir ', and down went the clay in showers, for the tailor had lost his senses. Of course the by-standers would not let the poor woman be buried against her own will; so they seized on Darby and his shovel, and when his short madness was checked, he fell in a stump on the sod. When poor Judy was brought to life, the first sight she beheld was her husband lyin' without a kick in him, and a wag of a neighbour proposed to her to let Darby be put down in her place, and not give so many people a disappointment after coming far and near. The dead woman, by way of thanks, gave him a slap across the face that he felt for two days; and not minding the figure she cut in her grave-clothes, fell on poor Darby, and roared and bawled for him to come to life, and she'd never say a conthrāry word to him again while she lived. So some way or other they brought the tailor round; but how *her* and him could bear to look each other in the face for a while, I do n't know. May be as there was a good deal of love under all the crossness, they found a way to get into their old habits again, and whenever she felt a tart answer coming to her tongue, she thought of the rattling of the clay on the coffin, and of the three geese that were only two after all; and if they did n't live happy——but that's the end they put to lying fairy stories, and as this one is so true and moral, it can afford to do without a tail".

After Owen's story had been commented on, and some counter-charges made against the men by the women present, and I had dwelt a little on Mr. Mac Gauran's discomforts, I asked Larry if his opinion about libraries continued the same. He answered:—

"Indeed it is not. I do n't doubt but that it is just as pleasant, and a little more healthy, to make hay, and lie down in the warm sun when you are tired, or mind the cows; and I 'm sure it is much more agreeable to be coming home with a good appetite for supper in the summer evenings, and see the smoke rising up straight in the calm air, and see the shady mountain beyond the smoke, and hear the cows lowing, and the dogs barking, than to sit in a dark shop, and have nothing to look at through the door but a dead wall, may be. Still I suppose the librarian in Patrick Street would not change with one of us".

"The longer I live", said Owen, " the surer I am that every body, if it is not his own fault, may enjoy a mid-

dling good share of happiness, and that it is foolish to be
pitying any one too much, without hearing his own
opinion of his state of life".

" I heard a story long ago that this talk brings to my
mind. Just as you go towards Bunclody from the Cross
of Kilmeashil, and as you get over the hill, and have the
view of the mountain, and the woods all running up its
sides from the town, and the walls of the deer-park over
them, and see the tops of the houses of the town through
the big trees, and the hill beyond the Slaney. Ovoch!
where is my head!—just from where you'd get that
view, there is a meadow, and two or three thorn trees
very old, standing here and there, with the bark rubbed
off the trunks by the cows and sheep, and the ground all
bare under them. A good many years ago, the people
took notice of one of the cows that used to be doing nothing all the day but licking the bark of one of these old
thorns. No one ever saw her clipping a blade of grass,
and still she looked as fat, and gave as much milk as any
of the others.

" Well, they drove her off and off, and they might as
well let her alone, she always came back again, and
licked away, till at last her master brought a hatchet, and
cut down the tree; and when it was falling, there it burst
open, and a beautiful statue of Saint Bride was found
within it safe and sound".

" Oh, dear, was n't that nice", said little Kitty; "and
what did they do with it?"

" I do n't think I ever heard: perhaps they sent it to
the chapel of Kilbride (*Saint Bridget's Church*), up in
Carlow; sure it's worth enquiring about any way. I
only mention this on account of what we were talking
about: every one pitied the poor animal, and no one could
know the pleasure she had in licking the old thorn or the
good it *done* her".

My godmother's sister was obliged to do the singing
on this evening. She was a woman of little imagination,
and undisturbed by romance. How she learned the lay
that follows is a mystery to me still.

The Unlucky Lover.

" In Davidstown, of high renown, there lives a lovely maid,
 Perfect, complete, and consumámte, she has my heart betrayed
 She outshines by far the morning star, or the moon that rules by
  night;
 When first I saw this lovely maid I lost my senses quite.

" Diania fair could not compare, nor Venus from the tide,
 Nor Dido sure—that virgin pure, that for her hero died.
 There 's none so rare, or can compare, to that damsel of renown.
 Had I command o'er all the land, my love should wear the crown.

" I stood amazed, and on her gazed with contemplation fair,
 Awhile I roved within the grove, and then at length drew near
 ' Are you the maid', to her I said, 'that 's mistress of this grove,
 Or Luna bright that rules the night, that from the seas did rove?'

" Like an organ sweet this maid discreet addressed herself straightway,
 Saying, ' I never roam so far from home, but through these woods
  do stray.
 I 've passed a vow, I tell you now, these seven long years and
  more;
 It is in vain for to complain, so trouble me no more'.

" With great disdain she crossed the plain, and left me there alone,
 The small birds joined in melody, bewailing my sad moan,
 Saying, ' Arise, young man, I pray march on, your heart it was
  betrayed,
 But do not blame that charming dame, that was before engaged'.

" I hearkened then within my mind to what the small birds said,
 Advising me for to go home, and quit these pleasant shades.
 Home I went with discontent, my mind oppressed with care,
 May powers divine with me combine, and free me from despair !

" Now all alone I sigh and moan down by yon valley wide,
 Since that angel bright—my heart's delight, refused to be my
  bride.
 Each night I dream, rave, and complain, and ne'er enjoy my rest,
 The pain I endure no man can cure, it lies within my breast".

The only other song achieved that evening was *Matt Hyland*, for a variety of which the reader may consult Gerald Griffin's poems.

CHAPTER XXV.

A LEARNED TREATISE ON MARRIAGE: FAIRIES OR NO FAIRIES.

ANOTHER spring went by, and we were at the end of summer, and I was looking out for a summons to Kildare Place in the ensuing winter, when my absence from my little kingdom would be attended with only little inconvenience, on account of the small attendance at that season. I expected news of Charley's marriage from day to day. Though Edward's letters occasionally expressed strong hopes, they were at times of a very despondent character. No one could set more vigorously to work, or pursue it with greater eagerness, but when he did not see his way, or had to make a choice in any important matter, and found his judgment unequal to the task, his mind became gloomy and depressed to the last degree. The women of the Lucas family employed themselves for a good part of the summer spinning wool, which was loosely woven, and then tucked, as the operation is called, in Mr. Hogan's tuck mill, *i.e.*, treated with soap-lees and other matters, and pressed against the sides of a wooden box by a pair of gigantic wooden hammers, which played alternately on the mass. The cloth is thickened by this process, but it must be watched, and taken out at times, night and day, and pulled between two persons' hands to prevent an unevenness in the thickness of the texture. H. W. often had the honour of acting *vis-a-vis* to Mrs. Hogan in the process. It is afterwards cleaned, and returned to the weaver, who stretches it on his tenters, cuts off the superabundant nap on one side with a pair of giant sheers, and presses it between thick, glazed, brown paper boards, over a heated metal plate. Finally, it is made into coats for the use of the family, or sent to Rathdrum fair. Our Tombrick manufacture was narrow cloth only, and it afforded pleasant employment to members of families between the heavy spring and autumn labours. Mrs.

Murphy and I spent some of our midday leisure talking to Margaret and Jane Lucas, as they moved along the cool clay floor of an out-house, and plied their wheel and spindle.   Murtagh and Matt would occasionally be present, so would Mrs. Lucas, and thus there were hostile interests watching each other.   We, *i.e.* Mrs. Murphy and H. W., were aware that Margaret had by dint of gentle obstinacy obtained a respite till next year, and was not to be urged to entertain Murtagh's proposals. Meanwhile the girls are spinning, and some old acquaintances of the reader are sitting and chatting, and Matt threatens that if some Tombrick girl will not have compassion on him, he will take a trip to the county Carlow. "Though, after all", said he, "I believe I will think twice about it.   Do n't I see how miserable my brother Thigue is, whenever his wife's head aches, or one of the children has a sore finger, or when any other háporth is the matter with one of them.   And if he takes a quart or a tumbler, when he goes to market or to a funeral, is n't he afraid of his life to show his nose to the women!   And how *lude* he looks next morning!   I suppose he did n't get a *keer hauling*, one gloomy morning, when he woke with a headache".

"I suppose", interposed Murtagh, "you feel it very comfortable to have your shirt and waistcoat now and then without buttons, and unwashed stockings an odd time; and when you wake in the morning, and look about your bare room, to feel that you have not one in the world that has a real warm feeling for you, or cares whether you are sick or well.   Only think how dismal it is when one becomes old and sickly, or old without being sickly, or sickly without being old, that you are a burthen to any one that is good-natured enough to do a hand's turn for you, and that when God calls you, you leave no one to offer up a prayer for you from the heart!"

"Do you ever", said Jane, "see little Josy and Bessy running to meet their father when he 's coming in at noon or evening, or when he 's sitting with one on each lap at the fire, when the day's work is over, or when he is

wet or tired after a fair or market? I suppose he feels no
pleasure or snugness, when the good woman is getting his
dry things, or making him comfortable in the warm corner, or laying his good supper before him, or when herself and himself and the youngsters are taking a pleasant
walk through the fields of a Sunday evening?"

"I saw him crying like a child, and wringing his
hands", snarled Matt, "when Josy was delaying about
making his first appearance in the world, and the wife
was between life and death for part of a day and night;
and by this stick in my fist, I would not suffer as much
for the finest woman that ever stepped in shoe leather".

"I dare say you took no notice of him sitting soon
after by the bedside with the wife's hand in his, and the
babe with his little mouth to her breast, and herself looking so happy, and himself as if he got a legacy of a
thousand pounds". "Oh, did n't I, the old fool! and
may be I did n't hear his groans and his moans, once
when there was a differ with the landlord, and he was
afraid the lease would n't be renewed; and I 'm sure that
full five quarters of his trouble was for the woman and
the children".

"I think it would be no harm to hear the opinion
of Mrs. Murphy, or my father and mother", said Margaret. Mrs. Murphy answered:

"I was married to as good-natured a man as you could
find in a field of boolians; still he was too easy led by his
relations and old comrades. More than once they pinned
him after Mass, and from that time, till early next morning, I did not lay my eyes on him. I was nursing at the
time, and would be awake from dawn (it was in the summer), and may be it was cheerful to see and hear the rats
squeeling and skelping along the walls under the thatch!
I believe that on the whole, my husband and myself were
as cordial as many other couples, but I give you my
word, that if I was to begin life again, and had my present feelings and experience, I would no more be tied
down in marriage, than I would throw myself into the
Slaney".

"You know something of the trials of a married woman", said Mrs. Lucas. "Did an old maid who had no objection to be married, ever tell you her repinings and sorrows?"

"After all", observed Mr. Lucas, "I believe it comes to this: Marriage is a sacrament, holy and beneficial when worthily received, and, moreover, absolutely necessary while Christianity endures. They that do not marry, do worse in many cases, and from the sentiments just uttered by Mrs. Murphy, we may guess that it would not be well for the world, if people could have the wisdom and experience of age, joined at the same time to the gift of youth".

A little lady of nine years enters with a flushed face. "Master, will you speak to Mary Hogan and Anne Whitty; they put me out of the play, and I doing nothing". "May be they wanted you to do *something*, and you would not please them. Ah, there is too much noise in the paddock, and play hour is over".

*　　　*　　　*　　　*　　　*

It need not be stated that my mind was at ease as far as regarded lodgings, except in those cases where I had no choice; for if two or three of the young folk disputed possession of me on an evening when the school was closed, it was a ticklish thing to show a preference; and sometimes the matter was decided by lot. On one unlucky evening, I was obliged to temporise between three high contending powers, as far as their ways coincided; but being come to the extreme boundary at which indecision was practicable, I made a full stop, hoping that some one, by withdrawing his or her claim, would simplify the matter.

No such thing: appeal was made literally to arms, for I was seized by the three factions, and might have been dismembered, but for a lucky fall I got on a heap of stones, good-natured and vehement little Mary K. being the immediate agent. A cut I received in the side of my head appeased the passions of the warm-hearted little

23

rogues; and Mary, my godmother's little daughter, taking
advantage of the fright occasioned by the accident, obtained the victory such as it was.

Having been employed during the greater part of the
day, endeavouring to enlighten the minds and form the
characters of my little flock, most of whom felt a considerable degree of affection for me, except perhaps at
the moments when the little palms might be smarting for
some fault or neglect; now when evening came, how re-
freshing was the walk along the side of the hill of Coolgarrow home to my godmother's! The heathy hill was on
our left, the murmuring Glasha far below us, the broad
shade of the mountain side in front, with the evening
rays chequering the cool mass; and the fields and farm
houses surrounded by trees on the other side of the
river, with their varied bright spots and dark shadows,
spreading away to the old burial ground of Kilmeashill.
My young friends gambolling around me, somewhat
hungry, but still with brisk spirits, kept up a lively conversation on all sorts of subjects. Poor little Kitty,
apropos to some remarks that were passing on natural
history, once made this very unexpected observation,
"Oh, bedad, sir, the frogs are very fierce animals"; but
she soon had good reason to regret her rashness, for
when any of her brothers, or sisters, or first cousins,
wished to plague her, they made a very ill-natured use
of her new discovery among the Amphibia.

Just at sunset we enter my godmother's hospitable
porch, and we are again among the old familiar personages.

Mr. W. K. asked little Kitty to bring her book till he
would hear how she read; and Kitty, whose only avail-
able manual for the time, was a volume of *Tabart's Fairy
Tales*, was soon entertaining the company with the exploits of Tom Thumb the Great.

I can never forget the unction with which she used to
read the passage where Tom was shaken down out of the
clouds, into the dish of frumity which was carrying across
the palace yard to the table of King Arthur himself. The

very words are engraved on my memory as on brass, such was the emphasis which the innocent little lamb laid on them, and here they are: "'Oh, dear! oh, dear!' cried Tom; 'Murder, murder!' cried the cook, and the whole dish of frumity ran off into the kennel".

The lesson being over, Kitty asked the senior portion in general, whether any of them had ever seen an individual fairy. All were obliged to acknowledge that they themselves never had the luck; though there was no one but could name some acquaintance who had either seen a *lurikeen*, a fairy, or a ghost, or the candle in the hand of Will-o'-the-Wisp. H. W. mentioned the positive assertion of his brother Diarmuid, that he had once heard the measured tramp, and the buzzing conversation of a large troop of fairies, exactly as if it was a funeral procession coming after him, one night as he was returning home at a late hour from a wake. He declared that he frequently stopped, and that the moment he did so, the train did the same, and the noise ceased instantaneously, and was renewed the moment he resumed his walk. At last as he turned from the road down a short lane that led to our house, he heard the crowd pass on, and the buzzing and trampling grew weaker and weaker, and at last died away. He could see nothing, but he heard the tramp of the feet and the muttering of the voices, as if a crowd of living people were carrying a corpse to be buried. H. W. himself hinted a suspicion, that all this might be the effect of an extra tumbler of punch, but his godmother said that her own grandfather had had a personal experience of the "Good People" without a doubt, and in this wise it came to pass.

CHAPTER XXVI.

NED DOYLE IN THE FAIRY PALACE: THE ENCHANTMENT OF EARL GARRETT: AND THE LEGEND OF CATHLEEN OF FERNS.

" My grandfather was returning from the county Carlow home through Scollagh Gap at a late hour, and was tired and hungry; and just as he came to what he took for Matty Doyle's public house, he heard from within jovial voices and singing; and all the windows were blazing with light, and the road in front was as bright as in the noon day. So he entered and found himself in the midst of a large, lighted, beautiful room, the tables laid out with the best of eating and drinking; and the ladies and gentlemen sitting at them, dressed in the richest stuffs, and silk and gold lace; and the king and queen of them all with gold crowns on their heads; and in a kind of gallery that ran along one wall, there were harpers, and fiddlers, and pipers, playing the most enchanting old Irish airs at times; and the dresses of the whole company were of an old fashion such as a body sees sometimes in pictures. My grandfather felt frightened enough, and could hardly get out his ' *Sith ye merry, genteels*'; but the king fixed his eye on him, and cried out, ' You 're welcome, Mr. Doyle, here 's towards your good health; sit down and enjoy yourself: make room there for Mr. Doyle, and fill him a tumbler of the best wine on the table'. As my grandfather was fumbling about for a seat, he saw several of his neighbours that had the reputation of being fairy men, and among the company he knew the faces of old acquaintances that had been lying in Templeshanbo and Kilmeashil church-yard for years. The strangest thing of all was, that he felt no surprise after the first minute or two; and when he got a seat beside an old sweetheart of his own that he had not seen for twenty years, and who was looking now as fresh as the day she last danced with him at the old rath of Cromoge, he began to praise her beauty: but she looked straight before her, and without opening her lips, she charged him not to let on that he found anything strange, but for his life and salvation not to touch food or drink.

"The voice seemed as if coming out of a vault: my grandfather stopped short in his compliments, but he resolved to take the friendly advice. Well, there seemed to be great merriment going on, and the big tumbler of wine was soon laid before him; but though the eyes of all were fixed on him, he contrived to spill the liquor down his bosom, while he pretended to drink. At that moment the strings of one of the harps rang dismally, and the bag-pipes gave a hollow groan, and the faces of the fine folk seemed to twist in pain; but when my grandfather looked steadily at any one, the features got composed in an instant, and a smile stole over the whole countenance. The queen now called on my grandfather for a song, and he gave them in Irish, *Thugamar fein an Savra linn* [We brought the summer along with us]. There was great clapping of hands and applause, and every one drank his health and song; and the goblet that was standing empty before him was filled again, and the queen hoped that he would have no objection to toast the ladies present.

"All the beauty around him, and the perfumes, and the music, were working on his head; and he felt so tired and thirsty that he forgot all, and was going to pour the enchanted liquor down his throat, when he felt the word *Remember* piercing through his head like an icicle; and, looking at his companion, he saw her face as pale as a sheet, and her eyes fixed, and down went the wine again inside his waistcoat. This time, it felt like a sheet of ice along his breast, and his teeth chattered with the chill he felt all over. Once more the harpstrings groaned and cracked, and the pipes roared; the lights shot up in blue flames, and the beautiful faces looked as if they belonged to lost souls. There was such a silence in the hall while you could count about ten, that the fluttering of the wing of a fly could be heard over their heads; and then the jollity, and the music, and laughter arose louder than ever. In about half an hour, an officer cried silence, as

the chief singing man of the great *Geroidh Iarla* (Gerald
the Earl), who had come to the meeting all the way from
the old Rath of Mullaghmast, where his master was lying
in an enchanted sleep, was going to entertain the king
and queen and their guests with a song.   Then did my
father hear such melody as he never thought nor dreamed
of: the sound filled his heart and brain with a kind of in-
cense, and seemed to be lifting him from the ground, so
that he felt as if he could rise and float over the heads of
the beautiful creatures that filled the hall.   The words of
the song were in Irish, and very immoral words they were,
but my grandfather was carried out of himself, and had
no more power to act or think aright, than to stop in
middle air if he was falling from a tower.

"When the song ceased, the red sparkling liquor was
once more pushed under his nose; and such was his
excited state, and so agreeable was the smell, that he
grasped the goblet, and in a moment its contents would
have been down his throat; but at the instant he felt an
icy cold foot placed on his instep: a sharp pang darted
through his body, and his right hand shook and dashed
the glass from the edge of the table, and it fell with a
harsh grating ring on the pavement.   The hall was filled
in a moment with shouts of rage and despair; the lights
were blown out by an earthly-smelling wind that seemed
to rush from the yawning floor of the building, and the
air was beat in the darkness with the strokes of wings
beyond reckoning.

"My grandfather, half between dead and alive, found
himself whipped up, and borne forwards in a stupid state,
neither asleep nor awake; and after a considerable time
he became somehow aware that he was getting towards
home, and hovering nearer and nearer to the earth.
At last he felt himself moving over the knoc above the
old place in Cromogue, and the tops of the bushes touching his legs.   He was found lying in a very uneasy sleep
in his own bed next morning; and when they roused
him, he mentioned a certain spot in the knoc, where they
would find one of his knee-buckles that had been scraped

off by a tall furze twig. The buckle was found, sure
enough; and there was a smell from his mouth for some
hours, as if some bad whiskey had got into his inside;
and he often afterwards sung a verse or two of the song
of *Geroidh Iarla's* bard. As we did not understand
Irish, and he always said that the sentiment of the song
was not very edifying, we were never the wiser for it;
but he always used to give a verse or so whenever any one
would contradict him about the Fairies' Castle, and ask
how he could remember the song so well if he had not
heard it sung by the Fairy-man. So he always had the
last word. God be good to his soul!"

"Amen, godmother. One of my earliest recollections is
the same old gentleman. Your father was just after returning from Dublin, and I heard some one say that he
had brought home a big Bible with him; so I found my
legs too short till I got over to the rath, and as it was a dark
winter's morning, they laid down the book on a low stool
near the blaze of the fire. I opened it at the beginning,
and was soon striving to get some idea of the garden of
Eden and its four rivers. The grandfather was just
coming out of his bed-room, and, seeing such a little
creature grappling with the big book, he shouted out,
'Ah, will yez take the book from the child before he tears
it'? Finding that I could read it, he changed his tone
in an instant, and seemed as if he would never tire hearing me read, and talking to me".

"It's himself was easily pleased, and easily vexed, my
poor dear old grandfather! He was not fond of speaking
English, as in his young days, Irish was more commonly
used in the country, and he could n't bear to be laughed at
when he pronounced any word wrong. He used to divide
his time pretty evenly between the rath of Cromogue and
my uncle's near Bunclody, and my uncle's up in the mountain; and when anything annoyed him wherever he happened to be at the time, he was off like a shot to one of
the other houses. One day he came down to us from the
mountain, where he had got some affront as he choosed to
think it; and after he had been sitting down at the fire a

bit, and was getting comfortable, he began to thank heaven
for the fine warm spring: 'See, the birch is *budging*
already', said he, and there was a titter at once among his
grandchildren. 'Ah, troth, yez are the graceful pack',
says he in a rage: 'I 'll not trouble yez with my company
much longer'. He put on his hat, and got his staff in a
twinkling; and though we all took hold of him, and began
to blubber and beg to be forgiven, he tore himself away
and set off towards Kilmeashill. My brother Myles took
the short cut to our uncle's house, and told the story; and
they soon saw the old gentleman coming up straight to
the house, muttering and thumping his staff on the ground.
Well, he had hardly time to take his seat, and begin to
warm his hands at the blaze, when one of my cousins took
up the discourse. 'Oh, grandfather, what a fine spring
we are getting, thank goodness! the birch is *budging*
beautiful, already'. This was like putting a match to the
touch-hole of a gun: he was off without even an oath, and
we had the pleasure of soon seeing him come up the road,
and he did not quit us afterwards for a whole week".

"Some of yez", observed Owen, "won't believe a word
about the fairies if a body was to take their oath; but I
am sure Jemmy Kennedy, of Rossard, is as long headed a
man as you could find, and he told me himself that he was
lying on the side of the hill over the little stream that
runs down under his own place, and on to Thuar Bridge,
and to the Glasha. It was a warm day, and he was half
asleep, when he heard a great rustle of wings on both
sides of the stream, and a clash just over the water as if
softish bodies were slapped together, and faint cries, and
even the smothered sound of shots, and the little pools of
the river disturbed by things falling into them. It went
on this way for a good while, till at last he heard sounds
of lamentation, and wings beating the air, and making
their way across towards Booladhurrogha. Then there
were faint shouts as if from the conquering party, and a
rising of the wings high up in the air, and then silence
again".

"May be Jemmy was entirely and not half asleep, and
dreamed it all in the hot sunny day?"

" I wish", said little Mary, "somebody would tell about *Geroidh Iarla*, and why he remains enchanted under Mullaghmast".

" I wish you were as inquisitive about the Rule of Three", said her mother; " but not to have your sleep disturbed, I 'll tell you the story as I heard it once".

The Transformation of Gearoidh Iarla.

" Garret or Gerald Fitzgerald, was the great Earl of Kildare long ago. All the Fitzgeralds in Ireland are of an old English stock, long settled here; and they always were so kind to their neighbours and followers of Irish race, that their name is as dear through Ireland as those of the old Royal Blood itself, such as the O'Connors, the O'Briens, the O'Neills, or the O'Donnells. Well my brave Geroidh Iarla was a magician, and could take on himself the form of any living thing he chose. His lady knew that he had this power, and often and often begged him to show himself to her in the form of some of her pet animals. The earl put her off for a long time, till at last she began to complain, and say that he had no love for her, or he would gratify her in so trifling a thing.

" He was so troubled at this, that at last he explained to her, that if she took the least fright, or gave a scream, while he was out of his real shape, he could never recover it till whole generations of living men and women had gone down to the grave one after another.

" She said that she was so stout that he need n't have the slightest fear; and she pestered him so, that at last one fine summer evening as they were sitting in the great state parlour of their castle, he took the shape of a blackbird, and flew round the room, and in and out through the window, and perched on his lady's shoulder, and fluttered his wings, and sung, and nothing could equal the delight she felt as she stroked down his feathers. In the midst of their enjoyment, up jumped a black cat from under the sofa, or whatever kind of a seat they used in the old castles long ago; the countess gave a scream, and blackbird or earl was never seen again. He lies entranced to this day

under the ruins of the old Rath. Once in every seven
years he is permitted to ride round the Curragh of Kildare on a white steed, whose shoes are made of solid
silver; and when those shoes become as thin as a cat's
ear, he will regain his human form, drive the English
away, and reign King of Ireland for seven-and-thirty
years. Others say that himself and a band of old Irish
warriors are lying asleep in a cavern, dressed in armour,
and every knight's steed saddled and bridled behind his
master; and when the hour comes, a fated knight will
enter the cavern and cry, that the hour is come, and then
the band will ride forth and restore the old race of kings".

"Oh, dear!" exclaimed Owen, "what a fine life the
great quality must have led in them big castles. The
walls of the old building at Ferns I 'm sure are twelve
feet thick; and they say while the great people were safe
inside of these walls, they had their sogers all armed with
soords, and pot-lids, and shirts made of iron rings, watchin'
from the battlements, and guardin' the gates, and lyin' in
wait in the woods to catch rich prisoners, and seize on
cattle to roast at their tundherin', big kitchen fires.
What fine divarshin they must have inside, atin' the best
of white loaves, and good fresh mate, and drinkin' tay,
and makin' curtchies, and never wettin' their foot, nor
slavin', nor bein' obliged to handle spade, nor shovel, nor
billuke. Ah! if I was born the owner of a castle in them
good ould times, would n't I lie down every mornin' after
my breakfast of tay and toast, and a good rasher of
bacon, on the sofia, and smoke, or go to sleep, or listen
to a piper till dinner; and afther my dinner and punch,
do the same till supper; an' when I went to bed, I 'd
dhrink off a good tumbler of punch again, and never
bother myself about risin' till the sun would be the hoith
o' the threes. Ay, an' some days, may be I would n't get
up at all, but make the butler bring up my males to the
bedside".

"That would be very good", observed Mrs. K., "if it
could last, Owen; but do you reckon how long your
health would stay with you, shut up inside close rooms,

or how long you would find such a life pleasant. Did
you ever see an unfortunate rich man with a big red
nose, and a gouty foot, and a shaky hand, and perhaps
not enjoying an hour's sleep at night, and all got by idleness and drinking and bad living; and how do you know
but if you led so lazy a life, but your soldiers might
make a rebellion some day, and drag you down your own
big stone stairs with your feet foremost, and chop off
your poor head with the red nose on it, on a chopping
block; and may be, the devil whispering in your ear while
they were dragging you down, 'Is n't this a pretty end
you are come to, you unfortunate old rogue? Where are
all the poor you relieved in your time? What good did
you do for the poor farmers, and labourers, and servants
under you? Your carbuncled nose, and thin legs, and
big belly do n't tell of fasting or mortification: you practised praying so little during your life, that it 's not
worth while to begin now; so there 's no help, Owen my
boy, no use in whimpering: I 'll have a warm corner
ready for you down below, in the chop of a hatchet'.
This is the comfort the 'Old Boy' would be giving you;
and now what do you think of the wrong side of the car-
pet, Owen?"

"Be the laws, ma'am, I do n't like it at all; so I 'll
work as long as the Lord laves me sthrenth, and say my
prayers, and go to my duty, and do what little good the
Lord may enable me to do, and not wish to be coddled up
in old castles; and that puts me in mind of Cathleen
Clare that owned Ferns Castle long ago. She was the
wickedest woman in Ireland; Cathleen of Moneyhore was
one sister, and Cathleen of some place else was another,
and they were all as bad as bad could be.

Cathleen Clare.

"Cathleen Clare lived in them old times in the castle
of Ferns as I mentioned, and she used to curl her hair,
and paint her face, and have ever so much company at her
castle, and whenever she knew any great lord or *duiné
uasal* to have a great deal of money, she would make him

stay afther the rest of the company, and be so sweet with
him, that butter would not melt in her mouth, and he
would be made to drink hearty, and once he went into his
bedroom, he was never seen again.   A great many bad
reports got abroad, and at last the bould Sir Art Mac
Murrogh O'Cavanagh, who lived there above in the castle
of Clonmullin, said he 'd pay Cathleen a visit, and shake
the devil out of her, if he found her at her tricks with
him.   Well, there was great doins, and politeness, and
bows, and curtchies, and Sir Art was shown to the room
where so many had come to their end. His foster brother,
Bryan Oge, that always carried a little clarseach along
with him to entertain his chief, just as they were passing
through the long corridor that led to the room, struck his
harp, and himself sung as loud as ever he could rise his
voice—'Son of the O'Cavanagh, *glac fuar agus the*' (pr.
the as in *theme*), that is, 'take of the hot and the cold'.
But in Irish these words also mean 'make your escape'.
Sir Art kept the haft of his soord ready to his hand, and
Bryan Oge did the same, and his little dog that was
barkin' as loud as he could, from the moment the harp
was struck, jumped into the bedroom, and there he was
leapin' and prancin' about on the thrap-door.   The dog
was so light, that the door only went down an inch
or two, and the moment Sir Arthur's eye fell on it,
he drew his soord, and dashed back on the villianous
servants that were follyin' him. Himself and his fosther-
brother soon put the vagabones to flight, but there was a
strong guard at the end of the corridor, and soords were
clashin' and shouts risin' from the wounded rascals that
were fallin' under M'Murrogh's arm.   Bryan seein' that
more reinforcements were rushin' up stairs, caught a
lighted piece of bog wood, and thrust it out through one
of the narrow openings in the wall, and waved it, and
cried out as loud as his voice could rise, 'O'Cavanagh
Aboo'; and then the fighters heard shouts from the outside, and from the bottom of the stairs.   The gates were
opened before this by a friend of Bryan's, who was tired
of his bad life, and wished to save the young chief; and

a band of the Clonmullin men that drew near the gates
as soon as it got dark, broke in and cut down the guards:
and between the two warriors at the top of the stairs,
and their friends at the bottom, the scoundrels were cut to
pieces. Cathleen was burned at the Market-Cross in
Wexford; and the bodies of many young men were found
decayed away a hundred feet under the thrap-door of the
bed-room. Cathleen had red hair more by token, and I
believe that, since or before, it is not considered lucky to
meet with a red-haired woman early on a Friday morning.

"Well, Owen", said Mrs. James, "I never *seen* the peer
of you for uncharitable remarks about women. How can
a woman be the worse for the colour of her hair, when she
had no hand in dyeing it herself? Did you ever see a picture of the Holiest among women with her hair an auburn
or rich brown colour?"

"To be sure I did; but how did the painther know anything about what colour it was, anymore nor you an' me?"

"Well, there's some truth in that", quoth Mr. William,
"although it was Owen Jourdan said it: but at any rate,
there is a prejudice in the country for dark hair—sure they
say it was owing to a woman with sandy locks that the
Cathedral of Ferns was left unfinished for a hundred and
fifty years", and the good man related the legend of St.
Mogue, which the reader has already heard. When it was
over Owen judiciously remarked:—

"Well, one man may steal a horse safer than another
look over the ditch at him. If I tould yez this story, you
would not believe a word of it; and it will go down with
every one now like milk, because you hear it from Mr. K.:
I suppose it 's because he has some of the larning".

CHAPTER XXVII.

COURSING AND FOWLING OF AN EXTRAORDINARY CHARACTER: THE EARL OF STAIRS' SON.

MR. JAMES now began to bear his part; he was a solemn
looking, hard-featured man, as I believe was before ob-

served, and seldom smiled, but delighted to tell lies with a grave face. He was the man of business of the farm, and did the head work; his elder brother, the nominal chief, being contented to do any labour needful, while James and my godmother went to fairs, and sold the farm produce.

"You are very right, Owen; it is a shame for Billy to be stuffing the heads of the children with romances. Any one that has an ounce of sense, can amuse a company with what happened to his own knowledge, if he had any luck or gumption, in his youth. There's myself that was going down the hollow of Glanamoin, one evening, to make peace between the two brothers, the D.'s, that lived near Castle-Dockrell, for they were for ever going to law with one another; and the eldest had a warrant out against the youngest fellow at that time. I had my gun on my arm, and I felt very lonesome. There was the heathy side of Coolgarrow on my left hand, and the wood running down from the top till it spread out over the near side of Tombrick; and on my right there was nothing but the bare fields with their stone fences on the top of Kilachdiarmuidhhill, with the sheep grazing through them; and down below were the meadows, and houses, and castles, and woods, as far as my eye could go, and the whitish fog that lay just over the Slaney as it flowed on between the green inches. There was hardly a sound except the bark of a dog that would sometimes be heard far away below me; and I remember getting a start by a stone tumbling down the rocky path when it was loosened by my foot. All at once I got a bigger start, as I heard something over my head crying, 'Quaick, quaick'; and looking up I saw a flock of wild geese flying towards Bunclody. 'Here's luck', says I, but when I tried the gun, there was neither ball nor shot in it, nothing but a pinch of powder at the bottom of the barrel, and a little in the pan. 'Murdher', says I to myself, 'is n't this a pity!' I scratched my head with the end of the ramrod, and all at once a lucky thought came into it. I popped the same ramrod blunt end foremost into the barrel, cocked the piece, clapped the butt

·end to my shoulder, took aim, and let fly (I was a powerful shot at the time). Crack went the charge, and up flew
the ramrod as straight as an arrow. Somehow or other,
that evening, the geese instead of flying like a V on a
level, were straight over one another; so in the way they
flew, the ramrod darted right through the eyes of the first
it met, and then through the eyes of the next, and the
next, till in less than a minute, I saw the whole flight,
twelve in number, fluttering and falling to the ground, all
spitted, as you may say, on the lucky ramrod. Gad, I returned home with my prize at once, and clean forgot the
good errand I was going on".

"Well to be sure", said Owen, "the things that does
happen to lucky people bangs Banagher. Now, if Mr.
Jem had loaded his piece carefully before he set out,
may be he would not have shot one bird; and there was
twelve geese, you may say, dropped into his lap, by way
of reward for his forgetfulness: just like Mr. Tade Kennedy that lives beyond the Slaney, under Slie Bui. He
was sent one day to look for twelve sheep of his father's
that were straying, just the same number as the unlucky
geese. Well, after a long hunt he got tired, and lay down
in a field, where the reapers were at their dinner, and began to Shanachus with them. In about half-an-hour, just
as he was thinking it time to go on his search, what should
walk in through the gap of the field but the very beasts
he was looking for; and that 's the way with the world.
If some people would be pitching their luck and their
wealth out of the door, it would come back in spite of them;
and other crathers may slave and starve themselves, and
work early and late, and never be a penny beyant a
beggar".

"But, Owen", said Mrs. K., "did you ever compare the
numbers that thrive by neglect with the numbers that
grow poor by it? You have lighted on one or two strange
things, and you are in a great hurry to make a rule from
them".

"But how did it happen", asked Larry, "that the ramrod went so neatly through the eyes of the wild fowl?

sure their eyes are on a level, instead of one lying above
the other.   Ah, ha, uncle ! have I found you out?"

"Indeed, Larry, it is a pity you were not the gander
that was flying at their head, I mean their tail.   You
remind me of many a wiseacre that passes remarks on
histories, and poems, and ballads, as if he had the wit of
Solomon, and the writers were all jackasses.   Now open
your long ears till I insense you of the geometry of the
thing.   The goose that was at the bottom of the flight"—
"You said a gander just now, uncle".

"And what harm if I did! is n't a goose a she gander?   As I was saying, the he goose, or the gander, if you
like it better, the moment he heard the click of the gun-
lock, turned his head sideways to see what was going on
under him; they are all mighty watchful, them wild fowl;
the other geese did the same, and they were all *skivered*
before they had time to look straight before them ; and I
am sure a child could understand the way it happened".
Here the company made that clucking noise with their
tongues against the palates, which expresses either admiration, or pity, or contempt.   The hero of the story took
the demonstration as a compliment, and Larry, after begging pardon, asked for information about the brothers D.
and their dispute.

"I think I can give some account of that affair myself",
said Owen.   "The elder gave a warrant that he had
against the other boy, to Tim Kerry the bailiff; but Tim
disliked so much to have anything to do between brothers
that he never looked after his prisoner, and invented all
sorts of excuses when he 'd be attacked by the other.
At last, as he was cutting faggots one day in Munfin,
who should bounce out on him but the white nagur of a
prosecutor, and, says he, with a face on him as red as a
coal: 'Kerry, you thief', says he, 'you 're circumventin''
me now these three months, pretending that you can 't
find Jack.   There he is now in the next field : come and
I 'll point him out to you ; and by this and by that, if you
do n't take him, I 'll make Captain Carey take you, and
give you a lesson you won't forget'.   'Oh, begonies!' says

Tim, 'show me the *villian*, and see if I do n't make him
bounce.   What am I a constable for, but to do the duty
of one?'   Well, they went along the ditch till they got a
view of Jack; and up jumped the bailiff, and out he
roared, shaking his billuke at him in the most vicious
manner, 'Jack D., you vagabone, I have a warrant against
you in my pocket: stay there till I 'rest you like an
honest man, for if I come up to you I 'll have your life,
so I will'.   With that he began to run after him, shouting,
and waving the billuke about his head, and swearing like
a trooper; but poor Jack, not liking the invitation
he got, laid leg to ground, and Tim contrived to gain
very little odds on him.   He still kept roaring after him
loud enough to frighten the Danes; but this only made
Jack run the faster; and the big Turk of an elder brother held on behind, cursing Tim, and bidding him run
like the divel.   By the time they got as far as the cross
of Ballycarney, they had a hundred men and their wives.
helping the lame dog over the stile.   They lost sight of
their prisoner just as they crossed the bridge, and as there
was a great number of doors, and bawns, and passages,
and every one was giving a different direction, and every,
one that was n't directing, was bursting his sides laughing,
there was no use in following the chase farther; and poor
Tim began to wipe his face and head, and beg some good
Christian to give him a dhrink of could wather, or he 'd
stugue up.   This was a hint, of course, to his employer
to threat him to a quart or a naggin; and the crowd
looked at him so hard that he saw he 'd be obleeged to,
shell out; and he got so shamed by the people, and so,
disgusted with Kerry's thrickery and love of his glass,,
that he gave up the law-shute".

"Talking of Munfin", observed Mr. James, "reminds,
me what a delightful thing it is to be sitting at your ease,
on the side of a car, on a fine summer morning, when
the grassy banks at each side of the road are covered with,
dew, and the sun shining through the big ash and oak
trees, and yourself jogging along by Munfin house with
its gray front, and the green lawn lying before it,

24

and everything so nice and cool on account of the trees by the side of the high road. The thought of the strong tumbler of punch after your marketing is over, is very pleasant along with all, and the feeling of having no hard labour to do till next day".

" Ah, Mr. James, you 'd make to-morrow's work very tiresome to me, only that I 've often seen men staggering out through Irishtown in the evening, or lying with red faces in their empty cars, and snorting, and their poor heads aching, and their stomachs sick, and may be a cut on the left side of the head, and a fine scolding before them at home".

" Ah, do n't spoil our evening's comfort with your bad constructions. I 'll tell you all what happened once to myself near Munfin, when I was a young man, and not bothered with Peggy and the children here".

Peggy not approving the allusion, gave his ear a pinch and made him bawl.

" I was fishing one evening in the Slaney below Cloghbemon, and I was not thinking about anything in particular, when I felt a great chuck at the line. I gave a pull, and then a stronger one, but the weight of the fish was so great that I could not stir it. 'If you were the *old boy* himself', says I at the third offer, ' I 'll have you out, so here goes'; and putting all my force to the rod, up there flew over my head, out of the water—what do you think, but a large griddle! I can't tell you how high it flew in the air; but down it came flourishing into a brake behind me, and hit a buck that was sitting there at his ease, and chewing his cud, and broke his thigh. I soon dispatched him, and throwing him across my shoulder, and taking my rod in my hand, I walked up to Captain Cuff's on the hill to make him a present of the venison. Well, the Captain was not at home; but out came his daughter, Miss Cuff, and I put my best leg forward, and made a flourish with my hat, and begged the lady to present the deer to the captain with my best wishes. 'Oh, Mr. K.', says she (she was pleased to say Mr. K. Ach! it 's your real quality that has none of the nasty, shabby conceit of your half-sirs, or buckeens, or squireens, or purse-proud shopkeepers: they are just as homely and as easily spoken to as one of ourselves), 'Mr. K.', says she, 'this is too great a compliment: how can we recompense you?' 'Indeed, Miss', says I, 'this is the only recompense I'll accept'; and I took the liberty of saluting her in my politest style. 'Oh, Jemmy', says she, 'I declare I'll tell Captain Cuff that you kissed his daughter'. ''Pon my veracity, ma'am', says I, 'if you do, all the excuse I can make to Captain Cuff is, that his daughter kissed me'. Well, to be sure, how she laughed at my impudent answer!" At this point of the tale, the woman-kind fell on the vain-glorious hero, and gave him such a pummelling, and pinching, and hair-pulling, and tickling, that he was obliged to roar out between laughing and crying, and ask public pardon for his misdeeds, and promise to be more circumspect for the future in his mode of telling facts. He then continued his adventures. "Well, now that I am muzzled like, I'll be as sedate as Solomon himself; and I defy the sharpest nose in the company to smell out anything immoral in my next adventure. 'T was about the year of Nelson's death, and Peggy and myself were courting at the time; and she took great huff one day when her brother Miley was treating us all at the fair of Bunclody, because she thought I winked at Judy O'Flanagan, a fine strapping lass that could put her in her pocket". Here the story-teller beheld Peggy approaching with hostile intentions, and roared out, "No, I am wrong: it was Miss O'Flanagan took huff because I winked at Peggy". Still the attack was imminent, and of a more threatening character. "I see, I am still at fault: it was the year when nobody winked at anybody, and nobody took huff. But as I was saying, or going to say, I had a fine young dog that year; we called him Boney, and he and I started a hare just above Nick Thumpkin's, beyond the stream. Away scoured puss in brave style past Dan and Jemmy Kennedy's, and Nick Gahan's, up hill and down valley, till we were just above Templeshanbo; and if you

were guessing till to-morrow, you would not chance on
what happened when we were not twenty yards asunder".
" O yes, uncle; the hare lay down to rest, Boney lay down
to rest twenty yards behind him, and you lay down to rest
two yards behind Boney". " And how did your wisdom
find out that?" " Ah, sure you told it to us yourself
ever so long ago". " Well, well, all this comes of talking
wisdom to fools : catch me telling you a good thing again.
' Oh, ho !', says I to myself, when I saw puss taking his
ease, ' we 'll put the hare's head against the goose's gib-
lets now'. I recollected the expression in an old book we
had, ' Don Quixote', though to this hour I do n't know
what it means. ' Now for it, Boney, you thief', says I,
' spring on him'. I might as well be whistling to a mile-
stone; and, what was stranger, I felt all at once so fatigued myself, that though I had the greatest desire to
secure the game, I could not persuade myself to put one
foot before the other; and down I lay on the sod, one eye
on the dog, the other on the hare, and my whole soul and
body as if I was lying under a ton weight of clammy
wool-packs. I could not tell how long I lay, when at last
he got up, stood on his hind legs, and cocked his ears.
I have seen some young farmers in their new stiff clothes
at fairs, the very *moral* of him. Well, after surveying
the dog and myself for a little bit, he gave a roguish
shake to his ears, turned about, kicked up his heels, and
hit Boney on the head with a small stone, cut a caper,
and away with him. The dog and myself recovered at
the same moment; and may be we did n't lay leg to ground
to chastise his impudence. Down the side of the hill we
powdered, crossed the Glasha, forked it up to Ballychristal,
and at the point where the bog of Cummor begins, down
lay the deceitful vagabond again; down lay the dog, and
down I was obliged to lie, my legs having no more
power than if the skin was stuffed with bran like a doll's.
The same thing took place again: he led us round the
rim of the bog in the big bason under Mount Leinster,
and on the rise of the far hill he refreshed himself again.
While we were watching him this third time he threw

pishrogues on our eyes, I suppose: we saw him lying on the sod with his eyes wide open; and the next moment it was as if the earth had opened and swallowed him, or as if his substance had turned into thin air. He was nowhere to be seen; and we had a fine weary walk back to Coolgarrow.

"Well, the next time we had the fortune to start him, I knew the rogue quite well. We worked him to oil, so that we might catch him, and break the charm before he'd be down. This time we were within ten yards of him when he stopped, but our prospects were not a bit better. There he lay with his big eyes staring me out of countenance: there was not a wink or a twinkle in them; and it seemed as if some hurtful thing was darting from them through my eyes, and frightening and stupefying me, beyond anything I could describe. If you want to get a weak idea of what I suffered, look at some ugly thing, and think of nothing else for a quarter of an hour. We met him the third time in the same spot, as you go towards Glanamoin. This time the poor dog nor myself was in a hurry to begin the chase; but what did the impudent tinker do? He cocked his ears as high as they could go, looked at Boney for a moment, and then charged at him like a mad bull. Well, if you were dying you'd laugh at the poor dog. He let his tail fall between his legs, gave a yowl out of him, and flew towards home, as if the divel was at his heels: they were soon out of sight. When I reached home, I found the poor brute in his bed in a cold shiver; and I do n't think he was ever the same dog again".

"Well, Mr. James", remarked Owen, "that beats all the hunts or chases I ever hear tell of; but I think it is hardly as curious as your chase from Rossard to Ballyprecus". "I don't recollect that chase at all". "Well then, it's no harm to remind you. It was n't Boney that helped you in this one, though. It was a fine she hound, and the hare was the same *sect:* you can't but recollect it. You were bringing home turf from Cummor; and just under Billy Prandy's of

Rossard, a fine big hare ran across the road, ' *Magh go Bragh*', with Sweetlips after her ; and to the heels with yourself after Sweetlips, letting the horses find their way home as well as they could. Poor puss was in such a fright, that she forgot she was about having a young family, and Sweetlips had n't a bit better thought about her own case. Down across the fields they went like the wind, jumped the stream, and along the ridge above Cromoge with them, crossing the very knoc where the mistress's grandfather lost his silver knee-buckles after he was in the fairies' palace. At last they came to the very meadow where the cow used to be licking the thorn tree in the short cut from above the Crosses to Bunclody. There poor puss was short taken, and had five beautiful little leverets; and at twelve ridges behind her, Sweetlips was obliged to bear her company. Well and good, you, like a true sportsman, never interfered till both mothers gave the first suckling to their young ; and then the hunt began again, Sweetlips after the hare, and the five pups in full cry after the five little ones. Every dog caught her hare just as they got to the old church yard of Kil-meashil. I hope that, in respect to the place, you rescued the young things and the poor mother".

"Owen, I would be glad to be able to rescue my youthful adventures out of your possession. I have seen good portraits of people that would make you laugh, on account of a little funny drawing out of some of the features, but I must compare you to a botcher that would twist and pull out the same features, till any desire of laughing or smiling would leave you, finding the picture neither pleasant to look at, nor like the person it was intended for. I do n't lay any claim to that lying story: always tell it as if it happened to yourself".

"Well, surely, it is hard times when a crane takes the liberty of checking a snipe for the length of his bill; but Mr. James, I do n't think you had as much gumption when you were a young man, as you 'd wish us to believe. When you made a present of the *vengeance*, why did you not follow up the courtship that looked so well at the beginning, and push wedlock at the young lady, and may be it's Captain Cuff you'd be now yourself; I mean Captain Cuff's son-in-law; and be commanding a whole barrack of soldiers, and have a feather out of your head like a turkey cock, or may be, be kilt abroad in Flandhers, or Gibralther, or Jamaiky, and be returned among the kilt, wounded, and missing, and be mentioned in the history of Buonaparte, and sung in ballads at the fair of Enniscorthy! Ah! you had n't the luck of the Earl of Stairs' son; but he was a good scholar, and knew Geomethry, and Latin, and Greek, Practice and the 'Rule of Three Direct', Gunnery and Fluxions.   Them is branches I heard read out of Tom K.'s advertisement that I pulled off the gatepost of the Chapel the other Sunday after every one read it, and I'm sure if little Tom's head could hold such a lot of things, my brave young Earl of Stairs, that was a foot taller, was able enough for them.   This is the way it happened:

The Earl of Stairs' son.

"The father was called the Earl of Stairs, because his little house was just on the side of Black Stairs, looking towards Puck's Bridge.   One cave rested on the side of the rock, and the walls were good strong stone walls (there is no scarcity of stones in them parts); and the roof was as snug as *scraws* and heath could make it.   The Earl enclosed as much land off the common as he could till; so there was no scarcity of oaten bread, or potatoes, or eggs, or goats' milk; and small thanks to him for keeping up a good fire, for the turf bog was within a hen's race of his castle.   Both he and his wife were of old respectable families; and so, as they had the good drop of blood, and some larning, and were mighty genteel in their manners, they were called Lady Stairs and the Earl of Stairs. One day, an ignorant omadhaun of a mountaineer came in on some business, and he sat down, and kept looking at a bunch of keys that was hanging from a table-drawer, and say she, after a long pause, 'Ma'am', says he, ' do you sell kays here ?'

"Well, when the little boy was about fifteen years old, and knew more nor any school-master within ten miles of him, he was so eager after the learning, that he set out over the mountain, and through Carlow, and Kilkenny, and whatever lies at the back of them, till he came to Munster.   He got into a capital school there, and learned all them branches I mentioned while ago, ay, and grammar along with them; I forgot the grammar. A Mr. Blundell teached in that school about twenty years ago, but I do n't know the name of the young Earl's master who lived long before that time.   He paid nothing for his knowledge, but helped the master now and then; and the farmers' children going to the school were glad to take him home at night, as he was so ready to share his knowledge with them.   No wonder he should find it so easy to pick up learning in Munster, where they say the little boys minding the cows converses with one another in Latin.

"At last and at long, he returned home, a fine genteel young man; and did not his poor mother cry with joy, when she heard him talking to the priest the next Sunday,. after Mass, and conversing with him in Latin, and French, and Portuguee.

"Well, there was nothing to hinder him now from being a priest himself, if he chose, as the old people had some guineas laid up in the thatch in an old stocking; but though he was pious enough in his own way, he said he had no vocation; and that any one becoming a priest with- out a vocation, would be only endangering his own soul and the souls of his flock.   Every week he used to get an in- vitation to some great farmer's house for tay and hot cake, and wherever the priest had a station, he was sure to be there.   The girls had an eye on him, but though he was polite enough, he paid no particular attention to any one; and then they began to find out that his parents were be- low their own rank in life, and that his geese were all swans in his own eyes, and that the conçait of some people was astonishing.   He used to ramble about the rocks with a book in his hands; and though he was ready enough to help the Earl at his work, the deuce a hand would the old fool let him lay to a single thing.

"At last as they were sitting round the fire on a winter's night, the young fellow up and told the old couple, that he was tired of doing nothing and having nothing to do, and that he would set out on his travels, and that he hoped he would have something pleasant to write home about, before long.

"The poor old people were sad enough at this; but after doing all they could to persuade him to stay at home, and marry, and take a farm, or open a shop in Newtownbarry (it was only Bunclody then), or Ennis-corthy, or New Ross, he still held out, and one fine day, he set forward to Dublin and took ship there, and tale or tidings were not heard from him for two years, except one letter that he sent them from Paris about five months after he set sail; and in this letter he said he was well off teaching English to a merchant's children.

"At last one fine summer afternoon, a fine looking gentleman with a foreign appearance, and speaking English in a queer style, and travelling in a post-chaise, stopped at the inn at the cross of Rathduff, and put up there till next day; but said he wanted a guide to show him the way to the Earl of Stairs' castle. The people knew the nickname well enough, and after he got some refreshment, a boy was sent to show him the way. When they came nigh the cabin which was on the open common, and near the ending of a lane that came up straight through the enclosed fields, they heard a great grunting and squeel-ing, and there they saw two stout two-year old pigs with their noses to the half door, shrovellin' at it with all their might, and only for the rings in their snouts they 'd have it down in less than no time; and the squeelin' they kept up all the time was enough to vex a saint. A puckawn and eleven *meenshogues* were surnadin' along the ridge of the roof, and cantherin' round the bawn, and givin' a puck now and then to the musicianers at the door to quicken the tune a bit. Well, the gorsoon got through the goats, and gave a welt or two to the pigs, and got

them out of the way, and then he bawled out, 'Earl of
Stairs, are you within if you please, Sir? Here 's a gentleman from foreign parts come to see you'. So with that
the Earl came and opened the half-door, and requested the
gentleman to walk in. There was as fine a dish of white
eyes on their little table as you could wish to see, and a
couple of noggins of boiled goats' milk by the side of it,
and a plate of butter, and the moment the gentleman entered, they pressed him to sit down and join them; and
Lady Stairs filled out a mug of milk, and laid a knife and
a pat of butter for the stranger.

"He thought to explain his business at once, but they
would not hear a word till he would first eat and drink.
So he hung his hat on a peg, and taking the knife in his
hand, he cut one of the potatoes in two, and watched to
see how the master and mistress managed their's. And
he was so polite that he laid down his knife, and began to
peel off the potato skins with his fingers. Well, he did
not relish that way of going to work much, so he took up
the knife again and dispatched a couple of potatoes, and
took a pull at the milk which I 'm sure was good enough
for a queen. Well, the table was small, and the mistress
thinking that the potatoes were not much to their visitor's
taste, took down a wooden bowl, filled with good home-
made cakes; and laying it on her lap, as the little table
was crowded, she buttered a good slice, and asked him to
try it if he pleased. He done his best to seem to relish
every thing, and the Earl holding a lighted dipped rush
in one hand, pressed him to make a hearty supper.

"When the cloth was off the table, the Earl wiped his
hands on a wisp of straw in the corner: you will know by
and by, why I mention this straw, and the other things.
When he was done with it he threw it into the blaze, and
it was burnt. Now, do n't forget the dish held on the lady's
lap, nor the rush in the Earl's hand, nor the straw.

"At last says the Frenchman in broken English, as soon
as they would let him speak, 'Madame, the mistress of the
house, have n't you a son that left you about two years
ago?' The poor woman got into such a tremble, that some

of the cakes fell out of the bowl, and the father opened his eyes and his mouth, but couldn't say a word. 'Oh sir dear', says the mother, 'have you seen our poor boy?'   'Yes', says he, 'I have seen him, and he is alive and well, and well to do, and likely to be better'.   'And when is he coming home, and why did n't he write, and how does he look, and why did n't he come with you?"

"'As I can't speak the English very easily, you may better let me tell my story in my own way', says the Frenchman, for a Frenchman he was: 'I am the head man of business to a merchant in Paris; and about a year and a half ago, a young genteel-looking Irishman was engaged by my employer to teach his children English.   There was something so mild and engaging about the young fellow, that the children and the elder people got very much attached to him, and the young lady their eldest daughter began to like him better than the others.   Your son, for so he was, never took any airs on himself, and the young lady seeing that he paid no particular attention to her, began to mope and be dismal, and at last took to her bed, and was sick in earnest.   The mother, by some means, found out what ailed her, and let her husband know; but he was very angry, and indeed herself was not much better, but still the girl was ailing without making any complaint.   The young teacher made a great many mistakes in the lessons from the first day he missed the young lady from her place; and some of the servants remarked him several nights in the street at late hours, and looking up at the light of one of the windows.   At last, fearing that they would lose their daughter altogether, the mother began to question the young Irishman about his family at home. He made no boast, except that he was descended from good old Irish families on both sides; and that the lands belonging to his forefathers were taken from them, because they would not renounce their religion nor their king; and he mentioned that his own father and mother were still called in jest, Earl and Lady Stairs.

"'Well they had no great occasion to ask him what he thought of their daughter, for one of her young brothers happening to call one day at his lodging, and stepping in on tiptoe, and peeping over his shoulder, he found him sobbing and kissing a little picture which he had made of his sister, unknown to any body.

" 'So the old gentleman at last gave his consent, on condition that a person he 'd send over to Ireland to his father's place, would be able to give a satisfactory account of the state of things here. I think he expected that by getting time, and leaving the lady to herself, she might change her mind; especially as there is no end to the balls and entertainments going on, and as all the young gentlemen of their acquaintance are invited to the house, night after night. Miss Mary is a very lively, rattling young damsel with dark sparkling eyes; and we all wondered how she was so taken with your son, who is very quiet in his manner, and used to say so little. My master hopes from the briskness of her character, that she will get tired of his quietness; but I am sure he will be mistaken; and now a good deal depends on the news I am to send home in a day or two'.

" 'Oh dear', says the poor mother, 'what will you be able to say about such humble people as we, to make your employer think well of the match?'

" 'At all events', says the stranger, 'I can say of you, that before you knew anything of my business, you shared the best you had with me, and what more could you do if you were a real lady? Now if you have any way for me to sleep, I 'll let my guide go back, and bring up my dressing-case from the inn; and we will take to-morrow to go to the top of this mountain here, and walk about, and settle how every thing is to be; and next day I 'll write home'.

" Well, then, he pulled out a letter from their son; and between laughing and crying, they read, how at first he wrote after getting into business, and then when the trouble came, he did not wish to send any letter till he would have something pleasant to say. He put in everything to make them cheerful; and now and then something about the young lady would slip out, and her

mother's kindness, and the love he had for the little
brothers, and what a charitable good young lady she was,
etc., etc. So when the evening got late, Mounseer was
put to rest in a snug little room where their son had his
bed long ago, and well he might sleep too, for there was
a feather pallet, with a nice dry mat under it; and the
fresh air of the mountain got in through chinks and cran-
nies, and did not let the place feel too close; and the
sheets were clean and well aired, and the quilt had all the
beautifulest flowers in the world cut out on it in the
neatest patterns.

"Lady Stairs going in and out took notice that he
spent a good deal of time about his razhurs and other
dressing implements; but if he passed any time on his
knees, it was a mighty short one entirely. Next morning
they contrived to give the Frenchman a decent breakfast
of tay, and white bread, and butter, though them things
did n't often get so high up in the mountains; and they
say that the French do n't use tay at breakfast; and after
that he walked in his thin boots along with the Earl, to
the very top of Blackstairs. I 'm sure they had a delightful view from it, over the castles and demesnes of Mr.
Colclough, Mr. Blacker, Mr. Carew, and all their plantations, and the woods of Kilaughrim, and Tombrick, and
the Slaney flowing along, and the towns of Enniscorthy
and New Ross looking so small, and all the snug farmers'
houses down in the county Carlow, with the green paddocks around them, and the bogs here and there, and the
dry stone fences to the fields, and the town of Carlow,
and the fine broad Barrow flowing off towards Graigue
and New Ross. If they turned round to the sunrise, they
could enjoy the view of Mount Leinster, and the Wicklow
hills, and Ferns, and Corrig Rua, and the far-off sea beyond all.

"Well, that evening he pulled out his letter paper, and
his pen, and ink-horn; and began a letter to the merchant
in Paris, and this is the way a part of it was wrote.

" 'Most respected Sir,

" 'I write these few lines to you, hoping they shall find

you in health as leaves me at present, thanks, etc., etc.,; and the mistress, and Miss Mary, and the young Irish gentleman, and the other children. This country is very different from France: land is so cheap and plenty that they cut away a great deal of every field to make a big· dyke, and they build up a great big ditch with the clay and stones they take out. The people are cheerful, and. hospitable, and obliging; but they are too fond of staying in their chapels, and saying long prayers. Our young gentleman was rather modest in speaking of his father's rank and possessions. I can hardly make a guess at the extent of the demesne that spreads round his mansion for miles and miles, without hedge or ditch, and the sheep and cattle that graze on it are beyond counting. When I drew nigh to the castle, up an avenue half a mile long, it was in the evening, and the Earl and his Lady were at their supper. There were two musicianers stationed before the hall-door, and they played during the whole time, such music as you never heard in your life at any entertainment, no nor the King of France himself. Twelve halberd-men were drawn up in front by way of royal guard; so venerable as they looked, and such beards as they had! and while they were on duty they would not return a salute, nor answer a question to the King nor the Lord Lieutenant himself. Though the Earl and his Lady were at their supper in state, they showed me the greatest respect, when they heard from where I came. Will I ever forget the splendour of that supper! The *side table* could not be valued by the owner at less than fifty thousand pounds; and I am sure that the Earl would not part with the chief *candlestick* that gave light to the feast for ten thousand, any way.

"'After supper, the nobleman dried his hands on a towel with gold fringes, at least they looked very like gold; and so little regard had he for it that when he was done he thrune it into the fire. Moreover, he need not go out of his own demesne for firing for a hundred years to come; and by the end of that time, I'm sure you would hardly miss the trees that would be cut down. Such is the wonderful splendour of every thing here that I can hardly believe my own account of it; and I 'm sure the young Earl when he came to Paris, and ever since, pretended to be poor, that he might find some good young lady who would marry him for his own sake, and not for his rank nor his riches.

"'I will take a look at Dublin, and the Wicklow and the Welsh mountains on my return; and I hope to see my young mistress with the ring on her hand when I get home.

"'I am, etc., etc'.

"Well, the clever Frenchman was asked to the priest's house to take tea that evening, and two or three of the gentlemen-farmers met him there. He was very glad to get in company with the priest, as he spoke French well, having studied at a place abroad called Louvain, and he told him the sort of letter he was sending home. The clergyman wondered at it, you may be sure, but he said that the young lady would be thankful for the invention; and that her mother was won over already; and that the father only wished to make the thing look well in the eyes of their acquaintance; and so the letter would satisfy every body; and from all he could hear of the young man from his old neighbours, his young mistress would never meet a better husband; 'for he had good manners and a good appearance, and was a good scholar, and what few young Paris gentlemen were, he was a good Christian into the bargain.

"Well, to make my long story short, the Earl of Stairs soon made an addition of two rooms to his castle, a parlour and a bed-room, and the next year, there was joy and merriment in his house, for his son and his beautiful black-eyed bride came home; and they brought only a boy and a girl to wait on them; and the servants were harder to please than their master and mistress; and the merry young lady ran about among the heath and rocks, and her serious young husband and she were as fond as fond could be of one another; and she laughed till the tears ran down her cheeks at the notion of the halberd-men, and the musicianers, and the demesne, and the side table, and

the candlestick, and the towel with the gold fringes; and
she was as serious and devout at the little chapel as the
poorest person there. They came to spend a part of
every summer at Blackstairs during the life of the old
people; and if they did n't live happy, THAT WE MAY!"

H. W., at the conclusion of the story, asked Owen to
let us know how he recollected the Frenchman's letter so
well, observing that the beginning of it looked very like.
what one of our own country people, not accustomed to
composition, would write.

Owen answered, that he had heard the story from an.
old schoolmaster that knew, long ago, an old herd that
was acquainted with a neighbour that lived near the earl's.
castle when he was young, and saw the letter, and heard
a good scholar of a weaver read it one night in winter.
"But you need n't wonder", added he; "the queerest things.
happens up in the mountains now and then. Some people.
long ago were coming to Mass one Sunday down from the
hills; and a young man who was minding sheep and
goats, asked them where they were going. They said, 'to.
Mass'; and he asked, 'What was the Mass, and might he.
go along with them'. They said he might, and as they,
went along, they found him as innocent and ignorant as a,
child, for he was always living up to that time in a little
cabin in a cleft of the rock, and had no one to speak to,
but his old grandmother. Well, when they came into.
the chapel of Kilmeashil, the young boy kept his eyes,
and his ears, and his mouth open in astonishment; and
feeling his coat too heavy on account of the heat, he,
took it off, and flung it over the sunbeam that came
slanting in through the window with all the little specks
of dust floating in it; and because he was entirely free
from sin since he was baptized, the sun-beam held up the
coat. You may be sure that there was more people looking at him then than at the altar, and he was made much
of all the way home again.

"You may be sure he was eager for the next Sunday.
to come round; and as soon as he saw the people go by,

he joined them, and came to the chapel, and flung his coat
on the sun-beam as he did before; but the coat this time
fell to the ground, for he had committed some sin or
other, may be pride or vanity, talking to the people going
or coming".

"Well, Owen", said Mrs. K., "this story has a moral
any how, though it does not look a bit more likely than
the others".

The only song executed on that evening was, on the
whole, of a sound moral tendency, though like those lofty-
minded regenerators of humanity, Victor Hugo and Eu-
gene Sue, the composer found himself unable to accom-
plish his high moral object without using objectionable
means.   He dwelt on the silliness and cruelty exercised
by an old man and a young girl towards each other in
committing matrimony; and the unhappy wife sings of
the miseries of her lot, one of the incidents being her
lord's peculiar mode of passing the night, the verse ending with this line—

"He turns his back unto me, his nose goes through the wall".

It is more than probable that she exaggerated the fact.
No nose that ever came under our notice could occupy the
breadth of the wall of a farm-house or cabin, say eighteen
inches.   He probably had a snug hole scooped out and
lined with cotton or wool, extending, say from four to
six inches, into the dry mud, and used it for the comfort
of that feature during the dead hours.   Of the egregious
composition, no more than the concluding verse has remained in our memory: perhaps the loss is not great.   The
aggrieved woman, after detailing her wrongs, thus an-
nounces her determination:—

"Some, they bid me take him, and *dhrownd* him in a well;
More, they bid me take him, and grind him in a mill;
But I 'll take my own advice, and I 'll carry him far away,
And I 'll tie him with a *thraneen* between two cocks of hay".

When the lay was concluded my godmother cried out,—
"I think we have lost enough of time for one evening in

25

nonsense. Harry, will you take *Father Gahan*, and read'
us the meditation for the day, and then we will all join in,
the rosary".

So said so done, the minds just now vacantly occupied
with exaggerated views of life, were, for the next fifteen
minutes, meditating on the chief events of the life of our
Redeemer, and striving to keep the powers of their souls
employed on the holy subjects. We may lose our old
traditions, and manners, and language, but let us never
lose that living spirit of piety, which for fourteen hundred years has animated our islanders, and descended un--
impaired from generation to generation.

CHAPTER XXVIII.

BAD NEWS FROM THE CITY.

ONE evening towards the end of the autumn of this year,.
Jane called in as I was nearly, concluding school business,.
ostensibly to get a couple of pens made for Margaret, but.
in reality to request me not to fail to spend the evening
at her father's. She then slipped into Mrs. Murphy's,.
and requested her also to call in. So about the regular
time of rest from field labours, the two Horans and Mrs.
Murphy and I were added to the ordinary family group.
Jane had a troubled expression on her features, and her
movements were uneasy, and there was sadness on Margaret's sweet features. Matt asked me if I had heard
lately from Edward, and was answered that a letter had'
come from him about a week since. "Was there any very
particular news in it?" "No, but he said that he expected
to have something to say of an agreeable kind in about a
week". "I believe that part of his letter was true enough;
but he need n't say, it would be agreeable to every body
if-he did n't like. He said nothing of reading his recantation, or getting a Dublin wife". "Dublin wife!" said

Mrs. Murphy. "Come, come, Matt; we all know that Mr. O'Brien and yourself use n't to drink out of the one mug, but that's no reason for inventing fables". "Mr. Horan", said H. W., "your informer is either a liar, or very much deceived. He has no more married nor changed his faith, than any one in the present company. How has this news come to you?" "Faith, I 'll give you chapter and verse for it. I was over in Coollattin yesterday evening at Joe Morrissy's about the new barn he 's building, and who should be taking tay there but that long gad of a master that does be teaching the new choir at the Crosses. Well, a man would be fit to beat his own father, to listen to the way he was going on, and the compliments he was paying the mistress of the house. It was, 'Mrs. Morrissy, will you gratify me by taking another cup of your delicious tay? Shall I help you to another slice of this charming cake, ma'am? Allow me to supply you with hot water, my dear madam'". "But about the news?" "Oh, we 'll be at that part of the business immediately. I was so *sharoose* to hear the long sthrā of a fellow pressing the woman in her own house, to use her own victuals, that I was about going away, when the discourse turned about the son Darby, that 's a clerk in a soft goods shop in Dame Street, in Dublin. '*Do* he ever see Mr. O'Brien that *tached* lately in Tombrick?' says myself, 'and how is he?' 'Oh', says Mrs. Morrissy, 'he 's very well, and likely to be better: I hope there is no girl waiting for him to come back and marry her?' 'How should I know'? says myself. 'Well', says she again, 'it 's likely enough that he 's married at this moment, and going to church'". Here there was a general movement of surprise and disbelief, and poor Margaret, as I could perceive, became as pale as a sheet, and was obliged to grasp the arm of the settle bed. She showed a surprising command over herself, however, but did not venture to speak, for her heart was beating violently, and the utterance of a word would have betrayed her agitation. Jane interposed: "Mr. Matt, if this is an invention of yours, may you get a sound thrashing the

next time you sit in a tent to drink a glass of punch!"
"Thank you for your good wishes, Miss Jane. I have
neither hand, act, or part in the matter; I 'm repating
Mrs. Morrissy's own words; I was taken back as much
as yourself on hearing them. 'This is very strange,
ma'am', says I, 'but may be you 'd let us know the
exact truth of what Darby says?' 'I 'll read you
the part of the letter', says she, and she did so ; and
I asked to see the letter after she was done". "But
Matt, people do be saying that you are not up to
making out handwriting, unless it bees very plain".
"Do n't fret yourself; the writing was plain; and I saw
from the few lines that I examined, that Mrs. Morrissy
made no mistake, nor invented nothing, and this is what
was in it. Darby said that himself and an acquaintance
was taking a walk the Sunday before up Castle Street
and Thomas Sreet, and out to the country that way,
and when they were going up Skinners' Row, who
should they see going before them, arm in arm, but
my brave master, and a very nicely-dressed, handsome
young woman. They got a full sight of her face
once that she turned about, and Darby said he thought he
never saw a handsomer one in his life, only she was a
little too pale. Well, that was n't the worst; they came
within hearing of them just at the turn into the open
place before Christ Church, and they heard her plain
enough mentioning the wedding that was to take place on
the next Thursday. Well, they went in through the gate,
and walked into the church, and Darby and his companion saw no more of them, and that 's the sum and
substance of what she read. If I have added a ha'porth,
I 'll give any body leave to tie my hands, and give me a
lambasting; but Mrs. Morrissy is easily found, and so
is the letter, and I 'm sure, Darby is rather a well-wisher
of the master's than otherwise, and would be very far
from inventing anything that would tell again him".

"But, Matt", observed Mrs. Murphy, "might not the
marriage be some body else's, and might n't they be going
into the church only to look at the *curosities* or monu-

ments?" "With all my heart: I have nothing to gain by the wedding, nor the recantation, but Darby heard 'our wedding' as plain as tongue could speak, and it was just twelve o'clock as they were going in. And do you suppose that they would go waumising about through the church looking at lions, and unicorns, and ould monuments, disturbing the people that would be praying or listening to the minister a preaching? I 'm sure they would n't. Maybe the little master got a letter lately to let us know something about the business?" "I have not got any news for ten days or so, as I said before. All you have said may be true in appearance, but Edward is no more a married man, nor a Protestant, than Father Cullen". "I am of the same opinion", said Mrs. Murphy. "And so am I", repeated Jane and Murtagh. "I will know more on the subject before I sleep", said H. W. "Good night to you all. I will go to Coollattin, and when I have looked over that dreadful letter, I 'll know better what to do". "Will we see you again to night?" said Mrs. Lucas. "I think not, ma'am: it will be too late to be disturbing you, unless I find the thing looking very bad; for it is not so unpleasant to know the worst, as to be tormented with doubt". I said this, wishing to spare Margaret a sleepless night, as I did not intend to make my appearance again.

I pushed on to Coollattin, got a sight of the fatal letter, and found that Matt had given the substance correctly enough. I was sadly perplexed, but my opinion of Edward's loyalty remained nearly in its usual state. I called in at Lucas's next morning before school business, declared my conviction that these appearances would be soon explained, and mentioned that I would write that very day. This I did; but before night, the report of Edward's marriage, and his change of religion, were the subjects of conversation at every hearth in Tombrick, Moyeady, Coollattin, and Coolgarrow. In three or four days I should receive an answer: one of the little fellows of the school was sent to Bunclody on the third day, another on the fourth day, but no letter was got. I

wrote a second letter on this fourth day. No notice was
taken of it, and in due course I addressed a third, but
this time to our old friend, Charley, at the College
Botanical Garden.

We were now nearly a fortnight in suspense, and
during that period Margaret's mind was in a pitiable
state. She was afflicted with a dull headache, as I afterwards learned from Jane, who suffered in her turn,
but of course not so intensely. A general disquiet prevailed through the neighbourhood, for Edward had many
well-wishers, and no enemy. Matt merely disliked him
through mean, bad feeling arising from the consciousness of his own inferiority. There was a report of some
one urging Father Cullen to denounce the scandal from
the altar, but the cautious good priest flatly refused, and
said there need be no hurry till the full truth would be
known. Matt was not sparing of moral observations in
his visits: they were general in their character, in order
not to irritate Margaret, but she was left at liberty to
make a personal application of them at her leisure. They
were to the effect of the uncertainty of everything human,
of the great change for the worse that often takes place
in country people, when they change their abode for
cities; and how foolish it is to dwell on the constancy
of young fellows, if you trust them away from you for a
couple of years or so. "Did n't he know more than one
young *khout* that was slaved for, and edicated by his
poor father and mother, and when they were growing old
and feeble, and their sons in a good way in Newfound-
land, not so much as a quintal of fish did they ever send
them. And only to think of the silliness of a country
girl that would be constant to such a weathercock as
Mr. O'Brien, who was not thinking a ha'porth about
her, but would go off and marry some flaunting town
girl, and leave her to break her heart, if that was any
consolation to her. And what a goosecap she would be
if she kept at arm's length from her, a worthy, honest
neighbour that would go through fire and water for her,
and give her a comfortable life in the way she was used

to, and would n't ever be found reading an *ould* novel by the side of a ditch when he ought to be working; and what a bad example it would be to the rest of her sisters, if she had any, seeing her fly in the faces of her father and mother! He declared if he was a father of a family, and had such a *glinkeen* of a girl, would n't he, etc., etc.!"

I happened to get an opportunity of speaking a few words to Jane about this time, and was not a little troubled to find that poor Margaret was not spared by the father and mother at all; that she guessed Matt to be still bent on getting her married to his brother, and that he gave no rest to Murtagh or the seniors of the family: for if the marriage took place, he considered the field would then be open to himself, and Jane should marry him, or endure another course of persecution. "And indeed", added the poor girl, "all his endeavours are useless; he has a bad heart, and I won't have him if he was to go down on his two knees to me. And Murtagh, the big easy slob! I think from his manner to me a long time now, that he would n't be a bit sorry to see Mr. O'Brien step in this moment, and take Margaret away with him. But after all the proposals he made at first, he 'll never move hand or foot till my father and mother and all refuse him, or till there is a certainty of my sister's marriage with some other person. Ah, Harry, I wish you, or some other body, would take a short stick in your fist, and start for the city, and let us know the best or the worst. This life is worse than breaking stones on the road!" And poor Jane, under the influence of more than one annoyance, burst into tears.

CHAPTER XXIX.

A WELCOME LETTER.

It was on a Sunday evening that I received this communication from Jane as she was returning from Mrs.

Owens' of Munfin. She and Margaret had come together as far as Mr. Donovan's, where Margaret staid till Jane would call for her on her return.

We were near the gate of the short lane leading to Donovan's from the road, when we saw behind us one of my pupils, steady, earnest-minded Mick Foley, stepping out at a brisk pace to overtake us. We stopped till he came up, as he was making signs with a letter which he had just taken from his pocket. The direction was not in Edward's hand writing, and my disappointment was not small. "Michael; who gave you this letter, or where has it come from?" "Mr. James Kennedy, the ironmonger in Main Street, called me as I was coming by, and gave it to me; he said it was from Dublin, and that he was arrived that morning, after spending Saturday night on the road; and that he was just on the look out for a messenger to come on with it to Tombrick, when he saw me. Maybe there's news about the master in it". "Very well, Mick; I am going up to Mrs. Murphy's; if you come up by and by, I'll tell you all that you will care to hear. I think from the bulk there is a good deal inside. I am much obliged to you Michael, and will do as much for you another time; good bye for an hour or so. You need not mention the matter, till after you see me again". Michael went on, and we turned up by Donovan's, Jane, hot and cold with curiosity, and H. W. not much better. "Ah! I now recognise the hand; it is from Charley, our old school-fellow; God send us good news! Go in for Margaret; I will go up the lane before, and wait for you in the fallow field inside the first gap".

Now at the upper end of this field in the angle, there was a stile leading into the wilder knoc above it; and on the sunny side was a snug grassy seat, where I intended that we should rest while getting at the contents of the packet. Before I was overtaken by the girls, I had opened the missive, and glanced at the concluding lines; and found, as I had conjectured, that the body of the communication was in the hand of our old facetious friend. When they came up, I saw that Margaret was so affected between.

hope and fear, that she was trembling, and obliged to hold
her sister's arm. There were few words used! She gave
me one arm, and when we got to the sheltery bank spoken
of, we sat down, and I displayed the packet, in which I
found a letter with a strip of paper wrapped round. On this
strip was written, "Not to be opened till the contents of the
enclosing letter are known"; so I put it by, and proceeded
to the reading of the long-expected communication.

"DEAR HARRY,
    "I have too much to say, and too little time for it,
to waste any unnecessary compliments on you. You and
others, I suppose, are anxious about our common friend.
Take comfort! He is alive, I can't say well, but he is
getting towards it; and he is attended to by those who
will neglect nothing to hasten his recovery. He has been
endeavouring for some time, to obtain from his employers
permission to live to himself, either by getting a separate
lodgment in the establishment, or permission to live outside the premises, and come to his business during certain
hours of the day. Hitherto, as you know, his presence
was required during the entire day and night, and the
heads of the institution did not see how the business could
get on, if this arrangement was altered. As they had
promised at first, his salary was to be raised from the first
of October; and he was anxiously watching for the success of his application and his advance in income, in order
to take a race to the old county for some girl to whom he
is attached as I think few people are".
    A bright flush of happiness coloured the face of the fair
girl beside me at these words; I found my hand grasped,
and saw tears of pleasure streaming from the eyes of the
two sisters".
    "I suppose he has told you, that I have determined to
enter the fatal state of matrimony myself, having been de-
luded, bewitched, and enthralled by a Wexford girl who
happened to be on a visit to her relations here, and who
for her sins, I suppose, was thrown into my company. I
dare say that poor Ned felt the loneliness of his fate the

more, from the sight of our happiness; and he was very much taken aback by the difficulty of obtaining the permission he was so anxiously seeking. I heard him complain of headaches two or three times; and I thought he was keeping too much within the house. So last Sunday was three weeks, Ellen and myself called on him, and insisted on his coming out, and spending the day in the country, *i.e.* the neighbourhood of Mount Pleasant, at my eldest sister's place. I had to call to the north side of the city; and as Ellen was wishing to see the nave of Christ Church, with its 'Friars' Walks', the monument of Strongbow, etc., I asked Edward to be her 'guide, philosopher, and friend' so far; and after the inspection, meet me at the south bason. You must know, most uninformed country bumpkin, that crowds of Catholics are seen pouring here into St. Patrick's and Christ Church Cathedrals, to inspect the monuments of the nave, while the Protestant service is going on in the chancel".

Here we all looked at one another, with varying expressions of sheepishness, ludicrous surprise, and great satisfaction passing over our features; and we would, at another time, have moralised on the mighty hubbub caused in our far-off locality by the common incident of a young man and woman entering Christ Church, with no graver purpose than mere curiosity. However, we wanted to get farther into the story, and kept the fetter-lock of restraint on the lips of impatience, as Hajji Baba would remark under similar circumstances.

" We met at the bason, and would have had a pleasant walk to our dinner, but for the all-absorbing trouble that brooded on Edward's spirit. He particularly dwelt on the vacation having arrived without any likelihood of his obtaining his object in any reasonable space; and great as would be his desire to see his relations and his Tombrick friends during the recess, he foresaw so many annoyances arising out of a visit, that he was determined not to leave town. It was evident that there was something wrong about him; for in ordinary cases he is not at all in the habit of inflicting his grievances on his company. We were not behind hand in asking the name and genealogy of the intended Mrs. O'Brien, but we were none the wiser for our diligence; and at this present writing I am supremely ignorant of even the name of her whom I am sure I love and respect already for the sake of our poor friend.

"I will hurry over the rest of the evening; and you will find it more than enough to know that poor Edward was in the beginning of a lively fever the same night. As there was a spare bedroom at my sister's, he would not be allowed to return to town; and from that evening till about three days since, he lay between life and death. My sister and Ellen minded him, administered the medicines, kept his head as cool as they could; and finally with God's blessing he has been pronounced out of danger". The increased colour in Margaret's face at this passage, the sparkling of her mild eyes, and the convulsive working of her fingers, made me feel a lively sympathy in her lately endured afflictions.

"I called at the institution the morning after Edward's falling ill; and nothing could be more gratifying than the interest shown by the principals during the whole time of his illness. Surgeon Wright called frequently; and to the observing of his directions, under God's good Providence, we may attribute the saving of our dear old Ned. Your letters were received; but I thought better to leave you in the dark altogether, than cast terror and grief among you all at once. So I have waited till I can say that recovery is morally certain, and so give joy to his country friends by the good news.

"Within two days, I have been speaking to Edward's immediate chief, and learned the gratifying news that it has been decided on engaging an assistant for him, as his duties are considered too heavy; and that this same assistant will be saddled with the evening duties, thus leaving him that portion of his time at his own disposal, and liberty to fix his residence in the neighbourhood of the establishment.

"I do not suppose that there was as constant a correspondence kept up with Castleboro as Tombrick. So as he had written home the day before his illness, I conclude that his family are under no anxiety on his account.

"While writing the last few words a letter from Mrs. Bryan Roche has come to our hands; I suppose that Edward, without soliciting aassistance or aid, had made his circumstances known to Theresa; for here she informs him that between her parents and herself they had put together fifty pounds to help to the house-warming, whenever he felt resolved to take the fatal spring.

"We keep him as quiet as we can: I mean the women, for I cannot devote much time from my polyanthuses and ranunculuses; but he has insisted on my writing all about it; and he himself has scrawled something inside this inclosure, which he would not permit me to see,—the jealous rogue! You will know what to do with it. He requires an answer without delay; and if this answer be agreeable, you will see him with you in a fortnight at farthest. Thank God I am at the end of the sheet, and no paper nearer than Charlemont Street.   Farewell for the present.

                    " CHARLES REDMOND.
"P.S.—My own wedding was deferred by the above concatenation: the worse luck now, the same always".

My hearers being in a very inquisitive state concerning the enclosure, I pulled off the envelope, and found written on the inside, " Dear Harry, give the enclosed or not, according to circumstances. I feel that the happiness or misery of my future life depends on it. God bless you!"

Without a moment's delay I presented it to Margaret, who soon ran over the contents with undisguised gladness and tender emotion visible in every lineament of her countenance. She handed it to me when read, that Jane and I might sympathise at once in her happy feelings. The words were few, but full of meaning.

" DEAR MARGARET,
"You will see by the hand that I cannot write a long

letter, but I am getting better from hour to hour. I have loved you tenderly and devotedly for many a day. My prospects enable me at present to think of marriage; and at the earliest moment, I send you this first note asking you to be my dear wife. If I get a welcome answer, I will as soon as strength comes, see your loved face again; and that I hope will arrive before a fortnight passes. Send me a line or two to hasten my recovery.

" Your devoted true lover,

" EDWARD".

There was another note in the same envelope addressed to Mrs. Lucas. Margaret did not leave the precious piece of paper in my hands a moment beyond the time necessary for reading. She placed both inside her handkerchief, and after a few words we arose and resumed the walk homewards. As we crossed the next bushy field, we were joined by Murtagh, and after a word or two which I exchanged with Margaret, I told him the state of things. He sincerely rejoiced at the good news about Edward; but told Margaret with a smile, that if she did not make out a good wife for him in place of the one she had deprived him of, his ghost would haunt her. " Mr. Murtagh", said she, " I suppose I will have too much to think about for a while; but there's Jane that will be more at leisure. I'll make her be on the look out; but I advise you to depend on no one so much as yourself". Margaret and H. W. walked on: we had abundant matter for conversation. I had old letters from Edward in my pocket, parts of which I read to her, and I dare say she found the tones of my voice very musical, for she herself was the everlasting subject. The length of the road was not felt by either; and I believe that our companions, now really at liberty to open their minds to each other, did not let the opportunity slip by. We reached Lucas's in a mood very different from that which had possession of us an hour before.

Margaret got her father and mother up into her own neat little bed-room, and they spent about twenty minutes

there in consultation. The kitchen was pretty well furnished with visitors when they came back, for it had
become known that a letter had arrived; and I gave the
mingled audience that part of the intelligence that was
expedient under the circumstances. We received during the
evening embassies from Coollattin, Ballyduff, Moyeady,
Coolgarrow, and the border district of Cran Rua; and all
departed well pleased to have heard good news of their
favourite, and to have the farther distribution thereof. So
the minds of the Donovans, the Hogans, the Whittys,
and the Kennedys are at peace, and in possession of a
new topic of conversation; and H. W. is admitted to a
secret conference with Mr. and Mrs. Lucas, and gets full
permission to write a cheering letter to his friend. This
privilege I avail myself of the same night; and Margaret gets the letter when one leaf is filled, and she writes
on the third page such a charm as will effect the speedy
recovery of the poor invalid. She makes me seal and
direct the note without daring to cast my eyes on the
magic characters; and though it is certain that Edward
could repeat them by rote from the hour in which they
met his eyes, he never communicated the form nor matter
to H. W., his bosom friend and trusty agent. So the
reader may sigh if it is of any relief, but must decidedly
submit to a disappointment. Murtagh spent the evening
with us; and after some cordial handshakings everyone
retired to rest, and several fervent acts of thanksgiving
were offered up on bended knees that night.

*   *   *   *   *

The big meadow of Tombrick has been mentioned. It
lay by the Slaney near Moyeady; and after the hay was
cut, all the farmers of the townland kept their cows there
at grass, it being a kind of common property something
in the nature of a village common in France. Sunday
evening during the grazing season was a bright spot in
the lives of the young men and women of the township.
Groups of milkers would be scattered over the extensive
meadow; or coming in with empty vessels; or departing

with full ones. It is a very different thing walking with dear friends or relations across the soft turf of such a meadow, or the path across a field, or by the side of a fence on a fine sunny evening, from the feel of the nasty grit under your thin soles in the streets or roads near the city, especially when you find yourself all alone, and no one to take a loving interest in your health or welfare.

On such a fine evening were Margaret, Jane, Sarah, Murtagh Horan, some of the Donovans, H. W., and some female servants employed or not employed in the big meadow. There was no lingering however, as Edward and Charley were expected to arrive later in the evening. So we were quitting the bank where there is a sort of ford to Srehearth on the east side, and directing our steps to the common entrance, when we saw two young men approaching from Mat Foley's field. I recognized Charley, and every other one in the field knew Edward. They made the distance between us as short as they could; we aided them on our side. I will not attempt to paint the emotion, almost painful, of Margaret and her betrothed till their hands were once more entwined in each other, and their eyes gratified with the long looked for sight of each other's faces. There was a joyful and incoherent series of questions, shaking of hands, and expressions of delight among us all. I seized on Charley, and as soon as I could be attended to, presented him to our friends; and with his peculiar absence of shyness, real good nature, and possession of good manners, he was at home in a very brief period, and begging the young women to put out of their minds that he was an engaged man, and afford him the treatment of a lonely bachelor. We soon broke into groups; Charley entertaining his portion on many subjects, and Edward and Margaret letting us precede them, and apparently wishing for no increase of seceders from the front body. I dare say that some amongst us would have wished for the invisible cloak of the story, so that he might listen to their discourse unreproved; but taking everything into account, I do not think we lost much valuable information by the distance that separated us from them.

Charley mentioned that they had reached Enniscorthy on Friday evening, got out to Castleboro next morning, and had the pleasure of finding the three families all in good health and comfort. "Indeed, I should have said four", added he, " as Tom and Joanna are as well off as any of their rank in Bantry; they have a small farm at a moderate rent, and are not in fear of seizure or ejectment. We came off after an early dinner, having shook fifty pairs of hands before and after Mass at Courtnacuddy, and not finding somebody at home when we came this side of yonder ridge, myself or my companion got so impatient, that we reneagued the society of our new parents in prospect, and here we are".

As we came near home Margaret and Edward condescended to join us, and I had time to observe the change made in his appearance by a year of anxious exertion and by his late illness. However, the happy feelings now in the ascendant seemed determined to obtain a complete victory over past anxiety and the lingering relics of the fever. When we entered, and the renewed bustle was allayed, and his hat was removed, we noticed that a silk cap was an indifferent substitute for the profusion of black hair which he had carried away with him from Tombrick on the previous year.

"Ah, master", said little Sarah, "take off that black cap: is that the fashion in Dublin? and let us see your thick black hair again". " Sarah, my darling", said he, " my friends in Dublin had a choice of sending me home to you, a dead cavalier or a living roundhead; you see their choice; I hope you approve of it". " Ah, master, I hope you 'll stay with us now till your hair is long again". "Never fear: I think a week more will ree this black milk-bowl flung into the potato-field".

But the discourse of the evening was so disjointed, so many questions were asked by each party of the other, on points of which the reader is already sufficiently cognizant, and so many new questions were inserted in the unfinished structure of the answers, that the confused proceedings of that Sunday night shall remain unrecorded.

It may be thought that the consent of the seniors was too facile; but let it be understood that Jane took the liberty of joining the group in Margaret's bedroom the day on which the letter came to hand, and a little piece of information she gave concerning an offer made to her by Murtagh on the walk home, is supposed to have had its influence. The determined course things had taken on Edward's side, together with the evident deep seated attachment, not concealed by their daughter, broke down all further opposition. So the suitor had now no reason to complain of an uncordial reception.

Great confusion was thrown on our immediate neighbourhood for the next day or two, by Charley endeavouring to let a little extra sun-shine in on the understanding of the farmers in respect to the necessity of draining land, and of adopting the succession of crops. Tombrick being nearly all on a slope, and the land of a somewhat dry character, the workers of the soil were more anxious for moisture in dry seasons, than for devising plans for its removal. As to the crop succession, they had nothing to object; but their faith in the virtue of long fallowing remained unshaken. Edward paid flying visits to his old friends, the Donovans, the Kennedys, the Hogans, the Whittys, and to my godmother's hill fortress, and was everywhere received as a son returned from abroad.

He had got leave of absence for a month, and a couple of rooms, with kitchen and closet, were at this very time being neatly, but not very expensively furnished by Charley's sister, Charley's betrothed, and her cousins, for himself and his bride. They were next door to a little paradise prepared for Ellen's betrothed and herself, and in the neighbourhood of Charlemont bridge. From their windows they will have a view in summer, through the upper boughs of the elms skirting the canal, over the green meadows to the convent of Ranelagh, surrounded by its fine old trees, through the open boughs of which it will be delightful to see the rays streaming down on the fields, and the thin dewy vapour softening the shadows made by the leafy groupings and the

26

buildings. The man or woman who can look on a tran-
quil scene like this without feeling delight accompanied by
gratitude to Providence, is much to be pitied. Our newly
wedded will also have the mountains above the Little
Dargle, and stretching beyond Tamlacht for the background
of their view; and with decent competence and tender attachment to each other, they will hardly grumble at their
lot. It is the happiest at all events afforded to mere human
aspirations and instincts.

CHAPTER XXX.

THE LAST EVENING.

SOME of our old acquaintance were asked to hot cake on
the next Thursday, and surely it was a bustling happy
evening; such a well assorted little party was assembled
of married folk, candidates for that state, youth and maids
still unfettered, and happily disposed children. Edward
inquired of one of the youngsters if any extraordinary
discoveries continued to be made under his successor in
the school, such as the "fierceness of frogs", and Gulliver's
discovery of the new world; and was surprised to see the
shyness of the little man as to giving an answer. Little
Sarah laughed heartily, and mentioned Charley's own last
discovery. This child was the most restless and troublesome of the whole school. No question stopped him;
without a moment's thought he blurted out some cock-and-
bull response; and he volunteered answers for every one in
hardship. Natural history was his delight; so to keep his
hands occupied and his tongue from doing mischief,
he had been set on that very day to write about the fox.
Strange to say, that when his work was fairly before him,
he could think of nothing more to the purpose, than that
the _wool_ of that roguish animal was in great request in
Africa! When the laugh subsided, Charley dexterously
turned the satirical feelings of the company to Mick Foley,

who, being appointed a monitor, ordered his class to *horāsh* instead of turn, guiding horses at plough being to him a more congenial occupation than drilling little boys. Having pretty well succeeded in this movement, he entertained us with a cunning device invented by little Thomas Sutton the other day, when he was down playing with himself and his sister Catherine. Mrs. S. was after giving him a fair supply of apples, but not to the extent of his wishes. So he put on Catherine's bib and bonnet, and boldly presented himself to his mamma, and asked for some fruit. "You little rogue", said she, "did n't I give you plenty just now?" "Oh, mother, sure I am not Thomas: I am Catherine".

Edward was asked if he had seen many things of this kind among the little pupils of Kildare Place? but he said he could for the moment recollect only one piece of absurdity, for which a north-country teacher and a pupil were jointly, but not equally responsible. He then adduced the questions and answers. "What is a *wudda*?" "A woman who lost her husband". "Could you call any woman a *wudda*, if she did n't lose her husband?" Here the pupil was taken aback. "May be if she died before she was married at all". "Jest so, and you may call her a young *wudda*". "Oh! now I recollect", added Edward, "a really ingenious mistake of a little boy. He was asked 'what is the feminine of *drake*?' He could not recollect, perhaps he never had seen the object: so he began to search for it by analogy, repeating these examples to himself;—'The man and woman are going down street—the drake and —— what is it at all? The dog and cat—(cat is the feminine of dog)—are going down street—the duke and duchess are walking down street—the drake and drakess—oh, bother it!—Mr. Brown and his wife—the drake and his wife—drake's wife is n't the thing—Mr. Brown and Mrs. Brown—I have it. Drake and Mrs. Drake are going—the very thing. The feminine of drake is Mrs. Drake, sir'".

"Mr. O'Brien", said my godmother, "when you are resting yourself after your return to the city, you will have to get for me a copy of *Evelina*. I have a curiosity about seeing if I can bring back any of the delight I felt, when I read it about twenty years ago".

"And master", added Larry, "wrap up *Don Belianis of Greece* in the parcel: it won't cost much: the dog tore my copy of it, before I had a quarter of it read".

"And as it will be the same trouble to send four books as two", said Mrs. Murphy, "if you can get a cheap *Philothea, or the Difference between Temporal and Eternal*, or the *Spiritual Combat*, do n't forget your old sweetheart".

"*God's relief is nearer than the threshold.* I have a little box half full of books, which I hope is safe at this moment in Castle Dockrell. There is a *Philothea* in it for you, Mrs. Murphy, and a *Robinson Crusoe*, for you, Larry. You must do without *Evelina*, Mrs. K.; but *Belinda* by Miss Edgworth will supply its place. I do not know whether *Belinda* is the best novel in the English language, but it is decidedly the best that ever fell into my hands".

"Well, in my opinion", observed Mat, "bad is the best of them sort of books. I heard some samples of one or two of them, and what was it all about! A conceited young fellow with curly hair, and that used scented soap, and lavender water on his pocket hankecher, bows and scrapes to a glinkeen of a young lady seventeen years of age, that never did a haporth of good for herself or any body else. Well, they are both as handsome as the sun, and thinks that if they are allowed to marry, all their life will be a honeymoon; they 'll find money hanging on the boughs for them; and children as handsome as angels, in the cups of the flowers. All sorts of spiteful people get round them to make mischief; and no one ever heard of such stoney-hearted parents as they 're afflicted with. After enduring more than six camels, the youth is going to shoot himself, and the maid is three quarters gone in consumption, but at last two mountains knocks their heads together, the sky falls, and ever so many larks are caught. An old building that was fit to stand a hundred years, falls on the rogue that's keeping them asunder, and a big bag of gold is found for them in the rubbish. Heart-burn and decay are cured without the apothecary; and the little-good-for pair are wedded; and all the world that would n't value them a thraneen if they were ever acquainted with them, are ordered to sing, and dance, and rejoice, just as if there would n't be quarrels and fights and calling names before a quarter of a year went over their heads".

" I protest, Mr. Horan", said Edward, "you ought to write an essay against novel reading. However, you need not fear any harm that *Belinda* will do Mrs. K., nor her godson, nor Larry either. The lady and gentleman in it find something else to do besides dressing themselves fashionably and going to entertainments. They think it necessary to do good, and avoid evil; and all their wishes are not to run selfishly and thoughtlessly into a marriage with each other, although they are very tenderly attached. No: each is prepared, from a principle of duty, to do what is very unpleasant, and give each other up; and if the tender-hearted lady who writes about them, takes some trouble to put obstacles out of their way, and allow them to form a very desirable union, I hope no one in this room will blame her. You may be quite sure they will employ their after life in giving the best education they can to their children, making each other's lives as agreeable as possible, and improving the condition of their tenants".

" Well, Edward", said Mr. Redmond, " I think there is one fault at any rate in this lady's works. In all her books written either for little men or women, such as Sarah and Charley there, or bigger men and women such as ourselves (by saying bigger I do n't mean wiser or better: God knows, it is often the very reverse), all the important characters are gathered together in the end, just like the last scene of a play; and the good little or big people are praised and rewarded, and the spiteful boy or girl is chastised, or banished from society; and generally the story is too skilfully constructed. If a story is to be a true picture of life, why did not Miss Edgeworth some-

times let her good people continue to struggle with poverty
or trouble, and leave them to be rewarded by God at the
end? Indeed she might also allow the bad-hearted characters to live on with comfort and splendour about them.
With their evil dispositions they won't be able to enjoy
them. And after all, who can take any real pleasure in
the punishment of the very worst people?. Does n't every
right-minded Christian wish that they should be converted, and go to Heaven in the end?"

"Then I suppose", resumed Matt, "your tender-heart
would not allow you, if you were a king or judge, to
punish criminals at all. You would merely tap them on
the back, and say, ' Now, Mr. Jemmy O'Brien, or Mr.
Hunter Gowan, you see what mischief you done. What
good is it to you now? See how all the court is looking
at you: go away and live peaceably with every one: be a
good boy, and people will bring you gingerbread and
nuts from the fair of Cloghamon".

"Not a bit, Mr. Horan. Kings and judges must do
what they can, first to frighten bad people from doing
wrong; but if they do n't succeed in that, then to put it
out of their power to do any more evil against society.
Do you wish to take up the cudgels, Edward, for your
favourite writer?"

"Did you ever take notice of the old ruins at Castleboro on a fine fresh dewy morning, or at sunset either,
when you would see some parts so bright, and the strong
colours in the bits of white plaster, and red and green
moss making such a fine combination; or the bright sky
and the white sheets, or the white cows, or the handkerchiefs of the milking girls, making such a contrast with
the dark masses under the trees or the sheds, or the
shadow thrown over every thing where the sun's rays
could not shine?" "I surely did, and often wished I
could make a picture of it". "And did you ever see the
same view on a dry harsh day, when there was no sunshine, and every thing looked like a patched gown spread
out on a hedge? If you could paint it, which time would
you select? A painter may make an outline of a place if
he likes, and lay on the colours as they met his eye on the

harsh dry day I spoke of, but will many people look the second time at his picture? If a story-teller makes a commonplace narrative without any trouble to arrange his facts, or bring those near that would set each other off best, his work will remain on the shelf".

"And that", said Mr. Lucas, "is the very place I would wish all books not written with a good intention, to remain. I knew a young girl at Ballycarney, who was very seldom found doing her ordinary business; but whenever she came across a novel, you would find her sitting over the fire, perusing her edifying author. So lazy was she, that she used to bend the book, so as to bring the covers together, the way she 'd have the less trouble holding it: I suppose the backs were often found cracked after the heat of the fire and the usage she gave them. The young people of her own rank were rather shy of proposing for the lazy young lady; and one of the neighbouring gentlemen's sons did not see anything amiss in stopping, and conversing with her about the adventures of the ladies and their lovers she was so fond of studying about. So she was delighted at finding some one at last, that resembled Sir Lionel Belfield or Sir Eustace Delafield; but the poor thing, instead of gaining a fine husband, lost her character, and went from bad to worse. So she left the neighbourhood, and some one saw her drinking with a soldier one market day in Enniscorthy".

"It would be a nice point", observed Charley, "to determine whether that girl's flighty notions and lazy disposition set her on novel reading, or the novel reading weakened her good principles".

"Would n't it be safest", asked Matt, "not to teach such girls to read at all? and then they could n't do themselves any harm by their novels".

"To be sure it would", said Charley, "and also to leave little boys without a knowledge of writing, for fear they 'd be hanged for forgery some day".

"And there is", quoth Mrs. K., "such disagreement often between married people, and misery caused by bad children; and so much sorrow felt when death takes one of them away from the other; and it is so dismal when one or may be both die, and leave a helpless family behind them, that no one ought to marry if Mr. Horan's reasoning is right".

"Oh, yez may all laugh at me; but now suppose,—at the same time, may God keep us from harm,—suppose, I say, that when Mr. O'Brien and his wife are a year or so married, she is taken ill in any way, and left all alone to suffer by herself, while her husband is away at his business; and may be when he comes home in the evening he finds her at the point of death, would n't he give the world that he had never coaxed her to leave her family to live and die all alone in a strange town? Or suppose again, that Mr. O'Brien would lose his employment, or his health, or may be his life, and leave her two or three helpless little things for a legacy, do you think that her fate would be very agreeable?"

"When I find myself in low spirits, Mr. Horan", said Charley, "I 'll send for you to bear me company, if you are to be got within the breadth of two counties. However, let us not be frightened too much. My good wife that is to be, will be next door to my friend and my friend's wife; and if they do n't love one another there is not a headache in a gallon of bad beer. Know also to your comfort, that there are not simpler nor more affectionate people to be found than the real Dublin citizens, and that a cunning country *kannat* after living in the city for half a year, would buy and sell a whole street of the natives; and that however newspaper writers and public speakers labour, the friendship and kindness of Protestant and Catholic neighbours to each other is beyond anything".

"And after all", said Mrs. Murphy, "it 's a comfort to think that God's care is as near us in the city as in the country; and that Mr. O'Brien and his wife can attend an early Mass every day of their lives; and that well-disposed people have better opportunities of practising devotion there than we have".

"And I believe", added Mrs. K., "it is the will of God that, except those who cannot support themselves, or those who have a vocation for a religious state, people in general should marry, so that the human race may continue till the Day of Judgment is at hand. And if they wish for a reasonable share of comfort, let them select partners that are disposed to live in the love and fear of God, and above all, use no deception as to their own character or circumstances before their union".

"And you may add, ma'am", said Charley, "that they may as well not marry too young, nor in too great a hurry. I knew a young fellow in Dublin: he lodged in Church Street, and his weekly earnings were not large. A young girl whose weekly earnings were still less, as you may suppose, happened to lodge in the same building. I suppose there were no less than six or eight families altogether under the same roof. This wise youth was wonderfully staid in manner, and the moral observations that fell continually from his lips, were most edifying. Coming down one fine morning to go to his business, he found the young maiden sitting on the stairs, and weeping. He asked her the cause of her sorrow, and so genuine appeared his interest, that she confided to his friendly bosom, the fact of being at the Strawberry Beds the evening before, in company with Jeremiah Traynor, her young man, and that he then and there affronted her in presence of their whole company with whom they had left the town, and openly showed a preference for Winefrid Soden, the unprincipled little hussey, for taking her beau from her, after they were engaged to be married as soon as the now false Traynor would have a little room furnished. Beauty in tears! Ah, susceptible though moral Mr. Tracy! why do you not slip down the stairs before the flood-gates of confidence are flung open? For once, let the Good Samaritan be admired but not imitated; let No. 1 be in the ascendant; take the selfish worldly Levite for your model. Alas! alas! Instead of taking that prudent step, he took his seat beside the inconsolable fair, and a fortnight after, young Mrs. Tracy had no place in her memory for the woes of that sad morning".

"A blessed match it must have been", said Mrs. Murphy, "and a faithful and prudent wife, young Mrs. Tracy, I 'm sure!"

"Do n't be harsh in judgment, Mrs. Murphy. You 'd scarcely suspect a dunghill cock to have any wish for nursing tender chickens; nor if he had, would you think he 'd do that duty with ordinary skill and success? But, Mrs. Murphy, if ever a tender brood is left on your hands, after a Munfin fox has carried away the careful and loving mother, remove the feathers as gently as you can from the breast and so forth of gallant chanticleer, and see what a capital dry nurse he 'll turn out. Now it happened that the young and inexperienced couple were temperate, and saving, and careful, and at the time of my making their acquaintance, a year and a half after their unpremeditated match, their condition seemed satisfactory enough, and their mutual affection strong. Still I will not enforce their example as suited for general imitation. I am anxious to know Mr. Jourdan's notions on the subject of matrimony, and why he has so long lived a life of loneliness?"

"Do n't pity me too much, Mr. Redmond. While I can live at free quarters at my employers' places, and am welcome to the warm corner in the evening; with the old and young people about me, sorra' bit lonesome I feel. May be if I was married, it 's the cold hearth and the cool welcome I 'd have before me on a cold or wet evening. I was once employed at Mr. Horneck's of Gurrawn, and happened to know a little of an honest English labourer that used to be working on Mr. Tom Whitney's land. This man did not know A from B, I believe, though he was married to a smart, purty, little schoolmistress. May be they might have lived happy enough, only for an old, mischief-making magpie of a mother that she happened to have; and the best name *she* had for her unfortunate son-in-law, was 'ugly Tom'. Well, to be sure! how she would dress herself *to the nines,* the daughter I mean, and walk with her neighbour, the schoolmaster, up and down the road of a fine summer

vening, and talk grammar and *Bell's letters.* I donnow
vhat sort of letters them is; but I heard them mention
he names more than once. I 'm not going to think
ɔr say they done worse; but it was an odd sight to
see poor Tom with his hoe or his spade on his shoulder,
ʒoing into his cabin after his weary day's work, and
ɛating a few potatoes out of the ashes, and his fine wife
ɛalking and laughing at the bawn gate with her entertaining companion. One day that I went in to light my
pipe, I saw the old damsel nipping about an inch off an
ɔunce of tobaccy that she was just after buying, and
handing it to her daughter; and says she, 'That I think
will be quite enough to satisfy the longing of Ugly Tom
till to-morrow'. Yerra, if poor Tom ever had the good
fortune to be robbed of his paycock, hen I mean, and his
magpie, and went back to England, what a fine notion
he could give them of Irish wives and mother-in-laws!
Well, for many a day, I could not let Tom's mistress out
of my head day or night; and I believe that is the chief
reason that I never pushed wedlock at any one". (Owen's
later and, on the whole, happy marriage, furnished a
curious comment on this speech).

"Well, Owen", said Mrs. Murphy, "I wish that you 'd
let into your delicate imagination a trifle of what the
poor slaves of wives have to expect, even when their
husbands are not very bad at all. You heard of Shān
Risthard of Ballyphilip?" "Oh! who did not hear of
Shān that would never speak the Irish he knew so well;
but would for ever be making offers at the English, though
he could n't put three words of it after one another. He
meant to tell a neighbour's child one day that 'she had a
nose like a weesel', but he could only settle the Irish sounds
in something like an English form: so says he, 'Och,
you lazy *Ceolān*, (c hard), you have a sock on you like a
planet'". "Owen, you want to put my argument aside,
but you sha'n't. Shān and his wife were sitting one evening
at the fire talking about their little farm. 'I think', says
he, 'I 'll buy some *see hades*, in Bunclody, next Saturday,
to sow the paddock'. 'Do so', says the wife, 'but Shān

asthore, don't call 'em *see hades*, but *hee sades*'. ' Do you
vont to larn me grammar, Molly?' says he: 'it 's not,
hee sades, but *see hades*, I tell you'. 'An if you vor a
grammarian fifty times', says she, ' *hee sades* is the word'.
At last Shān, by way of settling the argument and his
own bad temper, gave Molly a tap with a stick, and broke
her arm. And they were jogging to Bunclody half an
hour after, Molly on the pillion, and her arm in a sling;
and the surgeon had the best of the argument".

"I decidedly forbid any more discourse of this kind",
said my godmother, "A pretty joke if any of our young
people should be frightened, and run off and go live all
alone by themselves in some cavern under the hills, where
the water would be dripping down through the roofs, and
where they 'd get their death by rheumatism, We'd then
have to be bringing them home, and nursing and petting
the withered, cross creatures. I 'm sure it would be poison
to their eyes to see a man and wife sitting chatting by
the sunny side of a ditch on a Sunday evening with their
children chasing one another about". My godmother's
fears were groundless, for the three marriages took place
within a month.

The conclusion of a letter of Edward's, received many
years after was, "I love my dear Margaret more with
every day that passes over our heads". Charley's face-
tiousness and animal spirits had suffered no diminution at
the same period; and when Murtagh's day's work was
over, and Jane was preparing supper, he often told me
that he did not envy the king on his throne.

THE END.

NOTES.

The Milk Bath of the White Cows; p. 12.

This historical tale is mentioned in Keating's *History of Ireland.* The locality is named in the old chronicles, *Ard Leanachtha* (The Hill of New Milk). Some antiquaries fix the scene lower down the river. *Loch Carmain* (Wexford Bay) is the " Pool of Carmen", a Celtic goddess. The invaders were the *Tuath Fiodgha* (woodmen) of Wales. The memory of the battle, not derived from books, was green in our part of the county in the early part of this century.

The Star of Slane; p. 16.

Some specimens of our poetry which now only excite laughter were composed by men well acquainted with the prosody of native lays, of which assonance and alliteration were essential qualities. Whatever offences they commited against good taste, neglect of rhythm was not to be found in them. Most of them were composed by school-masters or weavers, who thought in Irish, but were obliged to communicate their ideas in English.

Lime Kilns; p. 33.

Among the debris of a Tombrick lime-kiln, and som etime between 1820 and 1823, one of the writer's little pupils found a curious lump of calcined matter of an irregular globular shape, and about two and a-half inches across. She presented it to her teacher, and he, after preserving it for several years, handed it over to Mr. John Veevers, superintendent of the Model School, Kildare Place. This gentleman afterwards filled the office of stipendiary magistrate at Mohill, in Leitrim, and Bailieboro' in Cavan. In a communication made to the writer about fifteen years since, he mentioned that the mineral was lost. A description is here subjoined in order that he may obtain from some man of learning an idea of how it could have acquired the strange marks by which it was distinguished. These were the imprints of the hoofs, paws, etc., of cows, horses, sheep, goats, and, to the best of my recollection, dogs, made as if lilliputian animals had thrust their feet into the mass, while in a soft state, and there left their mould-like marks. The depth of the cavities might be between one-eighth and one-quarter of an inch, and nothing could excel the accuracy and finish of the impressions. There was also the mark of the ferrule of a spindle. No ingenious artist ever cut out the once filling-up-matter of these little shafts. The substance—if the writer's memory has been faithful—resembled pumice, and was quite rough on the surface. If it could be supposed that the lump was once large, and of the consistence of mortar, and impressed by the feet of full grown animals, and had afterwards shrunk to the size of a child's fist, the thing might be accounted for. In this case, however, the antecedents and process would be more strange than the result. The compiler of this volume will be very grateful for any attempt at a rational explanation.

St. Mogue; p. 97.

If Owen had been consulted some twenty years later, he could have given the following additional information on the subject of St. Mogue. In the little town adjoining the cathedral a well has furnished refreshment to the inhabitants since Ferns knew an inhabitant. A fine large trout was tenant in perpetuity of this well, say thirty-five years since; how long before that time we are unable to say. The water-drawers would bring crumbs of bread for his use in their daily visits, and the greatest respect was paid him, as it was supposed he had existed there since the days of the saint, and was in fact the guardian of the spring. About the period mentioned, a reckless shoe-maker, Will Harden by name, *diabolo suadente*, took the trout from his cool abode, put him in a pot of water, set fire under the pot, and as he acknowledged afterwards to my informant, a living Dublin citizen, "if he burned the whole wood of Ferns a boil would not come". His wife coming in from a visit found him at this abominable task and obliged him to take the fish back again in a pail to the well, where it was found in its usual state by the next visitors.

In the changes consequent on the introduction of the rail-road, the ground was raised all round and over the well, and its water has since been distributed to the public by means of a pump. In the opinion of the consumers it does not enjoy the clear quality it once possessed. That Harden told the story we firmly believe, but we entertain strong doubts of his (Harden's) love of veracity. The cave of Cong and a well near Kells had similar tenants, and we were told some dozen years since by an inhabitant of the little burgh in Meath, a tale, the same in substance as Harden communicated to our authority.

Another incident connected with this well was got from the same quarter. A poor man who had lost his reason, was informed in one of his visions that he would be restored to health of mind on bathing in St. Mogue's well. He acted on the impression, and got into it, but was soon pulled out by the inhabitants who chased him naked a mile or so out of the town. He was really restored to the use of his lost reason, perhaps from a confidence in the operation, united with the cool shock and subsequent exercise.

Castle of Clonmullin; p. 327.

This name appears to be made up of *cluain*, meadow, and *mullan*, height or hillock. A curious archæologist ascending the slope from Bunclody towards the summit of Mount Leinster, will find where the fortress once stood, and if lucky, will also come on a druid's circle; the enclosed turf having all the properties of the dread *Feur Gorthach* (hungry grass). Some stingy or careless labourer having taken his dinner there very long ago, and omitted to leave some crumbs of bread or potatoes, or a few drops of milk after him for the *Duine Matha* (good people, fairies), they accordingly left the curse of hunger on the spot, and a person inadvertently crossing it, was afflicted with utter prostration till some food was administered to him. Of the curse inflicted on the Cromwellian chief, only two lines of the original Irish remained on the memory of the Duffrey Shanachies of sixty years since, viz., the last and third last in the lament.

Irishians must pardon the mistranslation of one word.

" *Biodh cac na gobhar le thaebh a leabha,*
Is nead an chreabhair le bun a gheatha!"

Castle Hyde; p. 161.

This serious attempt at the picturesque, not being noticed or patronised by the castellan, the affronted poet composed a satirical lay by way of revenge for the slight. It furnished the idea of the "Groves of Blarney" to the gifted bard, Mr. Milliken, of Cork.

Rose Mac Bruin or Treon; p. 223.

For a circumstantial account of the building of the fortifications of New Ross, and a most interesting romantic narrative connected with it, see Mr. Ferguson's beautiful little romance of *Rosabelle of Ross*, DUBLIN UNIVERSITY MAGAZINE, first vol. for 1836.

Munfin; passim.

Tradition relates that this fine old manor house, described in Michael Banim's story of the *Croppy*, was about two centuries since in the possession of Colonel Butler, brother of Lord Galmoy, and equally cruel. Once hearing from the road fence a woman say to her boy who was loitering behind, " Come on, you young thief! If Colonel Butler catches you, you'll be hung". Out spoke the colonel; " Oh ho! if he's a thief, I'll make short work with him". He jumped out, seized on the poor child, and had him executed. This story is told of other high personages of cruel memory. We vouch not for its truth. The word means Fair wood.

GLOSSARY OF IRISH AND CORRUPT EXPRESSIONS.

☞ *The second word in Italics is the correct Irish expression. For other useful hints towards the study of this Glossary, see that appended to the* Banks of the Boro, pp. 367, *etc.*

Antherantaarians the ordinary pronunciation of *Antitrinitarians*, a long spell in Fenning's *Universal Spelling Book,* the other jaw-breaker being co-essentiality, pronounced by now dead students, *cozzentiality.*

Arklow: *Arc,* impost; *Loch,* lake or bay. *Arc* also means small or swift; the payment of customs probably gave name to town and harbour.

Baithershin: *feidhir,* possibility: *sin,* so, thus, that, there. The slang term *chaff,* expresses its colloquial meaning.

Ballindaggin: beal, a mouth or pass; *daigh,* plunder, slaughter, fire.

Ballinlugg, *beal an luig,* mouth of the pit.

Ballinvegga; *beal an bhagha,* pass of the fight. It may also mean a pass or town in the marsh.

Ballycarney, the pass of the ford of the heap of stones (the several words before explained). The last we have ascertained of the old fortress was its being dismantled, and all its wood work burned, by a certain partizan of Cromwell named Carroll, in order to prevent it from affording shelter to Lord Ormonde and his Loyalists.

Ballyprecus: pracas, a mess of oatmeal and milk. Perhaps the name arose from the stingy proceedings of some early dwellers in the *Baile* (township).

Barcelona, silk handkerchief.

Behan: *beachan,* a bee.

Bawnard: *ard,* high; cattle enclosure on the height.

Boolian: *buachalan,* ragweed.

Boolavogue, before explained as "Mogue's cow-pen", is more probably, the cows' enclosure in the marsh.

Bullaan a rinka: *buaile,* a paddock where cows were milked; *rincé,* implies that dances were held there either by the fairies or mere young human beings.

Carnew: *cathair,* a fort; *nua,* new or strong.

Caroline, a beaver hat.

Carric Rua, red rock.

Choka, *cach.* For the recondite meaning of this word consult an Irish dictionary in repute.

Cloghamon: *abhan*, river; the stone in the river, or the wood, or the bog, or the stone by the thorn tree. For the separate names see the *Banks of the Boro*, p. 370.

Clonegal: *gal*, battle; *gaill*, foreigners; plain of battle, or plain of the foreigners.

Cnoc-an-Bocha, the hill in the marsh. This eminence is on the Carlow side of Mount Leinster. *Edward* was wrong in supposing it to be Sliabh Buidh.

Colclough, if a Celtic name, might be explained, the stone in the wood, or the retired nook. The name *Coquely* occurs in French nomenclature.

Comether, if not a corruption of "come hither", is probably a modification of *comharshan*, a neighbour.

Cool, beyond but not through the wicket, a hurling expression.

Coolgarrow: *gearbach*, rugged; rugged or uneven wood. There is now no wood, but the position is rugged and uneven enough.

Coollattin: *leathan*, broad; wide wood.

Coolycan: *cean*, cattle; the wood abounding in cattle.

Cromoge: *cro*, fortress; *bogach*, marshy. The reader is referred to the description of the old rath, pp. 21, 225.

Cuchulainn, Culann's dog. The hero, when a stripling, entering at night the premises of Culann the great blacksmith, then entertaining his (Cuchulainn's) uncle, king Conor, was obliged to kill his watch dog in self-defence. It being left to himself to decide on the amount of the *eric* to be paid to the smith, he consented to watch his house at night till a pup of the famous dog would be strong enough to undertake the duty. Hence the name. *Culainn* is the genitive case of *Culann*.

Cummor: *cumar*, a valley. The bog of Cummor forms a basin surrounded by Mount Leinster and its spurs. *Coombe*, so frequently met in Irish and English topography, has the same derivation.

Cumulum, a dance tune, getting its name from a frequent answer made by the dancer to the musician when asked what tune he would prefer—"*Cuma liom*", "(It is) indifferent to me". An attempt was made in the Glossary to the *Banks of the Boro* to explain the origin of the word, but it was not approved by Irish-speaking dancers.

Cushla: *cuishle*, pulse; *cuishle-mo-chroidhe*, pulse of my heart.

Drooghan, *droighean*, blackthorn, sloe tree.

Forth, Owen's pronunciation of fort, the old rath on the south bank of the Tombrick stream, opposite Mrs. Carey's house. It was not meddled with till 1850, when some spear-heads were discovered, with a coin of one of the Edwards, now, as we understand, in the possession of — Farmar, Esq., Dunsinane, near Enniscorthy.

Fringes, the Franchises (of Dublin) formerly marked by a procession on Lord Mayor's Day, as much of the sea at Irishtown being included, as a spear flung by a strong arm could reach.

Glanamoin, the defile between Coolgarrow and Kilachdiarmid hills. For explanation see *Glanmuin* in the vocabulary of *Banks of the Boro*.

Glasha, *glaishe*, stream.

Gra gal machree: *gradh*, love; *geal*, bright; *mo croidhe*, of my
heart. By an oversight, this ballad is reprinted, having already
appeared in the *Banks of the Boro.*

Granbrie: *brisde*, broken; crushed grain.

Grieshach, *grioshach*, live embers.

Gurtheen: *gearr*, short; *tain*, land; small garden; or *gorth*, garden,
with the diminutive termination *in.*

Haggard; *ioth*, corn; *cuirt*, a court or yard.

Hogan, *ogan* or *oganach*, a youth. In Irish *h* ranks no higher
than an aspiration.

Inagh, forsooth, probably from *eagnach*, expressive of reproach or
resentment.

Kennedy: *cinn*, genitive of *ceann*, head; *eidhe*, *eidheadh*, or *eidigh*,
armour;—helmet.

Kilachdiarmidh· *Cullach Diarmudha*, Diarmuidh's Boar. For the
legend of the peerless Diarmuidh, and his death from the bristles of
the magic boar, see *Ossianic Society's Transactions*, vol. 3. Diarmuidh met his fate on Ben Gulban in Sligo. The Highland Gael
point out the hill in Argyle where the tragedy occurred. Scarcely
a relic of the *Fionn Mac Cuil* stories has been preserved in Wexford.
They must have been popular there once, or the hill in question
would not have got the name.

Kilcavan: *caomhan*, a noble person; perhaps noble church, or
church of the nobles.

Lambasting is probably made up of the Irish *lamh*, hand, and the
English baste.

Lucharoe, *luachar*, pl. *luachra*, rushes.

Maurya: *mo bhreithe*, (on) my word, forsooth (said in derision).

Meenshogue : *minnseog*, a young she-goat.

Mishal: *Meisi*, spirits; *ail*, stone or rock; Fairy rock.

Moyeady: *magh Aoidh dubh*, the plain of Black Hugh; or *Magh
eideach*, plain of cloth. Perhaps cloth was manufactured and milled
there in ancient as well as modern times.

Mull, a corruption of mould.

Murphy, properly *Moroch : muir*, sea as well as wall. The Leinster
chiefs favoured with a long sea-board, probably derived their name
from the circumstance of being conversant with naval matters.

Murtagh or Muriertach: *muir*, a wall; *foirnigh*, build; *teach* or
teagh, a house; one who raised a stone fort. There is an Irish tract
taken up with the expedition of Muriertagh, who lived in the great
stone fortress of Aileach near Londonderry.

Musha: *maiseadh (ma is se)*, if it be so, then, therefore.

Omadhawn, *amadan*, madman, simpleton.

Onshuch, *oinsheach*, female simpleton.

Palinody, a word wrested from its original sense to denote a
rambling discourse, calculated to mislead the listeners.

Pew, a name as inseparably combined with the Protestant idea in
the minds of the writer's early acquaintance as the Thirty-nine Arti-

cles. It was occasionally associated with the habitual fire-side seat
of an old person.

Pool-a-phooka, *poll an phuic*, the goat's hole, or Puck's hole, that
fairy frequently committing havoc under the shape of a he-goat.
Poc is the nominative case. Poulpasty in Bantry, *Poll na peisthe*,
serpent's hole.

Puckawn, *pucan*, properly a small he-goat, but not used in that
sense by country folk.

Raimshogues; *reimseach*, heroic; romances, nonsensical stories.

Rathdrum, *rath druim*, the fort on the ridge.

Rossard; *ros*, promontory, isthmus, plain, arable land. The townland in question probably got its name from the spur thrown out
by Mount Leinster immediately above it.

Ryland, *roilbh*, wood, heath, common, the first name the most appropriate. Carlow visitors have this wooded ridge on their right
as they approach Bunclody.

Sausty, *sasdhach*, easy, comfortable.

Scarawalsh; *scirbh*, stony ford; Walsh, a proper name; Gaelic—
uaill, renowned. In Teuton *Walsch* is a stranger. There was once
of course a stony ford where the bridge now stands. *Scair* is
a drying ground.

Scraw, *scrath*, a thin broad sod.

Scullabogue; *scail*, rugged rock; rugged rock in the bog. The
isolated rock, Carrig-Byrne extends into the town-land of Scullabogue, a portion of which must have been marsh land. A much
esteemed correspondent of Harrystown, Ballymitty, has furnished
us with some interesting information on this point.

Sharoose; *searbh*, bitter, sore; *searbhais*, bitterness.

Shrehearth; *srath*, valley, hill-side over a stream, marsh, thicket,
bleaching place; *airthir*, eastern; eastern slope above the stream.
This suits the village and townland facing the big meadow of
Tombrick with the stony ford between.

Shroughmore. The principal word is the same as the one just quoted,
with the addition of *mor*.

Shuler; *siubhal*, walking, motion; a rambler, vagabond.

Skeogh, *sceach, sceagh*, whitethorn.

Skew, a corruption of *askew*.

Skithaan; *sgiothal*, ridiculous; a giddy person.

Slie Buie; *sliabh*, hill; yellow hill.

Taghmon, house of St. Munin; festival on 21st October.

Templeshanbo: *teampoll; sean*, old; *both*, hut, the church of the old
huts. The erection of the first church is attributed to St. Colman.
According to legends, some ducks belonging to this saint being
stolen, could not be boiled by the thief, and were therefore restored to the owner. No other appropriator ventured on a repetition, so the saint was left his fowl in surety.

Threenacheala; *thrid*, through; *cheile*, associate, companion; through
one another, confusion. The derivation in the glossary to the
Banks of the Boro, is erroneous.

Thraneen, *traithnin*, a long st alk of grass, the herb bennet.

☞ *The greater number of these derivations will, it is hoped, be found correct; some are mere conjectures. If any archæologist blessed with learning, leisure, and plenty of MSS., be prompted by the present imperfect attempt, to write at large upon the antiquities of the Duffrey and Bantry, he shall be considered as an enlarger of his country's literary treasures, and respected accordingly.*

Since writing the last sentence I have got a glance at the very valuable work of Mr. P. W. Joyce, M.R.I.A., who has effectually done for Ireland, what I have been striving to do for a small nook of it. This Glossary was in type before I got a sight of *The Origin and History of Irish Names and Places.*

INDEX.

Second Thousand; foolscap octavo, boards, 2s., by post. 2s. 3d.,

THE BANKS OF THE BORO,

A Chronicle of the County of Wexford.

BY PATRICK KENNEDY.

OPINIONS OF THE PRESS.

The Athenæum—" Under the cover of the tale, the author portrays scenes and incidents in Irish life in a simple unpretending manner. * * * On the thread of story are hung illustrations of Irish life, legends, morals, and poetry, which are the real staple of the book. * * * As a vehicle for conveying agreeably a large amount of information concerning men and manners in Ireland, this volume will be found most pleasant and profitable".

The Star—" Mr. Kennedy's plan is to group all kinds of local recollections, accounts of peculiar customs, and of gatherings for merriment, or for more solemn purposes, round a simple village story. * * * His ' Dance School', his ' Hurling Match', and his ' Wake at Pedher Mor's', are full, not of fun only, but of touches of finished character. * * * We can heartily recommend this book to any one who cares to know what quiet home life was in Ireland in happier days".

The Leader—" The actors in this Irish drama of real life are chiefly of the peasant class, and they, with their priests, farmers, teachers of dancing, and various odd characters, are delineated with much dry humour. *The Banks of the Boro* will be found a complete repertory of Irish songs, customs, and folk-lore. Its author has grafted them to a story, which, though of slight structure, will be perused with interest by the English reader".

The Dublin Evening Mail—" To the attraction of a picture of manners among a pious, primitive people, the story adds that of interest; for the author is possessed of constructive as well as pictorial power, and has woven his reminiscences into a tale of interest. Mr. Kennedy's picturesque sketches are as green, sunny, and vivid as a bit of landscape from a true artist's pencil. The scenes are full of character and innocent humour, which his pencil sharply and tenderly delineates. The feature most marked in his sketches is the *life* which animates every page. We ask no truer painter of the Irish character, in its simpler and tenderer aspects, than the author. At every Irish hearth the book ought to have a hearty welcome".

The Nation—" Mr. Kennedy's pen-and-ink sketches appear to be most faithfully executed. There is in them no exaggeration, no straining after effect, no outrageous caricatures of the people. Yet a great amount of mirth and oddity is to be found in his scenes, and a very effective representation of the warmth and intensity of Irish feelings under peculiar circumstances. We are taken to the wake, the dancing-school, the hurling match, and the harvest home, where the wit and humour of the country folk run on right merrily, and we are treated to the jokes they make, and the songs they sing, which are often exceedingly comic".

The Irish Times—" As a delineator of the people and their manners, the writer is perhaps unrivalled in a realistic sense. This present work is characterised by a quaint, sly humour, pungency, and raciness. The chronicle now before us is as remarkable for originality, for truthfulness, and simple philosophy, as for its wealth of information concerning curious customs, local traditions, and social gatherings, which the writer attaches to an interesting narrative of quiet country life".

The Freeman's Journal—" This little work rescues from oblivion the household stories, manners, and amusements of a most interesting people of half a century since. The style is pure, and as simple as the habits the writer describes, and the characters are well sustained. Not the least interesting in the collection are the songs and ballads of his youthful days. The author has rendered a great service to Irish literature".

Londonderry Standard—" The author has here collected a charming series of tales and sketches. * * * In the descriptions of natural scenery, Mr. Kennedy is exceedingly graphic. They exhibit poetic beauty of a high order. His characters, too, are distinctly marked, being unmistakeably living men and women, admirably portrayed, and consistently sustained. * * * The leading personages possess truly noble qualities, while a tone of unobtrusive piety, morality and universal kindness, pervades the whole narrative. There is not in the book one dishonouring blot of mere sectarianism. We have perused this little volume with a large amount of enjoyment. It presents a panorama of Irish social life in all its phases—grave, gay, humourous, and grotesque".

The Spectator—" For the somewhat numerous class who like to look at nations through a microscope, and those who are seeking to understand better many curious phases of Irish thought and feeling, this volume will have considerable interest".

The Wexford People—" The author has constructed a tale into which story, song, and legend, popular amusements, and habits are skilfully interwoven. * * * He delights in picturing the quiet household joys, the gentler pleasures and virtues, the harmless eccentricities, the sports and drolleries, that give us the calm and sunny aspect of Irish rural life. In the ' Banks of the Boro' all the shades and colours, all the characteristics and accessories that go to make up a perfect picture of Wexford social life fifty years ago, are merged, toned, contrasted, or harmonised with all the skill and cunning of the true artist".

The Imperial Review—"The author takes us to the Wexford village and farm of fifty years ago, and groups round a touching village story, a number of illustrative descriptions, which bear the stamp of perfectly true details of real occurrences. No extracts could give an idea of the quiet vein of humour which runs through the whole work. * * * We heartily recommend the story to those who would know what Irish country life used to be".

Kilkenny Moderator—"We have here a tale racy of the Irish soil. * * Admirers of the sensational novel had better not attempt to read it. * * * But those who retain a stomach for healthy literature will feel thankful to us for having brought it under their notice. All the scenes are clearly drawn from nature, and the characters are the living counterparts of personages photographed in the memory of the writer. They are produced with the most life-like effect. The tale is quietly told and not unartistically wrought out; but its great attraction lies in those pictures of olden manners and customs now fading so fast. For preserving their memory, Mr. Kennedy deserves the cordial thanks of every lover of his country".

The Irishman—"In the 'Banks of the Boro' we become a guest at the fireside of the comfortable farmer, and a confidant of the gossip that flows in fluent streams round his bright hearth. Episodes racy, rollicking, and genial, and ballads of the real natural type abound, and are strung together on a string of fiction, as country children string the wild flowers of the field".

☞ *Criticisms as favourable as the above, were furnished by twenty-five literary papers.*

J. F. Fowler, Steam Press Printer, 3 Crow Street, Dame Street, Dublin.

Anglesea St
July 12. 72

Dear Sir

I beg to thank you
for your liberality in the matter of my books The four books
before the present one were pub
lished at my own risk and
hitherto have not paid me but
there is every prospect of their
doing so. For the one about to
appear Messrs Routledge have
paid me a fair price I
hope it will amuse you

I do not think you have
a Copy of my Evenings in the
Dufffrey so I forward a Copy
If ever you are Cast on a de
sert isle or snowed up in a Low
land hut I hope you will read
it for it is worth reading The
Scenes are still to be found the
personages without exception all
were Known to me in my Youth
and there is Scarcely a shadow
of Invention in the incidents
However unartistic my Manage
ment the picture of Country

Society as known once to me is strictly true — There are several local legends and much rustic Minstrelsy scattered through the book. The tradition of the "Young Prophet" is preserved in my own family the victim's name being Anthony Kennedy. The book is the worst printed of all my two but I could not help it. I shall start three copies of the Anecdotes to you when I get them. I have corrected all but the Index.

With best wishes
I am Dear Sir
Yours faithfully &c
P. Kennedy

There is an index & the glossary & ballads

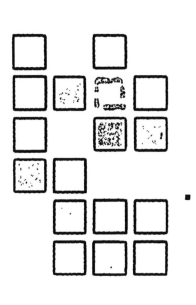

Lightning Source UK Ltd.
Milton Keynes UK
UKHW021003240822
407764UK00005B/575